Books by Inis L. Claude, Jr.

SWORDS INTO PLOWSHARES
The Problems and Progress of International Organization

POWER AND INTERNATIONAL RELATIONS

NATIONAL MINORITIES
An International Problem

SWORDS INTO PLOWSHARES

SWORDS INTO PLOWSHARES

The Problems *and* Progress *of* International Organization

BY

INIS·L·CLAUDE, Jr.
University of Michigan

THIRD EDITION, REVISED

Random House
NEW YORK

SECOND PRINTING

First edition, published in 1956
Second Edition, Revised and Enlarged, published in 1959
Third Edition, Revised, published in 1964

 Published in New York by Random House, Inc., and simultaneously in Toronto, Canada, by Random House of Canada, Limited.
Library of Congress Catalog Card Number: 64–12777
Manufactured in the United States of America by
H. Wolff Book Manufacturing Co., New York

DESIGN BY VINCENT TORRE

TO SUSAN, BOB, AND CATHY

who deserve a better world
to grow up in

Preface to the Third Edition

In preparing this new version of a book that was initially completed in 1955, I have been impressed by the extent to which the world has changed, the United Nations system has changed, and I have changed, in the brief space of eight years. I have undertaken to make the revised manuscript reflect these changes. To this end, I have added new material, deleted old material, revised judgments that no longer seem pertinent, and presented interpretations inspired by the facts of international life as they appear to me in 1964. The most significant addition is Chapter 14, which reflects my view that the most important development in the recent history of general international organization is the formulation of the theory and the beginning of the practice of preventive diplomacy.

Not everything has changed, of course, either in the field to which this book relates, or in the book itself. Many of the most recent developments in international organization represent movement along a line of continuity which was already discernible in 1955. The tendency of the United Nations to abjure the effort to construct a collective security system, and its increasing emphasis upon programs of economic development fit into this category.

I have retained the emphasis, which characterized the earlier editions of this book, upon analysis of the theoretical underpinnings and the operative problems and tendencies of international organization, particularly the United Nations. Thus, I have not undertaken to present a comprehensive survey of all the parts of the present-day international institutional system, or a digest of the activities of those organs. The student of international organization who would "keep up with the United Nations" is advised to give regular attention to such periodicals as the *United Nations Review* (an official publication of the organization) and *International Organization* (a quarterly journal, published by the World Peace Foundation, Boston), and to the annual survey of the issues currently before the General Assembly which is published each fall in an issue of *International Conciliation* (Carnegie Endowment for International Peace, New York). Essential information about the structure and the work of the United Nations may also be found in *Everyman's United Nations,* the recurrent volumes of the *Yearbook of the United Nations,* and the annual *Report of the Secretary-General,* all of them produced by the organization itself. I have attempted to provide not so much an account of the facts, or a chronicle of events, as an essay of interpretation.

As this book moves to a third edition, my obligations of gratitude multiply beyond the point where it is possible to list my benefactors. The unnamed others may forgive me if I confine myself to acknowledging my special indebtedness at Random House to Charles D. Lieber, Mrs. Leonore C. Hauck, and Miss Anne Dyer Murphy; at the University of Michigan to Professors Arthur W. Bromage and Harold K. Jacobson; and at home to my wife and children, innocent victims of my occupational diseases.

I. L. C., Jr.
January 1964

Preface

The process of international organization is a significant feature of the dynamic pattern of international relations in our time. World affairs move in many directions at once; one of the most persistent trends of the last century, and particularly of the last generation, has been the movement toward the organization of international relations. The creation of multilateral institutions has become a standard response of statesmen and peoples, for purposes both intensely realistic and highly idealistic, to the challenging problems and terrible dangers of international life in an era of increasing interdependence.

In this book, I have undertaken to analyze the development of the trend toward international organization and to examine the problems, progress, and prospects of some of the most important agencies in which it has found expression. I must disclaim any intention of producing a comprehensive handbook of international organizations or a digest of their activities and accomplishments. Rather, I have felt that the time is ripe for a study which focuses upon the theoretical bases, evolutionary trends, constitutional problems, and major operational issues of international agencies, without the inclusion of an unwieldy mass of detail regarding structure and function. That is what I have attempted to provide in this volume. I shall be happy if it promotes deeper understanding and stimulates thoughtful evaluation of the process of developing organization among nations.

There is a certain brashness about putting one's thoughts into public print which an author can only mitigate by making public acknowledgment of his debts. I would mention first my wife, who has worked, not tirelessly, but unceasingly, to assist me in this enterprise. I owe an incalculable debt to three inspiring teachers of my undergraduate days at Hendrix College—T. S. Staples, W. C. Buthman, and R. E. Yates—who first aroused and guided my interest in the political affairs of men and nations. I am grateful to my colleagues at Harvard University and to fellow students of international affairs elsewhere—notably Robert H. Cory, Lawrence H. Fuchs, Henry C. Galant, A. Burr Overstreet, and John G. Stoessinger—for the generous sharing of knowledge and tolerant discussion of disagreements which have done much to shape my own viewpoints. Special thanks are due to Walter F. Cronin, Rupert Emerson, and Payson S. Wild, who read parts of the manuscript and gave me the benefit of their valued judgments, without—I hasten to add—incurring any responsibility for the views expressed herein. Finally, I am indebted to my students at Harvard and Radcliffe, who have either taught me or forced me to learn most of what is contained in my modest treasury of understanding of the intriguing, complex, and important field of international organization.

I. L. C., Jr.
August 1, 1955

Contents

Constitutional Problems of International Organization

Approaches to Peace Through International Organization

The Future of World Order

Appendixes

Introduction

CHAPTER I

Introduction

"One World" is in some respects an ideal and an aspiration, born of modern interpretations of ancient moral insights and of rational estimates of the requirements for human survival; it is in other respects a pressing reality, an actual condition of mankind, produced by a century of change which has tied all the peoples of the earth together in an unprecedented intimacy of contact, interdependence of welfare, and mutuality of vulnerability. Whether or not we obey the religious injunction to behave like brothers, or attain the ethical objective of a peaceful world community, we human beings cannot escape the hard fact that all of us are, as John Donne put it, "involved in Mankinde." Given the existence of One World defined as a set of objective conditions, disaster may be the price of failure to achieve One World defined in terms of a moral and political ideal.

Sincere and sensible men may differ as to how much and what kind of world unity is possible and desirable, how it can or should be achieved, and how quickly it is likely to be or ought to be attempted. These are important questions, and some attention will be devoted to them in this book. However, we are not simply confronted with a debate about hypothetical possibilities for the future. The growing complexity of international relations has already produced international organizations; the world is engaged in the process of organizing. This process has a past which is not very long, as historians measure time, but which is nonetheless significant. It has a present which is confused and troubled, but which is not for that reason less important as an object of study. And, it may be confidently asserted, if man has a future, so has the process of international organization.

The present state of international organization, representing an attempt to adapt the institutions, procedures, and rules of international relations to the conditions of international interdependence, is far from satisfactory. But though much is lacking *in* international organizations, there is no lack *of* such agencies. Well over a hundred public international organizations, having states as their members, are in existence today, not to speak of a much greater number of nongovernmental organizations, composed of private citizens or groups in various countries. Indeed, the proliferation of such bodies has produced an International Union of International Associations, with headquarters in Brussels. International agencies vary greatly in size and scope, in structure, and in the ambitiousness of their programs. The amazing variety of the subjects with which international organizations have dealt may be illustrated by referring to such names as the International Congress on Vineyards and Wine, the International Commission of the Cape Spartel Light, the International Whaling Commission, and the Permanent Central Opium Board. Nations have joined together for such minor and specialized purposes as those of the Central Bureau of the International Map of the World on the Millionth Scale, and for such fundamental and far-reaching aims as those pursued by the United Nations. It cannot be emphasized too strongly that the organization of international affairs is not just a gleam in the eyes of idealists, to be judged in terms of its acceptability or feasibility as an ideal, but it is a process under way, to be studied with a view to understanding its causes and effects, its progress and limitations, its problems and prospects.

International *organization* is a process; international *organizations* are representative aspects of the phase of that process which has been reached at a given time. This is a book about international organization, based primarily upon an analysis of the organizational efforts in which governments participate as the official agencies of states. Thus, the realm occupied by nongovernmental organizations is largely excluded from its scope. It is a selective study, not a comprehensive digest, but its time range includes past, present, and possible future developments. It is written in the conviction that international organizations, as institutions, have a double significance: they are important, though not decisively important, factors in contemporary world affairs; and they are significant expressions of, and contributors to, the process of international organization, which may ultimately prove to be the most significant dynamic element in the developing reality of international relations.

APPROACHES TO THE STUDY OF INTERNATIONAL ORGANIZATION

Serious scholarship in the field of international organization is a relatively new enterprise, and the pioneer writers and teachers in this field have tended to approach the subject in a manner largely determined by the professional techniques and specialized emphases characteristic of the older and better established disciplines in which they have been trained. Thus, international lawyers have tended to treat the study of international organization as an exercise in rigorous analysis of the multilateral treaties which serve as the constitutional foundations of international agencies. Students of comparative governmental institutions have considered international organizations as sets of machinery, to be examined in terms of their structural and procedural characteristics. Specialists in world politics have focused on the role of international organizations in power conflicts and in the balancing process. Scholars with a sociological orientation have looked upon international organization as a phase of the secular community-building process, regarding its institutions as outward expressions of the nature of the world social situation and as instruments for influencing the development of basic patterns of human social behavior. These are all valid and useful approaches to the study of international organization, although too nearly exclusive reliance upon any one of them may result in failure to do justice to the complexities of the subject.

This book represents an effort to apply to the study of international organization a variety of approaches which have relevance and importance for understanding and evaluating developments in this field.

The historical approach is important first of all for the obvious reason that the present cannot be adequately understood, nor future prospects reasonably assessed, without a grasp of the tendencies and continuities which emerge from the past. Even so, it is well to be aware of the fact that in this field, as in others, the advantages of "learning from history" are somewhat offset by the perils of being "blinded by history." But an historical emphasis has an even more important function in this field of study: mere recognition of the fact that international organization *has* a history serves significantly to dispel the notion that contemporary international institutions are simply gadgets, arbitrarily contrived devices to deal with current problems, and to drive home the point that international organization is a characteristic phenomenon of the modern state system, an organic development rooted in the realities and conforming to the necessities of international relations. A sound understanding of historical backgrounds puts us on notice that, whatever the basic policy questions to be decided in our time may be, they do not include the question, "Shall we have international organization?" International organization is a distinctive modern phase of world politics; it is a recent growth, but it has become an established trend. International organizations may come and go, but international organization is here to stay. The collapse of the League of Nations led almost automatically to consideration of the question of what kind of international organization should next be attempted, and similar failure by the United Nations might be expected to produce the same reaction. Historical analysis is required to establish and explain the fact that international organization has become a necessary part of the system for dealing with international problems, and that "to organize or not to organize" is no longer an open question for statesmen of our time.

The theoretical approach, too often neglected in this field, is given substantial emphasis in this book. A well-established body of political theory has long provided guide posts and points of reference for the study of national government and politics, but the relevance of this theoretical material for international organization has not been adequately explored, nor has sufficient attention been given to the possibility of elaborating a special body of theory to serve as a framework for the study of international organization. It is true that the development of international organization has been marked by a strong pragmatic bent, and that this tendency has been a healthy one for the early and tentative stages. Nevertheless, the time has come when it would be useful to make explicit, and thus subject to critical evaluation, the unarticulated assumptions which have in fact served as the theoretical underpinnings of experiments in international organization. In addition, the theoretical approach has the merit of pointing up the relationship between international organization and other developments and problem areas in the general field of social studies. International organization is not an isolated phenomenon, but part of a general context; its foundations are embedded in the same theoretical stratum which supports other modern economic, social, and political developments. Thus, the theoretical approach may have the value of demonstrating the connection between the process of international organization and other things that are going on in the affairs of man-in-society, just as the historical approach clarifies the relationship between that process and the evolution of international relations.

A strong political emphasis pervades the treatment of international organization in this book. Legal and structural analysis of institutions is indispensable, but it contributes little to understanding unless international organization is placed squarely in the political context where it operates. One can learn something about his automobile by studying the blueprints, and something more by peering under the hood at its parts, but real understanding comes with checking its behavior in traffic. Similarly, international organization must be considered in terms of its inseparability from the political forces and trends of the time—the configuration of power, the impact of technological developments, the sweep of political unrest, the urge for political stability, the drives for domination, the clashes of interests and of ideologies. International organization is a product of international politics, which largely determines its shape and the course of its development. On the other hand, there is a mutuality of interaction, with international organization becoming a factor influencing the course of international politics. There is real danger in concentrating too heavily on the constitutional documents and formal structural arrangements of international agencies. Their actual operations can only be understood with reference to the world of politics, and their ultimate results can be properly evaluated only in terms of their impact upon that world.

Finally, it is recognized in this book that the problem of building effective international organizations is ultimately the problem of building a world community. This task involves more than devising foolproof legal structures or ingenious mechanical devices; it involves working on the underlying factors which shape international politics—the loyalties, values, prejudices, fears, hopes, and expectations of human beings. International organization is concerned with sociological problems on a grand scale. If the creation of individual life is the great mystery of biology, the creation of social life is the great mystery of sociology. We know that community-building takes place, but our knowledge of the process is not sufficient to enable us to produce by artificial means the unit of human cohesion which international organization requires as its basis. Thus, the study of international organization carries us to the frontiers of social exploration.

The purpose of this book is to promote the careful examination and intelligent understanding of international organization. The analysis will necessarily be inconclusive, but we can hope at least for a limited understanding of why international organization today is what it is, of why it is not what it is not, and of what factors will determine what international organization can do in our time and may do—and may become—in the future. This will require a critical analysis of the problems, limitations, failures, and inadequacies of international organization, as well as its growth and achievements.

The realization of the above purpose requires the devotion of serious attention to a multitude of relatively unspectacular issues and problems, and resistance to the temptation to concentrate too exclusively upon the big, basic, fundamental questions about international organization. Contemporary discussion of the United Nations tends to be dominated by excessive passion for reopening the question of its basic design, for dealing first, last, and always with such exciting Great Issues as whether the veto can be abolished or world federation should be introduced. The wisdom of this approach is questionable. A wise President of the United States does not spend his time pondering about whether we ought to adopt the British cabinet system of government, or substitute a unitary for the federal system, or discard the principle of a written constitution, or abolish the Senate; rather, he accepts the basic arrangements as they stand, assumes the need to make our government work as well as possible within its established framework, and focuses on the problems at hand. Students of international organization might do well to devote less energy to thinking about whether the United Nations is a suitable institution and more to considering what we can do with, and make of, the international agencies we now have. This is not to encourage complacency or the belief that more advanced forms of international organization cannot and should not be developed; it is to encourage the bestowal of something better than a contemptuous sneer upon the problems which exist within the present context of international organization. In this field, daring speculation directed toward the future is no substitute for patient analysis of the past and present, or adventurous idealism concerning grandiose possibilities for sober awareness of mundane realities.

THE NATURE OF INTERNATIONAL ORGANIZATION

Considered primarily in terms of its purposes, international organization may be said to exhibit a basically dualistic nature.

On the one hand, it may be regarded as a means for making the modern state system function more satisfactorily. From this point of view, international organization is set within the context of the multistate system; it accepts the sovereign state as the basic entity of world political life; it does not purport to create a supergovernment, destroying the sovereignty of states and taking over the functions of their governments. Instead, it provides modernized methods to supplement and in some measure to replace old ways of conducting interstate relations, new agencies for stimulating and facilitating voluntary cooperation of states and harmonization of their policies, improved channels for negotiation, and a more adequately organized framework for diplomacy. In this view, international organization represents nothing more revolutionary than an agreement of states to engage in regular consultation under set conditions and to establish machinery for the implementation of their joint decisions. Thus, it is a movement for reform, for modification, for adaptation of the multistate system to the requirements of international life in our time.

In contrast, international organization may be looked upon as a process of initiating steps in the direction of world government, of realizing the ageless aspiration for human brotherhood by transcending the national state system and substituting a fundamentally new system. In this interpretation, existing international agencies are intended not so much to assist states in solving the current problems of their common existence as to promote the development of more advanced types of world institutions. They are imperfect and inadequate—Model T devices to replace horse-and-buggy devices for dealing with the problems of a jet-propelled world—but they represent the necessary first stages of a movement toward a revolutionary advance in the management of human affairs.

Both these views have some validity. Existing agencies serve as aids in the conduct of international relations by the component parts of the traditional state system, and at the same time they exercise some measure of authority and function which is essentially governmental in nature. International organization owes its dualistic nature to the fact that it is a product of both realistic statesmen and idealistic dreamers.

This situation carries within it the seeds of conflict. Statesmen, by and large, are devoted to the first conception of the nature of international organization. In creating the United Nations, they meant that it should be an instrument for promoting national interests and purposes, including that of making it possible for the multistate system to operate tolerably well. Tell a United States Senator that the United Nations assists our sovereign nation in conducting its affairs in the modern world, and he may support it; tell him that it is a first step toward the elimination of national sovereignties, and he is likely to show hostility. On the other hand, many internationalists support contemporary international bodies primarily because of the hunch and the hope that such agencies may in the long run undermine the national state system and contribute to the building of world government. These people tend to think that international agencies should be forerunners of world governmental institutions, and hope that that is what they are.

Thus, international organization has created strange bedfellows, supporters whose conceptions of the actual and proper nature of international agencies are at variance. The truce between these two groups is an uneasy one. Statesmen, oriented toward the maintenance of sovereign states, hold the upper hand, for they control the very existence of international agencies. But they can hardly have the kind of agencies which they want and desperately need for their purposes without relying upon the support and service of individuals who are likely to entertain the hope that those agencies will develop into instruments of a world order based on a global unity which will transcend the divisive principle of national sovereignty.

This introduces the question of the potentialities of the United Nations. What may it become? What changes in the organization of international life is it likely to produce?

Again, we find two ways of looking at the "problem of becoming." The first might be characterized as the "seed" approach. A seed contains within itself a fixed pattern of potential development and forces of growth. Thus, an acorn may become an oak tree; it may, of course, die and become nothing; but if it becomes anything at all, it will become an oak tree, not an elm tree or a grape vine. Following this analogy, there are those who look at the United Nations itself, seeking to discover its inherent potentialities—rudimentary principles which may become dominant in a new and different world system, new ideas capable of growth, new forces capable of extension. Thus, they may conceive of the General Assembly as a potential world parliament, and the International Court of Justice as the world supreme court of the future. As one early analyst of the postwar organization put it:

> the potentiality of the world state is inherent in the United Nations. When I say that it is inherent, I mean that this is the end and the logic according to which the United Nations must evolve if they are to evolve at all toward an enduring world order. The world state is inherent in the United Nations as an oak tree is in an acorn. . . . In this sense, not another League of Nations but a world state, in the exact meaning of the term, is inherent and potential in the embryonic organism of the United Nations.[1]

This view stresses historical perspective, and accepts the application of the concept of organic evolution to human institutions. Those who adopt this theory may view the prospects with favor or with alarm, but they are agreed that the clue to future development lies in the institutions of the present.

The second approach to the problem of becoming might be described as the "building" theory. A building has no inexorable pattern of growth; it can be made and remade according to the desires of its builders and users. Within limits, a given foundation can be used to support different types of buildings. An existing structure can be left the same or remodeled; new rooms may be added or old parts torn away. Following this analogy, some observers emphasize the intentions, desires, and policies of the states whose property the United Nations is, rather than its own inherent qualities, as the determining factors in its future development. From this point of view, what the United Nations will become depends not upon what kind of seed it is, but upon what kind of building is wanted; its future depends upon what its members, especially the more powerful ones, wish it to become, allow it to become, and force it to become.

The first theory is essentially organismic and deterministic; the second is pragmatic and voluntaristic. Neither is entirely adequate. The latter theory, however, contributes more to an understanding of international organization. The development of the United Nations will be primarily determined by the conditions of the world political scene and the policies of governments; it will become what human beings make it become—not something that it must become because it is what it is.

Nevertheless, this view must be qualified by recognition of the fact that human institutions do some times and to some extent evolve in un-

---

[1] Walter Lippmann, "International Control of Atomic Energy," in Dexter Masters and Katherine Way, eds., *One World or None* (New York: McGraw-Hill, 1946), p. 74. Copyright, 1946, McGraw-Hill Book Company, Inc.

willed directions, violating the intentions and confounding the expectations of their founders and operators. The Founding Fathers of the United States did not entirely know what they were doing; our government has become something which they could not have predicted or intended and might not have approved. Similarly, the United Nations may become something which the statesmen of San Francisco, the state-oriented men of 1945, did not consciously intend. Moreover, the course of its development may be determined less by the consciously adopted plans of the governments which participate in its functions, or the officials who serve it, than by the cumulative influence of day-to-day pressures and case-by-case decisions.

One ought not to take too literally the formally stated purposes of the United Nations or of any other international institution. The Charter gives expression to a set of lofty purposes—including the maintenance of peace and security, the development of friendly international relations, and the promotion of cooperative solutions to basic problems of human welfare and human rights. This is not to say that the governments which formulated the Charter were in fact unanimously devoted to the realization of these purposes, through the United Nations or otherwise. We can say with assurance only that they were all willing to make this formal assertion of the ends for which the new organization should be used. In practice, statesmen use, or attempt to use, the United Nations for a variety of purposes, some of which were not mentioned in the Charter, and some of which are customarily regarded as unmentionable by the drafters of the constitutions of international organizations. In a very real sense, the United Nations has no purposes of its own; the purposes which it serves are set and altered by the operation of its political process, in which the clash and consensus of the aims of member states are the decisive elements.

What the United Nations will become, and what it will do—these are questions which can best be answered by reference not to the Charter, but to the political, ideological, psychological, technological, and economic features of the international scene.

THE BASIC ASSUMPTION OF INTERNATIONAL ORGANIZATION

However much men may differ as to the purposes which international organization should pursue or the manner of estimating its future prospects, it is clear that international organization as we know it rests upon a distinctive basic assumption about the nature of international politics. This assumption may be stated as both a denial and an affirmation.

International organization implies rejection of the idea that men and governments, in the era of the multistate system, are bound by inexorable laws which inhere in that system. This position contrasts with that of two groups of thinkers about international relations: the self-styled "realists" of the power politics school, and the champions of world government.

These groups, which come to very different conclusions and recommendations, share the basic contention that men-divided-into-states must inevitably clash. States enmeshed in a multistate system are driven inexorably by the laws of the system into a limitless struggle for dominance, a violent competition for power. Thus, Frederick L. Schuman has written that:

> Whenever two or more States, each "sovereign" and "independent" of others, confront one another . . . their relations will tend to be dominated by a competitive quest for power and by calculations of relative power.
>
> Every State is a system, precisely because it is a State in a system, seeks to extend its power over all others in its quest for security or empire.
>
> What is not justified . . . is the assumption that it is within the capacity of men to make right rather than might the test of statecraft in a system of competing sovereigns.[2]

Having started out together, these two groups go off in different directions. Exponents of the power politics line accept the multistate system, with its assumed laws of inevitable clash, as given, and advise statesmen to be realistic practitioners of the arts of national survival in the nastiest of all possible worlds. World governmentalists, agreeing that the laws of the system are fatally incompatible with any hope for decent relations among states, advise instead that it is possible and necessary to leap over the wall of the multistate system, entering into a new kind of world in which the old laws do not inhibit the achievement of peace and order. What they have in common is the fundamental belief that, within the framework of the existing state system, conflict and chaos are the ordained lot of mankind.

In rejecting this doctrinaire determinism, theorists of international organization repudiate both the pessimistic conclusions of the power politicians and the apocalyptic visions of believers in world government. International organization has been built, consciously or not, upon the assumption that nations are not prisoners of destiny but reasonably free agents. Its theory is that the relationships of states can be modified, even while the present system remains unchanged in its fundamentals. This constitutes an affirmation that men are in fact free, in the here and now, to formulate and pursue objectives relevant to international relations. Some believers in international organization envisage the ultimate transcending of the national state system, whereas others look to the development of a tolerable pattern of relations without systemic transformation; what

---

2 *The Commonwealth of Man* (New York: Knopf, 1952), pp. 22, 30, 38.

unites them is the conviction that men, organized in states, are confronted with a malleable international system. Thus, international organization reflects the view that it makes sense to hope and try for gradual reform of state behavior.

This fundamental aspect of the theory of international organization serves not only to distinguish it from other ways of looking at the problem of international relations, but also to identify its relationship to other theoretical positions in the general field of socio-political thought. The controversy concerning the limits of determinism and freedom is not limited to the theoretical realm of international relations.

There is a basic philosophical affinity between the movements for modifying international relations by international organization and for reforming economic and social relations by the political means of democracy, which suggests the need for a redefinition of that much used and abused term, liberalism. The essential concept of liberalism is the postulate that men are not inexorably constrained by the laws of a social system—that however compelling may be the restraints and determinants imposed by the structure of the arena within which they operate, men yet retain the possibility of empirical maneuvering within the limits of the system and perhaps of achieving the ultimate transformation of the system. In these terms, liberalism is not so much a doctrine committed to the *advocacy* of freedom as a doctrine based upon the conviction of the *reality* of freedom for man in the social universe.

International organization is clearly the typical expression of liberalism, thus defined, in the realm of international relations. Its philosophical assumptions have seldom been clearly articulated, but it is obvious that international organization makes sense only if it is assumed that there exists an area of freedom for action within the confines of the multistate system. The fundamental nature of this assumption was indicated by Dag Hammarskjold, the second Secretary-General of the United Nations, when he called for "a firm faith in the capacity of men and governments to have the common sense to find their way out of the awful labyrinth of seemingly irreconcilable conflicts and insoluble problems in which we are now wandering." [3] International organization rests upon the belief that man is at liberty, not only to surrender to the operation of the iron laws of the system, or to attempt an apocalyptic leap from an era of determinism into an era of freedom, but to shape his collective destiny in the here and now.

International organization has too often been described, by both its critics and its champions, as simply a venture in international cooperation, based upon the assumption of the harmony or harmonizability of the interests of states. It is more accurate to state that a dualistic conception of international relations—a view which takes into account the phenomena

---

[3] *United Nations Bulletin,* May 1, 1954, p. 353.

of both conflict and cooperation—provides the foundation for this enterprise. This is evidenced by the fact that the builders of international institutions have undertaken to equip them to serve both as arenas for conflict and as workshops for collaboration. Ideally, at least, international organization is an attempt to minimize the conflictual and maximize the cooperative aspects of international relations. The philosophy of international organization is idealistic—not in its view of the facts, but in its hope for changing those facts; not in the sense that it promises a panacea, but in the sense that it expresses an optimism sufficient to justify a reformist effort. It does not deny the reality of conflict, but asserts the conviction that it is necessary, and may be possible, to reduce that aspect of reality to manageable proportions.

This belief may be in error. Certainly there is no guarantee that international organization will be successful. It is easy to exaggerate the progress that has been made; supporters of international organization are often tempted to take too seriously the ostensible gains that exist only on paper—the fine words of constitutional documents, the noble sentiments of United Nations resolutions. But it is equally easy—and perilous—to adopt a pessimism which refuses to recognize the advances that have been made and denies the hypothesis that a meaningful opportunity exists for gradual taming of power, harmonizing of interests, and building of allegiance to the ideal of a world fit for human life.

SUGGESTED READINGS

Levi, Werner, *Fundamentals of World Organization,* Minneapolis: University of Minnesota Press, 1950.

Nicholas, H. G., *The United Nations as a Political Institution,* London: Oxford University Press, 1959.

Russell, Frank M., *Theories of International Relations,* New York: Appleton-Century-Crofts, 1936.

Schiffer, Walter, *The Legal Community of Mankind,* New York: Columbia University Press, 1954.

Historical Backgrounds of Contemporary International Organization

CHAPTER 2

The Development of International Organization in the Nineteenth Century

International organization—which ought, strictly speaking, to be called *interstate* organization—is a phenomenon of the multistate system. There are, in fact, four prerequisites for the development of international organization. The first two relate to the existence of objective facts or conditions: the world must be divided into a number of states which function as independent political units, and a substantial measure of contact must exist between these subdivisions. The other requirements are subjective in nature: the states must develop an awareness of the problems which arise out of their coexistence, and, on this basis, come to recognize the need for creation of institutional devices and systematic methods for regulating their relations with each other. Thus, the setting of the stage for international organization involves the development of the *facts* of division and interdependence in the external world, and of the *moods* of anxiety and dissatisfaction, coupled with hopeful determination and creative imagination, in the minds of men.

It was in the nineteenth century that these four prerequisites were satisfied in sufficient measure and in proper combination to bring about the birth of modern international organization. The multistate system can be traced back to the earlier breakup of the unity of medieval European Christendom, and historical reference may be made to such significant landmarks in its development as the Peace of Westphalia in 1648 and the Treaty of Utrecht in 1713. However, it remained for the nineteenth century to bring about the combination of the continuing proliferation and solidification of states, particularly under the impact of growing nationalism, and the emergence of a pattern of technologically-based contacts, unprecedented in range and intensity, which made the world situation ready for international organization.

At the same time, men were becoming ready for international organization, although their psychological preparation was much less complete than the preparation which had taken place in the conditions of the external world. The problem of war forced its way to the forefront of men's attention. It became increasingly apparent that military activity could no longer be regarded as a kind of professional sport, sponsored by royal patrons, but that it had become a menace to the welfare and happiness of humanity. It was also evident that the conditions of interdependence, growing out of phenomenal advances in transport, communication, and industrialism, had created complex problems which could not be solved, and great new possibilities which could not be realized, without changes in the management of international affairs.

Recognition of the complication of problems, the intensification of evils, and the attainability of unparalleled benefits was a necessary step toward awareness of the inadequacies of the established principles and methods of international relations. The multistate system, as it had developed up to the nineteenth century, was characterized by the doctrinal principle of sovereignty and the correlative institutional principle of decentralization.

Sovereignty has meant many things to many men, and it has been the subject of much learned discourse and disputation and of a great deal of hair-splitting, who's-got-the-thimble, how-many-angels-on-the-point-of-a-needle type of analysis. It suffices here to describe sovereignty as a principle of irresponsibility. Cervantes described it as well as legal or political philosophers when he had Don Quixote ask:

> who was that jolt-head that did subscribe or ratify a warrant for the attaching of such a knight as I am? Who was he that knows not how knights-errant are exempted from all tribunals? and how that their sword is the law, their valour the bench, and their wills the statutes of their courts? I say again, what madman was he that knows not how

> that no privilege of gentry enjoys so many preeminences, immunities, and exemptions as that which a knight-errant acquires the day wherein he is dubbed and undertakes the rigorous exercise of arms? [1]

In its original context, sovereignty denoted the authority without accountability which was the attribute of monarchs; its locus was shifted, but its essential nature was not altered, when monarchy began to share the international stage with republicanism, and abstract entities called national states appeared with the claim to act with a free hand in both internal affairs and external relations. The theoretical pretensions of sovereignty were seldom absolute. Doctrines of international legal obligation developed simultaneously with notions of sovereign irresponsibility, and the nineteenth century inherited a system of international law to which sovereigns, whether they were personal rulers or impersonal states, were presumably subject. But there was a joker in the pack; the international law which was to control sovereigns was itself controlled by them. The law was by no means completely ineffective in civilizing the relations of sovereign entities, in so far as they recognized common interests and reciprocal obligations, but it tended primarily to reflect their preoccupation with their own rights and status and dignity. It was not surprising that an international legal system, shaped and controlled by sovereigns, should have served the major function of ratifying the concept of sovereignty, sanctifying the rights of sovereigns, and legitimizing the irresponsibility of sovereigns. The major defect of the international legal system was not that it failed to enforce the obligations of sovereign states but that it conceded too much to their pretensions and claims of rights and privileges.

The traditional system of international relations translated the theoretical concept of sovereignty into the institutional principle of decentralization. In the operation of the system, the key word was *self:* self-limitation, self-judgment, self-help of states. The community had no central governing institutions, and no authority to impose central direction or control upon sovereign states. The law consisted of obligations which states imposed upon themselves; states served as judges in their own causes; states enjoyed a legal right to the arbitrary use of force. The theoretical predominance of sovereignty meant the operative predominance of unilateralism, qualified primarily by the techniques of diplomacy.

It was this sort of multistate system which was recognized as inadequate under the conditions of international life as they developed in the nineteenth century. The movement toward international organization reflected the conviction that it had become necessary and possible to modify the free-wheeling irresponsibility of sovereign states to a greater extent than had been done under traditional international law, and to remedy the

---

[1] *Don Quixote of the Mancha,* translated by Thomas Shelton; Charles W. Eliot, ed., *The Harvard Classics* (New York: Collier, 1909), XIV, 457.

international institutional vacuum by creating and putting to work some agencies which would serve the community of states as a whole.

This is not to say that drastic revision of the international system was contemplated or accomplished during the nineteenth century. No iconoclastic reaction to the sacred principle of sovereignty developed, and no concerted effort to substitute a fully elaborated and authoritative set of community institutions for the decentralized system of international relations was envisaged. It was true that the nineteenth century inherited, and added to, a venerable tradition of speculative projects for peace and order through unity on a world or European scale, produced by such men as Dante, Pierre Dubois, Emeric Crucé, the Duc de Sully, William Penn, the Abbé de Saint-Pierre, Rousseau, Bentham, and Kant.[2] These various utopian schemes, which had appeared in a steady procession from the fourteenth century, had never reflected or appealed to a strong sense of current need, nor did they in the nineteenth century. Far from repudiating the principle of separate and independent sovereignties, the world of the nineteenth century continued the glorification of that concept and insisted upon its eternal rightness, while it reacted to the awareness of new necessities by undertaking to achieve working restraints and functional innovations through the initiative, consent, and collaboration of sovereign states. International organization was thus brought into being not so much by prophets who saw it as the legitimate successor to sovereign states, as by statesmen who sought new arrangements and devices whereby the sovereign units of the old system could pursue their interests and manage their affairs in the altered circumstances of the age of communication and industrialism.

THE CONCERT OF EUROPE

The first of the three major streams of development whose rise may be traced to the nineteenth century is the system of multilateral, high-level, political conferences.

Diplomacy, the traditional technique for conduct of international affairs, was essentially a bilateral phenomenon, involving occasional consultation and negotiation between two sovereigns or their representatives. Larger-scale gatherings of the managers of foreign relations were not unknown before the nineteenth century, and the idea of such conferences had a respectable age. Thus, Hugo Grotius, the so-called "father of international law," opined in 1625 that:

> It would be advantageous, indeed in a degree necessary, to hold certain conferences of Christian powers, where those who have no inter-

[2] See S. J. Hemleben, *Plans for World Peace Through Six Centuries* (Chicago: University of Chicago Press, 1943).

est at stake may settle the disputes of others, and where, in fact, steps may be taken to compel parties to accept peace on fair terms.[3]

However, the Congress of Vienna in 1815 initiated a series of developments which made it possible to speak of a nineteenth-century conference *system* without precedent in the modern world.

The dazzling assemblage at Vienna was convoked to lay the diplomatic foundations for a new European order upon the ruins which had been created by the disastrous Napoleonic Wars. It was conceived by its leading participants as the forerunner of a series of regular consultations among the great powers which would serve as board meetings for the European community of nations. This ambitious concept quickly faded; four major conferences between 1815 and 1822 sufficed to reveal differences in policy and objective among the great powers which made it impossible for them to collaborate in the operation of such a systematic scheme for the management of Europe. Nevertheless, the techniques of diplomacy had been irrevocably changed. Europe was not ready for institutionalized management, but in practice the leaders of the major states constituted themselves a Concert of Europe which met sporadically, some thirty times in the course of the century, to deal with pressing political issues. The diplomatic history of this era is studded with such landmarks as the Congress of Paris in 1856, the London Conferences of 1871 and 1912-13, the Berlin Congresses of 1878 and 1884-85, and the Algeciras Conference of 1906. Diplomacy by conference became an established fact of life in the nineteenth century.

This development involved a great deal more than the mere multiplication of multilateral convocations. A major feature of the unsystematic system was the frank assumption of special status and responsibility by the most powerful states; the term, "great power," took on a definite meaning and became something like a formally established category after 1815. The Concert of Europe was an exclusive club for great powers, whose members were self-appointed guardians of the European community and executive directors of its affairs. They sometimes admitted European small fry to their Splendid Presence, and occasionally failed to dominate the scene as completely as they wished, but they left no room for doubt that the Concert of Europe was in fact a Concert of the Great Powers.

This hegemony of the powerful had its seamy side, as all dictatorships must. If it is true of individuals, it is surely even more true of states, that possession of extraordinary power and authority leads to abuse and selfish exploitation. In the case of this directorate, however, mutual jealousies tended to limit the misuse of power for the purposes of either corporate or

[3] Cited in H. Lauterpacht, *The Function of Law in the International Community* (Oxford: Clarendon Press, 1933), p. 7, n. 2.

individual selfishness. But what is more important for our purposes than the effects of great power predominance is the fact that the existence of a board of directors implied the existence of a corporation. If "great power" became a more concretely meaningful expression, so did "Europe." The Treaty of Paris in 1815, establishing the Quadruple Alliance, contained a reference to the function of the great powers to take measures "for the maintenance of the Peace of Europe." [4] A conception of European solidarity, of a community of nations, took root in the nineteenth century and found its expression in the operative agency of the Concert of Europe.

The great powers gave evidence in various ways of their assumption that Europe was a political community as well as a geographical category. The Concert decided on the admission of new members to "Europe," as when it accepted Greece and Belgium as independent states in 1830, and declared that non-Christian Turkey was entitled to full status in the European system in 1856. It undertook, from the conclusion of the Treaty of Chaumont in 1814, "to maintain the equilibrium of Europe," [5] and in pursuance of this aim, intervened in such matters as the Russo-Turkish conflicts of the 1850's with a view to preventing the disruption of the balance of power upon which European order was deemed to depend. It assumed the responsibility of formulating certain standards of European public policy, as when it insisted at the Congress of Berlin in 1878 that Serbia could "enter the European family" only if it recognized the religious liberty of its subjects, described as one of "the principles which are the basis of social organization in all States of Europe." [6] The Concert system was the manifestation of a rudimentary but growing sense of interdependence and community of interest among the states of Europe.

The functions which the Concert presumed to exercise on behalf of Europe point to another major aspect of the developing nineteenth-century system. Multilateral conferences became something more than "peace" conferences in the traditional sense—meetings of statesmen to conclude wars and agree upon treaties of peace. The occasions and purposes of consultation, and the subject matter of international discussion, became more varied. The numerous conferences which were held in the decades after the Congress of Vienna were concerned with the maintenance of existing peaceful conditions, the substitution of pacific for violent methods of manipulating the distribution of power, the agreement upon ground rules for playing the competitive game of imperialism, and the formulation of general international legislation applicable to the ordinary relations of states. The Concert system gave Europe, for the first time since the rise of na-

[4] See the excerpt in Gerard J. Mangone, *A Short History of International Organization* (New York: McGraw-Hill, 1954), p. 64.

[5] See Article XVI of the Treaty of Chaumont, Frederick H. Hartmann, ed., *Basic Documents of International Relations* (New York: McGraw-Hill, 1951), p. 3.

[6] Oscar I. Janowsky, *Nationalities and National Minorities* (New York: Macmillan, 1945), p. 180.

tional states, something imperfectly resembling an international parliament, which undertook to deal by collective action with current problems ranging from the regulation of international traffic on the great rivers of the Continent to the adjustment of relations between belligerent and neutral states, and from the re-division of Balkan territories to the carving up of Africa.

Not only was the principle of joint consultation established, and the expectation of collective diplomatic treatment of major international issues normalized, but important progress was made in developing the techniques and creating the psychological prerequisites of successful mutilateral negotiation. It should be emphasized that international cooperation requires a great deal more than good intentions. When the bachelor and the spinster get married, being in love will help them get along with each other, but they will find that they both have habits appropriate to single bliss rather than to matrimony, and they are confronted with a problem of learning to live together which is more a problem of the head than of the heart. The analogy applies to the relationships of states; it is no simple problem for sovereigns to develop the devices which are essential for the efficient conduct of multilateral conferences and to adopt the attitudes which are necessary for harmonious consultation.

Before the nineteenth century, the rulers of Europe were so preoccupied with their Sovereign Dignity that they were virtually unable to do anything more at international conferences than argue about questions of precedence and prestige. In planning for a peaceful European order, William Penn felt compelled to stipulate that sovereigns should meet in a round room with many doors, so that substantive discussions should not be delayed by long arguments about who should have the privilege of entering first into the room! Rousseau described international conferences as places "where we deliberate in common council whether the table will be round or square, whether the hall will have more doors or less, whether such and such a plenipotentiary will have his face or back turned toward the window." [7]

No subsequent developments have completely eliminated such seemingly trivial matters from the list of obstacles to effective international cooperation, but the experience gained and the procedural innovations adopted in the great conferences of the nineteenth century contributed notably to the facilitation of serious consideration of problems by the representatives or rulers of sovereign states. Statesmen learned something about the arrangements and procedures, and became imbued with some of the temperamental attributes, which make possible the give and take of genuine multilateral negotiation.

Sound evaluation of the nineteenth-century political conference sys-

[7] Cited in F. S. Dunn, *The Practice and Procedure of International Conferences* (Baltimore: Johns Hopkins, 1929), pp. 78-79.

tem requires caution against exaggerating its contribution to the development of international organization. It did not produce permanently functioning institutions for handling the problems of high politics and security. Conferences were sporadic rather than periodic; they were, in Sir Alfred Zimmern's phrase, "the medicine of Europe rather than its daily bread." [8] Collaboration was improvised, not regularized, and it rested upon the basis of the authority which the great powers arrogated to themselves rather than upon clearly established legal foundations.

The conference system did not inaugurate a rule of law, or produce an impartial agency politically superior to national states and capable of upholding the moral standards of a larger community. It was a system of *de facto* great power hegemony, and the fact that its arrangements frequently resulted in collective or international decisions did not mean that those decisions were necessarily wise or just. Indeed, the beginning of wisdom for the student of international organization—a start which can very well be made in the study of the Concert of Europe—is to learn to avoid the illusion that decisions made by many states, whether they be small or great powers, are, simply because of their collective origin, almost automatically superior in wisdom and righteousness to decisions made by individual states. Sitting around a conference table does not transform selfish nationalists and arrogant power politicians into a collegium of world-minded, justice-oriented statesmen of humanity.

When all is said and done, the political conference system contributed more to awareness of the problems of international collaboration than to their solution, and more to opening up the possibilities of multilateral diplomacy than to realizing them. But it produced the prototype of a major organ of modern international organization—the executive council of the great powers.

THE HAGUE SYSTEM

A new sort of international conclave was instituted at the Hague in 1899 and 1907. The conscious construction of a distinctive "Hague System" of international relations was interrupted all too soon by the outbreak of the First World War, but the beginning that had been made was significant enough to figure as one of the major contributions of the nineteenth century to present-day world organization.

The two "International Peace Conferences" held at the Hague, under the initial impetus provided by Czar Nicholas II of Russia, were notable as major diplomatic gatherings convoked in time of peace to deal with a variety of subjects involved in the business of international relations. While the original motivations behind the Hague Conferences were questionable (it

---

[8] *The League of Nations and the Rule of Law, 1918-1935* (London: Macmillan, 1936), p. 78.

has been alleged that the Czar was actuated less by sincere desire to promote peace than by worry about Russia's financial disadvantage in the armaments competition), and their immediate results were not universally regarded as promising (the London *Times* held that the conference of 1907 "was a sham, and has brought forth a progeny of shams, because it was founded on a sham" [9]), it is clear that the Hague meetings were envisaged as steps toward a more adequate organization of the state system, and it is from that point of view that they will be discussed here.

A leading feature of the Hague System was its approach toward universality. Whereas the first conference was attended by only twenty-six states, and was preponderantly European in composition, the second involved representatives of forty-four states, including the bulk of the Latin American republics. Thus, the world achieved in 1907 its first General Assembly; as the president of that conference put it, "This is the first time that the representatives of all constituted States have been gathered together to discuss interests which they have in common and which contemplate the good of all mankind." [10] This was a significant step toward broadening the focus of international diplomacy, toward escaping the increasingly unrealistic European-fixation and defining more accurately the boundaries of the community of nations with whose problems statesmen had to deal.

Universality had another implication than inclusion of non-European states; it meant the acceptance at major diplomatic assemblies of the small states on equal terms with the great powers. If the Concert of Europe had been a Board of Directors of the European corporation, the Hague System, particularly in 1907, was a Stockholders Meeting of a much more extensive corporation. At the Hague, the small states got a strong taste of independence and equality. The results were not uniformly good; there were some accusations that this first draught produced intoxication, evidenced by undue self-assertion and unseemly self-importance on the part of small power representatives, and angry mutterings were heard that the small states were incapable of holding the liquor of equal diplomatic status. Nevertheless, it was a foretaste of things to come. International organization got its first taste of the difficulties of solving the conflict between great and small states as to their relative status and function in the business of managing international affairs. The era of the Concert had been the period, *par excellence,* of great power hegemony; the Hague Conferences ushered in the heyday of the small states.

These conferences marked a new peak in the development of collective activity for the purpose of general permanent reform of the system of

---

[9] Cited in J. B. Scott, ed., *American Addresses at the Second Hague Peace Conference* (Boston: Ginn, 1910), p. xiii.

[10] J. B. Scott, ed., *The Reports to the Hague Conferences of 1899 and 1907* (Oxford: Humphrey Milford, 1917), p. 201.

international relations, as distinguished from the purpose of dealing with specific, temporary situations. More conspicuously than the Concert of Europe, the Hague System was divorced from the immediate problems raised by particular wars or disputes, and was concerned with international problems in the abstract. In an important sense, this statement justifies the contention that the conferences were a sham. The powers consented to meet largely because the original Russian initiative could not be spurned without diplomatic embarrassment and pacifistic public opinion could not be ignored without domestic embarrassment. Their willingness to consider general principles was but the reverse side of their unwillingness to submit specific issues, which were the real components of the contemporary problem of peace, to the judgment of a conference. In political terms, the conferences involved a considerable degree of multilateral insincerity, and met in an atmosphere heavy with unreality. Nevertheless, the statesmen of the Hague, for whatever reasons, contributed to the establishment of the precedent that collective diplomacy should be oriented toward such matters as the codification and further development of important branches of international law, the formulation of standing procedures for the peaceful settlement of disputes, and the promotion of the principle that pacific solutions should be sought by disputants and might properly be urged and facilitated by disinterested states.

The Hague concepts were not revolutionary; they pointed toward encouragement of avoidance of war and mitigation of the evils and barbarities of warfare rather than recision of the legal right of states to make war, and toward the evolution of tolerable conditions of international life within the multistate system rather than drastic transformation of the system itself. But the business of the Hague was clearly the reform of the rules and methods of the system, rather than the solution of the problems arising out of particular cases of conflict within the system.

This aspect of the Hague Conferences was emphasized by the attention which was given to the task of institution-building. For our purposes, the primary historical importance of the meetings of 1899 and 1907 lies in the fact that a major concern of the participants was to create devices and agencies which would be permanently at the disposal of states.

The urge toward institutionalization was expressed first in regard to the Hague Conferences themselves. At the 1907 assembly, the view clearly predominated that there should be not simply Hague Conferences, but a Hague System. The concept of regular, periodic international conferences, which had received acceptance only from 1815 to 1822 as a basic plank in the platform of the Concert of Europe, was reintroduced. The interval between the two Hague Conferences had been eight years, and the American representatives in 1907 favored the establishment of machinery by which future conferences would be regularly convened without the necessity of initiatory action by any state. This proposal was not fully accepted, but the second conference did recommend "the assembly of a Third Peace Conference, which might be held within a period corresponding to that which has elapsed since the preceding Conference, at a date to be fixed by common agreement between the Powers. . . ." [11] This action led Joseph H. Choate, a member of the American delegation, to comment:

> Friends of peace, friends of arbitration, may now depend upon it that every seven or eight years there will be a similar conference, and that where the last conference left the work unfinished the new conference will take it up, and so progress from time to time be steadily made. . . .[12]

The hope for a reunion at the Hague in 1915 was dashed by the outbreak of a general war, but the revitalization of the idea of a regular assembly of the nations was to prove a more significant event than the gentlemen of 1907 could have imagined.

In other important respects, the Hague Conferences tended toward systematization. Their very size conduced to the adoption of innovations in conference technique. Experimental use was made of the apparatus of chairmen, committees, and roll calls, even though "It seemed extraordinary to those not accustomed to it to see Governments, as ordinary individuals, responding to a roll-call." [13] Although the rule of unanimity formally prevailed, this traditional practice, resting upon the fundamental respect for sovereignty which characterized international law, was mitigated to the extent that *voeux,* or recommendations of the conference, were passed by a mere majority vote. Most significantly of all, the 1907 assembly anticipated the future by proposing that a preparatory committee should be established to collect and study suggested items of business and prepare an agenda for the next meeting, and to put forward a system of organization and procedure for adoption by the Third Hague Conference.[14] The statesmen gathered at the Hague, looking forward to the completion of a permanent home for their meetings which had been promised by Andrew Carnegie, clearly believed that they were favored to be the founding fathers of a permanently functioning, efficiently organized mechanism for the maintenance of world peace.

The Hague efforts at institutional creativity extended also to the erection of agencies which would be available for use by states involved in particular quarrels. In 1899, a Convention for the Pacific Settlement of International Disputes was adopted, containing provisions for the establishment and functioning of *ad hoc* International Commissions of Inquiry, at the option of the disputing parties, and for the creation of the Permanent

---

[11] *Ibid.,* p. 216.
[12] Scott, *American Addresses at the Second Hague Peace Conference,* p. xxv.
[13] Scott, *The Reports to the Hague Conferences of 1899 and 1907,* p. xxxi.
[14] *Ibid.,* pp. 216-217.

Court of Arbitration. The latter body was misnamed, since it in fact consisted of a standing list of persons who might be selected as arbitrators whenever states wished to avail themselves of their services. Nevertheless, it was "permanent" in the sense that it was equipped with a standing professional staff and diplomatic board of control, and with a set of rules for the process of arbitration. The establishment of this agency did not satisfy the ambitions of the Hague statesmen; they expended great energy in the effort to create two full-fledged judicial institutions, a Court of Arbitral Justice and an International Prize Court. These projects did not reach fruition, but the Hague Conferences nevertheless represented the climax of a century of development in which attention shifted more and more to the possibilities of international institutions as instruments of world peace.

The Hague Conferences were notable events in the history of international organization not so much because of their actual accomplishments as because of the conceptions to which they gave expression, the hopes which they dramatized, the proposals which they largely failed to put into effect, and the problems which they failed to solve but succeeded in exposing.

The abortive system of the Hague called attention to the emerging reality of a global, rather than a merely European, state system, the demands of small states for participation in the management of that system, and the need for institutionalized procedures, as well as improvised settlements, in the conduct of international relations.

The Hague approach to the problem of peace was distinctly rationalistic and legalistic. The focus on the peaceful settlement of disputes was a clear indication of the underlying assumption that war was a product of misunderstandings and emotional flurries that could be eliminated by elucidation of the facts in dispute, clarification of the applicable law, and invocation of the calmness and self-possession of reasonable men. This reliance upon rational prudence and the judicial temper may have been excessive. Postponing evaluation, let it be said here that it was, for better or for worse, a leading characteristic of the Hague approach which was transmitted to subsequent conferences on international organization and is today a significant element in the operative theory of international organization. The Hague ideal of rationally self-restrained states submitting to a kind of Olympian judgment has not been realized, but neither has it been abandoned.

The conferences of 1899 and 1907 also anticipated twentieth-century international organization in the measure of their concern for peace in the abstract. They were devoted to building a peaceful system and preventing or controlling war in general, rather than to maintaining peace in a particular crisis or liquidating a specific war. Such an emphasis, in some degree, must characterize any system of international organization. It marks the inherent differences between systems and organizations on the one hand,

and expedients and improvisations on the other. Nevertheless, it points to one of the standing difficulties and problems of balance in international organization.

Almost everyone is for peace in the abstract, and is likely to be for war in certain specific situations; thus, international organization is likely to attract a volume of enthusiastic verbal support from public opinion when it works against *war* which may prove to be meaningless and ephemeral when it throws its influence against *wars*. On the other hand, experience shows that statesmen are unlikely to develop deep interest in the process of international organization, conceived as an approach to problems of peace in the abstract. The leaders of governments are almost by definition men who are preoccupied with the events and dangers of the present, with the crises of the moment, and they are not inclined to attach much importance to activities directed toward the solution of less concrete and immediate problems. In the mid-twentieth century, few Western statesmen can avoid translating "peace through security against aggression" into "peace through precautions against Soviet aggression"; they are not so much concerned with the problem of war as with the danger of World War III. The really fundamental support of statesmen is reserved for agencies designed to cope with urgent situations, not for those devoted to building a world order. This problem cannot be solved simply by avowing that statesmen are selfish and short-sighted and should become world-minded and far-seeing. Some change in that direction is essential, but it is equally necessary for international organization to achieve a proper balance between the projects of building a world system and of solving current international difficulties, between transforming international relations in the long run and saving international peace in the short run. This persistent problem of international organization was foreshadowed at the Hague Conferences.

The Hague System rendered valuable service in calling attention to the fact that there are difficult problems of international organization itself—instrumental problems—which must be solved in some degree before the problems of international relations—substantive problems—can usefully be tackled by international organization. Its most significant contribution to the future of international organization lay perhaps in its identification of some of the most basic of these instrumental problems. Champions of a better world order might well reflect on the lesson of the Hague—that the most valuable support may not be enthusiastic advocacy which minimizes difficulties but sober analysis which contributes to fuller understanding of the problems that lie ahead.

THE PUBLIC INTERNATIONAL UNIONS

The third major stream of development in the organization of international life arose from the creation of public international unions—agencies concerned with problems in various essentially nonpolitical fields. Whereas both the Concert and the Hague reflected the significance of the quest for security and the importance of high political issues, this third phenomenon was a manifestation of the increasing complexity of the economic, social, technical, and cultural interconnections of the peoples of the modern world.

In the nineteenth century, particularly after 1850, a new type of organizational effort emerged as the response of governments to the difficulties posed and the opportunities offered by the unprecedented international flow of commerce in goods, services, people, ideas, germs, and social evils. This was truly a revolutionary era; only a short while before, the national state had been too large to serve as the appropriate administrative unit for many of the affairs of men-in-society; now, it had become too small. The first products of the groping of states to create a rough correspondence between the area of administration and the new scope of the affairs requiring administration were the various international river commissions of Europe, the International Telegraphic Union (1865), and the Universal Postal Union (1874). The process of international organization, thus begun, quickly resulted in the establishment of a profusion of agencies whose terms of reference touched upon such diverse fields as health, agriculture, tariffs, railroads, standards of weight and measurement, patents and copyrights, narcotic drugs, and prison conditions.

This trend, it should be emphasized, was not the product so much of proposals as of facts, conditions, and needs. It represented adaptation, not innovation; it was less the work of idealists with schemes to advance than of realists with problems to handle. This is not to say that idea-men played no part in the process. It was a typical historical development in that the imaginative initiative of individuals and groups sparked a process of conscious social contrivance to meet the requirements formulated by circumstances. Yet, the essentially organic character of this trend in international affairs may be buttressed by reference to parallel trends within individual countries. In the nations most affected by the technological and industrial revolution, central governments were gaining in importance, compared with local and provincial governments, as agencies of administrative regulation, and they were expanding their administrative jurisdiction to cover aspects of economic and social life which had for some time been regarded as outside the province of government. In the international realm, the development of public international unions represented fundamentally similar patterns of evolution: the creation of international bodies to supplement the administrative work of national governments with narrowly limited territorial spheres of competence, and the notable expansion of the subject matter of international relations to include many problems which had been outside the scope of traditional diplomacy.

It has often been asserted that these national trends were produced, in more or less conspiratorial fashion, by mysteriously powerful statists and socialists, and the analogous international trends by similarly potent and devious internationalists and world govermentalists. A much less romantic theory seems valid: that the world has witnessed appropriately similar and simultaneous national and international adaptations to new conditions of complexity, which necessitate the redefinition of jurisdictional boundaries to correspond with the expanding territorial scope of problems requiring solution, and the redefinition of the functional responsibility of governmental institutions to correspond with the expanding area of subject matter requiring regulation.

The nineteenth-century international organizations represented at most the initiation, not the consummation, of a trend toward international control of the subjects with which they were concerned. Although the national and international developments which have been pointed out were fundamentally similar, in terms of directional tendencies, they were profoundly different, in terms of immediate results; domestically, the agencies of expanded territorial and functional jurisdiction were instruments of authoritative government; internationally, the corresponding agencies were instruments of voluntary cooperation among states. Public international unions were not segments of governmental apparatus, drawing power from the circuits of a pre-established dynamo of sovereignty, but rudimentary pieces of a system of intergovernmental collaboration, dependent for their operation upon such power as could be generated in the new and drastically incomplete plant of international authority.

These agencies engaged in a range of activities which was something new under the international sun. Most importantly, they served as collection points and clearing houses for information, centers for discussion of common problems by governments, instruments for achieving the coordination by agreement of national policies and practices, and agencies for promoting the formulation and acceptance of uniform or minimum standards in the fields of their concern. To a lesser extent, some of them had functions of actual regulation and administration in limited spheres and of arbitration or conciliation in cases of conflict among states. On the whole, however, this was a system for the provision of services to governments and the facilitation of cooperative relations among governments, not for the management of affairs or the government of people.

It is obvious that, judged by such criteria as the possession of legislative competence, power of taxation, and executive authority, the public international unions of the nineteenth century were vastly inferior to those institutions which we call governments. However, the clue to their significance may be found not in the observation that they were *less than* governments, but in the observation that they were *different from* governments. It is perhaps less than absolutely self-evident that the necessary and proper approach to world order consists simply of the mimicry of the devices and methods of national government. In any event, the founders of these agencies did not set out to create supranational governmental institutions, and end up by creating incredibly inadequate ones; rather, they undertook to establish international mechanisms for doing a kind of job that had never been done before, and they succeeded in stimulating an experimental development of functional innovations in international relations which has not yet begun to reach the limits of its potential historical significance.

Turning from function to form, we find that the nonpolitical international bodies of the nineteenth century produced organizational inventions which were of fundamental importance for the future. The first genuinely permanent international machinery was the product and property of these agencies. The Bureau of the International Telegraphic Union, established in 1868, was the prototype of the secretariat, the vital core of any modern international organization. This development of a permanent staff to give continuity to the organization, to carry out functions of research, correspondence, and publication, and to prepare the business and make arrangements for future conferences, was the crucial step in the transformation of international organizations from sequences of disconnected conferences into genuine institutions. In addition to establishing bureaus, the public international unions of the nineteenth century introduced the dichotomy between the general policy-making conference of all the member states and the council or governing body, consisting of representatives of a few selected members and functioning as a policy directorate on behalf of the organization in the intervals between general conferences. Thus was established the structural pattern of bureau, council, and conference which, with many elaborations but few deviations, serves as the blueprint of international organization today.

Modest but significant advances in the techniques of international collaboration and breaches in the rigidity of principles impeding the development of collective action were brought about by public international unions. Valuable experience was gained in handling the myriad problems of language, documentation, internal organization, and procedure of large-scale international gatherings. The treaty, traditionally an agreement negotiated by the representatives of two or a few states for the establishment of particular legal rights and duties pertaining to themselves, was given the form of the multilateral convention, hammered out in committee and conference of many states, voted upon as if it were a legislative bill, and adopted to serve as a joint legislative enactment. Such a convention might relate to any one of a thousand subjects, ranging from the handling of international postal communications to the control of epidemic diseases, which were for the most part utterly foreign to the subject matter traditionally dealt with by treaties. Technically, multilateral conventions were still treaties, despite their unusual subject matter, the quasi-parliamentary nature of the proceedings leading to their formulation, and the fact that their participants resembled a congregation more than a partnership; this meant that each state was equally entitled to have a voice in their formation and to consider itself unaffected by them unless it consented to be bound by their terms. However, some minor revisions appeared even in regard to these sacrosanct implications of sovereignty. Arrangements for the unequal distribution of voting power were made in several unions, and the rules of unanimity and "no treaty obligation without ratification" were pushed aside, formally in the International Telegraphic Union and informally in the Universal Postal Union, to permit the easier adoption of generally applicable rules on essentially noncontroversial and technical matters. The multilateral convention was, and still is, a clumsy and inadequate device for international legislation, but the creation of this instrument out of the old materials of the treaty device was nevertheless a major triumph of nineteenth-century nonpolitical organizations.

This phase of the development of international organization was marked by the emergence of wholly new groups of participants in the business of international affairs, which had hitherto been virtually a monopoly of diplomats, foreign ministers, and other statesmen accustomed to wearing the mantle of sovereignty. The result could hardly have been otherwise when international relations began to include such matters as public health, telegraphic codes, and plant diseases, along with wars, alliances, and boundaries. The intruders included all manner of professional specialists and technical experts, members of the embryonic body of international civil servants, private interest-group and humanitarian organizations, and governmental officials and ministers outside the foreign offices. Many of the new agencies owed their creation to nondiplomats; for instance, David Lubin, a Sacramento merchant, was the instigator of the movement that produced the International Institute of Agriculture,[15] and American and German postal officials initiated the formation of the Universal Postal Union. Some international unions began as organizations of private associations, and were later transformed by the substitution of governmental for unofficial delegations; in a few cases, they remained mixed, private and public, in character. In operation, public international unions relied heavily upon the work of experts, and governments tended to entrust the representative function at conferences to subject-matter specialists from appropriate departments rather than, or in addition to, professional diplomats. This tendency for everyone to get in

[15] Mangone, *op. cit.*, pp. 88-89.

on the international act was not an unmixed blessing, but it was clearly a novel phenomenon, and another of the nineteenth-century portents of things to come.

In the final analysis, the most significant contribution of the early public international unions to the evolution of international organization was a cluster of ideas and attitudes. The most important of these was a derivative of the expanded concept of the subject matter of international relations: the implication that there is an area of international affairs within which sovereign states have a common interest in cooperative endeavor. If we conceive international relations narrowly enough, we can maintain the simple proposition that they are reducible to the terms of conflicting-interest relationships. If we conceive them broadly enough to embrace their total reality, our neat picture is rudely complicated by the necessity of recognizing that they also partake of the character of common-interest relationships. This was the lesson of the nonpolitical organizational system of the nineteenth century. The Concert stood for compromise; the Hague stood for regulation; the public international unions stood for cooperation. The cooperative concept is not essentially idealistic or altruistic. Its focus is on the satisfaction of needs, which demands not so much the sacrifice of sovereignty as the utilization of the resources of sovereignty to create institutions and methods capable of supplementing the functional activity of national governments. The creation of public international unions was indicative of the recognition of, and of a groping after compensation for, the functional inadequacy of sovereignty.

CONCLUSION

Twentieth-century international organization is very largely the product of the convergence of these three streams of development which arose in the nineteenth century. To a limited extent, international agencies established in the early formative period of international organization have simply continued to exist; the most notable instances are those of the Universal Postal Union and the International Telegraphic Union, now transformed into the International Telecommunication Union. To a much greater degree, the past century has influenced the present by providing the broad outlines of a general system of international organization, combining great power councils, universal conferences, specialized functional units, and permanent staffs. Current international organization owes much to the earlier period of experimentation in the elaboration of functions, the devising of structural patterns, and the invention of procedures for multilateral agencies. Most basically, the nineteenth century contributed a broadening concept of the nature and subject matter of international relations, an evolving sense of the need for joint decisions and actions by states, a growing recognition of the potential usefulness of international machinery, and an increasingly clear awareness of the problems of achieving effective international organization.

The question must be faced as to whether the nineteenth century did not leave us an inheritance more harmful than helpful to our endeavors for saving the world from chaos and our nations from destruction. The power politician might say that we were bequeathed a potentially fatal delusion which has diverted our attention from literally vital efforts to comprehend the grim reality of international relations and to master the arts of national survival in the international jungle. The world federalist might say that the nineteenth century set us off on the wrong foot; it encouraged us to attempt the impossible task of reforming the operations of the multistate system, when we should have been repudiating that system altogether and adopting a world government. Whether these criticisms are valid or not, it is clear that one part of the legacy was an ambiguity which is a persistent bane of the existence of international organization. Men and nations want the benefits of international organization, but they also want to retain the privileges of sovereignty which are inseparable from international disorganization. The development of international organization has been plagued by the failure of human beings to think logically and realistically about the inexorable relationships between the purchase and the price, between the having and the eating of the cake. The discrepancies among the objective need for international organization, the subjective awareness of that need, and the subjective capacity of men to create and maintain the organizational structure appropriate to that need are a part of the established tradition of international organization.

SUGGESTED READINGS

Choate, Joseph H., *The Two Hague Conferences,* Princeton: Princeton University Press, 1913.

Mangone, Gerald J., *A Short History of International Organization,* New York: McGraw-Hill, 1954.

Mitrany, David, *The Progress of International Government,* New Haven: Yale University Press, 1933.

Phillips, Walter Alison, *The Confederation of Europe,* Second Edition, London: Longmans, Green, 1920.

Reinsch, Paul S., *Public International Unions,* Boston: Ginn, 1911.

Webster, C. K., *The Congress of Vienna,* New York: Oxford University Press, 1919.

Woolf, L. S., *International Government,* London: George Allen and Unwin, 1916.

CHAPTER

3

The Establishment of the League of Nations

It is useful to consider the nineteenth century as the era of *preparation for* international organization, and, for this purpose, to treat 1815, the year of the Congress of Vienna, and 1914, the year of the outbreak of World War I, as its chronological boundaries. Starting thus, we establish the years which have passed since the momentous events of 1914 as the era of *establishment of* international organization, which, in these terms, comes to be regarded as a phenomenon of the twentieth century. There is an element of artificiality in this scheme, as in all efforts to divide history into distinct periods, but it is nevertheless a serviceable device for the study of the process of organizing international relations.

Clearly, the establishment of the League of Nations was an event of fundamental importance, worthy of being considered a decisive forward step in that evolutionary process. To change the figure, nineteenth-century institutions provided the ancestry, but the League of Nations provided the parentage, of international organization as we know it today.

The purpose of this chapter is to analyze the creation of the League, with particular emphasis upon the sources from which the new organization derived and the nature with which it was invested. The legal and structural pattern and operational experience of the League will be dealt with in segmental fashion in subsequent parts of this book. It suffices at this point to treat the establishment of the League as one of the great flurries of creativity in the historical development of international organization.

SOURCES OF THE LEAGUE

The immediate origins of the League of Nations are to be found in the development of both private and public schemes during the War of 1914-1918, particularly in the United States and Great Britain, and in the negotiations which took place at Paris as a part of the diplomatic enterprise of bringing the war to a formal conclusion. Unofficial consideration of the possibility of making a great new experiment in international organization flourished during the years of hostilities, under the leadership of such groups of prominent and influential citizens as those who united in the League to Enforce Peace, in the United States, and the League of Nations Society, in Britain.

Governmental leaders were not far behind. Lord Robert Cecil devoted himself to advocacy of a postwar organizational effort in the British Cabinet, with the result that a committee was established under Lord Phillimore to draft definite proposals. The French Government set up a similar planning body, headed by Léon Bourgeois. In the United States, President Wilson gave public support to the concept of a League of Nations as early as 1916. In his address of April 2, 1917, invoking a formal Congressional declaration of war upon Germany, he asserted the national purpose of fighting "for a universal dominion of right by such a concert of free peoples as shall bring peace and safety to all nations and make the world itself at last free,"[1] and he later included an even more explicit commitment to the formation of "a general association of nations" as the climactic point in his famous list of war aims known as the "Fourteen Points."[2] Wilson and his trusted adviser, Colonel House, undertook the preparation of American blueprints for the proposed organization. Finally, a pamphlet, *The League of Nations: A Practical Suggestion,* by the distinguished statesman of South Africa and the British Empire, Jan Christiaan Smuts, provided perhaps the most significant example of governmental thinking about international organization submitted to the peace conference.

The actual formulation of the Covenant of the League of Nations was the work of a special committee established by the Paris Peace Conference, which began its sessions in January 1919. The committee consisted of representatives of the five great powers—Britain, France, the United States, Italy, and Japan—and of at first five, then nine, of the smaller states. Wilson served as chairman, and the great powers effectively dominated

---

[1] Ray S. Baker and William E. Dodd, eds., *The Public Papers of Woodrow Wilson, War and Peace* (New York: Harper, n.d.), I, 16.

[2] *Ibid.*, p. 161.

the proceedings. More precisely, the drafting of the Covenant became a predominantly Anglo-American enterprise; the Hurst-Miller draft, a combination of British and American plans, was used as the basic working paper, and Wilson, Cecil, and Smuts earned the title of Fathers of the League.

Presented to the plenary conference on April 28, 1919, the Covenant became an integral part of the Treaty of Versailles, and assumed formal effectiveness on January 10, 1920. It was, in terms of its direct derivations, the product of specific wartime planning and postwar negotiations; in a more fundamental sense, however, it was a product of history, of contemporary circumstances, and of an emergent trend in international life.

We have already sketched, in Chapter 2, the preliminary developments in the field of international organization which contributed to the shaping of the Covenant. The formation of the League was in part a process of imitation of the organizational forms and types of the nineteenth century. But strict imitation was not so much in evidence as completion, elaboration, and progressive adaptation of the primitive prototypes of international organization. The Council of the League was a new edition of the Concert of Europe; but it was a significantly *revised* edition, incorporating the principles of legal definition of authority and terms of reference, institutional continuity, regularity of session, and balanced composition of great and small power representatives. The Assembly represented the realization of the hopes and plans of the Hague statesmen for a general conference of the nations, meeting periodically without dependence upon the initiative of a single state and equipped to develop standing rules of procedure. The Secretariat was an institutional flowering of the seminal concept of the international bureau which had been found in the earlier unions. The Permanent Court of International Justice, which was anticipated in Article 14 of the Covenant[3] but not definitively established until its Statute received ratification by a majority of the members of the League on August 20, 1921, constituted the full-fledged international judicial organ which the Hague Conferences, dissatisfied with the primitive Permanent Court of Arbitration, had vainly tried to create. The International Labor Organization, a partially autonomous agency but one closely related to the League, was the lineal descendant of the system of specialized functional organizations of the nineteenth century. The Covenant provided for some institutional innovations, such as a standing body to advise the Council on armaments and military matters and the Permanent Mandates Commission, but it represented primarily the continuation and evolution of organizational achievements and the realization of frustrated organizational hopes of the past century.

---

[3] See the text of the Covenant in Appendix I.

The creation of the League may also be regarded as a rationalization, focalization, and consolidation of previous organizational developments. The League was a composite of the institutional descendants of nineteenth-century agencies; it pulled together the separate lines of development into a coherent system. Although it never fully achieved the comprehensive control of international cooperative activities which was envisaged in Article 24 of the Covenant, the League did serve generally to convert organizations into organs of an organization. It provided what has been variously referred to as a "hub" or a "roof" element, giving the modern world its first taste of institutional centralization.

The League was also the product of nineteenth-century beginnings in the sense that it picked up the ideas, adopted the assumptions, and reacted to the awarenesses which had been emergent in that earlier period. It was a more mature response to the recognition of the need for, and the challenge of the possibilities of, international organization. Smuts showed an appreciation of the lessons of the past as well as a vision of the future when he wrote, in 1918:

> It is not sufficient for the League merely to be a sort of *deus ex machina,* called in in very grave emergencies when the spectre of war appears; if it is to last, it must be much more. It must become part and parcel of the common international life of States, it must be an ever visible, living, working organ of the polity of civilization. It must function so strongly in the ordinary peaceful intercourse of States that it becomes irresistible in their disputes; its peace activity must be the foundation and guarantee of its war power.[4]

More immediate historical events also contributed to the shaping of the new organization; the League was, in important respects, the product of the First World War.

In the first place, it was a response to the realization, now more widespread and intense than ever before, of the vital need to prevent wars. It is difficult for us, living in the second half of the twentieth century, to comprehend the optimism and blissful obliviousness to the problem of war which had characterized the pre-1914 generation. Gilbert Murray has given us an illuminating description of the mood of that era:

> the mass of educated people did not think much about the danger which actually brought the age to disaster—the international anarchy which led to the War. . . .
>
> Things were safe, and improving. And none of the critics seriously diagnosed the one real danger. They prophesied revolution, and all sorts of terrors which never came. But they did not see that the international anarchy of a world administered by some sixty sovereign independent states with no authority over them, admitting no

[4] Cited in F. P. Walters, *A History of the League of Nations* (London: Oxford University Press, 1952), I, 59.

reciprocal duties and nursing unlimited national ambitions, was a disease carrying the seeds of death. M. Seignobos, the French historian, wrote two articles in 1913 to explain that he considered a European war no longer a danger to be reckoned with. Mr. Brailsford said the same in his book *The War of Steel and Gold,* published in 1914. I am pretty sure I thought the same. The Cosmos, strong in self-confidence, vigorous in self-criticism, was not much troubled by thoughts of the precipice towards which it was actually moving.[5]

The Great War changed all this; it produced a fresh awareness of the horrors of war, a rather bewildered admission that modern European civilization was not immune from the destructive forces of military conflict, and a distressed feeling that "it must not happen again."

This emotional reaction produced the intellectual conviction that the war had been a horrible accident, resulting from stupid and indefensible negligence. Arthur Sweetser took a position which he correctly attributed also to Sir Edward Grey, British Foreign Minister in 1914, when he wrote soon after the end of the conflict:

> the war came into being largely by default, because the forces of negotiation and peaceful settlement marshalled against it suddenly collapsed . . . the world in 1914 got itself into a blind alley where all doors were closed except that to war. . . .
>
> The catastrophe began without a single conference. The nations were plunged into war by a handful of telegrams which in their portentous official phraseology are even today not fully understood. One false step led to another until the vicious circle was complete. No meeting ground was available, no obligation for discussion existent. The madmen who had worked for war could generate it without a pretence of discussion, without the simple human act of meeting their opponents face to face, without asking yea or nay of their peoples.[6]

The League was based on reaction against "the blind vagrant way in which the various publics blundered into hostilities in 1914."[7] The concept of the Accidental War underlay the system of prudent precautions which was outlined in the Covenant, providing guarantees that peoples and governments should have and utilize opportunities for cooling off, facing facts, and reaching decent settlements in any future crisis. This principle of a moratorium on violent expression of intemperate passions, designed to exploit the assumed avoidability of war, was pre-eminently a British contribution to the Covenant.

The League's dedication to the provision of safeguards against accidental and unnecessary war was illustrative of what is perhaps a general tendency for international organizations to exhibit a retrospective men-

---

[5] *From the League to U.N.* (London: Oxford University Press, 1948), pp. 18, 22.
[6] *The League of Nations at Work* (New York: Macmillan, 1920), pp. 5, 8-9.
[7] *Ibid.*, p. 58.

tality. Such a tendency is no monopoly of international organizations; if the League was created to prevent the outbreak of World War I, the French Maginot Line was also built to win the battles of World War I. But it is significant that the great organizational endeavors of the modern world have been parts of the aftermath of great wars, and it is possible to argue that they have tended to produce instruments better adapted to preventing the recently concluded tragedy than to dealing with the momentous issues of the future. The League, established to prevent the accidental war, was unable to cope with Hitler's deliberately plotted campaign of conquest; as we shall see later, the United Nations may with some justice be described as a device for nipping World War II, rather than World War III, in the bud, and some of its activities may be interpreted as post-mortem resistance to Hitler. There is a real danger that newly created international organizations may not be simply too little and too late, but also already out of date. The fundamental problem of modern man, not yet adequately appreciated, is to learn how to build his international organizations on the basis of a wise understanding of the lessons of history *and* a perceptive estimate of the issues and forces which will challenge his survival and welfare in the future.

The First World War not only aroused the nations to their responsibility for taking urgent measures to prevent the recurrence of war's disastrous effects, but it also stimulated them to ponder the lessons of the cooperative potentialities which it revealed. The beginning of wisdom about modern war is to recognize its dual character: it is a phenomenon of conflict, and it is a phenomenon of cooperation. In the realm of individual relations, its functional significance from a moral and psychological point of view is that it calls for the expression of both uninhibited hostility and uncommon devotion to a community of effort and purpose; if it operates primarily to release aggressive instincts in some men, it also imposes unparalleled demands upon the cooperative instincts of other men. In the realm of international relations, a similar dualism characterizes war. It reveals the awful potentialities of international conflict, but it also stimulates the extraordinary development of, and demonstrates unsuspected possibilities of, the capacity of nations for collaboration. World War I served to convince men that there existed great resources of international cooperation which had not previously been tapped.

The experience of wartime cooperation among the members of the victorious coalition inspired peoples to meet the moral challenge of proving that they could cooperate as readily to promote the values of peace and avoid the catastrophe of war as they had done to bring the war to a successful conclusion. This mood had a retrospective aspect; the chastisement of war had been visited upon nations which had been too sovereignly stiff-necked, too stubbornly uncooperative, to achieve in peacetime the creation of elementary devices for peaceful settlement of disputes. Allied collaboration had caused a shift of emphasis away from the sacrifice of sovereignty, the surrender of freedom of action, to the positive values—from the price to the reward—of united action by nations. Thus, the enterprise of the League reflected the ideal of continuing the collaboration which had produced victory. Alliance for war had laid the psychological foundations of alliance for peace.

Moreover, the conduct of the war had made a tangible contribution to the body of experience in creation and operation of multilateral agencies which was available to the founders of the League. Great Britain, France, and Italy, ultimately joined by the United States, had improvised an impressive network of joint bodies, including a Supreme War Council, a Revictualling Commission, an Allied Maritime Transport Council, and a Blockade Council. These agencies had proved invaluable in facilitating the complicated task of fighting together. They had seemed to prove that effective international cooperation could be achieved, without the necessity of creating an authoritative decision-making body to issue orders to national governments, by bringing together responsible officials of governments to get to know and trust each other, to confront the full and true facts of the situation together, and to harmonize their national policies on the basis of respect for the facts and appreciation of the positions of the various governments. There was some disappointment that the machinery of economic cooperation was dismantled at the end of the war, on the insistence of the United States. While the swords and spears were not themselves converted into plowshares and pruninghooks, the instruments of joint military effort nevertheless made an important addition to the stock of organizational models and techniques, and to the fund of optimism concerning the feasibility of cooperative achievement, which facilitated the creation of instruments of peaceful collaboration.

The coalition machinery also contributed to the future of international organization by aiding in the creation of a new breed of men—a group of officials and experts who had learned the techniques, acquired the attitudes, and developed the affirmative faith in international cooperation which are essential to its success. International organization depends heavily upon the work of such men, serving as national representatives and international officials. Since 1914, the modern world has produced its first generation of pioneers in international organization, men who have made their careers in the new professions of multilateral diplomacy and international administration. An outstanding example of this development is the career of Jean Monnet, a Frenchman who learned the skills of international service and statesmanship in the wartime coalition machinery, transferred his energies later to the League, and has most recently played an outstanding role in the creation and operation of European institutions. It would be easy to formulate a plausible "Great Man Theory" of international organization, emphasizing the role of the relatively small group of individuals whose names appear over and over again in the annals of twentieth-century international agencies as founding fathers, prominent participants on behalf of governments, and leading administrative officials. Resisting this temptation, we can at least recognize that the contributions of this group have been indispensable, particularly in view of the fact that the most thoroughly state-oriented professional groups involved in the management of international affairs along more orthodox lines, the diplomats, Foreign Office officials, and military specialists, have tended to show coolness, if not resistance, to the development of the newfangled ways and means of international organization. The rise of international organization to a place of vital importance in international life depends ultimately upon the support and participation of these latter groups, but it is clear that the preliminary development of a special class of experts in collaboration within the machinery of the World War I coalition was a phenomenon of real significance.

Wartime experience in the joint and coordinated use of the economic weapon against Germany implanted in the minds of Allied statesmen the new concept of nonmilitary sanctions, the economic squeeze, as an instrument for use by international organization to maintain world peace. This was one of the major contributions of World War I to the stock of ideas upon which the League was based.

In short, World War I influenced the creation of the League by stimulating efforts of the victorious powers to do in peacetime the things that should have been done before the war, in order to prevent it, and to continue doing the things which they had found it possible to do during the war, in order to win it.

Another cluster of factors affecting the formulation of the Covenant inhered in the general political situation existing in 1919. International organizations are never simply the products of creative planning and institutional evolution; they find their sources deep in the context of national interests and the power configuration of the international setting out of which they arise. Understanding of the nature of the League erected at the Paris Peace Conference requires analysis of the determinative political realities of the time.

A primary feature of the situation was the existence of a victorious military coalition. The international atmosphere was "still reeking with the fumes of war and still more or less dominated by the military spirit." [8] The psychology of conflict had merged into the mood of victory, and more than a trace of vindictiveness appeared in the proceedings at Paris. This points to a persistent dilemma of international organization: great organizational enterprises are dependent upon great wars to demonstrate their urgent necessity and to stimulate recognition of their feasibility, yet postwar

[8] Ray S. Baker, *Woodrow Wilson and the World Settlement* (Garden City: Doubleday, Page, 1922), I, 165.

periods are most inauspicious times for such undertakings, in the sense that they tend to be dominated by a temper of hatred, suspicion, and arrogant nationalism which bodes ill for the establishment of just foundations for a new world order. The world has not solved the problem of combining post war psychological readiness to organize with peacetime psychological fitness to organize.

In 1919, the triumphant Allies desired to harvest the fruits of victory, to keep the spoils which they had gained, to establish and uphold a new status quo reflecting the shift in power relations which military events had produced, and to maintain their coalition to keep Germany in a posture of defeat. In these terms, the function envisaged for the League was not so much to keep *peace,* but to keep *a specific peace*—to legitimize and stabilize a particular world settlement based upon victory. Woodrow Wilson perhaps wished to incorporate the Covenant into the peace treaties in order to make certain that the League should be established while the psychological iron was hot,[9] but it is clear that some other Allied statesmen approved this incorporation because they wished to symbolize the mission of the League as custodian of the architecture of the settlement imposed by victors upon vanquished.

A second determinative fact was the dominant position of the Principal Allied and Associated Powers; the world seemed to be the oyster of the great powers. The basic reality was not simply that Germany had been defeated, but that the great powers had done the job. Having won the war, they had the power, the prestige, and the inclination to determine the shape of the new regime.

This hegemony of the powerful few was strongly reflected in the preliminary planning for the League. Their nostalgic recollections focused on the Concert of Europe, not on the Hague Conferences. By and large, the great powers ran the show in 1919, and their conception of a world organization effectively under oligarchical direction and control was reflected in the Covenant provision for permanent membership of five great powers in the nine-power Council, and the clearly expressed expectation that the Assembly might meet only at four- or five-year intervals and would humbly play second fiddle to the Council in the new Concert. The major Allies asserted the right to make the settlement and assumed the responsibility to dominate the future course of events.

A countervailing fact of the politics of Paris was the resurgence of the small states; the world turned out to be a singularly reluctant and recalcitrant oyster of the great powers. The small states were multiplying in numbers, as the great multinational empires of Europe disintegrated under the impact of defeat and separatistic nationalism. They still cherished the

---

[9] Cf. Walters, *op. cit.,* I, 31.

taste of sovereign equality which they had had at the second Hague Conference, and a peculiar combination of factors supported their claims to play more than a modest and subservient role in the system of the future. They had the moral sympathy of Wilson, who had made the doctrine of national self-determination and the rights of small nations major ingredients in Allied propaganda. They were in a position to capitalize upon the determination of France to safeguard and enhance its position of Continental primacy by creating a bloc of European units oriented toward acceptance of French leadership. They benefited from the traditional concern of Britain to maintain the European configuration required by balance of power considerations, and from Britain's susceptibility to the pro-small-state influence of its Dominions. These factors gave the small states a measure of bargaining power which was utilized to extract such concessions from the great powers as four seats on the Council of the League, provision for equal participation of all members in the Assembly, and the general grant of an indiscriminate veto power in all the arrangements for voting in the new organization.

The small states hardly had a determining voice at Paris. They were still mainly objects of policy, rather than makers of policy, but the general interest in preserving fragmentation as a fact of the world political system enabled them to bring their influence to bear upon the shaping of the provisions of the Covenant.

The negotiations which produced the League of Nations were further marked by significant divergencies among the interests and policies of the great powers. Moreover, the complexity of the political pattern was increased by the fact that contradictory pressures emanated from individual powers. Thus, not only were compromises effected between British and American, and Anglo-American and French, conceptions of a world organization, but concessions were made to both Wilsonian idealism and Senatorial conservatism on the American side, and to both Léon Bourgeois' demand for an ambitious international military system and Clemenceau's skepticism concerning newfangled devices and methods on the French side. Political conflicts within the great powers, among the great powers, and between great and small power blocs, all played a part in determining the powers and limitations of the League and the distribution of power within the League.

Finally, the League was a product of the ideological climate of the time. Its sources included not only the heritage of past institutional inventions and the political realities of the present, but also the aspirations for the future which were embodied in current thinking. Like all great phenomena of human society, the establishment of the League derived from a combination of facts and ideas, circumstances and purposes, objective conditions and subjective conceptions. The new system reflected the philosophical assumptions and normative ideals which characterized the contemporary approach to international relations. These factors were not dominant, but they were important.

The figure of Woodrow Wilson dominated the ideological scene. He appeared as the prophet of a new era, making a dramatic appeal to peoples and governments; he symbolized the idea that the anarchy of power politics should be ended by the injection into international relations of the highest values evolved by political man. Sitting at the conference table, he had more than American power behind him; he was backed by the enthusiasm of masses of people in Western Europe who were newly conscious of international relations and conspicuously insistent that the lamb of peace not be devoured by the wolves of cynical diplomacy.

The scheme for a League of Nations adopted at Paris was, in ideological terms, an expression on the international level of nineteenth-century liberalism. It represented not so much a new set of ideas as a new area of expression for old ideas. While it was not, of course, a "pure" ideological product, the Covenant was predominantly liberal in tone.

This meant, first of all, that the League was intimately related to the assumptions and values of democratic theory. Wilson, following the thesis laid down more than a hundred years earlier by Immanuel Kant in his essay on *Perpetual Peace* (*Zum ewigen Frieden*), believed that world peace could be established only by a compact among democratically governed nations. Although the "self-governing" qualification for new members specified in Article 1 of the Covenant was in practice interpreted to mean only that approximate independence was the standard of eligibility for League membership, Wilson made it clear that he believed and intended that this provision should define the League as an organization of free peoples, enjoying the right of democratic self-government in their homelands.

> Only the free peoples of the world [Wilson asserted] can join the League of Nations. No nation is admitted to the League of Nations that cannot show that it has the institutions which we call free. No autocratic government can come into its membership, no government which is not controlled by the will and vote of its people.[10]

This Kantian-Wilsonian position rested upon the assumption that democracies, in contrast to autocracies, are inherently peaceful; "only a nation whose government was its servant and not its master could be trusted to preserve the peace of the world."[11] Common men are reasonable enough to abstain from rash hostilities which impose intolerable suffering upon themselves, and decent enough to respect the rights and

---

[10] Hamilton Foley, *Woodrow Wilson's Case for the League of Nations* (Princeton: Princeton University Press, 1923), p. 64.

[11] *Ibid.*

interests of other nations. War is caused by the selfish irresponsibility of rulers who can reap the benefits while they make their enslaved peoples pay the bitter price of war; when the people rule their nations, the nations will live in peace.

This version of political liberalism called for external, as well as internal, democracy. The League relied upon the beneficent impact of public opinion upon international relations. The new era was to be characterized by open diplomacy, the publication of treaties, the investigation and dissemination of the facts concerning international disputes, and the use of the League forum to submit grave issues to the moral consciousness of free peoples. Wilson envisaged the League as the "court of public opinion" in which the "conscience of the world" could render its verdict, "the general judgment of the world as to what is right."

> Nothing is going to keep this world fit to live in like exposing in public every crooked thing that is going on. . . . A bad cause will fare ill, but a good cause is bound to be triumphant in such a forum. You dare not lay a bad cause before mankind.[12]

Through the democratic process, the peoples of the world would control their governments and determine wise, peaceful, and cooperative policies; through the League, they would control the policies of other nations, injecting their wisdom and morality into international relations and saving the peace of mankind from the machinations of autocratic scoundrels.

Thus, the League rested upon two assumptions: that the age of democracy had arrived, providing a sufficient number of soundly democratic states to unite in an organization for maintaining world peace; and that the democratic method of arriving at agreement by civilized discussion rather than coercive dictation could be applied to the relations of democratic states as well as to those of individuals. Wilson had fought his war to make the world safe *for* democracy; he created his League to make the world safe *by* democracy.

The influence of nineteenth-century liberalism was evident, secondly, in the emphasis upon national self-determination which characterized Wilson's thinking about the organization of peace. This doctrine, so revolutionary in its implications, was not by any means absolutely dominant at the Peace Conference and it received no formal expression in the words of the Covenant, but it was nevertheless a major tenet of the Wilsonian faith. To the wartime President, national self-determination ranked as an essential corollary of democracy.[13] Just as the people had a right to govern themselves within the national system, so the nations had a right to govern themselves within the global system. The League was strongly imbued

[12] *Ibid.*, pp. 102, 106.

[13] Alfred Cobban, *National Self-Determination* (Chicago: University of Chicago Press, n.d.), p. 20.

with the Wilsonian conviction that the nation is the natural and proper unit of world politics, and that the only sound and moral basis for international order is a settlement which enables peoples to achieve autonomous existence within a system dedicated to the preservation of the independence and sovereignty of nations. Sovereignty was not a naughty word for the League; it was a symbol of liberty in international relations, comparable to democracy as a symbol of domestic freedom.

In the League philosophy, the realization of the ideals of democracy and self-determination was regarded as the essential means for minimizing the element of conflict in international relations. Given the proper division of the world into political units based upon considerations of nationality, those units would tend to develop along democratic lines. The diffusion of democracy and the elimination of frustrations stemming from denial of legitimate aspirations for national self-determination would combine to make international relations reasonably harmonious. Assuming these conditions, international organization appeared to be at once possible and almost—but not quite—unnecessary. The postulated international harmony was neither absolute nor automatic; there was enough harmony to make the operation of the League feasible, and sufficient need for harmonization to make its operation essential. The League would have to bolster its own foundations by providing devices of peaceful change which reasonable statesmen could use to perfect the realization of the ideal of equal justice to all nations. It would have to provide facilities for peaceful settlement of disputes and for effective restraints upon state behavior in the exceptional cases when appeal to reason and popular decency would not suffice. The League was to fill the international need for an accessible common judge and a method of coping with occasional outlaws. But, by and large, the League's function was to be that of providing a framework for the working out of possibilities of harmonious relations among free peoples, of holding the ring while offering facilities for such minimal collaboration as national interests might impel states to undertake.

This theoretical scheme was a logical projection of liberal political thought. It tied on not only to nineteenth-century liberalism but also to the liberal foundations which had been laid in the two preceding centuries. It represented a choice of John Locke over Thomas Hobbes. In the seventeenth century, Hobbes had postulated a social conflict so profound that peace and order could be achieved only under the iron rule of an all-powerful "Leviathan," while Locke had believed in a natural social order so nearly perfect that it required only a government with minimal powers and functions to remedy its inconveniences. It represented agreement with the eighteenth-century position of Adam Smith, who had relied mainly upon an "invisible hand" of nature and only secondarily upon the artificial contrivances of government to bring about harmonious relations among autonomous economic entrepreneurs. In the domestic sphere, liberalism had come to mean a limited government, performing important but minor functions, supplementing but not interfering with the natural harmonies which were assumed to exist in a society of self-interested but reasonable and decent men. In the international sphere, liberalism as embodied in the League meant a limited collective agency, supplying the relatively modest requirements of a system of free peoples, enjoying national self-realization and democratic self-government, for central direction and control.

The liberal ideal called for a government of law, in which might should not make right but should be tamed and subordinated to collective conceptions of right embodied in rules of law. The League represented an attempt to realize this ideal in international relations—to establish the principle that force should be used only in accordance with and in support of a legal order designed to make justice and peace prevail in the world.

In short, all the basic concepts of nineteenth-century liberalism—democracy, nationalism, natural harmony, law, limited government, rationalism, discussion, consent—made their imprint upon the Covenant of the League of Nations.

THE NATURE OF THE LEAGUE

The international organization which derived from the institutional developments of the nineteenth century, the First World War, the resultant political situation, and the prevalent ideological climate was not intended to be a revolutionary organization. Its founders approved the basic principles of the traditional multistate system; they accepted the independent sovereign state as the basic entity, the great powers as the predominant participants, and Europe as the central core of the world political system. They felt no sense of failure or inadequacy when they created a League which did not represent a fundamental alteration of the old system, since they regarded that system as basically sound and workable. They experienced no uneasy sense of futility when they undertook to get new results from an old system, for World War I was to them not an indication that war is the typical and necessary result of the existence of sovereign states but a warning that accidents can happen. The task to which they set themselves was that of creating safety devices to obviate the repetition of such an unfortunate breakdown as had occurred in 1914. The League was the manifestation of a reform movement, an effort to improve the procedures and assist the operation of the world political system.

Despite this essentially conservative attitude, a sense of pioneering, of exhilarating adventurousness, accompanied the founding of the League. This enterprise reflected an ambiguity of purpose, a combination of politicians' reaction to victory and desire to nail it down, with peoples' reaction to war and desire to build a durable peace. Nevertheless, there was a general enthusiasm about the modernization of the international system which had been effected. For the first time, a conscious effort had been made to create a systematic structural pattern for the organization of international relations; the multistate system had been equipped with a central institutional instrument of unprecedented utility. The retention of the traditional foundational principles was less striking than the introduction of what might be decisive new developments in the conduct of international relations: organized consultation, publicized diplomacy, institutionalized pacific settlement, codified outlines of basic principles of international law and morality, collectivized security. International law was to be imbued with higher normative standards and international diplomacy to be provided with greatly improved methods. The era of legally unrestricted right to resort to war, neutral indifference to aggressive use of force, rival alliances and competitive armaments, and cynical manipulation of power relationships was past. In the new era, war anywhere would be everybody's business, discussion at the bar of world public opinion would supersede Machiavellian browbeating tactics, and the security of nations would be a matter of collective responsibility.

The League, as designed at the Paris Peace Conference, combined much that was new with much that was old. The point is that it was intended to introduce radical changes in the operation of the multistate system, rather than to accomplish or even to presage the replacement of that system. It was established in the faith that the goals of peace and security were to be achieved not by the revolutionary repudiation of sovereignty but by the fulfillment of the constructive and cooperative potential of sovereign, self-governing peoples.

SUGGESTED READINGS

Cecil, Lord Robert, *A Great Experiment,* New York: Oxford University Press, 1941.

Foley, Hamilton, *Woodrow Wilson's Case for the League of Nations,* Princeton: Princeton University Press, 1923.

Salter, J. A., *Allied Shipping Control: An Experiment in International Administration,* Oxford: Clarendon Press, 1921.

Sweetser, Arthur, *The League of Nations at Work,* New York: Macmillan, 1920.

Walters, F. P., *A History of the League of Nations,* London: Oxford University Press, 1952, Vol. I, Chaps. 1-5.

Zimmern, Alfred, *The League of Nations and the Rule of Law, 1918-1935,* London: Macmillan, 1936.

CHAPTER

4

The Origins of the United Nations System

In the fall of 1939, Europe was the scene of the opening of hostilities which were destined to engulf the world. Only twenty years after the conclusion of a "war to end war" and "to make the world safe for democracy," and the establishment of a League to keep the peace, the forces of totalitarianism, international disorganization, and national irresponsibility produced the greatest and most disastrous of conflicts—World War II.

This total collapse of world order produced not so much a sense of the futility and hopelessness of international organization as a vivid awareness of the need for and a resolute determination to achieve an improved system of international organization. It became clear that the modern world had developed the habit of responding to catastrophe by intensifying its quest for effective organization.

The direct lines of origin of the United Nations may be traced to wartime declarations of intent to establish a postwar organizational system. Early statements by anti-Axis leaders were marked by a studied vagueness, but by October 1943, at Moscow, the Governments of the United States, Britain, the Soviet Union, and China were prepared to issue a clear statement of resolve to create a general international organization. Significant differences of approach to the problem remained, but the basic issue was settled; after the Moscow Conference, there was no open questioning of the principle that a new organization should be formed.

The war years were marked by an unprecedented volume of plans and proposals for postwar international agencies. From nongovernmental sources came suggestions ranging from the utopian blueprints of idealistic dreamers to the carefully considered proposals of well-organized groups of experts. Official consideration of the problems and possibilities of postwar organization was seriously undertaken, particularly in the United States and Britain. Secretary of State Hull initiated American preparatory work almost immediately after the war began in Europe, and was responsible for the most concentrated and elaborate study of international organization ever conducted by a government.[1] Although draft plans had been developed as early as July 1943, the American planning machinery did not go into high gear until after the Big Four placed their order for a general international organization at the Moscow Conference; in the months that followed, intensive preparations were carried out.

The actual construction of some parts of the projected international system took place during the period of blueprinting. A number of temporary agencies, most notably the United Nations Relief and Rehabilitation Administration, were set up in 1943 and subsequently, in order to perform essential tasks related to the war and its immediate aftermath. The process of establishing permanent bodies which would fit into the general system of postwar organization began with the convening of the United Nations Conference on Food and Agriculture at Hot Springs, Virginia, in May 1943, which laid the foundations for the Food and Agriculture Organization. In 1944, the establishment of the International Monetary Fund and the International Bank for Reconstruction and Development was initiated at the Bretton Woods Conference, and the constitution of the International Civil Aviation Organization was drafted at Chicago.

The decision to proceed piecemeal in the building of the postwar system reflected the belief that governments were ready to commit themselves in regard to economic, social, and technical matters even though they were not yet prepared to make permanent political arrangements, and that the gravity of the economic and social problems which would exist at the end of the war made it important to have agencies fully established and ready to go to work on those problems without delay. In addition, these organizational conferences were regarded as valuable trial runs; a supreme effort to negotiate the basis of world order was impending, and it was felt that preliminary negotiations on relatively noncontroversial matters would test the possibilities, reveal the difficulties, and facilitate the success of international cooperation in the creation of a new organization for peace and security.[2]

---

[1] The fascinating story of this enterprise is told in *Postwar Foreign Policy Preparation, 1939-1945*, Department of State Publication 3580 (Washington: Government Printing Office, 1949).

[2] *Ibid.*, p. 143.

The period of planning and experimental building of peripheral agencies merged into the period of major construction on August 21, 1944, when the Dumbarton Oaks Conversations began in Washington. Representatives of the United States, the Soviet Union, and the United Kingdom participated in the first and most important phase of these talks, while China joined American and British delegations in the second phase. In secret and informal negotiations at the technical level, the great powers exchanged views, hammered out compromises, identified differences which would require resolution at higher political levels, and produced a set of proposals which described the major outlines of a world organization for the future.[3]

Progress was made in filling the most notable gaps in the Dumbarton Oaks Proposals at the Yalta Conference in February 1945, where Churchill and Stalin accepted a text on voting arrangements in the Security Council presented by Roosevelt, and the leaders of the Big Three agreed on the basic principles which should characterize a supplementary chapter on trusteeship. An embarrassing issue which had been left over from Dumbarton Oaks, where the Soviets had dumfounded their fellow-delegates by insisting that the sixteen constituent republics of the USSR should have separate voting rights in the projected organization, was resolved by an agreement that the United States and Britain would support a Soviet request that two of them, the Ukraine and Byelorussia, be granted this peculiar status. The Big Three, considering that the stage was set for the great organizational effort, agreed to summon a general conference of the anti-Axis coalition at San Francisco on April 25, 1945.

Two additional conferences were important in preparing the way for the meeting at San Francisco. In February and March 1945, the United States consulted at Mexico City with its fellow-members of the Inter-American system, in order to gain support for the Dumbarton Oaks scheme and to promote the formulation of a general hemispheric position on questions of international organization, especially those involving the status of regional systems. A Committee of Jurists, representing virtually all the nations which were to participate in the San Francisco Conference, met in Washington in March and drafted a Statute for a judicial agency, to be submitted to that Conference.

The climactic event in the long process of building the new world organization was the United Nations Conference on International Organization at San Francisco. Here, representatives of fifty nations which were more or less closely identified with the still unfinished struggle to defeat the Axis Powers assembled in a meeting that was history's nearest approach to a global constitutional convention. In two months of arduous negotiation and debate, they created the Charter of the United Nations and its integral

---

[3] For the text of the Dumbarton Oaks Proposals, see *ibid.*, pp. 611-619.

supplement, the Statute of the International Court of Justice, out of the Dumbarton Oaks and Yalta proposals of the great powers, the draft Statute supplied by the Committee of Jurists, and the plethora of supplementary papers and amendments produced at the Conference by both great and small states. The formal completion of mankind's most ambitious international structure was celebrated on June 26, 1945, with the signing of the Charter.[4]

Only the final stages remained to be completed. The world's new ship had been ordered at the Moscow Conference, designed primarily in the United States and Britain, and constructed at a series of conferences culminating at San Francisco. Now, it was fitted out for sailing by a Preparatory Commission meeting in London; delivery was accepted by the purchasers on October 24, 1945, the date when a sufficient number of ratifications had been deposited to make the Charter effective; and it was launched on the perilous international seas on January 10, 1946, when the first session of the General Assembly commenced in London.

SOURCES OF THE UNITED NATIONS

As in the case of the League, the United Nations reflected the influence of a variety of formative factors. It was not simply a brainchild of idealists, a contrivance of nationally-oriented statesmen, a flowering of historically-planted seeds, or an excrescence upon the surface of contemporary world politics. It was all these things and more.

The influence of past developments in international organization was clearly evident. The major structural outlines which had been evolved in the nineteenth century were transmitted to the United Nations through the League of Nations, and that first great experimental system of the twentieth century contributed advances and modifications in organizational principles, worked out in its own experience, to its successor. The United Nations could be described, with considerable justification, as a revised version of the League. Many of its features were indicative of conscious effort to avoid the deficiencies of the previous world organization, to strengthen the institutional system at points where weakness had become evident, and to project into the future the progressive trends which had been initiated during the interwar period. In both negative and positive fashion, the old order influenced the creation of the new.

The United Nations system also drew upon the past in the sense that it simply adopted, without fundamental alteration, significant segments of the pre-existing complex of international machinery. Such special-purpose agencies as the Universal Postal Union, the International Telecommunication Union, the International Labor Organization, and the League's organ

---

[4] The text of the United Nations Charter is printed in Appendix II.

for international drug control were destined for integration in the new network. The Permanent Court of International Justice was formally superseded by a new agency, with a revised title, but the modifications in the Statute and the technical dissociation of the two judicial bodies were not significant enough to break the effective institutional continuity of the World Court. Thus, a century of organizational development bequeathed to the United Nations not only a pattern of ideas, a collection of object lessons, and a supply of used building materials, but also a group of working institutions which were durable enough for continued operation.

In a more specific sense, the United Nations was shaped by the influence of American planning and leadership. The primacy of the United States in this enterprise derived only in part from this country's unequaled weight in the scales of military and economic power. It depended also upon the world-wide prestige of America's wartime President, Franklin D. Roosevelt, who died before the San Francisco Conference began but was nevertheless the spiritual father of the United Nations in much the same sense that Woodrow Wilson had been the symbol of creative idealism in 1919. American predominance was related to the fact that the United States Government had had the opportunity, resources, and disposition to undertake the elaborate preparations which placed it in a unique position to offer guidance and leadership.

The deliberations at San Francisco reflected the interaction of national policies and viewpoints which were predominantly shaped by considerations of national interest and ambition. There was a great deal of talk about the objective requirements for creating an effective world order. Some of it was sheer hypocrisy, a kind of rhetorical camouflage for the pursuit of national goals. Some of it was meaningful, in the limited sense that governments tended to identify the purposes of serving national interest and achieving global order. But there is little evidence that delegates were either prepared to treat the ideal of building an adequate institutional structure as a consideration overriding national interest, or able to emancipate themselves from conceptions of the universal interest which were rooted in national biases. The Conference was not divided between pure national partisans and disinterested exponents of a global ideal; nationalist goals and internationalist aspirations were almost indistinguishably compounded in the positions of all the participating governments, which differed mainly in the degree of internationalism incorporated in their conceptions of national interest and in their ability to make their viewpoints prevail in multilateral diplomacy.

The position of the United States was peculiarly complex, and for that very reason exceptionally influential. The proposals of the American Government necessarily represented a mixture of ideas of national interest and conceptions of the essential principles of international organization, with provisions included primarily to avoid the danger of provoking the

Senate to veto American membership in the United Nations. The singular importance of ensuring the full participation of the United States in the new system impelled foreign statesmen at San Francisco to give weight not only to their own national claims and conceptions of world order, but also to the requirements for meeting the problems posed by the domestic political complexities of the United States. America's influence was based upon the cogency of its proposals, the positive force of its diplomatic strength, and the negative factor of its domestic political uncertainties. This combination of factors was effective in bringing about the adoption of a Charter which was fundamentally based upon principles advocated by the United States.

In broader terms, a dominant role in the creation of the United Nations was played by the élite class of great powers—including the United States, the Soviet Union, and Britain, and, in the second rank, France and China. The Big Three had borne the brunt of the military struggle, and would obviously constitute a power oligarchy in the postwar world. Considering the requirements of international security, it was clear that the collaboration of the military giants was vital to the United Nations. Considering the possibilities of meeting this condition, it was clear that the experience of great power cooperation during the war, and particularly the intimate and systematic pooling of effort in which the American and British partners had engaged, offered a potential basis for the creation of the coalition of power which was essential for the future success of the United Nations.

The great powers were keenly aware of their corporate indispensability, and were inclined to make the most of it. They had functioned as a kind of Global Executive Committee in preparing the blueprints for adoption at San Francisco, and they continued in this role at the Conference. Although formal equality and a two-thirds voting rule prevailed, the informal collegium of the Big Five, operating behind the scenes at San Francisco, had the ultimately decisive voice in the formulation of the Charter.

The influence of the great powers was not confined to their collective solidarity against unacceptable alterations of the Dumbarton Oaks-Yalta proposals. Their disagreements were as significant for the work of the San Francisco Conference as their agreements; indeed, at San Francisco and afterward, lesser states were never sure whether they should be more frightened of great power solidarity or of great power conflict. A complex pattern of divergencies of interest and viewpoint among the major states appeared at the Conference; if the USSR precipitated crises by insisting upon a more extensive veto right than the other great powers favored, the United Kingdom was equally at odds with its colleagues in regard to colonial questions. In the final analysis, the great powers left their imprint upon the Charter by negotiating compromises among themselves as much as by handing down dictates to their less potent allies.

Emphasis upon the hegemonic position of the Big Five should not be allowed to obscure the "democratic" aspect of the San Francisco Conference. Although the rank and file members of the wartime United Nations coalition had no significant share in shaping the preliminary drafts, except the provisional Statute of the International Court of Justice, they were permitted to make the San Francisco Conference an occasion for doing a great deal more than simply smiling politely and signing on the dotted line. They may have been expected to show more humility and acquiescence than they actually exhibited; in fact, they made the Conference a spirited affair, submitting amendments and counterproposals with abandon, participating vigorously in debates, and bravely challenging their great power betters.

By and large, the small states contributed constructively and realistically to the drafting of the United Nations Charter. This was not a foreordained result of the relative freedom of participation which they enjoyed. Small states are not necessarily the saints of the international community; if great nations are inclined to abuse their strength by behaving dictatorially, small ones are often tempted to abuse their weakness by behaving irresponsibly. But many small state representatives at San Francisco displayed a high degree of statesmanship. They did not challenge the principle of great power leadership. Indeed, they welcomed it and relied upon it, but they made great and somewhat successful exertions to modify it, and to confine its expression within tolerable bounds. There were definite limits beyond which the small states could not go in fighting for their conceptions of a new world order, but they made the most of their opportunities. In the final result, the United Nations Charter was to a surprising extent a "hammered-out" document, the product of the most extensively multilateral debate ever held for the shaping of the broad outlines of the world political system, and the reflection of the best ideas on international organization and the best compromises on points of national conflict that the statesmen of fifty nations could produce.

Finally, the Charter was influenced by the opinion, the psychological state, and the aspirations of millions of common and uncommon men in many of the states which were anticipating their approaching victory in the terrible global war. The phrase, "We the peoples of the United Nations," with which the Preamble of the Charter began, was something more than a cynically adopted euphemism. The Conference was conducted in an unprecedented glare of publicity, and under the pressure of popular demand for a vigorous attack upon the evils of international life. The American representatives, for instance, were constrained to give attention to the surge of idealistic enthusiasm for a cooperative approach to world order which was expressed in the press and other organs of public opinion, as well as to conservative fears of national embarkation upon new ventures. If they felt the breath of isolationist Senators upon their necks, they also heard the voices of the internationalist consultants, representing leading American private associations, who had accompanied them to San Francisco. The people never speak with absolute clarity, nor do they ever command implicit obedience, even in a mature democratic nation; but the men of San Francisco felt the dominant popular mood of support for an enterprising effort to build a decent world, and were influenced by it as never before in the history of international diplomacy.

To some extent, the concessions to idealistic public opinion were insubstantial, consisting more of verbal decoration than of genuine strengthening of the plan for a new organization. For instance, pressures for endowing the United Nations with competence in the field of human rights were met by multiplying references in the Charter to the objective of promoting human rights, rather than by providing clear authority and effective means for the development of an international guarantee of the rights of man. But it is doubtful if the response to popular idealism was much more deficient in substance than the idealism itself; the articulate public willed the end but it did not with equal clarity will the means, and it may have been better satisfied by the drafting of glowing phrases than it would have been by the adoption of provisions essential to the genuine effectuation of the ideals which it espoused. In large measure, the impact of public opinion upon the Charter took the form of ideological inflation.

The United Nations Charter was the composite product of past experience in the building and operation of international institutions, wartime planning, great power and particularly American leadership, intensive negotiation amid an intricate pattern of national disagreements and conflicts of interest, and popular pressures for realization of the desperate demand and noble aspiration for a just and durable peace.

THE NATURE OF THE UNITED NATIONS

The chronological setting of the San Francisco Conference offers a significant clue to the nature of the United Nations. When the Conference began, victory for the United Nations coalition seemed certain, but not necessarily imminent. In fact, Germany surrendered during the drafting of the Charter, but Japan held out for more than two months after the conclusion of the Conference. The construction of the new world organization before the end of the war was a deliberate act of policy, determined primarily by the United States. This decision seems to have represented a sophisticated attempt to capitalize upon the advantages and avoid the disadvantages of the traditionally close association between great wars and great projects of international organization. Cordell Hull, the leading proponent of this decision in the United States Government, emphasized the importance of early action to avoid the danger that postwar domestic disunity on foreign policy would imperil the whole project; if the Conference were delayed until after the close of hostilities, Hull warned, "peoples in all the democracies will be scattered in every direction under every sort of discordant influence. . . . As a result, nothing will be more impossible at that belated stage than for a country like mine to pursue a suitable postwar program and rally and unite all essential forces in support of it." [5]

While Hull stressed the danger that Americans would drift apart, another peril was that the major allies would drift apart. Wartime coalitions are notorious for their tendency toward dissolution after their military functions have been discharged, and there were already alarming signs of a break in the tenuous cooperation between the Soviet Union and the United States. If the grand alliance for war was to be preserved as a grand alliance for peace, it seemed that there was no time to be lost.

The timing of the Conference was planned not only to take advantage of wartime unity within nations and among allies, but also to avoid creating an unnecessarily close relationship between the United Nations and the peace settlement. Here was an obvious effort to profit from the mistakes of the founders of the League of Nations. The League had been handicapped by the tie between the Covenant and the Treaty of Versailles; critics of the League, especially in Germany and the United States, had made the most of the contention that the organization was an instrument for upholding a dictated and unjust peace, and its most idealistic supporters had suffered from qualms of conscience in the matter. The United Nations Charter was to embody the legal principles and operative mechanisms of the approaching peaceful era, and although the organization would necessarily have to function within the framework of the settlement between victors and vanquished, it would be spared the unfortunate symbolism of identification with an act of military triumph which had plagued the League. This purpose was promoted not only by formulating the Charter in advance of treaties of peace, but also by incorporating in it provisions explicitly excluding the organization from concern with the treatment of the defeated states of World War II.[6]

Thus, the United Nations was purportedly designed as an instrument of justice and orderliness in international relations, an agency of the world community at large—not as an adjunct of a victorious military coalition.

The United Nations was put forward, again for psychological reasons, as a decidedly *new* organization, rather than as a revived and remodeled League of Nations. In fact, its linkage with the earlier institutional system was quite close, and sensible steps were taken to make the United Na-

[5] *The Memoirs of Cordell Hull* (New York: Macmillan, 1948), II, 1294.
[6] Articles 53 and 107.

tions in some respects the legal heir of the defunct League. The understatement of this bond of continuity with the League was a tactic designed to avoid offending the Russians, who had been alternately distrustful of, disillusioned with, and outraged by the old organization, and the Americans, who would have found it embarrassing to join an organization from which they had so long made it a cardinal point of national policy to abstain. The general attitude of the United States toward the organizational past was well illustrated by a passage in the report of the American representatives to the London Conference, in November 1945, for the creation of the United Nations Educational, Scientific, and Cultural Organization (UNESCO):

> It was very strongly the opinion of the [American] Delegation that the new Organization should be conceived of as a new start in the work of international collaboration and that nothing in its location or personnel should relate it directly to earlier undertakings in its field.[7]

Moreover, the League was associated with creeping ineffectuality and ultimately disastrous failure. It was the considered judgment of the founders of the United Nations that it was worthwhile to sacrifice the possibility of creating a popular sense of historical perspective and awareness of evolutionary continuity in international organization in favor of stressing the newness of the leaf that had been turned, the hopeful freshness of the start that was being made. Thus, the United Nations was discourteous toward its ancestors, but solicitous of enthusiastic support for itself.

The adoption of the Charter represented the implementation of a fundamental decision which had been expressed in the Moscow Declaration of 1943: the decision to establish a *general* international organization, world-wide in membership and scope. The old debate between the proponents of universalism and regionalism had raged during the war, and the choice in favor of the former concept was made in the face of Prime Minister Churchill's pronounced preference for building the new order on the foundation of regional groupings. The Charter made concessions to the possibility that regional agencies might play important supplementary roles, in accordance with the demands of many nations which placed a high value upon actual or potential regional associations, but its primary feature was the establishment of a structural pattern of international organization which emphasized the unity, rather than the compartmentalization, of the modern world.

The United Nations was created as a general organization in the additional sense that it was to deal with a comprehensive range of subject matter. The world was its parish, and all the problems of mankind which required international attention were to fall within its area of concern. The

[7] *The Defenses of Peace,* State Department Publication 2457, Conference Series 80 (Washington: Government Printing Office, 1946), Part 1, p. 8.

Purposes of the United Nations, stated in Article 1 of the Charter, related to the promotion of a great variety of political, economic, social, cultural, and humanitarian objectives. The breadth of its intended sphere of activity was attested by the designation, in Article 7, of the Economic and Social Council and the Trusteeship Council as "principal organs," along with the General Assembly, the Security Council, the International Court of Justice, and the Secretariat. The generality of the United Nations in this sense represented a continuation of one of the most prominent trends which had emerged in the operative experience of the League, and a flat rejection of the Soviet concept of a United Nations which would be almost exclusively concerned with political and security matters. Churchill tended strongly to sympathize with this Soviet viewpoint; among the great powers, it was the United States which stood out for a broad definition of the new organization's functional sphere.[8] American leadership in regard to this issue struck a responsive chord in the hearts of statesmen at San Francisco representing peoples whose miseries in this life were patently too overwhelming to permit them to wax very enthusiastic over a mere collective security agency. The representative of Mexico undoubtedly expressed the hopes of millions when he said at one of the closing sessions at San Francisco:

> The Charter is not only an instrument of security against the horrors of war. It is also, for the people who have been fighting to uphold the principles of human dignity, an instrument of well-being and happiness against the horrors of a peace without hope, in which men would be subjected to humiliating privations and injustices. "Blood, sweat, and tears" comprised the glorious but provisional rule of war. It must not become the rule of peace.[9]

The bold definition of the terms of reference of the United Nations was not accompanied by a decision in favor of a highly centralized, tightly integrated institutional structure. Functionally speaking, the United Nations system was set up as a kind of loose confederation of international agencies. In contrast to the League, which had in theory and, to a lesser degree, in practice imposed central direction and control upon the operation of agencies in nonpolitical fields, the United Nations was committed to the concept of the coexistence of a "hub" organization and a group of autonomous "Specialized Agencies," looking to the United Nations proper for coordination and guidance but enjoying essential freedom of action in their respective fields. This principle of decentralization modified by persuasive coordination but not authoritative control from the center was

---

[8] Cf. Edward R. Stettinius, Jr., *Roosevelt and the Russians* (Garden City: Doubleday, 1949), pp. 17, 62, 316.

[9] From a speech by Ezequiel Padilla, *The United Nations Conference on International Organization: Selected Documents,* Department of State Publication 2490 (Washington: Government Printing Office, 1946), p. 932.

neither precisely defined nor exclusively applied in the Charter. An indeterminate amount of responsibility for the actual conduct of cooperative activities in nonpolitical fields was vested in the major organs of the United Nations and their directly subordinate bodies, rather than being delegated to the peripheral Specialized Agencies of the new system. No one could say exactly what and how much was supposed to be done by the United Nations itself, or how much control should be exercised over the autonomous agencies by the central organization. Nevertheless, it was clear that the United Nations, which was at its birth confronted with a number of already existing and operating international institutions, was intended to supplement, support, and coordinate organizations working in economic, social, humanitarian, and technical fields, rather than to dominate or absorb them. The die was cast in favor of a complicated network of international organizations, together constituting the United Nations system.

Within the United Nations proper, as distinct from the more comprehensive United Nations system, the division of functions and responsibilities was much more precise. The League Covenant had failed to delineate the respective spheres of the Council and Assembly; in practice, the Council had assumed supervisory authority over virtually the whole range of League activities, although the Assembly had consistently enlarged its area of operation, and a move had been afoot shortly before the outbreak of World War II to remove the direction of most nonpolitical endeavors from the sphere of the Council. The San Francisco Conference, acting in conformity with the trends which had prevailed in the operation of the League, adopted the principle of separation of powers. It assigned primary responsibility for matters relating to high politics and security to the Security Council, and entrusted virtually all other responsibilities to the General Assembly, which was to be equipped with specialized Councils on Trusteeship and Economic and Social matters, such other subordinate machinery as it might require, and facilities for establishing working relationships with the autonomous Specialized Agencies. The United Nations was a characteristic product of the era of specialization and division of labor.

In structural terms, the United Nations system may be described as a vast complex of international machinery, all-embracing in territorial and substantive scope, and characterized by internal decentralization and specialization.

The establishment of the United Nations represented a renewed effort to achieve world peace through *international organization,* as distinguished from *world government.* Like its predecessor, the League, the United Nations was dedicated to the proposition that it makes sense to try to eliminate war by improving the mechanisms and procedures of international relations and promoting higher standards of national behavior.

The creators of the new organization refused to accept the view that anything short of a revolutionary act of transformation of the international system would prove to be an exercise in sheer futility.

The essentially conservative, reformist conception of the United Nations dominated advance planning. It was clearly expressed in a statement issued by President Roosevelt on June 15, 1944:

> We are not thinking of a superstate with its own police forces and other paraphernalia of coercive power. We are seeking effective agreement and arrangements through which the nations would maintain, according to their capacities, adequate forces to meet the needs of preventing war and of making impossible deliberate preparation for war and to have such forces available for joint action when necessary. . . . the hope of a peaceful and advancing world will rest upon the willingness and ability of the peace-loving nations, large and small, bearing responsibility commensurate with their individual capacities, to work together for the maintenance of peace and security.[10]

The triumph of this point of view at San Francisco was evidenced by the declaration in Article 2, paragraph 1, of the Charter that "The Organization is based on the principle of the sovereign equality of all its Members." This formal provision violated the facts of international life and overstated the conservatism of the United Nations scheme; nevertheless, it spoke volumes about the doctrinal mood of the builders of the United Nations. National sovereignty was not regarded as a millstone fatally attached to the neck of humanity. It was not treated as an evil spirit which had to be exorcised before mankind could hope for salvation. The prevailing attitude toward this fundamental principle of the traditional international system was expressed in a speech by Senator Vandenberg during the debate on the Charter in the American Senate, when he concluded a listing of various powers generally regarded as aspects of sovereignty by declaring:

> These things we toiled at San Francisco to preserve. We can effectively cooperate for peace without the loss of these things. To cooperate is not to lose our sovereignty. It is to use our sovereignty in quest of the dearest boon which the prayers of humankind pursue.[11]

There was in this mood nothing of the obsessive passion for extirpating sovereignty, conceived as the root of all international evil, which characterizes so much of the theoretical advocacy of world government.

To some extent, verbal deference to the principle of sovereignty represented a tactical effort to avoid stimulating conservative opposition to the new international building project. In fact, the Charter made unprece-

---

[10] *Postwar Foreign Policy Preparation,* p. 269.
[11] *Congressional Record,* Vol. 91, Part 6, p. 7957 (July 23, 1945).

dented inroads into the preserve of sovereignty; for instance, all members of the United Nations except the permanent members of the Security Council relinquished the fundamental right not to be bound without their own consent by accepting the obligation to permit the Security Council to act on their behalf and bind them by its decisions.[12]

However, the claim that the organization was respectful of the concept of sovereignty was not a mere fiction. On the contrary, the very ambitiousness of the Charter was in considerable measure fictitious. The Conference displayed greater enthusiasm for declaring noble international ideals than for formulating national responsibilities for aiding in the effectuation of those ideals, and more willingness to state grand objectives of international organization than to equip and empower the United Nations to pursue those objectives. If sovereignty was modified more significantly than was explicitly admitted in Article 2, it was nonetheless subjected to less drastic revision than was logically necessary for the effective realization of the purposes stated in Article 1. The Charter left no room for doubt that San Francisco had launched a project for cooperation among independent states rather than for consolidation of the nations under a kind of super-sovereign.

In spite of the fact that the founding fathers of the United Nations adopted the same nonrevolutionary approach to their task that their predecessors of 1919 had followed, their mood was strikingly different. At San Francisco, it was not always clear whether abstinence from charting a drastic transformation of the international system resulted from a firm conviction that such action was unnecessary, or from a reluctant admission that it was politically impossible. The statesmen of Paris had radiated self-assurance; there had been skeptics, of course, but by and large the makers of the League had seemed to entertain few doubts that the world situation required only the limited changes which they were instituting. The statesmen of San Francisco, on the other hand, were more diffident, less enthusiastically certain of the adequacy of their handiwork. After witnessing the debacle of the League, they had to grapple with a disturbing doubt as to the possibility that the old system could be made to work without fundamental change. Although they proceeded on the assumption that national sovereignty and world order could be made compatible, they could not escape the reminder of the old adage about having and eating cake. The drafters of the Covenant had chided themselves for acting too late; ruefully, they thought about how easily they might have prevented the First World War. The drafters of the Charter were plagued by the fear that they were doing too little; apprehensively, they wondered whether their half-measures would suffice to give the world peace and order in the future.

---

[12] See Articles 24 and 25 of the Charter.

We have heard a great deal about the excessive optimism of 1945, and the alleged "over-selling" of the United Nations to the public. It is true that public opinion was often treated to glowing accounts of the brave new world which lay around the corner, but the atmosphere of the San Francisco Conference and the American Senate was not suffused by a spirit of naive optimism. The makers of the United Nations were conscious of the discrepancy, as the drafters of the Covenant had not been, between the objective requirements and the subjective possibilities of an effective world order. Their mood was less one of faith that they were doing all that was necessary than of grim determination that something—however inadequate—must be done to deal with the urgent problem of world war. If they had been asked to choose their epitaph, they might well have selected a paraphrase of President Truman's favorite: "We done our damndest."

The United Nations was erected upon the fundamental assumption of the need for great power unity, an assumption which was expressed in the Charter by provisions elaborately setting forth special responsibilities and privileges for the Big Five.[13] The notion that the future structure of world order should rest upon such a foundation prevailed without serious challenge throughout the war years. The great triumvirate of the allied bloc, Roosevelt, Churchill, and Stalin, held in their hands the mighty forces needed to win the war, and they could not conceive that the unity of their nations would be less indispensable as the basis for a peace-preserving organization than it had been as the foundation of a war-winning coalition. Co-opting France and China as formally equal members of the international élite, the great powers put themselves forward as the corporate nucleus of the United Nations.

No aspect of the United Nations has been more seriously misunderstood or subjected to more tendentious and unperceptive criticism than this basic premise regarding great power unity. It is vital to a genuine understanding of the United Nations that the rationale of this underlying concept should be grasped.

In the first place, the adoption of Big Five unity as the foundation stone has sometimes been regarded as a cynical device to foist an international oligarchy upon the rank and file of the United Nations. Instead of accepting international democracy, the giants of the earth conspired to establish themselves as global dictators. At San Francisco, so the argument runs, the great powers forced their hegemony upon a world which had fondly but vainly hoped for the dawn of a new day of international equity and justice.

There is an element of truth in this accusation. Certainly, innumerable quotations can be adduced to prove that the wartime leaders of the

---

[13] Articles 23, 27, 47, 86, 106, 108, 110.

major powers were resolved to dominate postwar international decisions and events, and that they were impatient of interference by representatives of small states.[14] The great powers maintained a solid front against the opponents of their veto privilege at San Francisco, and used their predominant position to force small state critics into reluctant acquiescence. It would be difficult to describe as "international democracy in action" the performance of Senator Tom Connally, an American delegate at the Conference, when he dramatically informed his fellow debaters that they could vote to kill the veto if they liked, but that there would be no United Nations if they did.[15]

Nevertheless, the argument misses the point. The great powers gained no degree of predominance at San Francisco which they did not already possess. The Charter registered power; it did not confer it. If anything, the Charter understated the actual disequilibrium of power between the great and small nations. Viewed in terms of historical relativism, the striking thing about the San Francisco Conference and the Charter which it formulated is the unprecedentedly wide gap between the effective capacity of the super-powers to dictate terms and the privileged status with which they were in fact endowed. The phenomenal feature of 1945 was not so much that the great powers extracted concessions to their strength as that they accepted far-reaching treaty obligations for the responsible use of their strength. It is true that they were somewhat hypocritical in their preference for the term, "special responsibilities," in place of "special privileges." Yet, in essence, the Charter scheme represented acceptance by the great powers of a framework of constitutional limitations within which their *de facto* power was to be exercised.

The most celebrated of the special privileges granted to the Big Five, the right of veto in the Security Council, was not so much an instrument of great power dictatorship over small states as a factor injected into the relationships of the great powers among themselves. Far from facilitating the corporate management of the world by the giants, it introduced the potentiality that the collegium of the powerful might be unable to act at all, either to dominate the world or to save it. This was the central point of the opposition to the veto at San Francisco. The leaders of the attack opposed the veto on the primary ground that it would hamstring effective collective action under the leadership of the Big Five—it would dash the hope that the United Nations could rely upon the great powers to act positively when the situation so required.

At San Francisco, the small states accepted the superiority of the mighty as a fact of life. Their first objective was to insure that all of the

---

[14] See, for instance, Robert E. Sherwood, *Roosevelt and Hopkins* (New York: Harper, 1948), pp. 710, 714, 717, 785, 852.

[15] *United Nations Conference on International Organization* (New York: United Nations Information Organizations, 1945-46), II, 493.

great powers would accept their place in the leadership corps of the new organization; in this they were successful, and this fact was perhaps the major basis for the hope that the United Nations would prove more effective than the League. Their second objective was to constitutionalize the power of the international oligarchy; toward this end, they achieved the incorporation in the Charter of a surprising array of limitations upon arbitrary behavior, including the procedural brake upon collective decisions by the great powers which was implicit in the rule of unanimity. Their third objective was to gain assurance that the most powerful members would initiate and support positive collective action within and on behalf of the organization in times of crisis; in this respect, there were serious apprehensions of failure, based largely upon the fact that the veto rule foreshadowed the possible paralysis of such undertakings.

All this adds up to demonstrate that the special position accorded to the Big Five in the United Nations reflected not so much a cynical insistence upon high-and-mightiness by the great powers as a faltering effort to solve the dilemma of arranging for great power leadership while erecting safeguards against unprincipled dictatorship by the great powers.

Another critical interpretation of the establishment of the United Nations begins with the proposition that the organization was based upon the assumption that harmony and collaboration would certainly prevail in great power relationships, and goes on to question the intelligence of statemen who would build an international institution upon such a shaky foundation. Arguing in the abstract, critics suggest that only fools could have been unaware of the plain lesson of history that wartime coalitions tend to disintegrate after their military purposes have been served, and that it is a law of international life that the greatest states at any given time inexorably become the bitterest rivals and most implacable foes. Arguing in more specific terms, they allege that only statesmen who were blind to the real nature of Communist ideology and to the clear evidence of Soviet aggressiveness could have been so stupid as to erect the United Nations on the premise that postwar relations among the great powers would be characterized by sweetness and light. The new organization was founded on an assumption that was not only invalid but was so patently invalid even in 1945, so the argument goes, that those who adopted it revealed themselves as fatuous idealists or soft-headed dupes of Communist hypocrisy who were unable to evaluate objectively the facts of Soviet doctrine and behavior.

Ignoring the fact that most critics who take this line refrained from public exhibition of their superior prescience in 1945, we can proceed to check the accuracy of their understanding of the premise upon which the United Nations was established. Sound wisdom would seem to dictate caution about jumping too easily to the conclusion that the gentlemen of San Francisco were a pack of extraordinarily ignorant fools.

In one sense, it is true that the founding fathers proposed and proceeded to build the United Nations upon the assumption of great power unity. As Secretary Hull explained to Roosevelt, in transmitting an early draft plan of organization:

> The entire plan is based on two central assumptions:
>
> *First,* that the four major powers [later expanded to five] will pledge themselves and will consider themselves morally bound not to go to war against each other or against any other nation, and to cooperate with each other and with other peace-loving states in maintaining the peace; and
>
> *Second*, that each of them will maintain adequate forces and will be willing to use such forces as circumstances require to prevent or suppress all cases of aggression.[16]

However, the point of this assumption was *not* that great power cooperation *would* infallibly take place, but that there was no hope for a peaceful world *unless it did* take place. There is abundant evidence that Anglo-American leaders were troubled by fears that the Soviet Union would not be a reliable and lawful collaborator in the postwar world, even before but especially after the first rumblings of the new Soviet expansionism began to be heard in early 1945.

In a radio address on April 9, 1944, Cordell Hull told the American people that:

> However difficult the road may be, there is no hope of turning victory into enduring peace unless the real interests of this country, the British Commonwealth, the Soviet Union, and China are harmonized and unless they agree and act together. This is the solid foundation upon which all future policy and international organization must be built.[17]

The Secretary of State went on to point out that disaster would result from any serious split among the wartime allies, and that "no machinery, as such, can produce this essential harmony and unity." [18] Hull has recorded that sober discussion of grave doubts concerning Soviet intentions, confirmed and emphasized by Ambassador Harriman in Moscow, took place within American official circles in the fall of 1944.[19] The weeks preceding the San Francisco Conference were a period of intensive worrying, in which British Foreign Secretary Eden shared, about the implications of the mounting evidence of Soviet unfriendliness.[20]

---

16 Memorandum for the President, December 29, 1943 (referring to the draft plan of December 23, 1943), *Postwar Foreign Policy Preparation,* p. 577.

17 *The Memoirs of Cordell Hull,* II, 1322-1323.

18 *Ibid.,* p. 1323.

19 *Ibid.,* pp. 1459-1460.

20 See Walter Millis, ed., *The Forrestal Diaries* (New York: Viking, 1951), pp. 38-41, 47-48.

Hull's analysis of the situation and prospects was clear. During the crucial planning stage in 1944, he assumed that "Russia held a deciding vote" [21] on the issue of future world order; an effective United Nations system would be possible with, and impossible without, genuine collaboration among the great powers, including the USSR. He was keenly aware of the fact that Soviet cooperation could not be assumed, but would have to be carefully and patiently sought after and cultivated.[22] Although he was disturbed by signs of Soviet straying from the course of peaceful cooperation, he adopted the philosophical attitude that such deviations would inevitably occur, and clung to the determination to exploit every possibility of maintaining unity for the future which might be offered as a result of the pressure of Soviet self-interest (*not* an assumed Soviet idealism) for continued collaboration. Hull declined to assume either that Soviet adherence to a pattern of future cooperation was inconceivable or that it was inevitable. He was certain that it was indispensable, and that the duty of prudent statesmen was to do their best to obtain it.[23]

This was the typical version of the basic assumption of the United Nations. The new organization would be able to function successfully if peacetime unity prevailed among the major wartime allies; it would not be able to function successfully if the great coalition should disintegrate. It was assumed not that the Big Five would maintain their unity, but that the United Nations plan would work if—and only if—they did. It was assumed that the world had no better alternative in 1945 than to build an organization which was dependent upon the possibility that great power unity would continue. It was assumed that the possibility was a meaningful one, and that it would be an act of criminal negligence for responsible statesmen to decline to build the only possible structure for world order because of a defeatist attitude stemming from the hypothesis that future coexistence would be impossible with a state which had existed for almost thirty years and whose record included some evidence of a capacity for cooperation. Finally, it was assumed that the harnessing of the Big Five into a team responsible for the successful operation of the new organization might help to promote the maintenance of their indispensable unity. Senator Vandenberg did not betray naive innocence about world affairs when he urged his colleagues on Capitol Hill to support ratification of the Charter; while he warned against the illusion that peace could be preserved by the new mechanism if the great powers should fall out among themselves, he added:

> But I assert, beyond any shadow of a doubt that this United Nations organization can minimize the frictions and stabilize the international

[21] *Op. cit.*, II, 1464.
[22] *Ibid.*, pp. 1659, 1722.
[23] *Ibid.*, pp. 1465, 1468-1469, 1639, 1651, 1703.

friendships and channel the orderly contacts which can go indefinitely far in saving us from any such disaster.[24]

The founding fathers of the United Nations were realistic enough to accept the necessity of operating within the confines of the existing power structure and to recognize the grave dangers of future conflict among the super-powers; they were idealistic enough to make a supreme effort to promote great power unity and to capitalize upon the chance that the wartime alliance might prove cohesive enough to uphold world peace.

The nature of the new organization, like that of the League, was in considerable measure determined by the prevailing understanding of the great war which occasioned its creation. If the League had been designed to prevent the accidental First World War, the United Nations was equally a product of retrospective thinking about the causes of World War II. Looking back to the outbreak of the second global conflict, "No one believed that we had merely stumbled into the War of 1939; it had obviously been deliberately planned. . . ."[25] The conviction was strongly held that the war had been brought about by the calculated decisions of ruthless dictators who had believed that the situation was favorable for the realization of designs for world conquest. The Axis dictators' miscalculations might have been averted, and their program of aggression indefinitely postponed, if the great powers which ultimately resisted the Axis had been clearly aligned in advance in determined opposition to any breach of the peace. In a very significant sense, the United Nations Charter, with its scheme for collective peace-preserving action under the unanimous sponsorship of the Big Five, represented the world's belated prescription for preventing the Second World War.

In still other respects, the United Nations was characterized by a retrospective orientation. Close analysis of the collective security provisions of the Charter leads to the suggestion that they were designed with a view to dealing with future threats to the peace by the same Axis powers which had launched World War II. As Brierly has observed, the founders of the United Nations clearly recognized that the veto power would make those provisions inoperative against an aggressively-inclined member of the Big Five; it cannot be supposed that they considered such elaborate provisions necessary to prevent aggression by small states; hence, they must have agreed upon the collective security arrangements with a view to the possible resurgence of Germany and Japan.[26]

Moreover, the emphasis in the Charter upon the promotion of

---

[24] Speech in the Senate, June 29, 1945, *Congressional Record,* Vol. 91, Part 5, p. 6984.

[25] J. L. Brierly, "The Covenant and the Charter," *British Yearbook of International Law* (London: Oxford University Press), 1946, p. 91.

[26] *The Law of Nations* (4th ed.; London: Oxford University Press, 1949), pp. 280-283.

respect for human rights lends color to the suggestion that the United Nations was built upon a conception hastily generalized from immediately preceding experience: the view that the danger of war emanates from totalitarian governments, that war is caused by the diabolical plots of ruthless dictators who are contemptuous of human rights. The United Nations could be interpreted as an attempt to equip the world for dealing with Hitlers—after Hitler was already dead.

However, the United Nations was designed with an eye to the future as well as to the past. In some respects, the new plan of world organization was extraordinarily forward-looking. For a world which habitually runs behind schedule in the development of institutional devices for coping with its problems, which is addicted to the collective policy of too little and too late, the global community as represented at San Francisco showed a surprising degree of concern for preventing future instead of past wars. The United Nations reflected a sharp awareness of the developing significance of non-European peoples as full participants in world affairs. Whereas the League had not represented a decisive break with the tradition of European-focused international politics, the new system was directed toward the problems of a world in which Europe would appear in drastically shrunken, and Asia and Africa in greatly enlarged, proportions. The Charter was decidedly futuristic in that it provided a basis for the concentration of international statesmanship upon the emergent issues relating to the liquidation of colonialism and the pressure of newly self-conscious and self-assertive peoples for status, development, and autonomy. Indeed, a case could be made for the proposition that the creators of the United Nations suffered from abnormal farsightedness—that they visualized more clearly, and thus made the new institutional system more appropriate to deal with, the potential causes of World War IV than the probable causes of World War III. At any rate, the world's latest great enterprise in organization featured an unparalleled attempt to open up the possibilities of long-range international action to prevent the development of situations conducive to war, as well as more traditional efforts to prevent war from growing out of existent or imminent situations.

The United Nations system, like the League, found its philosophical origins in liberalism. But if the liberalism which inspired the League was essentially a nineteenth-century phenomenon, the doctrinal foundation of the night-watchman state, the liberalism which underlay the new system was the twentieth-century version, the theoretical support of the welfare state.

The new liberalism contrasted with the old in that it reflected loss of confidence in the economic and social results of freewheeling individualism, and the substitution of reliance upon governmental planning for the earlier faith in the manipulations of the invisible hand postulated by Adam Smith. Applied to the international sphere, this change meant a decline in optimism concerning the results of the relatively unregimented behavior of free and nationally self-determined political entities, and rejection of the League's heavy dependence upon natural harmonies in favor of the principle that international order must be produced by deliberate contrivance and positive action. The old liberalism had produced governments which guarded the arena within which the principle of laissez faire operated, and which intruded only to impose a bare minimum of regulation. The new doctrine supported the assumption by governments of vastly expanded functional responsibilities and a capacity for regulatory intervention in many areas formerly considered outside the range of their appropriate concern. Correspondingly, the Charter reflected a newly enlarged conception of the necessary and proper role of international organization in world affairs; it envisaged for the United Nations and Specialized Agencies a functional sphere and an agenda of activity far more ambitious than that mapped out for the League in 1919. The dominant assumption at San Francisco was that international organization can do its job effectively only if it is free to explore the wide-spreading economic, social, and ideological root structure of the problem of war.

Just as the transformation of the role of government in the modern world was a gradual process, unaccompanied by a conscious and abrupt shift in political philosophy, the League in operation evolved toward the sort of international system which was more explicitly defined at San Francisco. The conception of international organization embodied in the Charter contrasted much more sharply with that written into the Covenant than with that actually inherited from the League system. Nevertheless, it was a profoundly significant event in the history of international organization when the San Francisco Conference ratified the change from the minimalist conception of the function of multilateral agencies to a kind of international New Dealism, an adaptation of the welfare state philosophy to the realm of world affairs.

This preliminary analysis of the nature of the system devised at San Francisco provides no answer to the question of what kind of organization the United Nations may ultimately become. The perils of prediction in this field are well illustrated by the experience of the League of Nations; that experimental institutional system did not turn out, in either its successes or it failures, exactly as had been expected or intended by its originators. In some respects, the League was less conservative than its constitutional design; in others, it fell far short of realizing the potentialities for transforming international relations with which it had theoretically been endowed.

The difficulties of forecasting the development of an international organization were compounded in the case of the United Nations by the fact that the San Francisco Conference postponed the effort to conclude agreements on a number of vitally important matters: the allocation of armed forces to serve the organization, arrangements for control and limitation of armaments, a scheme for the international protection of human rights, the pattern of relationships between the United Nations and Specialized Agencies, the territorial scope of the Trusteeship System, etc. In these and other respects, the Charter was an unfinished document, representing simply an agreement to seek agreement. In 1945, not even the final form of the original structural design, much less the course of evolutionary development or the fortunes of the United Nations in its efforts to fulfill its responsibilities, could be confidently predicted.

A few men hoped, and a few others feared, that an embryonic world government had been created. A few men hoped, and a few others feared, that what had been fashioned was merely a manageable tool for use by the representatives of sovereign states. The world was not sure what it had created, and most men did not particularly care; what they did care about was the result which they were fumbling to achieve—a just and lasting peace.

SUGGESTED READINGS

Brierly, J. L., "The Covenant and the Charter," *British Yearbook of International Law,* London: Oxford University Press, 1946.

Chase, Eugene P., *The United Nations in Action,* New York: McGraw-Hill, 1950, Chaps. 2-4.

Goodrich, L. M., "From League of Nations to United Nations," *International Organization,* February 1947, pp. 3-21.

Goodwin, Geoffrey L., *Britain and the United Nations,* New York: Manhattan Publishing Co., 1957, Chap. 1.

Report to the President on the Results of the San Francisco Conference . . . , Department of State Publication 2349, Conference Series 71, Washington: Government Printing Office, 1945.

Russell, Ruth B. (Assisted by Jeannette E. Muther), *A History of the United Nations Charter,* Washington: The Brookings Institution, 1958.

Constitutional Problems of International Organization

CHAPTER

5

The Problem of Membership

THE NATURE OF INTERNATIONAL CONSTITUTIONAL PROBLEMS

The problems confronted by international organizations may be divided into two categories: constitutional problems—the problems *of* international organizations, and substantive problems—the problems *with which* the organizations are designed to grapple. The first group consists of internal matters, related to the management and functioning of the organizations, while the second includes external issues requiring solution. Constitutional problems are occasioned *by* the establishment of international organizations; substantive problems are the occasions *for* the establishment of such agencies.

However definite the dividing line between these two classes of problems may be in logic, it is not so in practice. The nature and intensity of world problems determine the nature and scope of organizational efforts, and thereby define the constitutional problems which emerge. Decisions concerning the internal development of international agencies are inevitably influenced by external political considerations, and, conversely, the solution of substantive political problems is affected by the degree of constitutional development achieved by international organizations. The two problem areas cannot be divorced.

One of the major tasks of twentieth-century statesmanship is to strike a balance between obsessive concern with institutional problems, which makes international organization an end in itself, and exclusive concentration upon substantive issues of current world politics, which neglects the building of an adequate institutional apparatus for international relations. It is good that theorists and idealists should remind statesmen that the constitutional problems of international organization should be handled with a view to the creation of an effective system of order, and that statesmen should insist upon the importance of resolving the conflicts and averting the dangers of contemporary world politics. International organization is but a means to an end; however, it cannot be an effective means unless it is in some degree treated as an end in itself. To put it concretely, Western statesmen cannot be expected to give higher priority to building a well-developed United Nations system than to coping with the Soviet threat; but they cannot expect the United Nations to become a useful instrument for dealing with present and future problems of international life unless their policy regarding its internal problems is dictated by concern for its sound constitutional development rather than for their own immediate political advantage.

Nowhere—in international organization or in national government—are constitutional problems treated simply on their constitutional merits. In the United States, positions regarding the issue of states' rights are determined less by general conceptions of an ideal federal system than by specific interests in the shaping of policy concerning racial relations and economic regulation. Yet, in the final analysis, Americans are prepared to admit that whatever is good for the United States is good for them. This saving qualification does not exist in the international sphere. The constitutional problems of international organization are peculiarly subject to being treated in terms of their impact upon national interests in particular political conflicts, rather than in terms of their importance for healthy institutional development, and no government is prepared consistently to accept the position that whatever is good for the United Nations is good for itself.

Thus, as we analyze the constitutional problems of international organization, we should keep in mind the fact that they are inexorably related to the substantive problems of international politics, and that their solution is a function of calculations of political advantage as well as of wisdom concerning the requisites of a system of world order.

MEMBERSHIP AS A CONSTITUTIONAL PROBLEM

The problem of membership is clearly one of the basic constitutional questions for international organization. The kind of solution developed for this problem largely determines the nature of an international agency, the position that it can claim, and the role that it can play in world affairs.

Membership policy offers significant evidence concerning operative assumptions as to the purpose of an institution, the type of functions expected from it, and the kind of future development envisaged for it.

In general, two choices are open to the creators and managers of international organizations. They may opt for universality, of either a permissive or a compulsory nature, or they may choose some brand of selectivity. If they take the latter course, the criterion of selection assumes crucial importance. They may emphasize geographical factors, thus creating regional rather than general institutions. They may apply a standard of the objective importance of states in regard to matters within the organization's purview, stressing the inclusion of major producers and consumers of a given commodity in an agency concerned with the stabilization of the international market for that commodity, or basing a maritime organization on the membership of the leading participants in ocean-shipping activities. Finally, membership policy may reflect qualitative judgments of states. An organization may be conceived as an association of members sharing a particular form of government or economic system; thus, as we have seen, Wilson envisaged only democratic states as members of the League. The ideal of cultural homogeneity, or religious solidarity, or ethnic exclusiveness, or community of historical experience, may dominate membership policy, as in such groupings as the Arab League or the Commonwealth. The standard of judgment may relate to the internal quality of a state; for instance, adherence to a certain standard of respect for human rights may be regarded as a condition of admission, as in the case of the Council of Europe. The qualitative criterion may involve an evaluation of the actual or prospective international behavior of a state; thus, the United Nations purports to exclude states which are not "peace-loving." This type of exclusiveness has been sarcastically characterized as a means of saying to "bad" states: "You are not worthy to be allowed the privilege of keeping the rules of our beautiful Covenant. Kindly go away and follow your own nasty inclinations!" [1]

Controversy over membership questions is endemic in international organizations, and it is complicated by the fact that genuine differences concerning the constitutional merits of principles governing membership policy are subtly mixed with competing claims based upon calculations of political advantage. From a purely constitutional point of view, no principle can be singled out as the "right one," but the theoretical ideal might be formulated as the *rule of essentiality*. According to this concept, membership policy should be rationally adapted to the functional purposes of each specific institution. States should be accepted or excluded, sought after as members or left alone, on the basis of judgment as to whether

---

[1] Quotation from Arnold J. Toynbee, in Royal Institute of International Affairs, *The Future of the League of Nations* (New York: Oxford University Press, 1936), p. 10.

their participation is essential to, or incompatible with, the realization of the aims of the organization. Following this rule, the membership of Norway, for instance, might be deemed essential in a maritime shipping agency, desirable but unessential in a general health organization, and improper in an Asian regional system. This ideal standard challenges the dogmatism of champions of particular organizational theories as much as the arbitrariness of politically motivated nationalists.

MEMBERSHIP IN THE LEAGUE

The League of Nations, which had gleamed as a great power club in the eyes of some of its Allied fathers before the Paris Conference, emerged from its birthplace as a voluntary association of sovereign and almost-sovereign or prospectively-sovereign entities which had not been found on the "wrong" side in World War I. It was clearly a general, not a regional organization, and was regarded as potentially, though not immediately or automatically, universal in scope. Germany and the newly-established Communist regime in Russia were deliberately excluded at the start; however, the participation of all other great powers—and ultimately, of the major states without exception—was generally considered a vital necessity for the success of the League.[2]

In practice, the League did not hold to the Wilsonian interpretation of the "fully self-governing" requirement for admission stated in Article 1 of the Covenant, but treated this stipulation as a demand that new members have approximate sovereign independence rather than internal democracy. It began its life with forty-two original members and quickly admitted six more at the first session of the Assembly in 1920. The League attained its maximum size in 1934, when it brought its formal membership list up to sixty, although this figure included two states, Germany and Japan, which had already given notice of withdrawal and ceased actual participation. Admissions were not significantly offset by withdrawals until the middle 1930's, when a flight from the League began; the final record includes twenty admissions, seventeen withdrawals, and one expulsion, that of the Soviet Union in 1939.

The League never formally accepted the principle of indiscriminate universality which was espoused by Argentina at the first Assembly,[3] and it did sometimes balk at the admission of dubiously qualified or politically unpopular states, but, on the whole, it sought to attract rather than to repel potential applicants. This attitude of receptivity was symbolized by the development of the practice of "admission by invitation," as an alternative to application by would-be members.[4] Beginning with the first meet-

---

[2] See Article 1 of the Covenant.

[3] See Walters, *A History of the League of Nations,* I, 124.

[4] See Aleksander W. Rudzinski, "Admission of New Members: The United Na-

ing of the Council, when Clemenceau presided with an empty chair, vainly reserved for the United States, at his right, the League was conscious that its success was jeopardized by the defect of inadequate inclusiveness. As one observer said regarding the first Council meeting: "As the afternoon wore on, the sun which streamed across the Seine and through the windows cast the shadow of the empty chair across the table. The shadow lengthened that day and the days that followed until the League died." [5]

By and large, the membership problem of the League was recognized as the problem of the empty chair. The great experiment could work only if virtually universal support, and certainly the support of all the great powers, could be enlisted. This condition was never fulfilled. The United States never joined the League; Germany was a member, practically speaking, only from 1926 to 1933; the USSR joined in 1934 and was expelled five years later; Japan announced withdrawal in 1933 and Italy in 1937. Only Britain and France were continuous great power members of the organization; in the most critical situations, the League's most important pieces of furniture were largely unoccupied. Official membership lists did not tell the whole story. Some members were formally in but virtually out, while the United States was formally out but, on some occasions, virtually in. On balance, however, corrections to take into account the relativity of membership did not improve the statement of the League's position. The unsolved membership problem of the League was that of getting the right states in and of keeping them in as active, working members, making essential contributions to its successful functioning.

MEMBERSHIP IN THE UNITED NATIONS

In accordance with the Moscow Declaration of 1943, the United Nations was designed to be a general, or quasi-universal, international organization, embracing the "peace-loving" states of the world. Under the terms of the Charter, fifty-one original members took their place in the organization, and provision was made for admission of other states by concurrent decision of the Security Council and the General Assembly.[6]

The original membership list of the United Nations was a compilation of the acutal participants in the anti-Axis coalition in World War II, states which were willing to adhere nominally to that grouping, and other entities which were admitted to that company as the result of political bargaining among the leading powers. The adjectival qualification, "peace-

tions and the League of Nations," *International Conciliation,* No. 480, April 1952, pp. 164-169.

[5] This comment by Edwin L. James was quoted in his obituary, *New York Times,* December 4, 1951.

[6] For membership provisions of the United Nations Charter, see Articles 3-6.

loving," was not taken seriously except as a basis for excluding the defeated Axis states and Franco Spain, their largely nonbelligerent supporter and protégé. Although the new institution was, in principle, an association of sovereign states, it followed the precedent of 1919 in admitting as original members several entities which did not measure up to the technical standard. The drafters of the Charter were clearly willing to contemplate the voluntary abstention or withdrawal of states and the deliberate refusal of the organization to accept candidates for membership, but they also entertained the view that the probable destiny of the United Nations was to become a substantially universal organization and that its proper role was to serve as the central agency of the entire family of nations. The great powers were the vitally essential members, and the necessity of avoiding the reproduction of the League's melancholy picture of the lengthening shadows of their empty chairs was the ultimately decisive factor in the negotiations at San Francisco. A normal trend toward universality was assumed; the Big Five simply reserved to themselves the right, through their veto-grip on the Security Council, to regulate the tempo of the movement in that direction.

The history of the United Nations thus far has been marked by "growing pains": by expansion of membership, pressures for expansion, quarrels concerning expansion, and reactions to the implications of expansion. The following chart details the growth of the organization to the end of 1963:

	ADMISSIONS	TOTALS
Original membership		51
1946	4	55
1947	2	57
1948	1	58
1949	1	59
1950	1	60
1955	16	76
1956	4	80
1957	2	82
1958	1	82*
1960	17	99
1961	4	104†
1962	6	110
1963	3	113

* In 1958, Egypt and Syria relinquished their separate memberships, joining in the United Arab Republic which took its place as a single member of the United Nations. Thus, the total remained at 82, despite the admission of a new member.

† In 1961, Syria resumed its independent status, and was seated again as a separate member. The total for 1961 reflects this change of status by Syria as well as the admission of four new members.

Virtually every state in the world, old or new, has either joined the United Nations or sought to do so. Notable exceptions are Switzerland, which has deliberately stood aside, and West Germany, which has been deterred from application by political considerations related to the persistent issue of German reunification. Moreover, despite the dissatisfaction of many members with the working of the system and the acute disaffection of several, none has yet moved officially to abandon it.

During the first decade of the United Nations, the issue of the admission of new members was the focus of major political contention. A few applicants were successful in the first five years, bringing the membership total to 60 in 1950, but the doors of the organization were then firmly locked until the fall of 1955. By the latter time, a score of frustrated applications, many of them dated as early as 1946 or 1947, had been accumulated. Clearly, the League's problem of empty chairs in the chamber had been succeeded in the United Nations by the problem of overcrowding in the vestibule.

This situation was the result of the adoption by the United States and the Soviet Union of a policy of competitive exclusion. States desirous of membership fell into two groups: those supported by the Soviet Union, presumably as potential members of the Soviet bloc in the United Nations, which were denied the necessary support of seven members of the Security Council; and applicants regarded by the Soviet Union as potential adherents to the Western grouping, which were consistently blocked by the Soviet veto.

Thus, the membership question became entangled in the politics of the cold war. Nevertheless, even though the admission of the states assembled in the antechambers of the United Nations could be expected to have some effect upon the general character of the organization, it is not clear that either of the major powers was significantly motivated by a carefully calculated appraisal of the changes in voting patterns which might result from this expansion of membership. Still less did Soviet or American policy appear to rest upon a settled conviction as to the nature of the membership situation which would be most conducive to the healthy development and effective functioning of the United Nations. Rather, the great powers treated the matter as an issue of political prestige.

Beginning in 1947, the Soviet Union sponsored a series of "package proposals," designed to secure the admission, *en masse,* of the bulk of the applicants in both groups. Although the United States had put forward the first such proposal in 1946, only to have it defeated by the USSR, it rejected the Soviet packages and denounced them as improper, on the ground that each membership application should be judged separately with reference to the criteria stated in Article 4 of the Charter, and not linked by any sort of political deal to other applications. This American position was supported by the interpretation of the membership provisions of the Charter handed down by the World Court in 1948.[7] When Western opposition, led by the United States, prevented the approval of Soviet membership packages, the USSR retaliated by using its veto power in the Security Council to defeat recommendations for acceptance of would-be members supported by the West.

In this controversy, the United States was able to extract some propaganda value from the double-barreled charge that the Soviet Union was guilty both of attempting to push through cynical and unconstitutional package deals and of misusing its veto to exclude well-qualified states from the organization. If the healthy growth of the United Nations was frustrated, the blame lay squarely at the door of the Soviet Union.

This was hardly an objective and accurate view of the matter. The Soviet position, if weaker from the standpoint of strict law, was nonetheless more favorable than that of the United States to the growth of the organization. The Soviet Union acted to prevent the admission of non-Communist candidates unless its own protégés were simultaneously accepted; it aimed not to exclude the Western group but to secure admission of both groups. The United States, on the other hand, was determined to exclude the Soviet group even at the expense of the ambitions for membership of states acceptable to the West. While the Soviet Union was prepared to admit both groups, to get its own candidates in, the United States was willing to have both groups rejected, to keep Soviet candidates out. This struggle over the membership question was a typical display of the political tactics of a self-confident majority and a defensive minority. The United States, attempting to secure the admission of states supported by itself and the rejection of those supported by the USSR, sought a political victory, a demonstration of its primacy in the organization. The Soviet Union, fighting to make certain that its protégés would also gain entrance if the door were opened for Western candidates, sought to avoid a political defeat, a demonstration of its lack of influence in the United Nations.

For a time, the American tactic of pointing to the Soviet use of the veto as the impediment to the expansion of membership struck a responsive chord in the hearts of the smaller states in the United Nations. The lesser powers, eager to enhance their status in the organization, were sensitive to the veto as a symbol of inequality. They were inclined to deplore its use as a bar to the admission of new members, to insist that the veto was not constitutionally applicable to Security Council action on applications, and even to argue that the General Assembly was competent to admit new members whether recommendations for admission had been

---

[7] Advisory Opinion on Conditions of Admission of New Members to the United Nations, May 28, 1948. International Court of Justice, *Reports of Judgments, Advisory Opinions and Orders,* 1948, pp. 57-66.

approved in the Security Council or not. A move to secure endorsement by the World Court of this interpretation of the Charter provisions on admission failed,[8] but this campaign by the smaller states is significant as a phase of their persistent effort to increase the role of the General Assembly as compared with that of the Security Council, and thereby to reduce the preponderance of the great powers in the United Nations. Thus, the membership issue became a political football in the contest between great and small power groupings as well as in that between Western and Soviet teams.

By 1955, however, the American stand had lost most of its appeal. It had become evident that the ultimate barrier to the expansion of the United Nations was not the vetoing of individual applications but the rejection of politically balanced membership packages. Package deals could be denounced as illegal and cynical arrangements, but they could also be praised as constructive efforts at political compromise. It is one of the peculiarities of politics, national or international, that a given operation may be described as either a reprehensible maneuver or a statesmanlike quest for accommodation, depending upon the commentator's evaluation of the importance of the objective. In this case, the conviction that it was essential to make the organization that was global in principle more nearly global in fact, to make the United Nations more accurately representative of the multistate system, had become so widespread that willingness to "make a deal" was regarded as indispensable evidence of political virtue. What might earlier have been viewed as unseemly haggling was now characterized as appropriate negotiation; what might have been praised as resolute adherence to principle was now deplored as unreasonable obstinacy.

The result was that a group of sixteen applications received favorable action in the Security Council and was approved by the General Assembly on December 14, 1955. The underrepresentation of Western Europe in the United Nations was definitively ended; the Soviet bloc in Eastern Europe was brought up to full strength (except that East Germany, along with the anti-Soviet West Germany, remained outside); several non-European states which had been caught in the lock-out were admitted. Most importantly, the broad principle of the open door was established. The politics of competitive exclusion had not been totally repudiated—an occasional applicant would still encounter delay or indefinite postponement of admission for political reasons—but the way had been opened for the progressive universalization of the United Nations. Virtually unimpeded growth lay ahead for the organization.

The continued expansion of the United Nations since 1955, expressed

---

[8] See Advisory Opinion on the Competence of the General Assembly for the Admission of a State to the United Nations, March 3, 1950. International Court of Justice, *Reports* . . . , 1950, pp. 4-11.

most dramatically in the admission of seventeen states in 1960, has corresponded very closely to the proliferation of new states resulting from the liquidation of European colonial empires; of the 37 new members accepted in the period 1956-1963, only two, Japan and Mongolia, were not new states brought into being by that process. The United Nations has incorporated all states whose present status antedates its formation, save Switzerland. It has accepted all applicants resulting from decolonization, and the trend developed since the breaking of the impasse in 1955 seems likely to keep the expansion of membership moving in step with the continued emergence of ex-colonial states. In the broad sense, the membership question has been resolved in accordance with the doctrine of universality.

Yet, significant reservations must be attached both to the proposition that universality has triumphed and to the assertion that the membership question has been resolved. The roster of the United Nations does not include the rival regimes which control segments of the countries torn asunder by the politics of the cold war: Korea, Vietnam, and Germany. The latter case is particularly significant; given the importance of Germany in world affairs, its absence from the United Nations represents a gaping hole in the fabric of universality. The conflict between the Soviet and Western blocs is the decisive element in the membership question in these instances. Whether, and when, one or two member states will be admitted from each of these divided countries will be determined by the progress of political relationships among the major powers. Agreements on reunification, or mutual acceptance of the indefinite perpetuation of current division, would seem to be required before admission of new members representing these countries can become a meaningful issue.

Finally, the case of China demands our attention, as it has claimed the attention of the United Nations throughout the greater part of its history. China was a founding member of the organization, designated in the Charter as one of the privileged great powers having a permanent seat and veto power in the Security Council. In late 1949, the lengthy and oft-interrupted Chinese Civil War came to a halt, if not a formal conclusion, with the triumph of Soviet-backed Communist forces over the Nationalist Government, which enjoyed the support of the United States. A Communist regime was established at Peking, and the Nationalist Government set up shop on Formosa, an island which may or may not be regarded as technically or realistically a part of the territory of China, depending upon what one wishes to prove at any particular time. This set the stage for one of the most confused and politically vexatious issues that the United Nations has encountered.

The question of Chinese representation, which persists at this writing after arousing controversy for a dozen years, is technically a matter of credentials, closely tied to the problem of recognition: which of the rival Chinese regimes is to be treated as the Government of China, entitled to participate on behalf of that state in the United Nations and affiliated organizations? Thus far the determined leadership of the United States has succeeded in perpetuating the Nationalist occupancy of the Chinese seat, denying to the Communist regime any capability of speaking or acting for China.

The United States, leading the campaign against the seating of Communist China, began by insisting that the issue of Chinese representation should be treated as closely analogous to the question of admitting a state to membership, and has tended gradually to forget that the two questions are at most analogous, not identical. To a considerable degree, both supporters and opponents of the American position have come to share this approach to the issue; the technical question of representation—of the authority to issue credentials to Chinese spokesmen in the United Nations—has been transformed into the political question of membership. Thus, arguments concerning the acceptability of the Communist regime have tended to focus upon the question of whether it meets the standards of eligibility for admission to membership, prescribed in Article 4 of the Charter.

Falling in with this disregard for constitutional technicalities, we might agree that the Chinese question has become, in political reality, a membership issue—and go ahead to state the obvious implication that, again in terms of political reality rather than technical formality, China has not been for more than a decade a member of the United Nations. In a very real sense, the United States has succeeded in expelling China from the organization—without resort, of course, to the means prescribed in the Charter. The Nationalist regime, however willing it may be to carry out the obligations of the Charter on behalf of China, is clearly incapable of doing so; no state, not even the United States, takes seriously the fiction that this regime is the effective government of the Chinese state which remains technically a member of the United Nations. The United States does not recognize the Communist regime *as* the government of China, but it does recognize that that regime *is* the government of China. The meaning to be imputed to American policy is not that the United States denies, but that it deplores, this fact. In effect, China has been ousted from the United Nations, and is in the position of a nonmember state, applying for admission. This virtual exclusion of China constitutes a very large and significant qualification of the universality of the United Nations.

Moreover, the Chinese question, if it be regarded as what it has in fact become, indicates that the membership problem has not been totally "resolved," in the sense of ceasing to be involved in the competitive politics of the cold war. In this case, the United States continues to follow the pre-1955 policy of opposing the admission of states included within or oriented toward the Communist bloc, and the Soviet Union maintains the contrary position. The issue of granting meaningful membership to China remains a political issue in the fullest sense of the term. Correctly or not, the United States considers the exclusion of China, now that it has become a major Communist state, as an important political interest. The persistent success of the United States in holding the United Nations to the policy of excluding Communist China, despite the obvious disapproval of the policy by many of the states which have regularly voted to uphold it, must rankle in the Soviet mind as an extraordinary political victory for the United States, an impressive demonstration of the dominating influence of the United States in the United Nations. The ultimate defeat of the American policy, a denouement which appears as certain as its precise timing remains uncertain, will undoubtedly be scored as a significant victory for the Soviet Union and be regarded in the United States as an occasion for alarm and embitterment.

The arguments advanced by the United States and its supporters in the controversy over China constitute a classic case of the moralization of the membership question, a process which characterizes treatment of a great variety of issues in the United Nations. The potentiality of this development in regard to membership issues was implicit from the founding of the organization, with the dedication of the San Francisco Conference to pulling together the "good" states which had put down the "evil" Axis powers, to ostracizing the "morally tainted" Spanish regime, and to requiring "peace-lovingness" of new members. In contrast to the League, which lost little time in emptying its comparable provisions of their moral content, the United Nations has on occasion purported to give serious attention to its ethical standards for new members. Both political camps, the Soviet and the Western, have participated in the moralizing process, but circumstances and political interests have decreed that the United States should become the foremost exponent of the view that the United Nations should serve as a Moral Accreditation Agency, stamping governments judiciously with its *Good Housekeeping* Seal of Approval. This, of course, is not an unfamiliar or uncongenial role for the United States, with its tradition of regarding moral aspiration and moral indignation as instruments of foreign policy.

Since the general abandonment, in 1955, of its exclusion policy, the United States has not given broad application to the doctrine that states applying for membership should be subjected to the test of moral fitness; by and large, it has accepted the prevailing view that every actual state should be welcomed to the ranks of the United Nations. But in the Chinese case, American insistence upon moral judgment has survived and flourished. The heart of the argument publicly expressed against the seating of representatives of the Chinese Communists is that their regime disqualifies itself by action and policy incompatible with the standards of domestic and international conduct laid down in the United Nations

Charter. In effect, China has read itself out of the organization by producing a government too vicious and contemptuous of international legal rules and obligations to be tolerated in a "peace-loving" family of nations.

It must be noted that the United States has not found it possible or desirable to adhere consistently to the view that the United Nations should be maintained as a community of saints, from which sinners are to be rigorously excluded. In practice, the United States has accepted both the admission of new members and the retention of old ones whose respect for the standards prescribed in the Charter or expressed by the organs of the United Nations is extremely limited. The exceptional severity of judgment in the case of Communist China presumably reflects the particularly hostile political relations prevailing between that state and the United States, and the animosity of American public opinion toward the Peking regime.

In any event, the morally-based American resistance to the seating of Communist China does not appear to be an expression of a well considered and firmly established conviction as to the nature of the United Nations and the type of membership policy required for the effective performance of the functions which the United States would attribute to the organization. The late Secretary of State, John Foster Dulles, once justified the exclusion of aggressively-inclined regimes on the ground that

> the United Nations was not set up to be a reformatory. It was assumed that you would be good before you got in and not that being in would make you good.[9]

A few months earlier, however, he had argued that the special merit of the United Nations was that it "brought together . . . prospectively warring elements," helping to prevent difficulties among them from becoming so acute as to lead to war.[10]

As Dulles' wavering views suggest, the United States is not wholly committed to the proposition that international trouble-makers should be excluded from the United Nations. To some degree, American policy reflects an appreciation of the potential value of subjecting such states to the formal obligations of the Charter and the influences and pressures that may be generated within the organization. On the other hand, continued American opposition to the seating of Communist China indicates that the United States has not wholly accepted the doctrine of universality. The United States still adheres somewhat to the concept of admission to the United Nations as a reward reserved for the deserving.

I have devoted considerable attention to the American attitude to-

---

[9] *New York Times,* July 9, 1954.

[10] Testimony by Secretary Dulles on January 18, 1954, in *Review of the United Nations Charter, Hearing before a Subcommittee of the Committee on Foreign Relations, United States Senate, 83rd Congress, 2nd Session* (Washington: Government Printing Office, 1954), Part I, p. 19.

ward membership questions because it has been both so influential in the United Nations and so typical of national attitudes, in the sense that it has not been related primarily or consistently to a definite conception of what functions the United Nations should perform, or attempt to perform, in international relations. Narrow political considerations, rather than broad constitutional considerations, have been dominant in this area. Statesmen have largely left to the successive Secretaries-General the task of thinking about the membership problem in terms of the functional effectiveness of the organization.

To argue that statesmen should think about the problem in these terms is not to suggest that it is theoretically possible to use such a simple notion as "the good of the United Nations" as the guide to membership policy. The preliminary question is: what might and should the organization be good *for?* The task of statesmanship is first to determine the purposes which the United Nations should serve, and then to develop a membership policy compatible with and conducive to the realization of those purposes. The Charter does not in fact answer the preliminary question, even though it states the aims to which its drafters were willing to give verbal assent in 1945. It is the continuing responsibility of the member states to determine the working purposes of the organization. Ideally, there should be a consensus on this fundamentally important question; actually, there are, and will no doubt continue to be, profound differences of view. At the least, a given state should adapt its own attitude toward membership questions to its own conception of what the United Nations should be and do. The problem of membership can be intelligently treated only as a subsidiary of the problem of objectives.

If the United Nations is conceived as a mechanism for perfecting a coalition against an identifiable hostile bloc, and perhaps also as a device for giving semi-global sanction to the activities of such a coalition, a highly selective membership policy is obviously appropriate. To adopt the former version of this conception would be to put the United Nations in the category of regional security, or collective defense, institutions; in view of the fact that the world is already well supplied with such agencies, it is doubtful that it makes sense to convert the United Nations into another coalition. If the West is dissatisfied with NATO, the solution lies in improving NATO, not in making the United Nations a new version of it. To make the United Nations a source of reliable support for the policies of either the Western or the Soviet coalition would require a drastic revision of its existing membership list. Clearly, it is too late—the movement toward universality has gone too far—for the United Nations to serve as a coalition or an adjunct of a coalition in the political struggles of our time. If the United States should wish the United Nations to function as an anti-Soviet coalition combined with peripheral members which could be depended upon to bless and legitimize coalition policy, it would have to concern itself with expulsion, not admission, policy. The requisite transformation of the United Nations would hardly be distinguishable from its destruction.

For the promotion of the objectives of the United Nations as originally formulated, the rule of essentiality coincides approximately with the principle of universality. This is a point which the first Secretary-General, Trygve Lie, made as early as 1946 and never tired of reiterating.[11] If the organization is to serve as the focal point for efforts to settle the disputes, moderate the attitudes, solve the problems, and eliminate the conditions which make for war and insecurity, its ranks should be as wide as possible. If the United Nations is to be a mirror of the real world, a forum for the consideration of the dangers that threaten and the challenges that confront the human race, an agency for dealing with the implications of interdependence, and an instrument for helping states to control their conflicts and collaborate in the pursuit of common interests, then maximum breadth of membership is essential.

This, I should argue, is the general conception of the nature and function of the United Nations that not only conforms most closely to the spirit of the Charter but also provides the most distinctive and promising role for the organization. The mission of the United Nations is to serve a troubled world in whatever ways a full-fledged *world* organization can contrive. From this viewpoint, the surge toward universality makes eminently good sense; not the exclusion of Communist China but the inclusion of states of every description and disposition contributes to the proper shaping of the organization. If membership is to be conceived in moralistic terms, it should be viewed less as a reward for the righteous than as a penalty for the wicked, a means of subjecting the latter in unmistakable fashion to the duties and restrictions legally formulated in the Charter. If membership is considered in terms of the functional requirements of the organization, it should be regarded as particularly important to encompass trouble-spots and trouble-makers, to give the United Nations the best possible basis for dealing with the ills that plague the world.

The degree of universality thus far achieved by the United Nations is not measurable in precise, quantitative terms. As in the case of the League, the United Nations system is characterized by relativity of membership. Under various arrangements, formal and informal, a number of states—notably, West Germany and Switzerland—participate in many of the activities of the comprehensive organizational system without enjoying official membership in the United Nations itself, just as some members refrain from taking an active or even a nominal part in certain phases of the system's operations. Under various provisions of the Charter,[12] the

---

[11] *In the Cause of Peace* (New York: Macmillan, 1954), pp. 50, 100-101, 102, 254, 280, 301, 319, 428.

[12] See Articles 2 (paragraph 6), 32, 35, 50, and 93.

United Nations undertakes to impose restrictions upon and to provide certain privileges and safeguards for even nonmember states. Thus, it is impossible to say precisely how significant the formal membership list is for the working of the organizational system.

Neither the progress toward universality thus far achieved, as expressed in the dramatic increase in membership of the United Nations, nor the total realization of that ideal offers the prospect of certain or easy solution of the problems of international relations. The admission of a state, or the seating of a regime, in no sense guarantees conformity to the rules of decent international behavior, submission to the expressed will of United Nations organs, susceptibility to the influence of the organization, or meaningful participation in collaborative enterprises. The virtue of the expansive trend is not that it guarantees results, but that it opens possibilities; it represents the progressive realization of the prerequisites for the organization's doing whatever a global institution can do within the setting of contemporary world politics.

Moreover, the expansion of the United Nations, recent and prospective, carries with it the creation of new problems within the organization. What has happened, and is happening, is not mere enlargement but transformation. That the transformation of the United Nations can be regarded as but a necessary and proper concomitant of the transformation of the multistate system does not minimize the difficulties of adaptation to its impact. As we shall see in subsequent chapters, the quantitative increase and qualitative revision of the membership list affects virtually everything about the United Nations, from the physical adequacy of its meeting rooms to the voting patterns of the General Assembly, from the acceptability of an eleven-member Security Council to the ideological bias of resolutions and the functional emphasis of the United Nations budget.

If a choice were necessary, the student who seeks to understand the United Nations would do better to scan the membership roster than to read the Charter. Since this choice is not necessary, the recommended approach is to treat the Charter as the starting point of an evolutionary process in which membership questions and membership decisions have figured as fundamentally important elements.

SUGGESTED READINGS

Akzin, Benjamin, *New States and International Organizations,* Paris: UNESCO (for the International Political Science Association), 1955.

Fleming, Denna F., *The United States and the League of Nations, 1918-1920,* New York: Putnam's, 1932.

Jenks, C. W., "Some Constitutional Problems of International Organization,"

British Yearbook of International Law, London: Oxford University Press, 1945.

Rudzinski, Aleksander W., "Admission of New Members: The United Nations and the League of Nations," *International Conciliation,* No. 480, April 1952.

Stein, Eric, *Some Implications of Expanding United Nations Membership,* New York: Carnegie Endowment for International Peace, 1956.

Walters, F. P., *A History of the League of Nations,* London: Oxford University Press, 1952, Vol. I, Chaps. 6, 27, 30, 33; Vol. II, Chaps. 46, 48, 64.

CHAPTER

6

The Problem of Regionalism

The world has not yet adopted a settled and presumably permanent structural pattern for the organization of international relations. The development of international organization has been accompanied by a continuing debate concerning this problem, which is customarily regarded as involving a choice between the concepts of regional and general organization. In fact, the alternatives are not limited so narrowly. Conceivably, the world might be organized exclusively in regional compartments, or along strictly global lines; practically, the two organizational concepts may and do receive simultaneous application, and the real questions relate to the balance between them, the most appropriate fields for universal and for regional institutions, and the possible and desirable relationships between the two types of agency. Nevertheless, the theoretical conflict between the geographically limited and the geographically unlimited approaches is well worthy of note.

THE THEORY OF REGIONALISM

Regionalism is sometimes put forward as an *alternative* to globalism, a superior substitute for the principle of universality. Emphasis is placed upon the bigness and heterogeneity of the wide world, and the conclusion is drawn that only within limited segments of the globe can we find the cultural foundations of common loyalties, the objective similarity of national problems, and the potential awareness of common interests which are necessary for the effective functioning of multilateral institutions. The world is too diverse and unwieldy; the distances—physical, economic, cultural, administrative, and psychological—between peoples at opposite ends of the earth are too formidable to permit development of a working sense of common involvement and joint responsibility. Within a region, on the other hand, adaptation of international solutions to real problems can be intelligently carried out, and commitments by states to each other can be confined to manageable proportions and sanctioned by clearly evident bonds of mutuality.

> The lure of universality has had since 1919 a dangerous fascination for promoters of international order. The universality of any world organization almost inevitably tends to weaken its appeal to particular loyalties and particular interests. It was probably a weakness of the League of Nations that its commitments were general and anonymous: it imposed the same obligations on Albania as on Great Britain, and the same obligation on both to defend the independence of Belgium against Germany and that of Panama against the United States. These generalities could be justified in terms of pure reason but not translated into terms of concrete policy, so that the whole structure remained abstract and unreal. . . . A world organization may be a necessary convenience as well as a valuable symbol. But the intermediate unit is more likely to be the operative factor in the transition from nationalism to internationalism.[1]

The advocacy of regionalism can be, and often is, as doctrinaire and as heedless of concrete realities as the passion for all-encompassing organization. It should be stressed that the suitability of regionalism depends in the first place upon the nature of the problem to be dealt with. Some problems of the modern world are international in the largest sense, and can be effectively treated only by global agencies. Others are characteristically regional, and lend themselves to solution by correspondingly delimited bodies. Still others are regional in nature, but require for their solution the mobilization of extra-regional resources. Thus, the control of armaments is pre-eminently a problem demanding global action; the interlocking of national railway systems is a proper subject for an organization of merely continental scope; and the economic development of Asia requires not simply the pooling of Asian poverty but the fertilization of Asian resources by vital contributions from the West.

The nature of a problem is significant not only for the determination of the most appropriate means of solution, but also for the measurement of the range of its impact. A problem may be regional in location, and sus-

---

[1] Edward H. Carr, *Nationalism and After* (London: Macmillan, 1945), p. 45.

ceptible of regional management, and yet have such important implications for the whole world as to make it a fit subject for the concern of a general organization. The world-at-large cannot be disinterested in such "regional" matters as the demographic problem in South Asia or the status of forced laborers in the Soviet bloc. Thus, the question of the ramifications of a problem as well as that of its intrinsic quality affects the choice between regional and universal approaches.

At bottom, the regionalist position is that the regional unit is capable of more effective organizational action than the global unit; the stress is placed here on the nature of the unit rather than the nature of the problem. This consideration points to one of the basic dilemmas of international organization: the disparity between *needs* for organization and *capacity* for organization. The unanswerable question is whether institutional endeavors should be geared to the requirements posed by the objective situation or to the possibilities offered by and limited by the political situation. In terms of our present problem, this question means choosing between the treatment of global issues on the universal level, in accordance with the nature of the issues and their implications, or on the regional level, in accordance with the assumption that more effective collaboration is possible on that level.

However, that assumption should not go unchallenged. The world does not in fact break easily along neatly perforated lines. Rational regional divisions are difficult to establish, boundaries determined for one purpose are not necessarily appropriate for other purposes, and the most carefully chosen dividing lines have a perverse way of changing or coming to require change, and of overlapping. It is true that brave universalist experiments tend to give way to sober regionalist afterthoughts, but it is equally true that carefully cut regional patterns tend to lose their shape through persistent stretching in the direction of universalism. In a sense, the adoption of the universal approach is the line of least resistance, since it obviates the difficulties of defining regions and keeping them defined.

The status of the great powers offers particular difficulties for the development of regionalism. On the one hand, the segmentation process may take into realistic account the fact that the great powers are *world* powers, or states with a general interest. In that case, the regional body tends to include the multiregional great powers along with the local smaller fry, and loses its geographical sense as well as its assumed emancipation from involvement in the unwelcome complexities of the wide world. For instance, the United States is a member of such diverse regional associations as NATO, ANZUS, SEATO, and the Organization of American States, in the European, Pacific, Southeast Asian, and Western Hemispheric areas, and is a prominent participant in (though not a formal member of) CENTO, in the Middle Eastern zone.

On the other hand, regional organizations are often built around the local great power, taking on the character of a solar system, with subsidiary members revolving about the central sun. One might conceive of a world divided into, say, American, Soviet, and Chinese regional blocs, but this arrangement might not constitute anything more than a formalization of spheres of influence; it might contribute little or nothing to the elimination of conflicts among the great powers, or the alleviation of the anxieties of the small states with regard to their security against domination by the neighborhood giant.

This leads to the statement of a cautionary "it ain't necessarily so" in response to the proposition that organized action operates best within regional groupings. Intraregional affinities may be offset by historically rooted intraregional animosities, and geographical proximity may pose dangers which states wish to diminish by escaping into universalism, rather than collaborative possibilities which they wish to exploit in regional privacy. While global organization may be too large, in that it may ask states to be concerned with matters beyond the limited horizons of their interests, regional organization may be too small, in that it may represent a dangerous form of confinement for local rivalries. Global stretching, in short, may be no worse than regional cramping. It may make little sense to have Nepal and Bolivia as fellow-members of the United Nations, but it makes even less to think of Israeli participation in the Arab League.

A second statement of the case for regionalism stresses its utility as a stepping stone to globalism; regional agencies are not substitutes for, but preliminaries to, a world organization.

This position may be stated in terms of something like organic evolution, with emphasis upon the notion of a natural sequence of stages of growth. Just as the national state of today represents the consolidation of pre-existing fragmentary units, it will be superseded by larger regional entities, which will in turn be united in a single global system; regionalism is a necessary and desirable intermediate stage in the slow process of world integration. As Robert Boothby has put it: "On the purely practical plane, regional organization is an essential prelude to any kind of global organization. You must build, on firm foundations, from the bottom upwards." [2]

Aside from the dubious accuracy of the view that the rise of the national state is clearly indicative of a trend toward enlargement of political units, a position which requires the playing down of the disintegrative aspect of modern nationalism, this general concept has considerable plausibility. However, the assumption that regionalism leads either automatically or easily to globalism requires closer examination.

One way of dealing with the problem of the transition is illustrated by the thinking of Clarence K. Streit, who proposed a union of democracies, which he assumed would constitute a "nucleus world state," capable of at-

---

[2] Cited in Alan de Rusett, *Strengthening the Framework of Peace* (London: Royal Institute of International Affairs, 1950), p. 123.

tracting outside states and thereby growing into universality.[3] Another possibility is to assume that the ultimate world system would have not one but several cores—that it would be not a universalized regional organization but a regionalized world organization, formed by the combination of regional building blocks. Thus, it has been suggested that most European regionalists envisage lesser federations as "constituent and permanent elements of a World Government structure." [4]

The latter view seems sounder than Streit's in that it recognizes the probability that the adoption of a regional approach would lead to the creation of more than one sub-global organization; while a snowball may simply grow by accretion, a combination of states tends to stimulate its duplication elsewhere in the world. What the latter view fails to take into sufficient account is the prospect that the several regional groupings will be competitive, and that the task of bringing them into either unity or harmony will be at least as difficult as the task of dealing with the multiplicity of national states. To put it in snowball terms, the makers of the several snowballs are as likely to throw them at each other as to use them for creating a single snowman. It is far from self-evident that regionalism provides decisive progress toward the evolution of an effective general system for world order and welfare.

Another version of the theory that regionalism is a necessary preliminary to universalism is definable as the "pilot project" concept. According to this view, regional organizations do not expand or coalesce into a world system but rather provide working models and serve as training grounds for organization on a world scale. They invent techniques, conduct experiments in advanced forms of international collaboration, and develop among their participants the habits and attitudes which prepare the way for successful organization of the globe.

This kind of thinking has been especially characteristic of students of the British Commonwealth. Lord Elton combined the organic and the instructional concepts of regionalism in his suggestion that ". . . the gift of the British Empire to the future is likely . . . to be of the Empire-Commonwealth itself as the pattern, and in some sense the nucleus, of some wider organization yet to be. It may be that the island from which the world learnt the art of freedom will yet help teach it . . . the art of unity." [5] L. S. Amery has affirmed the belief that the Commonwealth represents the development of "a new constitutional principle of immense hopefulness, not only for ourselves, but for the world." [6] Another commentator has asserted:

---

[3] *Union Now* (9th ed.; New York: Harper and Brothers, n.d.), pp. 87, 111-113.

[4] De Rusett, *op. cit.*, p. 159.

[5] Lord Elton, *Imperial Commonwealth* (New York: Reynal and Hitchcock, 1946), p. 523.

[6] Cited in de Rusett, *op. cit.*, p. 196.

> the British Commonwealth is a Society of Nations which has worked: a visible instance. It represents the only practical experience men have had of an enduring and peaceful association among sovereign states. As a working model it should be developed for the further instruction and experience which the world needs in supranational organization.[7]

In fact, the Commonwealth is a poorly chosen example of what regionalism may offer as a pattern for world organization. While it is a wholly admirable phenomenon, it provides singularly little guidance for dealing with the problem of global integration. The Commonwealth represents a remarkable transformation of the bonds of imperial domination into ties of willing partnership. But it must not be forgotten that it began with an empire, not with a congeries of independent states; its development has not been so much a process of creating unity where none existed before as one of salvaging a pre-existent unity by making timely concessions to demands for independence, and thereby facilitating the substitution of new and perhaps more durable ties for the bonds which would have been snapped if they had not been released. In historical terms, the Commonwealth is a unique example of the arresting of centrifugal tendencies in a unitary system and the revitalization of residual unity. This, however, has doubtful relevance to the problems of a world which begins as a collection of independent states. The task with which the world is confronted is not the skillful relaxation of unifying bonds, but the forging of such bonds; not the unraveling of a fabric of imposed unity, but the knitting together of traditionally separate states. If the Commonwealth experience embodies a lesson of universal application, it would seem to be that the world ought to be fortunate enough to be conquered by a great power which should ultimately turn out to be as wise and moderate in its imperial policy as Great Britain.

In so far as the Commonwealth is a successful enterprise in international cooperation, its success derives from factors which are unique to the Commonwealth system, not subject to transfer to or reproduction by other groupings of states or the total collectivity of states. The world cannot rely upon the possibility of creating global analogues of the British Crown, the diffusion of attachment to the historical and cultural traditions of the British mother-country, or the identification of national self-interest with the maintenance of ties with the clearly preponderant but extraordinarily self-restrained British great power. The intangible bonds of the Commonwealth may properly be regarded as the objects of global envy, but not global imitation.

From another point of view, the lesson of the Commonwealth is positively discouraging. It is striking that a group of states possessing such

[7] Paul McGuire, *Experiment in World Order* (New York: William Morrow, 1948), p. 346. Copyright, 1948, by Paul McGuire.

substantial elements of consensus and community should have failed so completely to develop formal commitments, institutional arrangements, and multilateral procedures indicative of the corrosion of sovereignty; in these respects, the Commonwealth is in the rearguard, not the vanguard, of international organizations. The ready answer is that the nations of the British family can manage their cooperative relations without formal paraphernalia; but if this be accepted, the conclusion is that the Commonwealth offers evidence that under ideal circumstances—circumstances which clearly do not prevail in the world at large—international organization is *unnecessary,* not encouraging proof that effective international organization is possible, or useful clues as to the means of achieving that possibility.

In truth, the ready answer is altogether too facile. The Commonwealth has long considered proposals for creating such agencies as a Commonwealth Tribunal and joint parliamentary and executive institutions, all of which have foundered on the rock of sovereignty. True, it has evolved highly significant methods of informal consultation and collaboration, but its failure to create formal institutions has been less indicative of the happy realization that such devices are unnecessary than of the stubborn unwillingness of its members to compromise their progress toward, and achievement of, a full quota of national sovereignty. The record of cooperative accomplishment within the Commonwealth is impressive, but it does not offset the fact that the British system fails utterly to provide either an inspiring example or useful instruction for a larger family of nations which is confronted with the task of inducing its members to relax their vigilance against derogation of sovereignty sufficiently to create increasingly advanced forms of international organization.

It has been well said that "The structure of the British Commonwealth of Nations is peculiar. If it did not exist, you could not invent it." [8] The larger family of nations cannot hope to duplicate its psychic foundations, and it would have no hope if it did duplicate its structural deficiencies.

The general history of regional agencies does not consistently lend support to the thesis that the world may expect to learn its organizational lessons from such bodies. The Commonwealth is not alone among regional groupings in functioning as a laggard rather than a trail-blazer, with respect to institutional development. The flight of security-minded statesmen from the veto-bound Security Council of the United Nations to NATO was not an excape from a primitive to a more advanced form of international organization. The North Atlantic Treaty is more respectful of sovereignty, and of the traditional rule of unanimity, than the United Nations Charter. Neither on paper nor in practice does the Organization of Ameri-

---

[8] K. C. Wheare, "The Nature and Structure of the Commonwealth," *American Political Science Review,* December 1953, p. 1016.

can States represent a significantly higher form of institutional development than the United Nations. If progress toward world order involves the acceptance of majority voting, the creation of international executive and administrative competence, the submission of states to the jurisdiction of international agencies, and the assumption by states of explicit responsibilities, the pioneers have more often been general than regional organizations.

On the other hand, regional developments in Western Europe since World War II provide a notable demonstration of the possibilities of institutional creativity at the sub-global level. The Community of the Six (France, West Germany, Italy, Belgium, the Netherlands, and Luxembourg), which began with the establishment of the European Coal and Steel Community (ECSC) in 1952 and expanded its functional scope by creating the European Atomic Energy Community (Euratom) and the European Economic Community (Common Market) in 1958, represents a profoundly significant forward step in international organization. In these institutions, commissions composed of individuals committed to function as "ministers" of the Community share executive authority and responsibility with more orthodox councils of governmental spokesmen. The European Parliamentary Assembly consists of members of the national legislative bodies (although it is expected ultimately to be constituted by direct popular election), chosen on a multiparty basis and entitled to cast their votes individually, without regard to the position of their governments. National delegations vary in size, reflecting the inequalities of the member states, and their members tend to exhibit transnational party solidarity rather than to form coherent national groups. The judicial organ of the Community, the Court of Justice, has jurisdiction over cases involving organs of the Community and enterprises within the member states, as well as the states themselves. While ECSC, Euratom, and the Common Market vary considerably both in the scope of their functions and powers and in their manner of operation, the Community is competent to exercise, through each of these agencies, significant regulatory and directive authority over the governments and private firms of member countries.

Some of these innovations in structure, procedure, and legal competence have led to the description of the institutions of the European Community as "supranational" agencies. The concept of supranationality has not been precisely defined. Some observers stress as crucial the capacity to make binding decisions on important matters by majority vote, while others emphasize the substantial authority conferred upon organs composed of persons other than governmental representatives, and still others stress the competence of the agencies to deal directly and authoritatively with firms and individuals within member states. In any case, supranationality is associated with governmentlike qualities. To say that the institutions of the Six are supranational is to assert that they represent a partial and incipient federalism. Supranational institutions are conceived as falling between the poles of federal government and international organization; they are defined in terms of their approximation of the former and their deviation from the latter. In short, they are regarded as sufficiently advanced to be treated as different in kind from conventional international organizations. Whatever the particular emphasis adopted in the analysis of this crucial difference, the key point concerns the relationship between the so-called supranational agency and the governments of member states. In contrast to an international organization, a supranational body stands over, rather than between, states; it represents not so much the restriction as the partial transfer of sovereignty; it is less dependent upon the voluntary collaboration of states and more highly endowed with policy-making authority and executive vitality of its own. Supranationality stresses the demotion of the state, the emancipation of joint institutions from the dominating influence of the governments of member states. In this vein, the High Authority of the ECSC described itself, in its annual report for 1960, as "a body independent of the individual governments and able to weigh different interests involved while at the same time basing its decisions on the general interest of the Community as a whole." [9]

Does the invention by the Community of the Six of supranational institutions represent a real breakthrough in the field of international organization? Certainly an enthusiastic and optimistic reception of the concept of supranationality has tended to characterize students in this field. This reaction may be traced in part to discouragement concerning the performance of conventional international institutions, and in part to acceptance of the philosophy of world government, according to which international agencies offer meaningful promise only to the extent that they acquire governmentlike characteristics. Nevertheless, the question demands a cautiously developed answer.

The case for skepticism involves, first of all, the recognition that the achievement of supranationality in the European Community, in the sense of the emancipation of the common institutions from dependence upon and ultimate control by national governments, is both incomplete and tenuous. These institutions, created by governments, can be operated successfully only to the extent that the willing support of governments can be enlisted. Their future development—or demise—is ultimately in the hands of governments. As the *Bulletin from the European Community* put it, in discussing the difficulties of the High Authority of the ECSC in handling the coal crisis of 1959:

[9] *Bulletin from the European Community* (Washington), No. 45, April 1961, p. 6.

> Yet observers were under no illusion about the essential role of the six governments, which retain practically the whole of the panoply of sovereignty. It is clear that if one or more of the governments . . . should decide systematically to defy the High Authority or refuse to carry out the obligations they have solemnly undertaken in the Treaties of Paris and Rome, the whole progress and even the structure of the new Europe could be undermined. For some considerable time yet, the building of Europe will depend on the good will of the governments.[10]

The creation of ECSC and, subsequently, of Euratom and the Common Market, was clearly conceived as the beginning of a dynamic process of integration which might culminate in the establishment of a full-fledged federal union of the participating states. The attempt to move quickly and directly from ECSC to political integration of the Six, expressed in the projects for a European Defense Community and a European Political Community, was defeated when France rejected the EDC in 1954, but the political drive gained new momentum in 1957, when the Treaty of Rome laid the foundations for Euratom and the Common Market. The movement to enlarge the membership of the Community was stalled, at least temporarily, by France's blocking of British entry in 1963, and the uncertainty as to the ultimate scope of the group complicates the already difficult problem of forecasting the nature of the future political development of the Community. In any case, it is evident that the long-term evolution as well as the current functioning of Community institutions is fundamentally a matter to be determined by the national governments concerned. Supranationality has contrived no genuine escape from sovereign states. It may be a step toward federal unity, but it is a step taken by *governments,* which retain the capacity to decide whether to take further steps forward, to stand still, or to retreat.

Secondly, there is room for doubt as to whether the quality of supranationality really endows the institutions of the European Community with a capacity to operate in a genuinely distinctive manner. Academic enthusiasm for supranationality reflects a tendency to rejoice in the possibility that spokesmen for states can be ignored, circumvented, and overruled by representatives of a larger community. Yet the actual operators of Community institutions have been, by and large, as free of supranational pretensions as of supranational illusions. They have not so much rejoiced in the conviction that they can dispense with the support of governments as they have been sustained by the hope that they can enlist that support. Generally, they have not exploited to the full the limited capacity with which they have been formally endowed for operating independently of governmental approval. They have frequently consulted with gov-

---

[10] No. 38, Oct./Nov. 1959, p. 9.

ernments even when they have been constitutionally free not to do so, sought support when they have been required only to inform, and attempted to achieve unanimity when a majority would suffice.

To some degree, this behavior can be explained in terms of timidity or prudence. Bearers of supranational authority may have thought it wise to move cautiously, in recognition of the ultimate power and in deference to the traditional sensitivity of governments. A realistic appraisal of their unprecedented position *vis à vis* governments may have suggested the tactical wisdom of modesty in self-assertion. On the other hand, this policy of moderation in the exploitation of supranational possibilities may be interpreted as an expression of the pragmatic urge to find the means for dealing most effectively with the tasks at hand. It may reflect the conviction that the collaboration of governments is practically indispensable even when it is not legally required for decision and action. In these terms, supranationality is not so much a fragile treasure as a possession of limited utility.

In any case, there is little evidence thus far that supranationality is a key that opens the door to institutional operations of a fundamentally new and distinctive kind. The impressive achievements of the Community of the Six are attributable less to the formal capacity of its institutions to function without the cooperation of governments than to their success in stimulating that cooperation. The effectiveness of these institutions has rested not upon the elimination of the veto in theory but upon the achievement of unanimity in practice. They have not escaped from the requirements of successful international organization, but have met those requirements in unusual degree.

This deflationary view of supranationality should not be taken as a denial of its importance and value. While the doctrinaire proponent of global or regional federalism may be disappointed if supranationality does not represent the transformation of international organization, a more pragmatic man may take heart from the observation that supranationality contributes to the effective working of international agencies. There can be no doubt that the supranational features of the Community institutions, notably the executive commissions charged with responsibility for exercising important functions with a view to promoting the interests of the entire grouping of states, make such a contribution.

Moreover, the extraordinary significance of the institutional developments within the European Community is not limited to the invention of supranationality. These institutions have *infra*national aspects, in that they impinge directly upon individuals and associations within member states, and, particularly in the Assembly, involve the official participation of persons who speak from a level lower than that of national government. They provide a stimulus and a setting for the development and functioning of *trans*national political parties and interest groups. The fact that they set officials *above* the state level may be no more important than that they reach *below* the state level and encourage affiliation *across* the plane of state boundaries; all this may be essential for effective collaboration *at* the state level. The genius of the European Community, conceived both as a working concern and as a dynamic organism evolving toward a form not yet clearly discernible, is that it uniquely combines international, supranational, infranational, and transnational features. Its own ultimate scope is as unpredictable as its ultimate form, and the possibility of its being successfully emulated in other regions or by the global family of states is even more obscure. Nevertheless, the European Community stands as the most striking confirmation of the thesis that organizational creativity may flourish at the regional level.

The underlying basis of the actual working balance between regionalism and universalism which has evolved in the twentieth century has been the conception of regional agencies as concomitant supplements to organizations of unlimited geographical scope. In this conception, regional institutions may function as subordinate pieces of international machinery, sharing the load, diverting some of the tensions of international relations from the central world organization, and serving as agents of the larger community in handling problems which pertain primarily to their own regional localities. They may be regarded as "backstops" for general international organization, providing a second line of defense upon which reliance may be placed if the global institutions fail to cope with the major problems of peace and security. They may be envisaged as temporary props for precariously grounded general agencies, saving them for future development by dealing with crucial issues which threaten to destroy them. This conception gives no theoretical priority to the principle of regionalism and concedes no inherent superiority to the institutions based upon that principle; rather, it assumes the compatibility of regional and general approaches, minimizing their competitive aspects, and looks toward the development of a pragmatic sharing of the tasks of international organization.

REGIONALISM AND THE UNITED NATIONS

The history of the United Nations, from the San Francisco Conference to the present, offers a case study in this sort of eclecticism. The atmosphere of San Francisco was affected by the necessity of making the bow to regionalism which was demanded by those states that had already made heavy political investments in such arrangements as the Inter-American system, the Commonwealth, and the Arab League. It was also impossible to ignore the prevalence of the wartime Churchillian view that "there should be several regional councils, august but subordinate, [and] that these should form the massive pillars upon which the world organisation would be founded in majesty and calm." [11]

However, the dominant characteristic of the Conference was a certain wariness about the acceptance of regionalist doctrine. The Wilsonian tendency to identify regionalism with war-breeding competitive alliances survived, and unhappy memories of the League's disintegration buttressed the suspicion that undue receptivity to regionalist schemes might open the door to the renunciation, tacit or otherwise, of all-encompassing protective responsibilities and to the fatal decomposition of the principle of centralized control over the behavior of rival blocs. It was considered essential that concessions to regionalist pressures should not establish "a precedent which might engender rivalry between regional groups at the expense of world security." [12]

The interaction between theoretical preference for universalism and political pressures for regionalism at San Francisco produced an ambiguous compromise. The finished Charter conferred general approval upon existing and anticipated regional organizations, but contained provisions indicating the purpose of making them serve as adjuncts to the United Nations and subjecting them in considerable measure to the direction and control of the central organization. The Charter reflected the premise that the United Nations should be supreme, and accepted regionalism conditionally, with evidence of anxious concern that lesser agencies should be subordinated to and harmonized with the United Nations.[13] The original conception of the United Nations, as expressed in the Charter, involved permissive concessions to regionalism; it did not, as Churchill had urged, involve fundamental reliance upon regional agencies as the "massive pillars" of the world system.

In the evolutionary development of the United Nations, the role of regional organizations has been in some respects smaller, and in other respects greater, than might have been expected. So far as the ideal of relieving the general organization of the burden of settling intraregional disputes is concerned, the record thus far gives very limited support to the notion of the usefulness of regional agencies. The Commonwealth, which made a great point during the League era of reserving disputes among its members for treatment *inter se,* has been a prominent exporter

---

[11] Churchill described his wartime thought in these terms in a speech at the Hague on May 7, 1948. See Randolph S. Churchill, ed., *Europe Unite* (Boston: Houghton Mifflin, 1950), p. 314.

[12] *Report to the President on the Results of the San Francisco Conference by the Chairman of the United States Delegation, the Secretary of State,* June 26, 1945, Department of State Publication 2349, Conference Series 71 (Washington: Government Printing Office, 1945), p. 108. This document will be cited hereafter as *Stettinius Report.*

[13] See Articles 51-54 and 103.

of political troubles to the United Nations; far from reducing the workload of the world organization, it has presented that body with such dubiously welcome gifts as the persistent conflict between India and the Union of South Africa over the treatment of non-Europeans in the latter country, and the Kashmir dispute between India and Pakistan. Indeed, such an atmosphere of brotherly love as the Commonwealth is able to maintain in its own gatherings is largely dependent upon the possibility of diverting gusts of interfilial animosity to the United Nations. When Greece and Britain—and, less prominently, Turkey—developed an acute conflict over the status of Cyprus, they took their troubles not to NATO but to the United Nations. Only the Organization of American States has functioned significantly as an agency of intraregional conciliation. In the case of the OAS, its use has been motivated in some instances less by the ideal of preventing the overburdening of the United Nations, or capitalizing upon the effectiveness of regional machinery, than by the insistence of the United States upon handling disputes in a forum which it dominates with less difficulty than the world organization. Latin American states involved directly or indirectly in disputes with the United States are inclined to prefer the global forum, while the latter presses for regional action; under such circumstances, use of the OAS must be regarded primarily as a political victory for the United States, not as a tribute to the peace-making efficacy of the organization. By and large, neither the states involved in disputes nor the political agencies of the United Nations have shown a strong disposition to exploit the possibilities envisaged in Article 52 of the Charter for utilization of regional instrumentalities for pacific settlement.

In most other respects, however, regionalism has achieved a gradually increasing importance in the global system. In considerable measure, the United Nations and the Specialized Agencies have decentralized their operations on the basis of geographical segmentation, and working cooperation between United Nations and regional bodies has been established in many functional areas.

The greatest upsurge of regionalism has taken place in the sphere of high politics and security. The period since 1945 has seen the development of the regimented Soviet bloc of nations and the North Atlantic Treaty grouping, the launching of the Southeast Asia Treaty Organization, the elaborate reconstitution of the Organization of American States, and the conclusion of numerous other alliances and special arrangements. The regionalist ferment has been particularly active in Western Europe, where, in addition to the institutions of the Six already discussed, such bodies as the Council of Europe, the Organization for European Economic Cooperation (supplanted in 1961 by the Organization for Economic Cooperation and Development, with Canada and the United States as full members), the Western European Union, Benelux, and the Nordic Council have been formed. Many of the European agencies have been concerned primarily with economic, social, and technical problems, but the European unification movement as a whole has been profoundly related to the quest for political and military advantage which has been the characteristic motivating force behind post-World War II regionalizing tendencies.

It has been customary since 1945 for the constituent treaties of regional agencies to provide verbal assurance of their conformity with and subordination to the United Nations Charter; for instance, the North Atlantic Treaty commits its parties to conform to the rules of international behavior laid down in the Charter, provides that the activities of the regional organization will be conducted within the authorization and limitations prescribed in Article 51 of the Charter, and disavows any intent to revise the rights or duties of parties which are members of the United Nations or to infringe upon the established responsibilities of the Security Council.[14] Moreover, it has been authoritatively suggested that such a regional agency as NATO might become an operating arm of the United Nations, serving as its military component whenever circumstances require.[15]

Nevertheless, regional security agencies have acquired a more nearly autonomous status, and a much more prominent status, in relation to the United Nations than was envisaged at San Francisco. Despite formal stipulations to the contrary, regional organizations are not in reality subject to the overriding control and authority of the world organization. The Soviet regional structure is justified largely in terms of Articles 53 and 107 of the Charter, which provide a convenient loophole for Soviet-sponsored action without reference to any higher authority, whenever such action is purportedly aimed at preventing the aggressive resurgence of enemy states of World War II.[16] The Western bloc-builders have usually avoided basing their arrangements upon the provision of Article 53 which requires previous authorization by the Security Council before regional agencies may legally resort to enforcement action, and have instead invoked Article 51, which recognizes the legitimacy of "collective self-defense," subject only to *subsequent* controlling action by the Security Council. Since the Security Council can be prevented from intervening in such a situation by the use of the great power veto, the practical effect of

---

[14] The North Atlantic Treaty, April 4, 1949, preamble and Articles 1, 5, 7. See Appendix III.

[15] See First Report of the Collective Measures Committee, 1951 (UN Document A/1891), in *Review of the United Nations Charter: A Collection of Documents*, Senate Document No. 87, 83rd Congress, 2nd Session (Washington: Government Printing Office, 1954), p. 650. This volume will be cited hereafter as *Charter Review Documents.* See also Sir Gladwyn Jebb, "The Free World and the United Nations," *Foreign Affairs,* April 1953, pp. 385-386.

[16] W. W. Kulski, "The Soviet System of Collective Security Compared with the Western System," *American Journal of International Law,* July 1950, pp. 453-476.

the legal position adopted by the Western powers, like that of the Soviet bloc, is to emancipate the regional groupings from any unwelcome assertion of controlling authority by the Security Council. In cases involving Guatemala in 1954, the Dominican Republic in 1960, and Cuba in 1960-1962, the United States has consistently resisted efforts to subordinate the OAS in any sense to the United Nations, and has minimized if not eliminated the impact of Article 53 upon the OAS. Thus, regional agencies have been able to acquire plausible legal justification and, more importantly, strenuous political justification, for being what they are intended by their creators to be: independently operating coalitions, unhampered by external controls. They *may* place themselves at the service of the United Nations and voluntarily accept its restraining influence, but they have escaped the subordinate status which was intended for them by the makers of the Charter.[17]

The constitutional problem of achieving a balance between regional and universal approaches to international organization is far from solved. The record of experience suggests that the weight of emphasis tends to fluctuate; inaugurate a great universalist experiment and regionalism will make its demand for attention; cut the world into subdivisions and the urge to create global institutions for harmonizing the policies and activities of regional agencies will arise. This is perhaps not a problem to be *solved,* but rather a process to be *managed.* The maintenance of equilibrium between opposing tendencies operating in a dynamic context is a task requiring great skill and statesmanlike capacity for judging the circumstantial requirements for and possibilities of adaptation. Beyond this, it requires an intelligent evaluation of the merits and demerits of the opposing tendencies which has not been notably present in the management of the shifting balance between regional and universal approaches to international organization.

SUGGESTED READINGS

Dreier, John C., *The Organization of American States and the Hemisphere Crisis,* New York: Harper and Row, for the Council on Foreign Relations, 1962.

Haas, Ernst B., "Regional Integration and National Policy," *International Conciliation,* No. 513, May 1957.

Haas, Ernst B., *The Uniting of Europe,* Stanford: Stanford University Press, 1958.

Lawson, Ruth C., ed., *International Regional Organizations,* New York: Praeger, 1962.

---

[17] For fuller discussion of regional security agencies, see Chapter 12.

Manger, William, *Pan America in Crisis: The Future of the OAS,* Washington: Public Affairs Press, 1961.

Mason, Henry L., *The European Coal and Steel Community,* The Hague: Nijhoff, 1955.

Moore, Ben T., *NATO and the Future of Europe,* New York: Harper, 1958.

Osgood, Robert E., *NATO: The Entangling Alliance,* Chicago: University of Chicago Press, 1962.

Political and Economic Planning, *European Organisations,* London: George Allen and Unwin, 1959.

Robertson, A. H., *The Council of Europe,* New York: Praeger, 1957.

Underhill, Frank H., *The British Commonwealth—An Experiment in Co-operation Among Nations,* Durham: Duke University Press, 1956.

CHAPTER

7

The Problem of Voting

Constitutional issues of the first importance for international organization are posed by the problem of voting. How should voting power be distributed among member states? What concentration of voting power should be required to validate decisions? Given the probability of disagreement within international agencies, the determination of the manner in which the international mind shall be made up and words put in the international mouth is clearly a matter of utmost significance.

Voting is a concept alien to the traditional system for the management of international relations, imported into this sphere as a result of the development of international organization. In consequence, much of the thinking about the international voting question has rested upon assumptions borrowed from outside, rather than upon principles developed with specific reference to the requirements of international organization. Thus, the equalitarianism of traditional international law, the majoritarianism of democratic philosophy, and the élitism of European great power diplomacy have been transferred to the sphere of international organization to serve as competing elements in shaping the approach to international decision-making. Should voting arrangements be determined by legal assumptions about the nature of the state, paying respect to the concept of sovereignty? Should they be governed by the ideal of making international agencies conform to the normative patterns of democratic institutions, adopting the principle of majority rule? Should they be designed to reflect the configuration of power in the real political world, giving special status to the great powers? All these considerations have entered into the development of voting systems in international agencies, and they have almost—but not quite—excluded the consideration which is of fundamental importance for sound constitutional evolution: what voting arrangements are most appropriate to the functional nature which international institutions are expected and desired to achieve?

Traditional international law contributed the rule which served as the historic starting point for international voting, and still serves as its basing point: the rule that every state has an equal voice in international proceedings, and that no state can be bound without its consent. The ingredients of sovereign equality and sovereign immunity from externally imposed legislation were combined in the rule of unanimity. In old-fashioned diplomacy, this meant simply that a state might abstain from treaty relationships which others might enter into at their pleasure; in new fangled international organization, the rule of unanimity tended to be transformed into the rule of *liberum veto,* according to which no organizational decision could be reached if any member of the organization dissented. The theoretical distinction between these two rules has seldom been insisted upon; in the vocabulary of multilateral diplomacy, the principle of unanimity implies the right of one state to prevent a collective decision.

Doctrinal insistence upon this principle was expressed by the President of the Second Hague Conference in 1907:

> The first principle of every Conference is that of unanimity; it is not an empty form, but the basis of every political understanding . . . in an International Conference each delegation represents a different State of equal sovereignty. No delegation has the right to accept a decision of the majority which would be contrary to the will of its Government.[1]

Lord Robert Cecil asserted at the Paris Conference of 1919 that "all international decisions must by the nature of things be unanimous,"[2] and the Covenant incorporated the unanimity rule in Article 5 as the basic premise of its voting arrangements. In its Advisory Opinion of November 21, 1925, the World Court noted that the rule of unanimity was "in accordance with the unvarying tradition of all diplomatic meetings or conferences," and held that it was "naturally and even necessarily" applicable to intergovernmental bodies such as the League Council, save only in explicitly excepted cases.[3]

---

1 Cited in Leonard S. Woolf, *International Government* (London: George Allen and Unwin, 1916), p. 109.

2 Cited in L. Larry Leonard, *International Organization* (New York: McGraw-Hill, 1951), p. 89.

3 Advisory Opinion No. 12 (Series B/12), Manley O. Hudson, ed., *World Court Reports* (Washington: Carnegie Endowment for International Peace, 1934), I, 740-741.

THE DEVELOPMENT OF INTERNATIONAL MAJORITARIANISM

The history of international organization is the story of efforts to achieve progressive emancipation from the tradition-based rule of equality and unanimity. In its equalitarian aspect, this rule makes for unrealism by masking the tremendous differences in the capacities, resources, interests, and involvements of states, and bestows upon lesser states a disproportionate influence in international agencies which discourages powers whose role is thus artificially minimized from taking the agencies seriously or entrusting important functions to them. In posing the requirement of unanimity, the rule ignores the hard fact that differences of interest and judgment make universal agreement a rare phenomenon in any society, whether of states or of individuals; "to lay down the principle that in an international organization every important decision must be adopted unanimously . . . is to admit that among nations no real organization is possible, for the rule of unanimity may lead to paralysis and anarchy."[4]

These two aspects are intimately interrelated. The unrealism of equality is practically insignificant, although it may be offensive to the national pride of underprivileged great powers, so long as the rule of unanimity makes one vote as effective as two or twenty for blocking action. The two concepts break down together; when the universal veto gives way to some brand of majoritarianism, distribution of voting power takes on real importance, and the search for a realistic pattern begins in earnest. Moreover, the significance of both equality and unanimity is decisively related to the legal quality of the authority vested in international institutions. So long as the latter have constitutional competence only to decide to advise or recommend, or to make binding decisions relevant to minor technical matters or internal housekeeping details, voting arrangements are relatively inconsequential; great powers may acquiesce in formal equality and all states may be willing to dispense with the veto. However, an increase in the legal authoritativeness and political weightiness of the decisions which lie within the competence of international organization carries with it a corresponding increase in the sensitivity of issues related to voting arrangements.

The process of international organization has involved the steady lifting of the dead hand of the unanimity rule. Minor modifications of the rule were achieved in a number of public international unions in the nineteenth century. The Hague Conferences departed from diplomatic orthodoxy by permitting the passage of *voeux* ("wishes" or recommendations) by majority vote. The League of Nations gave impetus to the majoritarian trend by developing a variety of methods for expanding the limited number of exceptions to the unanimity rule stipulated in the

---

[4] Nicolas Politis, *The New Aspects of International Law* (Washington: Carnegie Endowment for International Peace, 1928), p. 10.

Covenant.[5] The International Labor Organization, established in close relationship to the League, reversed the traditional principle by making simple majority voting the rule, and more stringent voting requirements the exception.

When the world inaugurated a new phase of institution-building during and after the Second World War, it effected the general repudiation of the unanimity rule. In contrast to the League Covenant, which merely made concessions to majoritarianism, the United Nations Charter and the constitutional documents of the Specialized Agencies establish the rule of simple or extraordinary majorities in all the organs, major and minor, of the post-war organizational system. The old-fashioned principle of unanimity, in its pure form, survives only in some of the regional organizations and some *ad hoc* international conferences. As C. W. Jenks has commented, "The battle to substitute majority decision for the requirement of unanimity in international organization has now been largely won." After noting the changes which have taken place since World War I, he writes that "The cumulative effect of these developments has been to make majority rule in some form normal practice instead of a strictly limited exception to normal practice. The process of development has reached its culmination in the provisions of the Charter of the United Nations which involve the complete abandonment of the requirement of unanimity in respect of the new general international organization." Jenks concludes that we have seen "the completion of a revolution of decisive importance for the future development of international organizations." [6]

We would do well to hold our applause for the victory of the majority principle, because, in the first place, the triumph is not so complete as it superficially appears, and in the second place, there is reason to doubt that the total victory of majoritarianism would be the occasion for unmitigated joy.

The most obvious remnant of the principle of unanimity is the veto power held by the five permanent members of the Security Council of the United Nations over the most important activities of that body and the adoption of amendments to the Charter. This power is not rendered less significant by the fact that it derives from the exceptional provision rather than the rule. Indeed, it is important enough to claim full treatment in a separate chapter.[7] Aside from symbolizing the fact that the great powers have not yet developed the readiness to renounce the unanimity rule which virtually all other states have demonstrated, either by joining or by

---

[5] Cromwell A. Riches, *The Unanimity Rule and the League of Nations* (Baltimore: Johns Hopkins, 1933).

[6] "Some Constitutional Problems of International Organizations," *British Yearbook of International Law*, 1945, pp. 34, 35, 36.

[7] See Chapter 8.

seeking to join the United Nations as unprivileged members, the extraordinary veto provision illustrates the possibility that nominally majoritarian voting rules may be almost as difficult to apply for effective decision-making as strict unanimity requirements. The less-than-unanimity rule of the Security Council is a far cry from real majority rule. Beyond this, the extra-constitutional resources for determination of international policy which are possessed by great powers often give them an informal veto power which reduces majority rule to a mere formality; for instance, the indispensability of American financial support gives the United States a voice which can, and frequently does, drown out the expression of majority will in virtually all agencies of the United Nations system.

A realistic analysis of the extent to which majority rule has become genuinely operative in international organizations must deal not only with the question of *whether* agencies can decide by majority vote but also with the question of *what* they can decide in that manner. A decision to recommend or to propose is not the same as a decision to impose legal obligation, and it is clear that the triumph of majoritarianism has been achieved primarily in regard to the former, not the latter, type of decision. Today's typical international body applies the majority rule to passage of recommendations which states may respect or ignore at their pleasure, to adoption of legislative conventions which bind each member state only if it chooses to ratify them, and to proposal of amendments to organizational constitutions which in many cases become effective for a state only upon its formal acceptance and which in any case a state may evade by resort to the expedient of withdrawing from the organization.

The question as to what may be decided by majority vote pertains also to the nature of the subject matter to which organizational decisions refer. In general, there is an inverse relationship between the importance attached to a subject and the disposition of states to permit international agencies to act on the subject by majority vote. In the present stage of international organization, nonunanimous decisions with binding effect tend to be constitutionally confined to matters of mainly technical importance or of not more than minor political concern. When fundamental security questions are involved, the traditional unanimity rule applies, as in the NATO Council; when major political issues are involved, the technique of legislation *ad referendum* is utilized, as in the General Assembly's approval of the Genocide Convention for submission to the states for voluntary ratification, or mere nonbinding resolutions are passed.

All this is not to minimize the significance of the advances toward majoritarianism which have taken place. A survey of the basic documents of the United Nations and its affiliated organizations reveals that truly remarkable strides have been made in the direction of determining organizational policy and controlling organizational activities by majority vote, as well as applying the majority principle to the adoption of regulations binding upon member states.

For instance, the General Assembly operates without any semblance of the veto principle in carrying out its functions of policy direction and administrative management for virtually all parts of the United Nations machinery except the Security Council. In this sense, the Assembly is a genuine international legislature, acting by simple or two-thirds majority—and it becomes clear that this is not a minor sense when we reflect that a large and increasing proportion of the legislative activity of such national bodies as the United States Congress or the British Parliament is concerned with authorizing, directing, and controlling the operations of government departments and agencies rather than addressing commands and prohibitions to private citizens. An approach to majority-based legislation in the latter sense can be seen in the provisions of most organizations of the United Nations system for assigning budgetary shares to member states, in the competence of such agencies as the World Health Organization and the International Civil Aviation Organization to adopt technical regulations applicable to all members unless they explicitly opt out, and in the capacity of such agencies as the International Labor Organization and the Food and Agriculture Organization to adopt conventions and recommendations which member states are bound, if not to accept, at least to take into consideration and to recognize as policy standards in regular reports to be submitted to the agencies. These illustrations, which could be multiplied,[8] bear out the thesis that minor and quasi-legislative powers of the citizen-commanding as distinguished from the bureaucrat-directing variety are being increasingly entrusted to voting majorities of international organizations.

THE MERITS OF INTERNATIONAL MAJORITARIANISM

As I have already suggested, unrestrained rejoicing over the victory of majority rule in international organization is perhaps inappropriate as well as premature. It is not clear that "A respect for the expressed will of the majority is as fundamental to international organization as it is to democracy." [9] The merits of international majoritarianism require careful evaluation.

The case for applauding the progress toward majority voting and deploring the incompleteness of that development rests first upon the assumption that this is a logical and eminently proper extension of "the

[8] See the collection of constitutional documents of the Specialized Agencies in *A Decade of American Foreign Policy: Basic Documents, 1941-49,* Senate Document No. 123, 81st Congress, 1st Session (Washington: Government Printing Office, 1950), Part IV.

[9] Dean Acheson, quoted in McGeorge Bundy, ed., *The Pattern of Responsibility* (Boston: Houghton Mifflin, 1952), p. 38.

democratic way." The ideological justification is powerfully supplemented by the conviction that the repudiation of unanimity is an essential step toward endowing international organizations with the capacity to act effectively. From a purely practical point of view, it seems desirable not to permit the world to be held to the lowest common denominator of cooperation, or to allow the use or threat of the veto by a single adamant member to inhibit the activities of the entire organized community. Moral and pragmatic objections to the unanimity rule are often combined, particularly with regard to situations in which a lawless state can avail itself of the veto to prevent a condemnatory judgment in its own case and to forestall the imposition of international sanctions upon itself.

It requires little effort to establish the criticism that majority voting in international institutions is not a genuinely democratic procedure, so long as the rule of "one state, one vote" persists. Given the equal voting power of states so disparate in population as, say, India and Iceland, it is clear that resolutions adopted by the General Assembly may not have the formal support of the majority of the total population of the United Nations, as expressed by the votes of governmental representatives. Theoretically, a collection of small states, representing only a very minor fraction of the population, could exercise negative or even positive control over the decision-making processes of the Assembly. The fiction of state personality, according to which we say that "France demands" or "Britain rejects" a certain policy, is useful and perhaps indispensable for some purposes, but we carry it too far if we assume that the will of a majority of states is necessarily entitled to the ideological prestige which democracy confers upon majority decision.

Even if the development of majority voting in international organization could be described as a genuinely democratic trend, its desirability would still be open to question.

Majority rule is not a natural law of social morality. Intranationally, it seems to have developed first as an expedient, a convenient procedural device, and later to have been rationalized in ideological terms. In democratic thought, majoritarianism has a moral flavor only in so far as it is substituted for *minority* rule; if moral legitimacy rests upon the "consent of the governed" principle, unanimous decision certainly has the edge over majority consent. In these terms, the shift from unanimity to majority rule is something other than a triumph of political morality.

However, the real objection to the principle of the *liberum veto* is not that it means unanimity rule but that it in fact means *minority* rule; it confers upon a minority of one the procedural competence and the moral authority to determine policy in a negative fashion. In these terms, the acceptance of majority rule represents both moral progress, so far as the minority is concerned, and a triumph for the possibility of effectively operating institutions, so far as the majority is concerned. Unanimity is the best guarantee of a "just" decision, but it carries the danger of the imposition of "no decision" by a minority; majority rule increases the probability of "some decision" and invests that decision with a moral force intermediate in strength between that afforded by unanimous and minority actions.

The institutional-efficiency basis for international majoritarianism is decidedly sounder than the moral-legitimacy basis. Yet, in the final analysis, the two considerations cannot be separated. Majority rule works, and thus acquires pragmatic justification, only if its moral legitimacy is generally accepted. Progress in political morality is not so much a product of majoritarianism, to be achieved by acceptance of majority rule, as a precondition for majoritarianism; the majority principle is not "better" than the unanimity principle, but it is a basis for more effective action which exists only in so far as an appropriately advanced moral consensus has been realized in the community. The problem is not to find moral justification for majority rule, but to build moral foundations for the pragmatically justifiable majority rule. And there is the rub so far as international organization is concerned.

The limits of effective majoritarian action within the formal voting provisions already established in international agencies, and of the expansibility of the majoritarian aspect of those provisions, are set by the attitudes of majorities and minorities toward each other and toward the larger community. Majority rule works only when the minority has such confidence in the ultimate reasonableness of the majority and such conviction of the ultimate community of majority and minority interests that it can afford to respect the right of the majority to rule without undue obstruction. Conversely, the situation demands that the majority recognize the rights of the minority and assume its basic loyalty to the rules of the game and the interests of the community, so that the majority can be prepared to rule without undue suppression. This condition exists only to a very limited extent in the international community. By and large, neither majorities nor minorities in the United Nations are spiritually fit to play their roles in a majoritarian system. Within areas of recognized common interest and relatively slight involvement of fundamental political concerns, acceptance of the majority principle has become feasible; but, as Riches has put it, "In the absence of a recognized community of interest and of agreement upon objectives, majority decision is impossible for the reason that the minority sees no reason for acquiescing in the decisions which might be reached by the majority." [10]

Indeed, majority rule has no valid claim of legitimacy apart from the existence of a basic moral consensus. We ought to be on guard against the naive tendency of some internationalists to assume that decisions of international majorities are infallibly just and impartial; national-minded sin-

[10] Cromwell A. Riches, *Majority Rule in International Organization* (Baltimore: Johns Hopkins, 1940), p. 296.

ners are not transformed into world-minded saints by coalescing to form a majority voting bloc in the General Assembly.

Karl Marx regarded the state as an inherently oppressive body, an agency by which the ruling class enforced and perpetuated its dictatorship over the underdogs. It could be nothing else, he argued, because national societies were nothing but arenas of inexorable class conflict. Marx was wrong about his facts; some national societies were already, and others were on the verge of becoming, genuine communities capable of using their states as agencies for harmonizing particular interests within the framework of a conception of community interest. But he was right about his theory; if and when group conflicts are as irreconcilable as Marx thought they were and had to be in capitalist countries, the state can be nothing other than what Marx thought it was in capitalist countries.

Marx's insight can be transferred to the realm of international organization. If states are so fundamentally divided that international society is essentially an arena of national struggle rather than a community, there is no real possibility that an international government or international organization can be anything other than an instrument which competitive states and blocs seek to capture for use in waging the bitter struggle. Such an agency can function as an impartial servant and guardian of community interests only to the extent that a genuine community has emerged. It is clear that contemporary world society has hardly begun to develop the consensual basis for giving majority rule the moral dignity that it has in an integrated community.

Under these circumstances, it may be doubted whether the trend toward registration of the will of a majority of member states as "international decisions" represents sound progress for international organization. Majority decisions in the equalitarian General Assembly are likely to be undemocratic in the sense that they do not represent a majority of the world's population, unrealistic in the sense that they do not reflect the greater portion of the world's real power, morally unimpressive in the sense that they cannot be identified as expressions of the dominant will of a genuine community, and for all these reasons ineffectual and perhaps even dangerous.

THE POLITICS OF INTERNATIONAL MAJORITARIANISM

We have been discussing the concept of majority rule in international organization in essentially theoretical terms, treating it as an issue related to democratic ideology and principles of political legitimacy. Majority control of international organization, however, is no longer merely a topic for philosophical disputation; it is a live political issue, impinging upon concrete political interests as well as abstract political principles. Hence, we turn now to consideration of the down-to-earth political implications of developments associated with majoritarianism in the United Nations system.

The position of the Soviet Union with respect to majority rule in the United Nations has been consistent and unambiguous. The USSR, with its small cluster of satellites, has functioned as a permanent minority—and has exhibited the disdain for and dislike of majoritarianism that is characteristic of permanent minorities. Indeed, it entered the United Nations with the apprehension that the organization might be dominated by "a majority on whose benevolent attitude toward the Soviet Union the Soviet people cannot count." [11] It clutched the veto power in the Security Council as a shield for defending its interests against hostile majorities. Nothing has happened in the history of the United Nations to convince the Soviet Union that it was unduly pessimistic in anticipating a minority position, or that it was unnecessarily cautious in providing itself with a defensive mechanism. On the contrary, Soviet leaders have regularly had occasion to regret that they were not equipped to frustrate the process of majority decision in organs other than the Security Council.

Viewing that process from the wrong side of the majoritarian tracks, the Soviet leaders have not been inspired by the thought that they are enveloped in a world community in which majority rule provides the valid expression of a community will. From that vantage point, "a majority in the United Nations, no matter how arithmetically overpowering, represents no distillation of the moral and political conclusions of mankind as a whole but only the manipulated votes of a hostile capitalist-dominated coalition to which only as much attention is due as the danger it may carry for the USSR." [12]

In the second decade of the operation of the United Nations, the increasing numerical strength of African and Asian states in the General Assembly has created a situation potentially much more favorable to the interests of the Soviet Union. Neutralist tendencies among the new states reduce the probability that the Western powers can continue to mobilize overwhelming majorities in support of distinctly anti-Soviet resolutions. The coincidence of Soviet anti-Westernism with Afro-Asian anticolonialism provides opportunities for the Soviet bloc to align itself with a majority in passing resolutions critical of and opposed by the Western powers. In short, this situation appears to offer the Soviet Union escape from its role as perpetual loser in voting contests; it does not promise the USSR the capacity to dominate the Assembly, but it does promise to deprive the

---

[11] The phrase is from Andrei Gromyko, speaking in the Security Council on March 5, 1947. Security Council, Official Records: 2nd Year, No. 22, p. 453.

[12] Rupert Emerson and Inis L. Claude, Jr., "The Soviet Union and the United Nations: An Essay in Interpretation," *International Organization,* February 1952, p. 7.

United States of that capacity and to permit the Soviets the occasional luxury of joining the majority on contentious issues.

There is little evidence, however, that the Soviet Union has begun to abandon the mentality of the permanent minority. Soviet leaders may exude ideological confidence that the USSR will someday preside over a massive collection of states which have seen the Communist light, but they have not responded to the altered situation in the Assembly by betraying more hopeful expectations regarding the outcome of the voting process. Understandably, they enjoy the opportunity to play back Western sermons on the virtues of respecting the majority will whenever they find themselves on the winning side, and the Western powers on the losing side, of a vote. But in general, they maintain the attitude of a defensive minority, convinced that majority decisions will run against them and that their task is therefore to resist majoritarian trends. Thus, in 1960 the Soviets introduced the "troika" proposal, a scheme for placing the administration of the United Nations under a board of three officials, representatives of the Communist, Western, and uncommitted groups, each of which would in effect have a veto power over the execution of United Nations programs and policies. Similarly, the USSR in recent years has denied the competence of the Assembly to bind member states to provide financial support for extraordinary peace-keeping operations, and has adhered to its earlier position that significant political matters should be dealt with in the Security Council, where the Soviet veto power is operative. Clearly, these are not the policies of a state which expects to dominate the United Nations, but of a state which foresees the continuing necessity of utilizing whatever capacity a minority may possess or acquire to frustrate the projects of an unfriendly majority.

As a minority power, the Soviet Union denies the legitimacy of the principle of majority rule, defies the decisions of the majority whenever it considers that its interests so demand, and concentrates upon inhibiting the effective operation of the United Nations as an instrument of the will and purpose of the majority. Should the USSR ever become a champion of majority rule in the United Nations, this might well be regarded as cause for dismay rather than delight in the West—for it would be less likely to reflect a Soviet conversion to higher principles of political morality than a Soviet conviction that the Communist bloc had gained, or was on the verge of gaining, a dominant position in the United Nations.

The attitude of the United States toward the principle of majority rule in the United Nations usually has been exactly the reverse of the Soviet attitude. American ideological sympathy for majoritarianism has been happily reinforced by the pragmatic consideration that Western voting victories have occurred with almost monotonous regularity. Over the greater part of the history of the United Nations, the United States has been able to mobilize overwhelming support in the Assembly for its policies and proposals; at worst, it has failed occasionally to amass an adequate majority. It has rarely tasted the actual defeat of being in a minority overridden by majority votes. Under these circumstances, American enthusiasm for the majority principle is as understandable as it may be superficial; nobody enjoys majority rule so much as the majority leader.

There is reason to doubt that the period when the United States was virtually assured of victory on issues which it regarded as significant, and the Soviet Union virtually foredoomed to defeat, was a healthy one for the United Nations—or for either of the two major powers. Genuine acceptance of majoritarianism is as unlikely to be fostered by the experience of winning consistently as by that of losing consistently. It is the minority that must learn to respect the will of the majority, but it is only a minority which has a reasonable prospect of being sometimes in the majority that can realistically be expected to learn this lesson. By the same token, it is the majority that must learn to respect the rights of the minority, but it is only a majority which has some experience of being in the minority position that can realistically be expected to learn this lesson. In these terms, the situation has not conduced to the development of attitudes appropriate to international majoritarianism in either the United States or the Soviet Union.

During its majoritarian heyday, the United States tended to exploit its capacity to inflict defeats upon the USSR to the point of undermining the potential usefulness of the United Nations as a mediating force, able to command the confidence of both the cold war contestants and thus to serve their common interest in helping them avoid mutually disastrous explosions of conflict. The Soviet Union developed the conviction that the United Nations was an instrument of American foreign policy, devoted to the support of American interests. The American position was ambiguous. On the one hand, leaders of the United States valued the organization, and encouraged the American public to value it, as a reliable instrument of American policy in opposition to the Soviet Union; on the other hand, they insisted that the Soviet leaders should regard the United Nations as an impartial agency of the world community, ready to serve neutrally in the solution of conflicts, and entitled to the support of all states.

As might be expected, it proved difficult to have it both ways. To the degree that the United States succeeded in using the United Nations as a pro-Western device, it reduced the utility of the organization as an agency of conciliation and stabilization in the cold war situation. American reaction was to minimize the need for neutral service by the organization; if a choice had to be made, it was clearly preferable that the United Nations should function as a member of the Western team, rather than as an umpire between East and West. The urge to exploit the possibility of outvoting the Soviet Union was stronger than the sense of necessity to negotiate with that power. The situation of American dominance in the United Nations that produced this attitude on the part of the United States led the Soviet Union to deny the possibility of neutral service by the organization. Soviet leaders, ideologically conditioned to expect hostility rather than neutrality from international agencies, found it impossible to conceive that a United Nations which operated primarily as a Western-controlled agency could function secondarily as a neutral element in the East-West conflict. Finally, the extended experience of having the United Nations serve as the locus of Western voting triumphs, and of justifying American participation in the organization on the ground that it did so serve, made the American public ill-prepared to come to terms with an emerging situation marked by the diminution of the Western capacity to control the United Nations.

Like Robert Frost's oven bird, the West has been confronted with the question of "what to make of a diminished thing." The drastic expansion of membership of the United Nations, initiated at the end of 1955, has carried with it the steady enlargement of the list of states whose votes in the Assembly are not readily or dependably available to create pro-Western majorities on cold war issues. Moreover, these states, largely newly independent entities in Asia and Africa, have come to constitute a grouping which holds roughly half the votes in the Assembly and can frequently mobilize overwhelming majorities for resolutions expressing its focal interest in decolonization and economic development. As the new states grow in numbers and develop their international parliamentary skills, they will presumably put the stamp of their political and doctrinal concerns more frequently and more prominently upon the decisions of the Assembly. The era of Western domination of the Assembly's processes is coming to an end.

Western reactions to the preliminary manifestations and the prospective development of this trend have been varied and confused. Official attitudes toward the changing United Nations have ranged from Belgian bitterness and French contempt to British indifference and American anxiety. Some commentators have confused hypothetical possibilities with present realities or imminent inevitabilities, arguing that the West is or must soon be a helpless minority, constantly abused by an overpowering Afro-Asian voting cabal which is aided and abetted—and perhaps manipulated—by the Soviet bloc. Others have paid closer attention to the developing record, noting that reports of the death of Western influence in the United Nations have been grossly exaggerated, and have argued that the West can, if it displays political wisdom and diplomatic skill, maintain a position of leadership.

A leading feature of the Western reaction to the political revolution which has transformed the Assembly is the development of interest in the concept of weighted voting. The disposition of the Western powers to challenge the rule which assigns equal voting power in the Assembly to every state, regardless of size or importance, was not strong so long as they were confident of their ability to mobilize comfortable majorities. Its growth correlates directly with the decline of Western confidence on this point.

As we have noted, the "one state, one vote" rule is susceptible to criticism on democratic grounds, but this line of attack, carrying the implication that population disparities should be accurately reflected in the distribution of voting power, is a rather dangerous one for the Western powers. It would be small comfort for the United States to escape from a situation in which Iceland has as much voting power as the United States into one in which India would have more than twice as much, and Communist China, should it enter the United Nations, would have more than three times as much. Understandably, Western criticism of the egalitarian rule has tended to concentrate on the issue of *realism,* not democracy, and to imply that voting power should be proportioned to real power and influence in the world, defined by some formula which would give weight, but not exclusive weight, to the population factor. Clearly, it is senseless and unrealistic to treat Finland and the Soviet Union, or Panama and the United States, or Gabon and France, as equal weights in the scale of international affairs.

In the historical development of international organization, various devices for giving institutional recognition to the real inequalities of states have been invented. The Universal Postal Union introduced the practice of assigning extra votes to colonial powers by according membership status to overseas possessions under their control. The International Institute of Agriculture, established in 1905, set a precedent for such present-day agencies as the International Bank, the International Monetary Fund, the International Finance Corporation, and the International Development Association, by allocating voting power to members in correspondence with the size of their financial contributions. In a number of agencies dealing with problems of international commerce in particular commodities, voting power has been distributed so as to create a balance between importing and exporting states, and to give special weight to the more important participants in international trade. Several of the regional institutions created in Western Europe since World War II have established organs in which voting inequalities are roughly correlated with population differences.

In some cases, weighting has been accomplished without tampering with the formal rule of "one state, one vote." For instance, the technique of granting permanent or constitutionally assured membership in organs of the "executive committee" type to the more important states was introduced in the treaty provisions concerning the composition of the Governing Body of the International Labor Organization and the Council of the League. This technique, sometimes supplemented by the device of giving the major states "bigger" votes without giving them "more" votes, has found increasing favor in organizational developments since World War II.

The United Nations Charter, for example, nowhere permits one member to cast more than one vote, except in the sense that it allows the Soviet Union multiple voting power through its control over the Ukrainian S.S.R. and Byelorussian S.S.R. and that it does not exclude the great powers generally from dominating the voting behavior of members which are factually if not legally subject to their control. However, it manipulates the pattern of voting strength by guaranteeing a balance between administering powers and nonadministering powers in the Trusteeship Council, and gives institutional recognition to a heavyweight class of five great powers by providing them with permanent membership in the Security and Trusteeship Councils, a monopoly of membership in the Military Staff Committee, special status in connection with the Transitional Security Arrangements described in Chapter XVII of the Charter, and decisively "big" single votes in major activities of the Security Council, in the process of bringing the Charter into force, and in the amending process. The United Nations Special Fund, established in 1959, is directed by a Governing Council which is equally divided between major contributors and recipients of the technical and developmental aid administered by the agency. This composition, coupled with the requirement of a two-thirds majority for important decisions, assures the primary backers of the Fund that they will have an important role in determining policy. Somewhat similarly, the Statute of the International Atomic Energy Agency contains a complicated formula for constituting the Board of Governors, designed to give special influence to the states most advanced in nuclear technology and the production of source materials.

These instances suggest that the distribution of voting power within the various components of the United Nations system already reflects to a considerable degree the principle of proportionality. If the General Assembly is considered, not in isolation, but in the larger context of the United Nations, it is apparent that the disproportionate weight given to small states in that organ is counterbalanced by the special importance assigned to great powers elsewhere in the system. Viewed as a whole, the United Nations represents not the triumph of the unrealistic concept of equality, but a compromise between the claims of great and small states for status and formal power to participate in decision-making processes. Moreover, it should be emphasized that formal voting power is significantly supplemented by informal capacity to affect decisions, a capacity which tends to accrue to states in rough proportion to their military, political, and economic weight. The fact that Upper Volta has voting power in the Assembly equal to that of the Soviet Union certainly does not mean that its influence is equivalent to that of the Soviet Union; the fact that the United States has less than one per cent of the votes should not be taken to indicate that the American impact on the operation of the Assembly is negligible. Indeed, the unrealism reflected in the rule of equal voting power for all members in the Assembly is matched by the unrealism exhibited by those who ignore the fact that the major states exercise an influence in that body far out of proportion to their formal voting capacity. Precise measurement is not possible in this area, but it is doubtful that the great powers carry less weight in the Assembly than considerations of political realism would dictate. As a member of the United States Mission to the United Nations put it:

> By and large, the influence of a nation in the Assembly reflects its position in the world. Although there are exceptions to this rule—for example, because of the particular qualities of a delegate or because of the unpopularity of a member's policies—the United States is not one of the exceptions.[13]

While an objective observer might conclude that a reasonable compromise between the principle of equality and the fact of inequality of states has been developed in the United Nations system, no one should be surprised that there has been persistent political dissatisfaction with the arrangement. In the early years, when the Security Council appeared destined to rank as the central political organ, the small states protested against the inferiority of position assigned to them in that organ and regarded their equality of status in the General Assembly as inadequate compensation. In more recent years, as the Assembly has become the primary organ within the system, the major powers have displayed dissatisfaction; they have not considered that their underrepresentation in the voting procedures of the Assembly is offset by the special status accorded them elsewhere in the system. Given the overriding importance of the role which the Assembly has assumed in the United Nations, it is clear that the demand for a balancing of the concepts of equality and inequality within that organ will continue to swell. Major powers, not content with their informal capacity to exert substantial influence upon Assembly decisions, will seek to institutionalize it, thus enhancing its reliability and its symbolic value. The small states, treasuring both the symbolic status of equality and the political influence which the "one state, one vote" rule places in their hands, will resist the alteration of voting arrangements in the Assembly.

The outcome of this struggle is not easy to predict. The vested interest of the small states in the egalitarian status quo is protected by two features of the amending process prescribed in Article 108 of the Charter. First, the requirement of unanimous ratification of amendments by the Big Five minimizes the likelihood of constitutional alteration, for the prospect of agreement among the great powers as to how differential voting weights should be allocated is very small, even though they might agree in

---

13 Jonathan B. Bingham, "One Nation, One Vote—and One U.N.," *New York Times Magazine,* September 16, 1962, p. 86.

principle on the need for institutionalizing inequality in the Assembly. Secondly, the provision that change can be accomplished only with the consent of two-thirds of the members of the United Nations, expressed ultimately in acts of ratification, puts the small states in a strong defensive position. The rigidities of the established pattern are in their favor.

On the other hand, the Western powers—particularly the United States—have a persuasive instrument in their capacity to grant or to withhold the financial resources required for support of United Nations programs of assistance to developing states. The record shows that in several instances the urge for formal equality has been subordinated to the desire for international aid. What appears most likely is that the general voting procedure of the Assembly will remain unchanged, but that particular programs and activities launched by the Assembly will, with increasing frequency, be operated under special arrangements which incorporate concessions to the principle of weighted voting.

Closely related to the development of pressure for redistribution of voting power in the Assembly is a second feature of Western reaction to the radical transformation of the political character of that body: the denunciation of bloc politics, and the accompanying charge of irresponsibility levied against states which adhere to blocs.

"Bloc" bids fair to join "veto" at the top of the list of opprobrious terms in the international vocabulary of the West. As new Asian and African members have crowded the halls of United Nations Headquarters, observers in the United States and Western Europe have noted with increasing concern the developing solidarities among those states—frequently exaggerating the actual achievement or the imminent probability of effective cohesiveness. The older Soviet bloc can be regarded with some equanimity, for it is a familiar fixture of the Assembly, its regimentation so thorough as to excite amused contempt, and its ineffectual role as a minority in Assembly voting has long been established. The Afro-Asian bloc, however, stirs raw emotion. It is new and growing—and the limits of its potential growth are not yet clearly discernible. It is not a troublesome minority which the West can expect to keep in its parliamentary place, but an incipient majority which threatens to displace the West as the dominant force in the Assembly's proceedings. In many cases, its members are states which are poor, weak, and small, doubtfully viable as economic and political entities, inexperienced and ill-equipped to function on the international scene. The reaction of many Westerners to the rise to power within the Assembly of this group of states is reminiscent of the standard reaction of aristocratic ruling classes to the domestic political intrusions of the common masses; one can expect the rude barbarians to exhibit ruthless solidarity in humiliating their betters, overturning established order, mismanaging the affairs of society, soaking the rich—and they may even get ideas about marrying one's daughters!

There is an unmistakable tinge of racial and cultural condescension, a residue of the colonialist's attitude toward the natives, a touch of the defensive arrogance of a beleaguered elite, in the attitude of those Westerners so confidently pessimistic about the irresponsibility of the Afro-Asian bloc.

It might be observed that certain subjective elements enter into the terms we are considering here. A state behaves irresponsibly when it votes "the wrong way" on an issue; no vote cast, for whatever reason, in support of a position favored by the United States has ever been cited by American observers as evidence of irresponsibility. A bloc is a group of states which opposes, or refuses to support, one's own position. Western commentators, for instance, have not cited Latin American solidarity with the United States as evidence of a deplorable tendency toward bloc voting—but Indian publicists have done so. A Madras newspaper commented on the defeat in 1953 of a proposal for Indian participation in the peace conference on Korea:

> This brought into sharp focus the fact that the Latin American bloc constitutes the only veto in the General Assembly which, under the Charter, is otherwise veto-free. The U.S. with 19 Latin Americans, can block any proposal in the Assembly and yesterday she made it plain that she won't hesitate to resort to it to get her way.[14]

Clearly, the "viewing with alarm" which has tended to characterize much of the Western response to the increasing Afro-Asian membership in the United Nations is a defensive reaction to the decline of Western dominance in the Assembly. The claim that inordinate influence has fallen into the hands of Afro-Asians, who allegedly will use it irresponsibly, may be used to support the demand for weighted voting, so as to redress the position of the West. It may serve as the basis for proposals that the West abandon the United Nations, or at the least shift its major emphasis to existing or proposed new "free world" institutions, in which Western predominance would presumably be assured. Finally, it may be used to establish an ideological basis for the proposition that majority voting in the Assembly does not necessarily produce resolutions deserving of respect; formal actions of the Assembly may reflect neither the consensus of "world public opinion" nor the views of responsible statesmen in command of the major portion of the power that counts in international politics, and may therefore be both properly and safely ignored when national judgment and interest so dictate. The West, threatened with the loss of its majority, is beginning to articulate the case against international

---

[14] Cited, from *The Hindu* (Madras), August 30, 1953, in *India and the United Nations,* Report of a Study Group set up by The Indian Council of World Affairs (New York: Manhattan Publishers, for the Carnegie Endowment for International Peace, 1957), p. 69.

majoritarianism which the Soviet Union, ensconced in its minority position, has argued—and the West denounced—from the earliest days of the United Nations. The argument that the voice of the Assembly may be regarded as an expression of the selfish will of an irresponsible majority, organized in a monolithic bloc, is the first resort of a permanent minority and the last resort of a majority which feels itself slipping into minority status.

It should not be assumed, however, that the United States has clearly and decisively shifted from the attitude and policy appropriate to the self-confident leader of the majority to the stand that might be expected of a state which finds itself, or expects soon to find itself, defending a minority position. Just as the Soviet Union has continued to behave like a member of the permanent minority, even when the decline of anti-Soviet majoritarianism has been increasingly in evidence, so the United States has in many ways maintained the outlook of the dominant power in the Assembly, despite its apprehensions regarding the shift of voting patterns in that body. In part, this may reflect a residual optimism—the conviction that the West may yet salvage its capacity to control the Assembly. Even more, it may express the inertia of policy—the lag between anticipation of minority status and the adaptation of policy to fit the emerging situation. The United States appears to confront what might be called a majority-minority dilemma. With respect to the Soviet bloc, the Western powers are in a majority position, and are motivated to enhance the world organization's capacity to overcome minority obstructionism. With respect to the Afro-Asian group, the United States and its allies are in a minority position, and might be expected to concentrate on developing safeguards against abusive action by the majority. It is not easy for a state to shift from a policy appropriate to a majority role to one consonant with a minority role, or to pursue both types of policy simultaneously. In effect, the United States has adopted the worried look of an actual or prospective member of the minority, but has otherwise continued to function as if its role as leader of a dominant majority were unchallenged; it has begun to feel like a minority power, but persists in thinking like a majority power.

This is illustrated by the strong support given by the United States to the proposition, enunciated by the International Court of Justice in 1962,[15] that the General Assembly is competent to impose binding obligations upon member states for payment of the costs of special peace-keeping operations, and, by extension, of any other programs which the United Nations might launch for the realization of the purposes stated in the Charter. In insisting that the Assembly be recognized as having the authority, by two-thirds vote, to exercise this power, the United States appeared to cast aside its anxieties about the domination of the Assembly by

---

[15] *Certain Expenses of the United Nations (Article 17, paragraph 2, of the Charter)*, Advisory Opinion of July 20, 1962: I. C. J. Reports 1962, p. 151.

an irresponsible majority of weak and impecunious states. The American position probably did not mean that the United States was willing to accept whatever financial obligations might be imposed upon it for the support of United Nations programs, including programs which it might disapprove; rather, that position appears to be an expression of confidence that the Western powers will not find themselves in the role of an outvoted minority in the Assembly. As I have suggested, the United States no longer has this confident outlook—yet, American policy seems still to reflect such confidence.

Throughout the history of the United Nations, the United States and the Soviet Union have undertaken, respectively, to enhance and to frustrate the effectiveness of the United Nations as an operative mechanism. At one level of analysis, this might be taken to mean that the United States has been dedicated, and the Soviet Union opposed, to the development of a potent instrument of world order. At another, and deeper, level, these contrasting policies might be interpreted as reflecting the differing estimates of the two major powers as to their capability for directing and controlling the activities of the organization. The urge to enlarge the functions and powers of an international agency is characteristic of majority mentality; the demand for restriction and inhibition, the outlook of a minority. Viewed from the minority position, effectiveness is a euphemism for majority domination. From the vantage point of the majority, the protective tactics of the minority represent perverse obstructionism. In the present international system, states are not so much committed to supporting or opposing a strong and active United Nations, or the majoritarian principle in the United Nations, as to enhancing their ability to promote international action favorable to their interests, and to prevent international action unfavorable to their interests. At bottom, the doctrinal controversies regarding international majoritarianism are ideological reflections of differing expectations regarding the politics of control.

Given the continuing expansion of the membership of the United Nations, and the shifting patterns of relationship among its members, we can anticipate changes in the attitudes of states and blocs toward the principle of majority rule. The Afro-Asian states will presumably replace the West as the group most enthusiastically devoted to the sanctity of that rule and to the expansion of its realm of applicability in the United Nations.

If the world organization is to realize its full potential as an international political agency, the states which enjoy the capacity to exercise parliamentary dominance at any given time must be restrained in their exploitation of that capacity by a sober recognition of the limitations of its genuine utility within the multistate system. The weakness of community consensus makes it impossible to rely upon the moral appeal of majoritarianism to produce minority acquiescence in decisions. It is premature to expect states to operate as if they were enveloped in a world community in which majoritarianism provides the valid expression of a community will. In the present moral context, voting tends to produce a specious sense of moral superiority among the majority, which exacerbates irritation, encourages uncompromising attitudes, and tempts the majority to stress outvoting members of the minority rather than reaching agreement with them. In the present power context, it promotes decision-making without a sense of responsibility to the realistic limits of policy.

Possibly, a minimal community of interest may sooner or later be discovered or developed by the states and groups of states whose relationships are now so fundamentally discordant; the assumption that international conflicts are eternally irreconcilable is no more tenable than Marx's similar assumption concerning the class struggle. But the exploitation of this possibility is more likely to be impeded than promoted by competitive voting. The substitution of the battle of the ballot box for violent conflict is the result, not the cause, of the transformation of a society from a bundle of profound antagonisms into a meaningful community.

Excessive emphasis upon the power to mobilize a voting majority obscures the fundamental truth that, in the world as it really is, voting does not solve problems or resolve conflicts. The case for old-fashioned unanimity is not that it comports with the old-fashioned doctrine of sovereignty, but that it focuses attention upon the present reality that the great issues of international conflict will yield only to the process of persuasion, compromise, and agreement. Majoritarianism serves the world badly by putting a premium upon the unacceptable proposal which can be voted over minority opposition rather than the bargaining proposal which may be tailored to agreement with the minority.

All this is not to say that voting will never become a proper and effective device for managing the problems of the world. It may; but this depends upon developments in the nature of the world political system, not upon innovations in the mechanics of the organizational voting system. Majority voting has achieved a significant role in international organization; at the moment, it appears that the world has more, not less, majoritarianism than it is morally equipped to handle or realistically capable of putting to effective use.

SUGGESTED READINGS

Hadwen, John G., and Johan Kaufmann, *How United Nations Decisions Are Made,* Leyden: A. W. Sythoff, 1960.

Hovet, Thomas, Jr., *Bloc Politics in the United Nations,* Cambridge: Harvard University Press, 1960.

Koo, Wellington, Jr., *Voting Procedures in International Political Organizations,* New York: Columbia University Press, 1947.

Riches, Cromwell A., *Majority Rule in International Organization,* Baltimore: Johns Hopkins, 1940.

Riches, Cromwell A., *The Unanimity Rule and the League of Nations,* Baltimore: Johns Hopkins, 1933.

Riggs, Robert E., *Politics in the United Nations: A Study of United States Influence in the General Assembly,* Urbana: University of Illinois Press, 1958.

CHAPTER

8

The Veto Problem in the United Nations

By all odds the best publicized constitutional problem of the United Nations is that of the great power veto. Scratch the consciousness of an apolitical American citizen with the initials, "U.N.," and he will respond with one word—"veto." The veto problem has become the symbol of the cold war and of the inadequacies of current efforts to deal with that phenomenon through international organization. Accurately or not, the veto is generally understood to be the critical defect of the United Nations.

The veto problem is a specialized version of the general problems which were considered in Chapter 7. It is at once an expression of the progressive trend toward abandonment of the unrealistic and undemocratic proposition that every state, however large or small, should have the same voice in international decisions, and a product of conservative resistance to the general tendency to introduce the majority voting rule in international agencies. That is to say, analysis of the veto arrangement should include Article 23 as well as Article 27 of the Charter; it is as significant that the designated "Big Five" powers—China, France, the Soviet Union, Britain, and the United States—are given permanent membership in the Security Council and peculiar responsibility for its operation, as that they are allowed the competence to block action of the Council on nonprocedural matters by withholding their concurrence. In the former sense, the arrangement constitutes an important segment of the Charter's progress toward institutionalization of the special role of great powers in international organization, which goes well beyond the League Covenant's limited attribution of unequal weight to the major states.[1] In the latter sense, the arrangement represents a lagging point in the general development toward majoritarianism; the great power veto in the Security Council and in the amending process is the sole surviving relic of the traditional unanimity requirement which still occupied a place of formal supremacy in the Covenant. From one point of view, the veto represents a holding out against the new principle of majority decision; from another, it represents the understandable demand of great powers for weighting of votes which derives from acceptance of the new principle.

In constitutional terms, the veto rule derives from the provisions of Article 27 of the Charter, which states that Security Council decisions "on procedural matters" shall be made by the affirmative votes of any seven of that body's eleven members, but that decisions on "all other matters" shall require seven affirmative votes "including the concurring votes of the permanent members." Thus, any of the Big Five can unilaterally defeat any Security Council proposal other than one relating to procedure, except that it, like ordinary members of the Council, must refrain from voting when the Council considers the possible means of peaceful settlement of disputes to which it is a party. In general, the veto power applies to pacific settlement under Chapter VI as well as to enforcement measures to maintain peace under Chapter VII; a great power can veto a proposal for enforcement action even if it is directed against itself; a particular great power is debarred from using its veto only if it is directly involved in a dispute which is the subject of peaceful settlement efforts, and even in that case the veto power of the other permanent members remains effective; a great power can use its right of veto to frustrate either pacific settlement or more drastic action in cases involving its friends, allies, or satellites.

Moreover, the great powers agreed among themselves at San Francisco, in a Statement of Interpretation submitted to the Conference,[2] that the unanimity rule should prevail in voting on the preliminary question as to whether or not a matter should be considered procedural and thus not subject to veto. This "double veto" principle seemed to authorize any great power to veto any effort to remove matters from the range of its veto, thereby permitting the indefinite extension of the capacity for negation assigned to the permanent members. Finally, in Articles 108 and

---

1 The Covenant provided for permanent membership of the great powers in the Council (Article 4, paragraph 1), but it gave them no powers or functions beyond those of other Council members.

2 For the text of this statement, see L. M. Goodrich and E. Hambro, *Charter of the United Nations: Commentary and Documents* (2d ed.; Boston: World Peace Foundation, 1949), pp. 216-218.

109, the great powers were given the competence to veto any possible efforts to abolish their veto right by constitutional amendment. There can be no doubt that the principle of great power unanimity was implanted in the Charter with deliberate firmness.

An interpretation of this action of the San Francisco Conference can best be stated in negative terms. In the present-day climate of reaction against the veto and misunderstanding of the veto, it is most essential to be clear about what the veto is not, what it was not intended to be, and what it was not expected to be.

THE ADOPTION OF THE VETO RULE

In the first place, the veto provision was not an illiberal rule insisted upon by the Soviet Union over the opposition of the more progressive-minded great powers of the West. American resentment of the Soviet use of the veto has tended to give birth to this myth; even so estimable a statesman as Senator John Sherman Cooper was moved to ask in 1954, "Isn't it true that the United States, at the time of the approval of the charter, was opposed to the veto?" [3] Nothing could be further from the truth. Provisions for the veto right of the great powers appeared regularly in the preliminary drafts for a general international organization which were made by planners in the United States Government.[4] Throughout the negotiations looking toward the establishment of the United Nations—at Dumbarton Oaks, at Yalta, and at San Francisco—the United States stood shoulder to shoulder with the other leading powers in supporting this concept. Indeed, Secretary of State Hull, in discussing a preliminary draft Charter with a group of Senators in May 1944, asserted that the veto principle was incorporated in it "primarily on account of the United States," and, with respect to the proposed Security Council, that "our Government would not remain there a day without retaining its veto power." [5]

Nevertheless, it has frequently been alleged that the United States stood for a more modest version of the veto power than the Soviet Union desired, and that the formula worked out at Yalta and ultimately adopted at San Francisco represented a "compromise" between the two positions.[6] It is true that the USSR entered the negotiations with a more nearly absolutist view of the essential veto power than its Western great power colleagues, but it would appear from the available evidence that the final arrangement represented a defeat for the Soviet Union rather than a compromise with that state. The Soviet Union gave up its claim of right to

[3] *Charter Review Hearing,* Part 1, p. 17.

[4] See *Postwar Foreign Policy Preparation,* Appendixes 13, 23, 35, 38, 42, 52, 53, 57.

[5] *The Memoirs of Cordell Hull,* II, 1662, 1664.

[6] For the "compromise" concept, see, for instance, Dwight E. Lee, "The Genesis of the Veto," *International Organization,* February 1947, p. 37.

veto acceptance of disputes for discussion by the Security Council, in response to pressure from the United States and other Western powers.[7]

The central issue in the debate concerning the veto among the great powers at Dumbarton Oaks and Yalta was the extent to which a permanent member of the Security Council should be required to abstain from voting in regard to disputes involving itself as a party. The Soviet Union fought vigorously for the veto right in all cases, with complete disregard for the ideal concept that no one should be a judge in his own case, but it was finally prevailed upon to accept the formula suggested by Roosevelt at the Yalta Conference, barring members of the Council from voting or vetoing in proceedings looking toward peaceful settlement of disputes in which they were directly involved and permitting interested parties to use their normal voting power in all other circumstances.[8]

So far as the United States was concerned, it appears that this was a clear-cut victory. It could be described as a compromise only if the United States had clearly and firmly stood for the absolute exclusion of parties from voting in their own cases, at all stages of Security Council consideration of disputes. However, this was not the case. In pre-Dumbarton Oaks drafts, the State Department planners had wavered indecisively in regard to this problem. In two 1943 drafts, which assumed the grant of permanent seats in the Council to the Big Four (excluding France from the great power team), they had proposed the compulsory abstention of parties from votes on peaceful settlement but not from votes on enforcement measures, although they favored the rule that only three of the Big Four votes should be required for decisions of the latter sort.[9] In December 1943, they had suggested the total exclusion of a great power's vote in disputes to which it might be a party, whereas in April 1944, they had dropped altogether the notion of compulsory abstention of interested parties.[10]

The American mind, after having considered all these possibilities, was not made up at the beginning of the consultations at Dumbarton Oaks; the United States proposals presented at this conference referred to the problem of voting by parties to disputes as one with respect to which "Provisions will need to be worked out. . . ."[11] In these crucial discussions among the great powers, the United States took the side of Britain, which had consistently stood for complete application of the rule against

---

[7] This Soviet concession was registered in the Statement of Interpretation agreed to by the sponsoring powers and France at San Francisco. See Goodrich and Hambro, *loc. cit.*

[8] Stettinius, *Roosevelt and the Russians,* p. 171.

[9] See the Draft of July 14, 1943, Articles 4, 9, 10; and the Draft of August 14, 1943, Articles 4, 7, 8. *Postwar Foreign Policy Preparation,* Appendixes 13 and 23.

[10] *Ibid.,* Appendixes 33 and 35.

[11] Draft of July 18, 1944, III-C-5. *Ibid.,* Appendix 38.

voting in one's own case in contrast to the Soviet Union's consistent demand for the complete rejection of that rule, but even then the American delegation was internally divided as to whether the rule should be applied beyond the pacific settlement stage.[12] Subsequently, leading British statesmen, including Churchill and Cripps, swung strongly toward complete acceptance of the Soviet view.[13]

In the light of this record of vacillation by the United States and, to a lesser degree, by Britain, it appears that the final decision, as expressed in the Yalta voting formula, represented precisely what the Western powers finally decided they really wanted, not a middle ground between what they wanted and what the USSR demanded. This conclusion is supported by the fact that the United States has never, in its various suggestions for reducing the scope of the veto power, intimated a desire to introduce a barrier to a great power's using the veto to kill proposals for enforcement action directed against itself.

The provision permitting a permanent member of the Security Council to block action on disputes involving itself, except action relating to peaceful adjustment, is one of the most damaging parts of the entire veto arrangement from the standpoint of those who favor the progressive development of the effective operating capacity of international organization. Indeed, one scholar has asserted that "The main defect of the voting provisions of the Charter does not lie in the requirement of the unanimity of the permanent members . . . but in the limited scope of the compulsory abstention."[14] Nevertheless, this aspect of the veto power commanded the full support of *all* the Big Five in their successful campaign to make constitutional recognition of their special status an essential condition for the creation of the United Nations. The veto rule, as it stands, was *not* a reluctant concession by "enlightened" great powers to the reactionary demands of the Soviet Union.

A second negative proposition which needs to be established is that the adoption of the principle of great power unanimity as a prerequisite for Security Council action did not reflect an ignorant and simple-minded inability to assimilate the lessons concerning the requirements for effective international organization which the experience of the League had made available.

The League had failed, and it had been founded upon the principle of unanimity. However, there was little in the record to support the view that the League had collapsed primarily because of the veto, or that

---

[12] *Hull, op. cit.*, II, 1677-1678.

[13] Stettinius, *op. cit.*, pp. 45, 54, 55, 115-116.

[14] Eduardo Jiménez de Aréchaga, *Voting and the Handling of Disputes in the Security Council* (New York: Carnegie Endowment for International Peace, 1950), p. 33.

it had been obviously doomed from the beginning because it had incorporated that concept in its foundations. Viscount Cecil (formerly Lord Robert Cecil) had written that:

> I do not . . . regard the so-called unanimity rule as a blot upon League procedure. At the worst it may have made the Council and Assembly cautious in discussing radical proposals, but that, I am inclined to think, is, in international affairs, a good thing.
>
> The number of cases in which a decision has been prevented by failure to obtain unanimity is not great. Indeed I do not think any such case has occurred in any coercive action by the League.[15]

It is notable that many of the best informed commentators on the history of the League have regarded that organization not as a ghastly mistake, condemned from the start to tragic failure by almost ludicrously inadequate and inappropriate constitutional provisions, but as a near-miss—an experiment that might very well have succeeded, that worked very well for a time, and that finally broke down primarily because of unfortunate circumstances and the mistaken policies and unenlightened attitudes of statesmen rather than because of intrinsic defects.[16] As a British spokesman at San Francisco put it, "Hard things are said nowadays about the League of Nations, that, by its very nature, it was inevitably doomed to failure. . . . I would say that the principal weakness of the League was not in its constitution or in its nature, but lay in the unwillingness of the nations to make the necessary sacrifices to achieve its purposes." [17]

In fact, the San Francisco decision concerning the veto was deliberately contrived to prevent the new organization from being plagued by what was regarded as the critical defect of the League: the nonmembership of some of the great powers. Official American spokesmen never tired of reiterating the thesis that if they had to present a vetoless Charter to the Senate and public of the United States, they would be unable to prevent the United Nations from being burdened with the same handicap of American abstention which had proved too much for the previous world organization. The veto right was treated as the guarantee that the United Nations would include the great powers among its members; nothing in the history of the League suggested that the retention of the great power veto would be as disastrous as the failure to retain the interest of the great powers.

Moreover, the great power unanimity rule was designed with a view to avoidance of international fiascoes like the League's effort to squelch Italian aggression in Ethiopia in 1935-36. Looked at negatively, this rule is a veto provision, enabling a great power to prevent the launching of

---

15 *A Great Experiment* (New York: Oxford University Press, 1941), pp. 72, 94.

16 Cf. Cecil, *op. cit.*, and Walters, *A History of the League of Nations.*

17 *The United Nations Conference on International Organization: Selected Documents,* p. 671.

organizational action; looked at positively, it is a unanimity provision, providing a guarantee that whatever acton is undertaken will be supported by the states which control the bulk of the world's economic, military, and political power, and that its success will therefore be almost a foregone conclusion. The "chain of events" logic of the great powers' Statement of Interpretation at San Francisco aimed at this point: the United Nations ought not to get out on a limb, or to start something which it cannot finish; if it takes a decision which initiates a chain of events leading to the possible necessity of enforcement action, it should make certain that the great powers whose combined strength is necessary and probably sufficient for carrying out sanctions are wholeheartedly in agreement with that policy from the beginning to the end of the chain. As Philip C. Jessup has stated, the veto is "the safety-valve that prevents the United Nations from undertaking commitments in the political field which it presently lacks the power to fulfill." [18]

Thirdly, it is not to be supposed that the framers of the Charter believed they were creating an ideal mechanism for maintaining international peace and security when they wrote the veto provision into the chapter on the Security Council. They did believe that this arrangement had the merit of precluding irresponsible decisions, voted in the Security Council by states which might have neither the power nor the disposition to enforce them, and they thought correctly that this was more than a minor virtue for international organization. Indeed, one of the most valid general criticisms of international agencies is that they "resolve" too much, too heedlessly, too piously, too ineffectually.

Beyond this, the founding fathers abjured the quest for the abstractly perfect organizational system which any schoolboy could have formulated but which no mere human beings could have implemented in the real world. Their acceptance of the veto was a testament to their awareness that the great powers would not consent, on paper and still less in fact, to put their power resources at the disposal of a sheer majority for the implementation of decisions with which they might not be in accord. Still more, it was a symbol of their recognition that if one of the great powers should go on the aggressive warpath, the other leading states—all states, for that matter—would insist upon determining their responses in the light of their own conceptions of national interest. The incapacity of the Security Council to decide on enforcement action against a great power, which clearly derives from Article 27 of the Charter, is not the result of an oversight, or of a naive faith in the eternal peacefulness of all great powers, or of a silly conviction that an ideal international system can exist without depriving great powers of the capacity for throwing legal monkey wrenches into the machinery of international sanctions.

---

[18] *New York Times Magazine,* October 23, 1949. Cited in Leonard, *International Organization,* p. 208.

Envisioning the possibility that one of the Big Five might become an aggressor and use its veto to block Security Council action against itself, Secretary of State Stettinius asserted that the plain answer was that "a major war would result, no matter what the membership and voting provisions of the Security Council might be." [19] The official British Commentary on the Charter recognized that "if such a situation arises, the United Nations will have failed in its purpose and all members will have to act as seems best in the circumstances." [20] According to Leo Pasvolsky, a leading American participant in the formulation of the Charter:

> The underlying theory, however, was that if one of the major nations were to prove recalcitrant, or were to refuse to abide by the rules of international behavior that were being inscribed in the Charter, a situation would be created in which the recalcitrant nation might have to be coerced; and it was apparent that no major nation could be coerced except by the combined forces of the other major nations. This would be the equivalent of a world war, and a decision to embark upon such a war would necessarily have to be made by each of the other major nations for itself and not by any international organization.[21]

These comments reflect no tendency to confuse a veto-hobbled Security Council with an ideal mechanism for maintaining world order; rather they indicate that the veto was incorporated in the Charter as a concession to the realities of the existing power configuration and policy orientation in the world of 1945.

THE VETO IN PRACTICE

Turning to the actual operation of the United Nations, it should be pointed out that the great power veto has not been the constantly growing, indefinitely expansible, cancerous factor in the life of the organization which has sometimes been supposed.

The veto has been used by all the permanent members of the Security Council except the United States, but only the Soviet Union has resorted to it frequently; in 1962, the total list of Soviet vetoes passed the 100-mark. From the standpoint of the effective working of international organization, as well as that of the interest of non-Communist states, it has clearly been *abused* by the Soviet Union. It has been hung over the

---

[19] *The Charter of the United Nations, Hearings before the Committee on Foreign Relations, United States Senate, 79th Congress, 1st Session* (Washington: Government Printing Office, 1945), p. 216.

[20] Cited by Sir Gladwyn Jebb, "The Role of the United Nations," *International Organization,* November 1952, p. 512.

[21] "The United Nations in Action," *Edmund J. James Lectures on Government* (Urbana: University of Illinois Press, 1951), pp. 80-81. Cited in Schuman, *The Commonwealth of Man,* p. 373.

Security Council like a sword of Damocles, posing a constant threat to its operations, discouraging statesmen from attempting to do serious business in the Council, and breeding contempt for that body in the minds of people everywhere. It has made difficult the realization of the universalist urge of the United Nations and damaged the capacity of the Security Council as an instrument of conciliation. Few observers would argue that the prophecy contained in the interpretative statement of the great powers at San Francisco—that the veto would be used with moderation and restraint, proving it a relatively innocuous as well as a vitally important provision—has been confirmed by events.

Nevertheless, the veto has assumed larger proportions in the minds of cynical critics and disillusioned idealists than in the workings of the United Nations. The size of the veto problem cannot be accurately measured by tabulating the instances of its use. Approximately half of the Soviet vetoes have been used to prevent the admission of new members; five of them were devoted to the exclusion of Italy.[22] In such cases, the number of vetoes is obviously controllable by those who push proposals to a vote; the Soviet purpose of keeping Italy out of the United Nations might just as well have required two or ten or fifty or a thousand vetoes as five. The arbitrariness of a list is also borne out by the fact that it cannot include the vetoes which were effective without being cast. For instance, the United States let it be known in 1950 that it would veto any candidate to replace Trygve Lie as Secretary-General; [23] as it turned out, this threat was sufficient to prevent the necessity of the American representative's casting a veto, but there is no limit to the number of vetoes which the United States *might* have had to inscribe on the record in order to uphold its policy.

The "double veto" concept which was enunciated by the great powers at San Francisco carried with it the theoretical possibility that the range of matters potentially vulnerable to the veto in the Security Council might be expanded without limit. Taken literally, the rule that a permanent member can prevent a matter from being designated as procedural means that anything is vetoable which a great power wishes to veto. In practice, however, the tragically absurd potentialities opened up by the double veto have not been realized. Although this device was used successfully by the Soviet Union on three occasions in the earliest years of the United Nations, its availability to the great powers has been uncertain since September 1950, when a parliamentary technique for frustrating its use was worked out within the Security Council and implemented against China. This technique involves a ruling by the President of the Council that the negative vote of a permanent member on the preliminary ques-

---

[22] See the table on "Use of the Veto in the Security Council Through 1953," *Charter Review Documents*, pp. 577-580.

[23] Lie, *In the Cause of Peace*, pp. 379-381.

tion of the procedural character of a given issue does not constitute a veto; once the chair rules that a vote of the Council has established the non-vetoable quality of a draft resolution, that ruling stands unless seven or more members vote to overturn it. Thus, a situation is created in which only a majority can determine whether a matter is subject to the application of the unanimity rule.[24] By this method, a Soviet attempt to use the double veto for preventing the creation of a body to investigate the situation in Laos was defeated in September 1959.[25]

It is not certain that this procedure can or will be used consistently to thwart the double veto; much depends, for instance, upon the political inclination and the parliamentary skill of the person occupying the chair of the Security Council when a particular case arises. Moreover, it is not clear that the double veto *should* be permanently eliminated by use of this gadget, since the former is just as much an instrument for protecting the great powers against the unconstitutional reduction of their veto rights as for permitting them to effect the unreasonable expansion of those rights.[26]

The point here is that, far from serving as the basis for the indefinite expansion of the scope of the veto power, the double veto rule has been exploited only to a negligible extent and its very availability for that purpose has become uncertain. The history of the double veto supports the proposition that it is the better part of wisdom in the study of international organization to recognize that the worst does not always happen.

Indeed, despite the popular assumption based upon exaggerated inferences from the Soviet Union's record of using the veto frequently and sometimes even frivolously, there has been a tendency in the Security Council to trim down rather than to extend the scope of the veto power. Following the precedent provided by the League of Nations, the Security Council established, very early in its history, the principle that the *abstention* of a great power should not constitute a veto.[27] This usage has been accepted by all the Big Five with the intention and the result of reducing significantly the negative impact of the veto upon the working of the Council, despite the fact that a strict interpretation of the Charter would have required the positive concurrence, rather than mere acquiescence signified by abstention, of the permanent members for a Security Council decision on matters of substance.[28]

In addition, the Council has adopted the proposition that the *absence*

---

[24] For a fuller description of this antidouble veto device, see Jiménez de Aréchaga, *op. cit.,* pp. 12-15.

[25] See Leo Gross, "The Question of Laos and the Double Veto in the Security Council," *American Journal of International Law,* January 1960, pp. 118-131.

[26] Leo Gross, "The Double Veto and the Four-Power Statement on Voting in the Security Council," *Harvard Law Review,* December 1953, pp. 251-280.

[27] See Jiménez de Aréchaga, *op. cit.,* pp. 17-23.

[28] See Article 27, paragraph 3.

of a great power is analogous to abstention and therefore does not have the effect of a veto. It was rather hesitant and unsure of itself in taking this position, but it asserted this view strongly in its handling of the Korean crisis in June 1950, and did not back down in the face of Soviet protests.[29] The Soviet Union, whose absence made possible the passage of the decisions for action against North Korean aggression, denied the legality of those resolutions, but it has not in fact consistently opposed the thesis that the absence of a permanent member should be construed as acquiescent abstention rather than veto in *absentia.*[30]

Although the efforts sponsored by the General Assembly to secure a formal listing of matters not subject to the veto or made immune to the veto by great power agreement [31] have come to naught, the Security Council has in practice treated as procedural questions a wide range of substantially important matters, including such significant questions as the acceptance and removal of agenda items. A careful student of the Council's voting procedure wrote in 1950: "Decisions during the past five years have established a growing body of precedents which have increased the range of procedural questions far beyond anticipation and which give promise of progressive development in the future.[32]

The veto is not a matter of negligible importance, and the range of its potential impact is broad enough to make it a seriously obstructive factor in the operations of the Security Council. Nevertheless, it is a fact that the veto has not been exploited for all it is worth, and the range of its application has been more modest than might have been expected.

A final negative proposition which should be stated is that the veto is not a decisive, insuperable, uncircumventable block to action which the majority of the Security Council believes to be necessary or desirable. Having already rejected the view that it is a cancer, subject to uncontrollable growth in the United Nations organism, we might now deny that it is a paralyzing malady, dooming the victim to complete inactivity whenever it strikes; it is rather a kind of deformity—incurable so long as the world is unwilling to submit itself to drastic and untried surgical procedures, but not necessarily fatal, and certainly not fully incapacitating. It necessitates determined and imaginative compensatory adjustment, but it does not doom to invalidism.

The striking thing about the list of vetoes which have been cast in the Security Council is how little they have finally mattered. The first Soviet

---

[29] Jiménez de Aréchaga, *op. cit.*, pp. 23-25.

[30] See the remarks by A. H. Rudzinski, in Clyde Eagleton and Richard N. Swift, eds., *Annual Review of United Nations Affairs, 1950* (New York: New York University Press, 1951), pp. 137-138.

[31] See the texts of Assembly Resolutions of November 21, 1947, and April 14, 1949, in *Charter Review Documents*, pp. 569-570, 572-575.

[32] Jiménez de Aréchaga, *op. cit.*, p. 181.

veto, on February 16, 1946, prevented adoption of a proposal expressing confidence that Britain and France would withdraw their forces from Syria and Lebanon; the two powers carried out that action despite the defeat of the resolution. In the same year, the USSR cast four vetoes to prevent passing the issue of United Nations action concerning Franco Spain over to the General Assembly; the Assembly subsequently took up the matter and dealt with it. In 1946 and 1947, the USSR cast six vetoes relating to the Balkan case; the dispute was taken up and disposed of with ultimate success by the General Assembly. On December 13, 1949, the same great power prevented the official congratulation of the Dutch and Indonesians for their successful negotiations at the Hague; the states concerned considered themselves nonetheless congratulated. In October 1950, a Soviet veto blocked the re-election of Secretary-General Lie; his term of office was "extended" by the General Assembly. As we shall demonstrate in Chapter 9, the evolution of the General Assembly has provided a means by which many proposals that have been defeated for lack of great power unanimity in the Security Council have subsequently been approved and put into effect.

It is true that the veto provides a theoretically absolute check against the admission of new members to the United Nations. Nevertheless, virtually all candidates for membership that have encountered the Soviet veto have been blocked only temporarily. Stalemates over membership questions are attributable to sheer political intransigence, and it is evident that the obstacle of the veto may be removed in most instances by political bargaining, even though it cannot be circumvented by legal maneuvering.

It is also true that the veto stands as an absolute barrier to the formal amendment of the Charter. However, the Charter can be, and has been, modified in substance if not in formal terms by means which are invulnerable to the veto.

Attention might be drawn to the Soviet Union's unilateral blocking of the development of plans for international control of atomic and other armaments; surely this is one vitally important sphere in which no method has been found for overcoming the effect of the veto. But in this case the veto is etched deeply into the realities of international power politics, not simply inscribed on the surface of a constitutional document. Regardless of what voting scheme might be used in the Security Council, effectuation of a world armaments control plan would require the consent of all the states with significant military strength. Erasure of the veto from the Charter would not affect the veto which is written, indelibly for all presently practical purposes, in the pattern of world power. A veto is at fault here, but it is not the veto of Article 27 of the United Nations Charter.

The point is that the ambiguities and alternatives provided by the

Charter afford opportunities for circumventing the roadblock of the veto in virtually every significant case in which it is the veto of Security Council procedure, rather than the veto of sheer military-political reality, that impedes action. As we shall see in subsequent chapters, these opportunities have been recognized and utilized to a very considerable extent.

From the point of view of the United States, the Soviet veto is a troublesome handicap to the functioning of the United Nations, an organizational deformity which unfortunately can be offset only in part by compensatory devices. From the Soviet standpoint, the veto power is an essential but regrettably limited and indecisive instrument of defense against Western utilization of the organization for anti-Communist purposes. The West deplores the excessive obstructive capability which the veto gives to the Soviet Union; the latter deplores the inadequacy of the protection which it affords. The Soviet attitude was dramatically expressed in the "troika" proposal, put forward in the fall of 1960, calling for the replacement of the Secretary-General by a committee of three men, representatives of the Eastern, Western, and uncommitted states, each of them empowered to exercise a veto over executive operations of the United Nations. This proposal was a reaction to the considerable success of Western efforts to diminish the negative force of the Soviet veto power in the Security Council. The USSR was, in effect, demanding a veto in the executive directorate of the Secretariat in order to block the escape route from its veto in the Council. The troika proposal also represented a Soviet urge to acquire the capacity to stop a United Nations action already begun, rather than merely to prevent the initiation of such an action. This proposal was put forward in the context of Soviet disenchantment with the Congo operation, which the Soviet Union had initially approved in the Security Council; turning against the operation as actually conducted, the USSR sought the capacity to force its termination or the revision of its guiding policy. In short, the troika proposal was an effort to repair the Soviet line of defense against Western domination of the United Nations—to buttress the veto power assigned to the USSR in the Security Council, and to provide a means for countering the Western tactic of outflanking the Security Council. The battle over the troika is but an episode in the persistent struggle of the West to deprive the Soviet Union of an effective veto power, and of the USSR to maintain such a power, in the United Nations.

Obviously, the veto power is a serious blemish on the organizational face of an international institution, considered in the abstract. Nevertheless, it is not self-evident that the strengthening of the United Nations is to be achieved by the formal or informal reduction of the capacity for negation which the Charter confers upon the great powers. The trouble with the United Nations is not that special provision is made for the registration and effectuation of great power dissent, but that dissension exists among the great powers. This is a matter of great consequence, and the United Nations would be fundamentally unsound if it treated the matter as one of little consequence. In organizations not characterized by deep cleavages among their members, the veto power is a symbol of the importance of achieving consensus; it provides a formal incentive for seeking unanimity. In an institution such as the United Nations, with its fundamental division between Soviet and Western blocs, the veto has other functions. The original hope that the requirement of unanimity of the great powers on major issues in the Security Council would stimulate the achievement of unanimity has been disappointed and, for the foreseeable future, must be abandoned. In the cold war era, the function of the veto is not to promote unanimity but to inspire a sober recognition of the implications of the cleavage between East and West. The veto protects the uncommitted states from being dragged by their membership in the United Nations into the clashes between the great antagonists; in concrete terms, this means essentially that the Soviet veto inhibits American use of the world organization as a Western instrument. The veto serves as a reminder to the West that the problem of dealing with the Soviet Union cannot realistically be reduced to that of mobilizing overwhelming numbers of votes. It tells the West—if the West will listen—that the United Nations will become ineffectual, and may even be destroyed, if the effort is persistently made to have the organization function in violation of what the Soviet Union strenuously regards as its interests. The veto rule represents the proposition that the potential value of the United Nations with respect to the problems of war and peace at the highest political level is defined and limited by the degree to which the major powers can discover a mutual interest in having it function as a stabilizing element within the context of the cold war. Viewed in this way, the veto is not so much an obstacle to be circumvented, or a defect to be remedied, as a salutary reminder of facts that must be acknowledged and of realities that must be respected. It is a safety valve—and the problem is not to shut it off, but to cope with the situation which is signaled by its operation.

SUGGESTED READINGS

Goodrich, Leland M., "The UN Security Council," *International Organization,* Summer 1958, pp. 273-287.

Jiménez de Aréchaga, Eduardo, *Voting and the Handling of Disputes in the Security Council,* New York: Carnegie Endowment for International Peace, 1950.

Lee, Dwight E., "The Genesis of the Veto," *International Organization,* February 1947, pp. 33-42.

Moldaver, Arlette, "Repertoire of the Veto in the Security Council, 1946-1956," *International Organization,* Spring 1957, pp. 261-274.

Padelford, Norman J., "The Use of the Veto," *International Organization,* June 1948, pp. 227-246.

CHAPTER

9

Problems of Constitutional Interpretation and Development

The United Nations is a complex system of international machinery, established to supplement and in some measure to supervise other multilateral agencies and to provide procedures additional to the traditional methods for managing international business, and designed to coexist with the institutional structures of national states. In these circumstances, the problem of defining relationships, delimiting jurisdictions, allocating functions, and distributing powers among the component parts of the global institutional complex presents great difficulties. Moreover, this is not just a problem to be solved, but a process to be continued. A static analysis will be out of date when it is completed. The world is on the move, and nothing is more subject to change and demands for change than the constitutional relationships of the elements of its untidy institutional structure.

This situation should not appear unfamiliar to an American, who is accustomed to living under one of the most complicated systems of government which men have ever devised or political evolution has ever produced. The relational issues which affect contemporary international organization are closely analogous to—and, as we shall see, are substantively connected with—the questions of constitutional definition and redefinition which bedevil the United States. The United Nations has problems of relationship between its major organs which are not unlike those arising out of the principle of "separation of powers" in the United States Government, and issues pertaining to the balance between the general organization and specialized, regional, and national state institutions which are reminiscent of the problems engendered by the federal principle, with its "division of powers," in the United States.

Such analogies as these should always be approached with an eye to the danger of inaccuracy stemming from the fact of incomplete comparability, but the comparison suggested here has sufficient potential values to justify our taking the risk. What is striking is that Americans spontaneously resort to the analogy, but do not, by and large, transfer the wisdom of their own constitutional experience to their thinking about the problems of international organization. How can anyone familiar with American history expect a written constitution to be precisely self-explanatory, or a judicial organ to serve or be permitted to serve as the exclusive authoritative interpreter of such a document, or an originally formulated jurisdictional equilibrium to stay put, or political factors to be excluded from influencing the evolution of constitutional relationships? If American experience proves anything, it indicates that international constitutional development will be marked by legalistic controversies that mask the realities of political conflict, by issues that defy permanent solution and constantly reappear in different guises, and by the emergence of trends which reflect new combinations of interests and new political conceptions more than they derive from legal principles sanctified by constitutional scriptures. Strictly speaking, the United Nations system is neither federal nor governmental, but the vicissitudes of the federal governmental experiment carried out in the United States may offer many useful clues as to its prospective constitutional problems.

EVOLUTION OF THE CHARTER

In the first instance, the problem of constitutional relationships is one of *interpretation.* A basic document has been accepted as the blueprint for the system. What hierarchical arrangements does it establish, what jurisdictional lines does it draw, what assignments of competence does it make? What substantive agreements did its drafters intend to incorporate in its terms? To move to the procedural plane, who or what agency has authority to interpret the constitution? What rules of interpretation are to be applicable? On what basis, in the light of what considerations, in accordance with what system of values, are interpretative judgments to be made?

The process of international organization has not been marked by conditions making for the provision of easy answers to these questions. The multilateral treaties which serve as constitutional foundations for international agencies are seldom models of precision; diplomatic negotiators are likely on occasion to formulate ambiguities which mask disagreements, rather than to succeed in drafting clear provisions which express genuine compromise of their differences. Thus, international constitutions are heavily—although not uniquely—dependent upon interpretation to supply as well as to elucidate their meaning. No American literate enough to read his own national Constitution ought to be guilty of exaggerating the uniqueness of the United Nations Charter as a device for indefinite postponement of embarrassing issues as well as indefinite perpetuation of sacred principles.

Although the charters of most contemporary Specialized Agencies contain articles prescribing methods of resolving disputes concerning the meaning of basic provisions, the major constitutional documents of international organization—the Covenant of the League and the United Nations Charter—have been notably deficient in this respect. This negligence might be taken as evidence of a conservative intention to perpetuate the old rule of sovereignty-oriented international law: in the absence of agreement to the contrary, international treaties can be authoritatively interpreted only by the unanimous judgment of the parties, and failing such unanimity, each party has legal freedom to attribute to them whatever meaning it wishes. However, it would appear that in fact the blankness of major constitutional treaties in this regard has reflected the inability of statesmen to reach formal agreement on an alternative and their disposition to rely on the informal evolution of an alternative, rather than a determination that there shall be no alternative. Whereas, in the past, governments have often been more willing to forswear sovereignty on paper than in fact, the reverse is now becoming increasingly the case; the trimming of sovereignty may be facilitated if states are not pushed to make formal admission of their subjection to that process.

The United Nations Charter hints at various possibilities. First, its silence might imply that members retain the sovereign right of unilateral interpretation; secondly, its designation of the International Court of Justice as "the principal judicial organ of the United Nations" [1] might serve as the logical basis for exclusive reliance upon the court as an interpretative organ; finally, its attribution to the General Assembly of competence to "discuss any questions or any matters . . . relating to the powers and functions of any organs provided for in the present Charter" [2] might be

[1] Article 92.
[2] Article 10.

regarded as a mandate for that body to serve as a constitutional umpire.

In fact, the San Francisco Conference opted to leave the question of interpretation open. It declined to accept proposals to make the International Court of Justice "a supreme court within the international administrative system," with "the power to settle conflicts of competence between international bodies," or to determine the boundaries between international and domestic jurisdiction.[3] It did not adopt a Belgian scheme to invest the General Assembly with "sovereign competence to interpret the provisions of the Charter." [4] It seemed to flirt with the concept of individual interpretation by member states when it adopted a domestic jurisdiction clause which pointedly omitted the League's rule that national "no trespassing" signs are invalid unless approved by an international body,[5] yet it clearly rejected the general application of that concept. The records of the Conference summarize the thinking of the founding fathers of the United Nations on the problem of constitutional interpretation: it was regarded as inevitable that each organ would interpret for itself the relevant parts of the Charter; this process was so natural that it need not be mentioned; interpretations of competence made by the various organs might conflict or be challenged by member states, in which case legal assistance might be obtained from the International Court or from *ad hoc* committees of jurists; if it were necessary to obtain an authoritative interpretation which all members would be bound to respect, the only method available was the ordinary process of Charter amendment.[6]

The statesmen of San Francisco expected organs of the United Nations to become living, working bodies, interpreting their terms of reference in accordance with the requirements of their tasks, and they hoped for general acquiescence in this process. They provided for a judicial organ, which would be available if required for the work of constitutional interpretation. But, in the final analysis, they refrained from explicit repudiation of the old rule of sovereign competence to interpret—or even to explain away—treaty provisions.

To the stickler for constitutional neatness, the San Francisco decision not to decide how the precise meaning of Charter provisions could be officially and unchallengeably stated is reprehensible. Americans in particular are likely to be offended by the spectacle of a constitutional system in which organs are encouraged to determine the limits of their own competence, parts are not definitely excluded from rendering their own interpretations of their relationship to the whole, the principle of legal

[3] See *The United Nations Conference on International Organization: Selected Documents,* pp. 162, 179-181.

[4] *Ibid.,* p. 130.

[5] Cf. Article 15, paragraph 8, of the Covenant, and Article 2, paragraph 7, of the Charter.

[6] *The United Nations Conference on International Organization: Selected Documents,* pp. 879-880.

rather than political interpretation is not solemnly enshrined on high, and no guarantee is provided that anyone can say with assurance, "*this* is what the constitution means."

It should be noted, however, that the situation of the United Nations in these respects contrasts much more strongly with the mythology than with the actuality of the American constitutional system. Our national Founding Fathers wrote no provision for a supreme arbiter of all constitutional questions. The notion that the states were competent to interpret the Constitution for themselves flourished in this country from the Kentucky and Virginia Resolves of 1798 to the secession movement which precipitated the Civil War. The Supreme Court propounded its doctrine of judicial review without explicit constitutional warrant, in an atmosphere of partisan political maneuvering, and it established its role of supreme constitutional umpire in the face of powerful opposition. Despite this development, the Court is only the ultimately available and the not-quite-decisive reader of the American Constitution; most routine interpretations of the basic rules of the game are made by the working organs of government, and "final" decisions are evolved through the democratic political process, only to be supplanted by later "final" decisions, produced in the same way. In the long run, constitutional interpretation in the United States is a function of the political development of the nation, and even though the Supreme Court plays what Americans have come to regard as an indispensable part in that process, at any given time there are uncertainties as to what is or is not "constitutional" for which not even the existence of the Supreme Court provides an assured remedy. The United Nations Charter is by no means uniquely deficient with respect to the problem of constitutional interpretation.

At this point it becomes clear that, even though the problem of constitutional relationships *starts* as a problem of *interpretation,* it *ends* as a problem of *development.* Statically considered, the Charter has to be interpreted; dynamically considered, it has to evolve. The process of interpretation has to do with the clarification of constitutionally prescribed relationships at a given moment. It equally relates to the registration and, to some degree, the shaping, promotion, and impeding, of developmental trends essentially political in nature. Sound constitutional interpretation, in international organization as in national government, balances insistence upon the legally formulated consensus of the past, awareness of the political configuration of the present, and consciousness of the community's requirements and demands for the future. This is not an easy stunt to perform in the United States, and it is immensely more difficult in the United Nations.

It is hard to say whether the operative system of interpretation in the United Nations is subject to criticism more because of the identity of the agencies utilized for that purpose or because of the substantive nature of the interpretations produced. Indeed, these are closely related matters. To some extent, the International Court of Justice, speaking through advisory opinions, has been called upon to serve as a constitutional arbiter.[7] In spite of the good intentions registered by member states when the General Assembly recommended in 1947 that organs of the United Nations system utilize the Court "to the greatest practicable extent in the progressive development of international law . . . in regard to constitutional interpretation,"[8] the Court has not significantly approached the status of primary expositor of the Charter.

The question of resorting to the Court has frequently been introduced as a conservative device by a state which has been placed on the political defensive and is desirous of obtaining a strict construction of its obligations and its vulnerability to United Nations interference and criticism. Almost as frequently, this move has met with the opposition of states which are on the political offensive, and the latter have been able to carry their point by appealing to the corporate jealousy of the political organ involved against attempts to limit its competence. For instance, South Africa has been unable to test its hope that the Court would rule against United Nations intrusion in its domestic racial affairs because critics of its racial policy have succeeded in capitalizing upon the General Assembly's sensitivity to the danger of subjecting its future development to the impediment of a judicial re-emphasis upon the constitutional understandings of 1945. Proposals to invoke the opinion of the Court have not always been conservatively motivated, but, rightly or wrongly, the prevalent view in the United Nations has been that judicial interpretation is inherently an exercise in the restatement of the legalities of the past. The political antagonists of the present, competing for immediate advantage, divide between invoking the respectability of the law established in the past and the idealism of the organizational development envisaged for the future.

In general, the latter tactic has been more successful. Antijudicialism has largely prevailed, and the prophecy of the San Francisco Conference has been confirmed: the political organs of the United Nations have tended to interpret the Charter for themselves. They have acted so as to require the inference that certain constitutional decisions have been reached, more often than they have adopted formal statements of con-

[7] See the following advisory opinions, officially reported in the annual volumes of the International Court of Justice, *Reports of Judgments, Advisory Opinions and Orders:* Conditions of Admission of a State to Membership in the United Nations (1948); Reparation for Injuries Suffered in the Service of the United Nations (1949); Competence of the General Assembly for the Admission of a State to the United Nations (1950); International Status of South-West Africa (1950); Effect of Awards of Compensation Made by the United Nations Administrative Tribunal (1954); Voting Procedure on Questions Relating to Reports and Petitions Concerning the Territory of South-West Africa (1955); Admissibility of Hearings of Petitioners by the Committee on South-West Africa (1956); Certain Expenses of the United Nations (1962).

[8] General Assembly Resolution 171 (III), November 14, 1947.

stitutional positions precedent to action. They have overridden allegations of their incompetence, and have paid little heed to the notion that members may unilaterally interpret the Charter to their own advantage, even though they have had no means of compelling member states formally to recant their outraged claims of unconstitutionality. The Soviet Union, for instance, has raised that contention on numerous occasions; the United Nations cannot gain the satisfaction of extracting a confession of error from the Soviets, but it can—and does—ignore the claim and act as if it had been decisively rejected.[9]

The antijudicialism of the United Nations is not an unmixed good. In so far as it is a symbol and an instrument of the urge to release the agencies of the system from the restraints and limitations established at San Francisco, it points to significant dangers. We cannot dismiss as fantastic the anxiety that international organization might prove itself a new variety of tyranny, global in scope; in the long historical view, any tendency of international agencies to exhibit contempt for constitutional limitations is a bad augury. Quite apart from this, the short-term prospects of the United Nations will be worsened if it gains the reputation of constitutional unruliness. The impression that the world organization casually rewrites its Charter to suit itself will have the effect of strengthening the hands and increasing the numbers of its enemies, ranging from Americans who make a fetish of the "rule of law" to Russians who are ever alert to evidence that non-Communist states are unreliable treaty-partners. The stretching of the Charter through undisciplined political interpretation is a poor way to increase the psychological readiness of states to make significant grants of competence to international agencies, or the ideological receptivity of states which are frequently or permanently in a minority position to the doctrine of majority rule in international organization.

Aside from the psychological danger of constitutional unruliness, there is the objective danger of constitutional unwieldiness. There is no necessary correlation between the capacity of interested states to secure the expansion of the theoretical competence of the United Nations or its particular organs and the capacity of the organization to deal effectively with the matters brought to it. Good health is not promoted by biting off more than one can chew; the United Nations, like all infants, has developed its incisors before its molars, and its most urgent need is increased evidence of ability to chew, not expanded opportunities to bite.

In the final analysis, antijudicialism as a device for protecting the United Nations against legalistic sterilization is simply unnecessary. The notion that international lawyers are a caste devoted to strapping fledgling international organizations in the straitjacket of sovereignty dies hard, but it deserves an obituary in which the following facts are cited: In 1923,

---

[9] Lie, *In the Cause of Peace,* pp. 432-433.

the Permanent Court of International Justice held that the domestic jurisdiction of states, within which they are sovereignly immune from the intrusions of international organization, is a relative expanse, subject to reduction in the course of the development of international relations.[10] In 1926, the same body found in the Constitution of the International Labor Organization an implied grant of authority for that agency to extend its activities into areas bearing upon, but not explicitly included within, its defined realm of competence.[11] In 1949, the new World Court continued this tradition by deducing a status of international personality for the United Nations from the general intentions of its founders, and produced the truly Marshallian dictum that "Under international law, the Organization must be deemed to have those powers which, though not expressly provided in the Charter, are conferred upon it by necessary implication as being essential to the performance of its duties." [12] In 1954, the Court held that the capacity of the General Assembly to promote its proper objects by creating an Administrative Tribunal "arises by necessary intendment out of the Charter." [13] In a series of advisory opinions relating to South-West Africa, the Court has expressed liberal views concerning the competence of the General Assembly to develop special techniques for exercising supervision over South Africa's administration of that former League mandate. The Advisory Opinion on Certain Expenses of the United Nations, issued in 1962, confirmed the Assembly's assertion of authority to impose financial responsibility upon member states for support of extraordinary peace-keeping operations and, by implication, other large-scale programs.

In the light of this judicial record, it would appear that the future development of the United Nations could be in worse hands than those of the members of the World Court. This is not to say that the job of interpreting the Charter should be turned over exclusively to the judges. It is unrealistic to suppose that the task of initiating, guiding, and controlling the process of constitutional creativity is ever, anywhere, entrusted wholly or even primarily to judicial agencies. John Marshall did not create the living American Constitution; he registered the developments, rationalized them, and contrived to keep the Court from standing in the way of constitutional progress. But it is probable that the World Court offers values which the United Nations is tending to neglect. No harm would be

---

[10] Nationality Decrees Issued in Tunis and Morocco . . . , Advisory Opinion No. 4, February 7, 1923, Hudson, *World Court Reports,* I, 143-162.

[11] Competence of the International Labor Organization to Regulate, Incidentally, the Personal Work of the Employer, Advisory Opinion No. 13, July 23, 1926, *ibid.,* pp. 745-760.

[12] Advisory Opinion Concerning Reparation for Injuries Suffered in the Service of the United Nations, *International Organization,* August 1949, p. 575.

[13] Advisory Opinion on Effect of Awards of Compensation Made by the United Nations Administrative Tribunal, *American Journal of International Law,* October 1954, p. 658.

done if it held the organization closer to the stipulations of the Charter, particularly if it did this while maintaining a keen awareness of the necessity of creative adaptation to realize basic purposes, as the evidence suggests that the Court would do.

The foregoing analysis is not intended to suggest that the members of the United Nations normally take positions on substantive or procedural questions of interpretation in accordance with settled convictions concerning the desirable pattern of organizational development. True, some nations have a general liberal bias and others a general conservative bias in regard to the future of international organization. But national statesmen are mainly concerned with political gains and losses in immediate situations, and they can switch the roles of strict and loose constructionists at the drop of a political hat. It is good clean academic fun to keep a running documentation on the inconsistencies of states in regard to questions of interpretation, but it merely confirms the existence of a universal human tendency, evident in the political-legal context of the United States as well as that of the United Nations, to cloak the pursuit of selfish interests in temporarily eternal devotion to the most convenient of available fundamental constitutional principles. In so far as states are consciously concerned to promote a particular trend of long-term development in the United Nations, their choice is likely to reflect a conception of national interest rather than a considered view of the ultimate organizational requirements of the world community. Statesmen are still Frenchmen or Indians, Communists or anti-Communists, colonialists or anticolonialists, great power representatives or small state spokesmen.

Nevertheless, it can be maintained that the development of contemporary international organization represents a groping toward the realization of an imperfectly apprehended conception of a global interest. To postulate this conception is to approach the area of what may best be called the metaphysics of politics. No one, from Rousseau to A. D. Lindsay, has been able to dispel the haze of mysticism from the idea of the "general will," and yet no hardheaded realist can deny that a meaningful notion of community interest sometimes emerges from a society of selfish men and competing interest groups. For instance, American society is divided in a thousand ways, but in the final analysis there is a phenomenon of unity, of common concern, which defies assured analysis but cannot realistically be dismissed as pious cant.

The concept of community interest is relatively underdeveloped but not altogether missing from the international scene. In part, it is served unwittingly and fortuitously by states which consciously aim only at promoting their particular interests, and incidentally by states which promote it only because they have discovered that the global interest is identifiable with their own national interests, viewed in enlightened fashion. Considered in this way, the concept of community interest is not a sublime expression of man's moral capacity—but the accidental or self-interested promotion of the common good is typical of such a well-developed national society as the United States, where entrepreneurs contribute to the nation in seeking profit, minority groups improve the health of the body politic by seeking status for themselves, and politicians serve the national interest in a quest for partisan advantage and electoral victories.

Ultimately, however, it would seem that *someone* must *will* the general good, making it a primary value to be pursued directly and for its own sake. A community requires at the least a devoted minority, and that is all any human community is likely to have, except that it may possess the ultimately essential capacity to evoke sporadically the supreme allegiance of virtually all its members. This is very much the situation of the United States. Most of us are Americans last, but not first and always; in a critical emergency, we can be counted on to offer to the national interest our last full measure of devotion, but most of the time the national interest must get along with contributions which are a by-product of our particularistic strivings, supplemented by the services of a few who are prepared to be Americans first and always, as well as last. The evolutionary development of the American constitutional system is a function of the combination of tendencies released from selfish antagonisms and of objectives deliberately pursued by the few whose vision embraces only the national good.

The situation of the United Nations is not very different from this. The world organization lacks the capacity to command the ultimate allegiance of more than a handful of human beings, but it should be noted that the national state also lacks this except for the purpose of its crucial dealings with other states; patriots do not die *for* their countries so much as they die *against* other countries, and it is probably unrealistic to expect that the United Nations of the earth can ever mobilize a massive human loyalty-to-the-death unless it can manage to stir up a mortal conflict with the United Nations of Mars. However, the progressive development of international organization in the twentieth century, initiated and carried along by the antagonisms and self-interests of slightly but perhaps increasingly enlightened states, is supported by the growth of a minute but vital body of sentiment which elevates the international community interest to the peak of the pyramid of values.

As we have seen, the International Court of Justice has treated constitutional issues of the United Nations as questions bearing upon the development of an effectively organized world order. If the cynic insists upon looking for national political motivations behind the opinions of the Court, the clear retort is that the World Court is decidedly less partisan than was John Marshall's Supreme Court of the United States.

The first Secretary-General of the United Nations, Trygve Lie, regarded himself in that capacity as a "spokesman for a world interest overriding any national interests in the councils of the nations." [14] In playing that role, he advised the Security Council that it had implied powers to accept governing responsibilities in the Free Territory of Trieste and to assume the task of implementing the Palestine partition scheme;[15] he sponsored the position that the United Nations was competent to press claims under international law against states, which won the approval of the World Court; he tried vainly to secure a settlement of the Chinese representation issue which would promote the approach to effective universality by the world organization; he gave vigorous support to the decision that the United Nations should act against aggression in Korea; he proposed, with meager success, that an international guard force be established; he supported the expansion of the security functions of the General Assembly to compensate for the ineffectuality of the Security Council; and he formulated a broad program for the long-term strengthening of the United Nations system.[16]

Lie's successor, Dag Hammarskjold, carried on in the same spirit, developing the practice of establishing a United Nations Presence in troubled areas, making his office available for "quiet diplomacy" whenever he saw opportunities to be helpful, playing a decisive role in the improvisation and direction of United Nations interventions in the Suez crisis of 1956 and the Congo crisis in 1960, and launching a program for supplying essential administrative personnel to understaffed governments (OPEX). U Thant, the third Secretary-General, has similarly taken the initiative in placing his office at the service of states involved in difficult and dangerous crises—for instance, in the cases relating to West Irian and Cuba in 1962.

The initiatives undertaken by these holders of the chief office of the United Nations are subject to legitimate criticism, but they have clearly been the efforts of men whose primary concern has been the development of the organization to meet the needs of the world community, rather than to serve as the instrument of a particular state or bloc. No Secretary-General has achieved absolute purity as an internationalist—but what national statesman has exhibited total commitment to the general interest of his society, entirely devoid of the taint of partisan or other particularistic bias? Devotion to the international interest is still a rare phenomenon and a relative one, but so is devotion to the national interest. International organization is slowly acquiring its vital minority of men who view its evolution in terms of the general needs of humanity rather than the particular interests of nations.

---

[14] Lie, *op. cit.*, p. 12.

[15] Stephen M. Schwebel, *The Secretary-General of the United Nations* (Cambridge: Harvard University Press, 1952), pp. 96-97.

[16] On these points, see Lie, *op. cit., passim.*

Finally, there are some indications that the General Assembly is capable of functioning as the institutional embodiment of concern for the healthy development of the United Nations system. True, it is a collection of national-minded and bloc-oriented statesmen, as its action normally demonstrates; but on occasion, it acts as if it were an entity charged with responsibility for promoting the long-range interests of the world community. This is perhaps so inexplicable as to be unbelievable, but it is no more mysterious than the phenomenon of a collection of party politicians, sectionalists, and interest group representatives who constitute a Congress which sometimes gives expression to the national interests of the United States.

The constitutional development of the United Nations, carried out through and expressed in the process of Charter interpretation, is the product of a complex network of factors: the legal stipulations of the Charter, the clash of national interests, the shifting of political alignments, the rise of institutional jealousies, and the impact of emergent conceptions of the global interest. What the United Nations has become up to this point is not what a legal technician might have deduced from the Charter, or what a diplomat might have constructed for the promotion of national interests, or what an internationalist might have designed for the realization of the ideal of world order; it is something of all these things.

THE CHANGING ROLE OF THE GENERAL ASSEMBLY

The first great area of constitutional controversy and change in the United Nations is the sphere of competence of the General Assembly. The transformation of the relationships between this and other organs of the global institutional system is a case study in the operation of the entire complex of factors already described.

A leading concept of the San Francisco Charter was that of the "separation of powers" of the Assembly and the Security Council. The League Covenant had failed to establish a distinct line of functional differentiation between the major organs; it had assigned to the Assembly and the Council an identical competence to deal "with any matter within the sphere of action of the League or affecting the peace of the world." [17] The framers of the Covenant had placed primary emphasis upon the role of the Council. Adding the Assembly almost as an afterthought to their structural scheme, they had expected it to meet infrequently, and consequently had not seen fit to endow it with a considerable sphere of action all its own. The Covenant had provided for concurrent action by the two major organs on a number of matters and for submission of certain

---

[17] See Article 3, paragraph 3, and Article 4, paragraph 4.

issues alternatively to the Council or Assembly, but it had neglected the principle of a division of labor.

In deliberate contrast, the great powers set out to create a post-World War II organization which would be characterized by a high degree of internal specialization. The Dumbarton Oaks Proposals reflected a clear intent to assign primary responsibility for problems of high politics and security to the Security Council, and to make the General Assembly the supervisor of organizational housekeeping arrangements and activities in economic and social fields.

At San Francisco, limited success attended the vigorous efforts of a number of states, particularly small ones, to expand the potential significance of the General Assembly as a political organ. Articles 10-15 and 35 of the Charter, as finally adopted, gave the Assembly a very respectable role in the management of the political activities of the projected organization. Nevertheless, the completed Charter contained a definite assignment of "primary responsibility for the maintenance of peace and security" to the Security Council, which was designated as the authoritative agent of all member states for this purpose, and gave it clear priority in the handling of political matters and exclusive capacity to decide on action to safeguard the peace in critical situations.[18]

The alterations in the organizational plan which were made at San Francisco certainly blurred the line of functional division between the General Assembly and the Security Council, but they did not obliterate it. The American Secretary of State, Stettinius, expressed a legitimate view of the results of the Conference when he reported that the demand of the great powers for making a "sharp distinction" between the functions of the two organs had prevailed, citing the rejection by "large majorities" of amendments "which attempted to place a share of the ultimate responsibility for peace and security on the General Assembly," and that the Conference had approved the "separation of powers" as "the basic concept of the Organization." [19] He summarized the situation in these terms:

> Perhaps the basic difference between the constitutional arrangement of the United Nations and that of the League of Nations, is that instead of the Assembly and the Council having identical functions, as was the case under the League, the General Assembly and the Security Council will each have different functions assigned to it. The General Assembly is primarily a body for deliberation and recommendation, while the Security Council is given powers to act in the maintenance of international peace and security whenever it deems necessary.[20]

---

[18] See Articles 11, 12, 24, 25, and 39-54.
[19] *Stettinius Report,* pp. 69, 77, 78, 84, 94.
[20] *Ibid.,* p. 60.

In the same vein, the chairman of the responsible committee at San Francisco asserted:

> The strength of the future world Organization rests on perfect equilibrium between the functions of the Assembly and those of the Security Council. Neither of these two bodies should try to dominate the other nor trespass on the other's peculiar sphere of activities and responsibilities. . . . The Assembly, as the supreme representative body of the world, is to establish the principles on which world peace and the ideal of solidarity must rest; and, on the other hand, the Security Council is to act in accordance with those principles and with the speed necessary to prevent any attempted breach of international peace and security. In other words, the former is a creative body and the latter an organ of action.[21]

In the actual operation of the United Nations, the breaking down of this concept of specialization has assumed the proportions of a major constitutional revolution. Gradually and increasingly, the General Assembly has intruded into the Security Council's "peculiar sphere." It began by becoming a more frequently used alternative forum for the consideration of political disputes; it acquired "the character of an organ of second recourse, an organ of appeal with relation to the Security Council";[22] in passing the Uniting for Peace Resolution on November 3, 1950,[23] it assumed the power to reverse the Security Council by calling for enforcement action in situations where that body, acting under its Charter-prescribed rule of great power unanimity, has decided negatively on proposals for such action; it has, in fact, virtually replaced the Council as the agency bearing primary political responsibility within the United Nations.

This trend can be documented by reference to the Assembly's taking over the Spanish and Greek questions from the Council in 1946 and 1947, its establishment in 1947 of the Interim Committee to provide continuous Assembly machinery for dealing with political disputes, its significant participation in the Palestine case in 1947 and afterwards, its adoption of a comprehensive plan for serving as a security agency in 1950, its replacement of the Security Council as the responsible United Nations body in the management of the Korean action, its handling of the Hungarian and Middle Eastern crises of 1956 after the Security Council was immobilized by great power vetoes, and its important role in the direction of United Nations activities undertaken in the Congo in 1960.

---

[21] *The United Nations Conference on International Organization: Selected Documents,* p. 706.

[22] Alexandre Parodi, "Peaceful Settlement of Disputes," *International Conciliation,* No. 445, November 1948, p. 626.

[23] General Assembly Resolution 377A(V). For the text, see *Charter Review Documents,* pp. 557-561.

The expansion of the political and security role of the General Assembly is in large part attributable to the leadership of the United States, exercised for the purpose of nullifying the Soviet veto power in the Security Council. American response to frustration in the Council has been to transfer important functions to the majoritarian Assembly, where the Soviet Union has had only the status of leader of a pitifully ineffectual minority bloc. In the narrow terms of national self-interest, the United States has worked to transform the United Nations into a more serviceable instrument of its cold war policies, and it has, understandably, encountered the opposition of the USSR in this project. Rationalized in terms of broad principle, American policy has aimed at adapting the procedures of the United Nations to the requirements of institutional effectiveness; viewed in these terms, the policy has commanded the support of the overwhelming majority of the organization's members.

Yet neither the American desire to minimize the capacity of the Soviet Union to prevent the United Nations from being used as a tool of the West nor the disinterested devotion of states to the ideal of sound constitutional development provides a full explanation of the Assembly's encroachment upon the sphere of the Security Council. At least two other factors have contributed to the process.

One is the persistent assertiveness of the small states which constitute the great bulk of the membership. They would clearly have had the desire, if not the ability, to enhance the position of the General Assembly *vis à vis* the Security Council even if the cold war had not developed; indeed, the harmonious comradeship of the Big Five might have made them even more desperately eager to elevate the Assembly. That body is the residual symbol of their cherished equality, and the primary vehicle available for the exertion of their influence upon world affairs. They got less than they wanted in their San Francisco campaign to establish the predominance of the General Assembly, and they left the Conference with the firm resolve to exploit every opportunity to advance the cause of "the democratic core of the Organization," which they hopefully regarded as "the great focal point from which all other United Nations bodies draw their source and to which they must all look for ultimate guidance and support." [24]

We may take it as a permanent feature of the politics of international organization that the small states will press for the concentration of powers in the agency where their inferiority to the great powers is least recognized; this was true of the League, in which the Assembly was able to gain steadily increasing prominence largely because the nonmembership of great powers weakened the competitive vigor of the Council; it is true of the United Nations, in which the General Assembly profits from the fact

[24] The quotations are from Herbert V. Evatt, *The Task of Nations* (New York: Duell, Sloan and Pearce, 1949), p. 12.

that the conflict of great powers minimizes the institutional self-assertiveness and efficiency of the Security Council.

Finally, the great powers as a group, and not just the United States as an anti-Soviet leader, have advanced the cause of the General Assembly. The Soviet Union has objected to the rise of the Assembly only to the extent that this trend has represented an American-sponsored movement to erase the effects of the Soviet veto power, as when it denounced the Uniting for Peace proposal as an unconstitutional alteration of relationships between the Security Council and the Assembly. Generally, Soviet leaders have treated this principle of constitutional conservatism in a way which should be familiar to students of American national politics; they have asserted it when they wished to block Assembly action, but have conveniently forgotten it on other occasions. In many instances, the USSR has initiated or supported proposals implying a broad view of the Assembly's competence, thereby adding its contribution to the development of an enlarged role for that body.

It would seem that the leading states have discovered that the negative capacity to block Security Council action is not so valuable as the positive capacity to win friends and influence people in the General Assembly. The rise of great power enthusiasm for the Assembly reflects a change in the conception of the political mission of the United Nations. So long as the Big Five entertained the notion of jointly managing the world's political business, they found the Security Council chamber a cozy consultation room for the top directorate. When they shifted to the concept of creating competitive alliances, the very coziness of that chamber became a drawback, and they came to appreciate the superior political and ideological acoustics of the Assembly hall. Giving up negotiation among themselves for drumming up a following among the smaller states, the great powers have marched into the Assembly.

The General Assembly has not only encroached upon the jurisdictional preserve of the Security Council, but it has also tended to revoke the Charter-prescribed delegation of specialized functions to the Trusteeship and Economic and Social Councils. This is particularly true of the Trusteeship Council, and the reasons for this shift of constitutional relationships are analogous to those discussed in connection with the displacement of the Security Council.

The Charter formally assigns the management of the Trusteeship System to the General Assembly, but it also designates the Trusteeship Council as the operating arm of the Assembly for that purpose.[25] Despite the obvious intention of the San Francisco Conference that the Trusteeship Council should conduct its business more or less autonomously, within the framework of its ultimate responsibility to the Assembly, there has been a

---

[25] See Articles 85-91.

steady trend toward the transfer of trusteeship questions to the plenary body itself.

This phenomenon is clearly an expression of the politics of anticolonialism. Just as the Soviet veto power inspires the United States to move from the Security Council to the Assembly, the prescribed balance of voting power between administering and nonadministering states in the Trusteeship Council inspires the anticolonial forces to shift from that body to the Assembly. Just as the great powers have learned to use the rostrum of the Assembly to build support for their competing cold war blocs, the anticolonial powers have learned to use that forum to mobilize support for their cause.

There is some reason to believe that the General Assembly may eventually achieve a hegemonic position in relation to the Specialized Agencies which are independently associated with the United Nations. In accordance with the Charter, the Assembly exercises, directly and through the Economic and Social Council, the coordinating functions to which those agencies have agreed.[26] The formal looseness of this control system is already somewhat offset by the Assembly's ultimate managerial power over the Expanded Technical Assistance Program, which it launched in 1949, and upon which a number of the Specialized Agencies depend for a very substantial proportion of their operating funds. Moreover, there have been persistent criticisms, notably in the United States, of the decentralized character of the United Nations family of organizations, which may presage an effort to strengthen the supervisory role of the Assembly.

The developmental process has made the General Assembly a court of appeal against the decisions, particularly the negative decisions, of virtually all the other organs. It is frequently treated as a substitute for the other organs by states anticipating a more favorable response to their demands in the Assembly than in the Councils having limited representation of the United Nations membership. Additionally, the Assembly's central position in the administrative system of the organization—typified by its electoral, budgetary, and supervisory powers—makes it the institutional hub of the United Nations. Thus, the evolution of constitutional relationships within the United Nations system has tended to make the General Assembly the unrivaled principal organ of the entire system.

DOMESTIC JURISDICTION AND INTERNATIONAL COMPETENCE

An even more critical area of constitutional interpretation and development than that pertaining to relationships among the organs of the United Nations system is the area of jurisdictional problems involving the world organization, on the one hand, and the member states, on the other hand.

---

[26] See Articles 13, 17 (paragraph 3), and 57-72.

In the United States, the division of power between the Federal Government and the states produces a persistent problem of "states' rights"; in the United Nations, the coexistence of international organization and national states produces an analogous problem of "domestic jurisdiction."

To the calm observer, the problem of domestic jurisdiction looked fairly simple at the time of the formulation of the League Covenant. In the light of settled legal principles, it was clear that the League should have only such competence as was delegated to it, and that the sovereignty of the state, not the authority of the organization, should receive the benefit of any doubt that might arise. Nevertheless, American Senators were far from calm observers, and the framers of the Covenant sought to allay their morbid fears of a world government which would meddle in such American affairs as tariff and immigration policy[27] by inserting in the article regarding peaceful settlement of disputes the proviso that:

> If the dispute between the parties is claimed by one of them, and is found by the Council, to arise out of a matter which by international law is solely within the domestic jurisdiction of that party, the Council shall so report, and shall make no recommendation as to its settlement.[28]

The experience of the League in applying this formula provided no great excitement. When the allegation was made that the Council had no business intruding in a particular dispute, the Council customarily treated it as a legal question, and relied heavily upon the advice of international jurists. This procedure brought about the formulation of a constitutional principle which is of major importance for the long-term development of international organization: the doctrine, stated by the Permanent Court of International Justice in its Advisory Opinion on Nationality Decrees Issued in Tunis and Morocco (1923), that acceptance by a state of treaty obligations relating to a given subject has the effect of removing that subject from the purely domestic domain.[29] Nothing in the experience of the League prepared the world for the intensely political battle over the question of domestic jurisdiction which was to arise in the United Nations.

The San Francisco Conference, in designing an organizational system with a much broader functional range than that of the League, formulated a domestic jurisdiction clause with a correspondingly greater range of application. Article 2, paragraph 7, of the Charter provides that:

> Nothing contained in the present Charter shall authorize the United Nations to intervene in matters which are essentially within the domestic jurisdiction of any state or shall require the Members to sub-

---

[27] Cf. Henry Cabot Lodge, *The Senate and the League of Nations* (New York: Scribner's, 1925), pp. 236-237, 391-395.

[28] Article 15, paragraph 8.

[29] Hudson, *op. cit.*, I, 156-157.

mit such matters to settlement under the present Charter; but this principle shall not prejudice the application of enforcement measures under Chapter VII.

It is notable that this formula was deliberately made applicable to the entire body of United Nations operations under the Charter except those pertaining to enforcement of the peace. This point was emphasized, on the insistence of the United States, in a statement for the record that the committee responsible for drafting the chapter on international economic and social cooperation was agreed that "nothing contained in Chapter IX can be construed as giving authority to the Organization to intervene in the domestic affairs of member states." [30] Moreover, the Conference deliberately refrained from indicating where the competence to decide on disputed jurisdictional issues should be lodged, and from citing international law as the relevant standard of judgment.

Lawyers so dispassionate as to be not of this world would have a hard time deciding individually or agreeing collectively on the abstract meaning or practical application of the Charter's formula for the delimitation of domestic and international jurisdiction.

From one point of view, the restriction on the United Nations means almost nothing. Ratification of the Charter by a state puts practically every conceivable subject—from the use of force to the civil rights of citizens, from territorial disputes to the management of the national economy—into the international domain, so that there is precious little domestic jurisdiction left to be infringed upon. The same conclusion can be reached by defining "intervention" strictly, and arguing that Article 2, paragraph 7, permits United Nations criticism, advice, and recommendation on matters which are within domestic jurisdiction, and that the concluding exceptional clause permits genuine intervention—coercive interference—in any matter which the organization deems related to the problem of international peace.

From another point of view, the domestic jurisdiction clause vitiates almost the whole Charter. If both "intervention" and "domestic jurisdiction" are broadly defined, to mean that international investigation, discussion, and recommendation are proscribed in relation to the domestic affairs and internal problems of states, it would appear that there is little activity in which the United Nations can constitutionally engage.

Either of these extreme interpretations reduces some part of the Charter to meaninglessness. The former makes the domestic jurisdiction clause an abortive attempt to limit the competence of the organization; the latter makes virtually the entire Charter, excluding Article 2, paragraph 7, a waste of words.[31]

---

[30] *The United Nations Conference on International Organization: Selected Documents*, p. 637.

[31] Cf. Quincy Wright, *Problems of Stability and Progress in International Relations* (Berkeley: University of California Press, 1954), p. 32.

In truth, the effort to discover the precise legal meaning of the jurisdictional text is a hopeless enterprise, since it was

> a formula which left everyone free to place his own interpretation upon the article in the future in the hope that he would make it prevail. Far from representing a definite concept which would be a clear guide for future action and which would resolve conflicts in this very delicate field of international action, the adoption of article 2(7) merely postponed the division of opinion which would be certain to arise in the future.[32]

Such an enterprise is also essentially irrelevant, because the question of the constitutional relationship between the world organization and its component states has been treated as preeminently a political matter.

In analyzing the operating experience of the United Nations, we can first of all discern a definite trend toward the enlargement of the subject matter with which international organization undertakes to deal. This trend was foreshadowed by the comprehensiveness of the functional range of the original constitutional documents of the United Nations. Compared to the Charter, the League Covenant was a narrowly political document. Governments do not create an organization with an Economic and Social Council if they wish to exclude international consideration of economic and social problems; they do not ratify a Charter containing a Declaration Regarding Non-Self-Governing Territories if they are convinced that colonial policy is purely a domestic concern of imperial powers; they do not commit themselves to a collaborative effort to promote the universal enjoyment of human rights if they adhere to the belief that every state has the sovereign right to treat its citizens as arbitrarily as it pleases. Having done these things, the members of the United Nations had committed themselves to a broad conception of the proper business of international organization from the very start.

The development of the trend has been a political process in more than one sense. In the first place, jurisdictional questions have been disposed of by the political organs of the system, without customary reference to the World Court or other legal advisory agencies. In the second place, the articulated criterion of judgment has been political in the best sense of that word—in the sense that concern has been expressed for creating a system of international organization capable of realizing the ideal purposes formulated at San Francisco. This sort of politicalism, which looks to the future to find opportunities for creative adaptation, stands in contrast to the kind of legalism which looks to the past to

---

[32] Statement by Lawrence Preuss, July 12, 1946, *Compulsory Jurisdiction of the International Court of Justice, Hearings before a Subcommittee of the Committee on Foreign Relations, United States Senate, 79th Congress, 2nd Session* (Washingtion: Government Printing Office, 1946), p. 82.

find permission for whatever activities might be contemplated. Finally, the motivating forces involved in the process have been political in the lower sense—in the sense that considerations of national self-interest have played a decisive part, and that national or bloc partisanship, in the manner of all partisanship, has produced expediential shifting from one constitutional position to another.

In general terms, the result of this process has been that the various organs of the United Nations have asserted the competence to deal with virtually any matter which might be presented to their attention. They have sometimes dealt in a gingerly fashion with matters which have been strongly alleged to lie within the domestic jurisdiction of member states, but they have not conceded the right of a state unilaterally to impose a restrictive definition of international jurisdiction. They have exploited to the full the World Court's doctrine of the treaty-obligation test of jurisdictional competence, and they have gone far toward developing a new constitutional principle which has not as yet been sanctified by the imprimatur of a court: the concept that the technical validity of a claim of domestic jurisdiction cannot prevent the United Nations from concerning itself with a case which it judges to bear significantly upon the preservation of world peace and the realization of the basic purposes enshrined in the Charter.

This principle was adumbrated at San Francisco in a subcommittee report which acknowledged that the problem of human rights was primarily a domestic matter, but asserted that if the fundamental freedoms of individuals "were grievously outraged so as to create conditions which threaten peace or to obstruct the application of provisions of the Charter, then they cease to be the sole concern of each state." [33] It has been invoked by both the United States and the Soviet Union. In discussing the Indonesian case, the American spokesman told the Security Council that "when there is shooting and men are killed the Council has full right to take the case in its hands," [34] and a United States representative declared to the General Assembly in 1950 that the Formosa issue "was not one of purely domestic jurisdiction since the case could lead to differences among nations, and even war." [35]

In similar vein, the Soviet Union argued in 1946 that the Security Council could properly intervene in Spain, on the ground that internal conditions in that country constituted "a threat to international peace and se-

---

[33] *United Nations Conference on International Organization: Selected Documents,* p. 483.

[34] Cited in Henri Rolin, "The International Court of Justice and Domestic Jurisdiction," *International Organization,* February 1954, p. 41.

[35] Report of speech by Ambassador Warren Austin, *New York Times,* October 8, 1950.

curity," [36] and its Ukrainian spokesman justified the demand for action concerning the maintenance of British troops in Indonesia in these terms:

> There are matters, however, which, though formally comprised in the domestic jurisdiction of a given State, border upon external political relations, or even encroach directly upon external political relations, threatening the peace and security of the peoples. Such matters cannot be left to be settled by the State itself, notwithstanding the principle of sovereignty.[37]

This doctrine has served repeatedly as the basis of action by the political organs of the United Nations.

The upshot of all this is a situation described approvingly by Charles Malik of Lebanon:

> Thus, any Member of the United Nations can bring before the Assembly any question falling within the scope of the Charter and, if he can muster the necessary votes, he will have that question both included in the agenda and discussed. Whether we like it or not, such is the structure of the United Nations that, if there is sufficiently strong feeling about any matter within the scope of the Charter—and this scope, as we all know, is practically all-embracing—then no legalistic protestations can possibly prevent its full discussion by the Assembly.[38]

Clyde Eagleton said the same thing in terms of disapprobation:

> United Nations organs have ridden roughshod over the domestic-questions clause of the Charter. In practice, granted a proper majority, that obstacle may now be regarded as removed; an organ of the United Nations may now do whatever it has the votes to do.[39]

This confrontation of Malik with Eagleton is indicative of another trend which we must note: the constitutional evolution of the United Nations has produced not only a trend toward the enlargement of international jurisdiction at the expense of domestic jurisdiction, but also a trend toward a bitter struggle over the question of the jurisdictional balance between international organization and national states. These two trends go hand in hand, as American experience in the development of federal centralization demonstrates. It is open to question whether the more significant fact in United Nations history is the emergence of the trend toward reducing the sphere of domestic jurisdiction or of the trend toward increasing the political sensitivity of that issue, just as it is doubtful whether

---

[36] Cited in H. Lauterpacht, *International Law and Human Rights* (London: Stevens, 1950), p. 190.

[37] *Ibid.*, p. 200.

[38] *United Nations Bulletin*, October 15, 1953, p. 370.

[39] "Excesses of Self-Determination," *Foreign Affairs*, July 1953, p. 594.

American history should be described as chiefly characterized by the gradual defeat of states' rights or by the persistent struggle of the champions of states' rights.

The political struggle over the domestic jurisdiction issue is a confused one, in which we find the USSR alternately denouncing international efforts to penetrate the sacred barrier of a state's sovereignty and joining gleefully in the effort to probe into the colonial affairs of Western European powers, India urging the United Nations to make racial conditions in South Africa its own business and defiantly asserting that it will tolerate no interference by the United Nations in its sovereign realm and no attempt to tell its government "what we should do in India or in any part of the Indian Union," [40] and the United States oscillating in much the same manner. Like the doctrine of states' rights, the principle of domestic jurisdiction is a concept which no participant in the political process can resist invoking when it serves his purposes or denouncing when it thwarts his purposes.

Nevertheless, the major battle has shaped up with reasonable clarity in the United Nations. The principle that the organization's business is whatever it chooses to make its business has become the chosen instrument of the rebellious, impatient, anticolonial, and self-consciously non-European bloc of states which is keenly aware of its increasing capacity to dominate the decisions of the General Assembly and determined to use that capacity to strike down the last vestiges of the white man's structure of political and racial superiority. Thus challenged, the embattled bearers of the white man's burden and protectors of the white man's civilization have collaborated in the project of erecting bigger and better "no trespassing" signs. Most of the colonial powers of Western Europe, busily engaged in attempting to achieve the constructive liquidation of the colonial heritage, would prefer to rely upon signs reading "Quiet—men thinking" or "Slow—men at work," but they have been exasperated to the point of accepting the wording preferred by the Union of South Africa, which is busily engaged in attempting to achieve the liquidation of the Western liberal heritage in its territory. The United States, ill at ease in the role of obstructing anticolonial campaigns but with its European alliances to think about, and profoundly uncomfortable in the role of giving aid and comfort to the aggressive racialism of South Africa but with its own imperfect racial situation to worry about, has shifted nervously from case to case and experienced difficulty in developing a position compatible with both its concrete national interests and its abstract national ideals. For a time, in the mid-'fifties, the United States appeared ready to take a firm stand with the forces advocating a conservative interpretation of the organ-

---

[40] *New York Times,* June 12, 1951.

ization's authority regarding colonial and racial issues. In 1953, an American spokesman, commenting on the race issue in South Africa, expressed the growing concern of his government about "the tendency of the General Assembly to place on its agenda subjects the international character of which is doubtful." [41] Two years later, the United States for the first time opposed the inscription of a colonial issue—the Algerian question—on the agenda of the Assembly, with explicit reference to the barrier of domestic jurisdiction.[42] However, this phase was of brief duration. By 1960, the United States reached the point of asserting that tensions deriving from governmental policies of racial discrimination, as in South Africa, posed problems that fell clearly within the jurisdiction of the political organs of the United Nations.[43] In the opening years of the Kennedy Administration, the American position on jurisdictional questions moved perceptibly toward that of the anticolonial bloc. But this shift by no means indicates that the issue of the expansion of competence of the United Nations is near resolution. The international battle over domestic jurisdiction bids fair to be as permanent a feature of the constitutional history of the United Nations as the domestic battle over states' rights has been in American history.

The question of domestic jurisdiction has given rise to an internal political conflict in the United States which is intimately related to the international struggle just described. It is in part a debate concerning the extent to which the United States should submit to the intrusions of international organization. The tradition of adherence to a doctrinaire conception of absolute sovereignty is well established in this country, and its most vigorous supporters have long been characterized by a neurotic anxiety and a suspiciousness of their opponents which have militated against their taking an accurate look at the facts or assuming a consistently logical position. As D. F. Fleming has pointed out, the Senate voted overwhelmingly in 1920 in favor of a reservation to the League Covenant which stated the intention of the United States to decide for itself what matters lay within its domestic jurisdiction and specified seven such matters: immigration, labor, coastwise traffic, the tariff, commerce, traffic in women and children, and traffic in opium and other dangerous drugs. Yet, the United States had already ratified treaties regulating all of those subjects, thereby admitting that they were *not* matters of purely domestic concern, and in 1924 Congress approved the sending of delegates to an Opium Conference sponsored by the League, with instructions to express the view that international regulation of the production of dangerous drugs was

[41] See the statement by Henry Cabot Lodge, Jr., on September 16, 1953, *Charter Review Documents,* p. 283.

[42] Robert E. Asher, *et al., The United Nations and Promotion of the General Welfare* (Washington: The Brookings Institution, 1957), p. 758.

[43] Security Council, Official Records: 15th Year, 855th Meeting, April 1, 1960, p. 3.

essential to the solution of the evils of the international narcotics traffic.[44]

That episode was fairly typical of "sovereigntyism" in action in the United States. The same outlook was expressed in 1946, when the Senate insisted upon encumbering American ratification of the optional clause of the Statute of the International Court of Justice, which involves a limited commitment to accept the compulsory jurisdiction of the Court, with the so-called Connally Amendment, an assertion of the right of the United States unilaterally to withhold cases from the Court on the ground that they pertain to matters within its domestic jurisdiction.

The most notable manifestation of American political sensitivity to the possibility of external interference within the realm which the United States may regard as its domestic preserve was the movement, reaching its peak in the early 'fifties, to amend the Constitution of the United States so as to inhibit the treaty-making process and to limit the impact of international engagements upon American internal affairs. In part, the campaign for adoption of one or another of the proposals—which acquired the generic label of the Bricker Amendment—reflected a reaction of conservative nationalism against the broadening jurisdictional sweep of the United Nations and other international agencies.

Probing more deeply into the American political context, we find that this reaction was intertwined with, and not merely analogous to, a reaction against the expanding functional competence of the Federal Government within the domestic system. Campaigners for the Bricker Amendment had only one wary eye focused on foreigners who might stick their noses into American affairs; the other eye, equally suspicious, was trained upon Washington, which might, in accordance with the constitutional doctrine pronounced in the *Missouri v. Holland* case (1920), derive from international commitments an additional power to intervene in the realm hitherto reserved to the states. The urge to protect states' rights—or, more basically, to protect interests which are favored by restriction of federal authority—lay behind the insistence upon curtailing American involvement in the expanding sphere of international organization. In short, Brickerism reflected as much concern about the enlargement of the sovereign competence of Washington within the United States, as about the diminution of the sovereign competence of Washington in the international context.

The Bricker Amendment movement was formally unsuccessful, but the dramatization of the political strength of the mood it represented has clearly inspired caution in the development of the American position with respect to international activities affecting the boundaries of domestic and international jurisdiction; it has had a greater effect upon policy than upon constitutional law. Moreover, the mood persists even after the cam-

---

[44] D. F. Fleming, *The United States and the League of Nations, 1918-1920* (New York: Putnam's, 1932), pp. 422-423.

paign has subsided. In the United States, and in most if not all other states, political forces sensitive to intrusions upon domestic jurisdiction can be expected recurrently to make themselves heard and felt. There may be an evolution of the competence of international institutions, but there is little prospect that it will be a quiet evolution.

The reaction against the jurisdictional expansiveness of the United Nations stems from such various sources as the concern of internationalists lest the organization attempt to do too much too fast and succeed only in exacerbating problems which it cannot solve, the nationalistic sensitivity of South Africans to outside criticism of domestic racial policies, the legalistic fear of American conservatives that Washington might amend the Constitution to its advantage by the treaty-making process, and the moral indignation of statesmen of colonial powers at the persistent stretching of their commitments regarding non-self-governing territories. This reaction is a significant one, and while there is little probability that it will produce a reversal of the trend toward maximizing the scope of United Nations activities, it will certainly maintain the trend toward making the jurisdictional problem one of the most controversial issues of United Nations constitutional development.

SUGGESTED READINGS

Cohen, Benjamin V., *The United Nations: Constitutional Developments, Growth, and Possibilities,* Cambridge: Harvard University Press, 1961.

Gross, Ernest A., *The United Nations: Structure for Peace,* New York: Harper, for the Council on Foreign Relations, 1962.

Haviland, H. Field, Jr., *The Political Role of the General Assembly,* New York: Carnegie Endowment for International Peace, 1951.

Lauterpacht, Sir Hersch, *The Development of International Law by the International Court,* New York: Praeger, 1958.

CHAPTER

10

The Problem of the International Secretariat

In a very significant sense, the identity of every organization—be it a giant industrial corporation, a community welfare agency, a labor union, a national government, or an international organization—is lodged in its professional staff. Members, stockholders, or citizens may control the organization, but they cannot *be* it; the staff *is* the organization.

This concept is nowhere more applicable than in the realm of international organization. The secretariat of an international agency has a peculiar importance, since it is normally the sole tangible evidence, in human form, of the continuous existence of the agency. In the case of the United Nations, the permanent missions of member states have tended to supplement the secretariat in providing an element of continuity, but they, of course, represent their governments rather than the organization. The secretariat is the major organ which best expresses the continuing vitality of the whole, as distinguished from its parts. In international organization, the member states are "organized," but the staff is the "international" component.

Indeed, the invention of the international secretariat may be described as the real beginning of international organization. In institutional terms, nothing essentially new has been added by the multilateralization and regularization of diplomacy until the secretariat is introduced; this is the innovation that transforms a series of conferences into an organization.

The problems presented by the need for an adequate secretariat and by the opportunity for developing the potentialities of this unique institutional invention are among the most basic constitutional issues of international organization. The international civil service is not only peculiarly important, but it also poses difficulties of a special order.

In part, these derive from its very newness. There are no long-established patterns of administrative structure and procedure in the international field, or traditional values of international public service. National precedents are available, and may be copied, but they are inconsistent with each other and they may be, singly or in combination, inconsistent with the requirements of international administration. Twentieth-century secretariats have had to experiment in a new area, undertaking to decide what can and should be borrowed from various national traditions and how to combine the borrowings, and to develop new patterns and norms specifically designed for their unique tasks. The technical difficulty of this job is enhanced by the diversity—linguistic, cultural, political, and professional—of the human material involved. The stubborn remnants of national administrative traditions, deeply embedded in the preconceptions of secretariat members, make the effective application of new international methods and standards, however rationally conceived, a formidable task.

The special difficulties of the international civil service also derive in part from a kind of institutional loneliness. A national bureaucracy fits comfortably into a governmental context; it has its bosses and its supporters, those to whom it is responsible and who are responsible for it, its institutional critics and defenders. The international secretariat, by its very uniqueness as a government-like institution on the international level, is condemned to function in something uncomfortably like an institutional vacuum. Its departments are ministries without ministers. In organizations like the League and the United Nations, the secretariat may be conceived in the dual role of staff and executive, with the Secretary-General serving as chief bureaucrat and prime minister, but this is an anomalous and delicate position; as one commentator has put it, the Secretary-General of the League had to try to get his budget "voted by a Parliament where everyone belonged to the Opposition." [1]

There is a sense in which it is true that the complex of governmental structures necessarily forms an integral whole, and one of the persistent

[1] C. Howard-Ellis, *The Origin, Structure and Working of the League of Nations* (London: George Allen and Unwin, 1928), p. 438.

delusions of thinking about international organization is the notion that a single element of a governmental pattern—for instance, a court or a police force—can function effectively in institutional isolation. Certainly, a civil service which is part of an international organization must be expected to perform differently and to confront different problems than a civil service which is part of a fully elaborated governmental structure.

Finally, the peculiar difficulties of the international secretariat are attributable to what we may call its "internationality." It is not only a bureaucracy without a government, but also a bureaucracy without a country; it lacks not only the appropriate institutional envelopment, but also the essential underpinnings of a community of political allegiance. A bureaucracy requires more than administrative patterns and integration in a governmental structure. A civil service is not just a technical achievement but an outgrowth of a political community; a good civil service is one of the rarest of human social achievements, reserved for societies which have reached an unusual degree of solidarity in respect to fundamental values and purposes. The United Nations secretariat can hardly be expected to rise far above the political quality of the United Nations; if it is also true that the United Nations can hardly rise above the quality of its secretariat, that is only one of many instances of the perverse circularity of international problems.

The history of the international secretariat effectively begins with the creation of the League of Nations and the International Labor Organization after World War I. Although certain public international unions had previously established permanent bureaus, these were of more importance as anticipations of the idea of an international staff than as precedents for the actual mechanisms of the League secretariat and the International Labor Office. These two bodies, which at their maximum included a combined total of hardly more than a thousand persons, were the trail-blazers of international administration.

The basic direction of the trail was established at once by Sir Eric Drummond, the first Secretary-General of the League. His decision to build a strictly international staff, composed of persons from many nations serving as individual members of a unitary international body rather than of contingents of national representatives, was a bold and imaginative innovation which has been generally acclaimed as "one of the most important events in the history of international politics." [2]

As to the manner of proceeding along the path, Drummond and Albert Thomas, the original Director of the International Labor Office, developed such contrasting patterns of operation as to present their descendants of the United Nations generation with a clear awareness of the fundamental alternatives. Drummond, a British civil servant by temperament

[2] Walters, *A History of the League of Nations,* I, 76. Cf. Lie, *In the Cause of Peace,* p. 41.

and conviction as well as experience, established the prototype of an efficient and unobtrusive administrative direction, while Thomas, an irrepressible veteran of French politics and labor activity, created the pattern of articulate and dynamic leadership in matters of policy. The categories which they established will dominate the concept of secretary-generalship for generations to come.

The pioneer secretariats discovered and left a record of the major pitfalls to be encountered along the path of international administration, even though they did not manage to pave an easy way to success. Their successors have the advantage of their experience in grappling with the difficulties, and the consolation—dubiously gratifying, perhaps, but the best available to builders of international order—of knowing that the problems which beset them have been encountered before.

Most significantly, the trail-blazing agencies demonstrated conclusively that the way was not impassable. The feasibility of an international civil service had previously been not only questioned, but "confidently denied." [3] Egon Ranshofen-Wertheimer expressed the conclusions of virtually all serious students of international administration when he wrote of the two pioneering secretariats: "Both had proved that international administration is feasible, that it can be efficient, and that the concept of international civil service is practical." [4] In contrast to the expectation that the difficulties of creating a workable team out of diverse multinational materials could not be surmounted, the League secretariat was "from a technical standpoint at least, one of the most efficient administrations the world has ever known." [5]

In general terms, the United Nations was built on the assumption that the League's failure had not been conclusive; in respect to the secretariat, it was built on the assumption that the League's failure had not been comprehensive. Whereas some aspects of the League experiment were continued by the formulators of the new international system for want of something better, or in the hope of building future success on past failure, this part at least of the institutional heritage was retained because it had proved outstandingly successful. In the formulation of the Charter and the early planning for its implementation, the basic principles of the League secretariat system were adopted: the United Nations was to have a unitary staff, multinational in composition but strictly international in character, headed by a Secretary-General through whom the secretariat was to be responsible solely to the organization and under whom it was to function independently of national governments.[6]

---

[3] Walters, *loc. cit.*

[4] *The International Secretariat: A Great Experiment in International Administration* (Washington: Carnegie Endowment for International Peace, 1945), p. 390.

[5] *Ibid.*, p. 151.

[6] See Articles 97 and 100-101 of the Charter.

In keeping with the general concept of organizational decentralization, the autonomous Specialized Agencies of the new system were to create their own versions of the international secretariat, each responsible only to its own agency and all subject only to such coordination and administrative unification as might be agreed upon by the agencies which they served. These decisions resulted in the creation of more than a dozen secretariats, having a total strength of approximately fifteen thousand, within the United Nations family of organizations. In addition, such regional agencies as NATO and the Organization of American States have developed flourishing staff organizations, further increasing the corps of international civil servants.

THE PROBLEM OF EFFICIENT ADMINISTRATION

The first major secretariat problem confronting the United Nations, and, analogously, other contemporary international organizations, is that of basic bureaucratic efficiency. The United Nations secretariat has at its disposal the administrative wisdom painfully accumulated by its predecessors, but it also has a combined list of unsolved old problems and difficult new ones.

Trygve Lie began his work on the basis of structural plans carefully elaborated by the Preparatory Commission of the United Nations, whereas Sir Eric Drummond had had to start from a scratch provided by himself, but, unlike the League, the United Nations commenced its operations in such a flurry that its original Secretary-General had to recruit and organize his staff with extraordinary haste. As Lie has reported, his task admitted of no delay, and he was forced to appoint, on a temporary basis, some 2,900 secretariat members—four times as many as the League had ever employed—in 1946.[7] This hectic beginning had its inexorable effects, and the subsequent history of the secretariat has been in large degree a process of correcting imbalances, rationalizing procedures, eliminating misfits, and reorganizing the structure for long-term operations—a task which might have been much less demanding if Lie's original decisions and choices could have been made at a more leisurely pace.

The sheer bigness of the United Nations secretariat poses problems of efficiency which are unprecedented in the international field. The League secretariat was dwarfed by that of the new organization, which was stabilized at a figure of roughly five thousand. Moreover, a considerable percentage of the latter group is stationed away from the New York headquarters, making difficult the effective application of the concept of centralized administrative control.

Even more significant is the extraordinary diversity of the human re-

---

[7] Lie, *op. cit.*, pp. 43-44, 54.

sources upon which the United Nations secretariat has drawn. The League had a general European orientation which was distinctly reflected in the composition of its staff. Although the geographical distribution of posts was progressively broadened, the League secretariat remained from first to last predominantly a collection of Europeans and therefore a relatively homogeneous institution in important respects. Switzerland, as host country, provided the bulk of lower-level employees; Britain and France supplied the core of the professional staff, its standard languages, and its administrative techniques. The differences between these two linguistic and technical contributions were real, but in the retrospection of the United Nations era they appear minor.

The United Nations began with a Charter provision which formalized the operative principle evolved by the League that "Due regard shall be paid to the importance of recruiting the staff on as wide a geographical basis as possible," [8] and with a *de facto* situation of excessive Americanization of the staff which was primarily a consequence of the haste with which early recruitment had to be carried out. Subsequent adjustments have reduced the United States contingent to reasonable proportions, and produced a pattern of geographical distribution which corresponds more closely to the increasingly global scope of the organization. In this pattern, nationals of the United States and Western European countries occupy a very considerable percentage of staff positions, but the geographical range has been broadened to take in persons from virtually all the member states. "Underrepresented" as most peoples not of Western European nationality or ethnic background still are, in terms of their quantitative importance in world population figures, they have nevertheless produced secretariat members in sufficient numbers to give the United Nations offices a much more heterogeneous character than the League headquarters possessed. The task of welding together men and women of different nationalities, languages, and cultural traditions into an efficient administrative team presents a much larger problem to the United Nations than to the League.

Aside from the difficulties of operating a decidedly multinational staff organization, once it is formed, the problem of reconciling the principle of equitable geographical distribution of recruits with that of "securing the highest standards of efficiency, competence, and integrity" [9] is a formidable one. This delicate task was politically imposed upon the League Secretary-General, and is constitutionally required of his counterpart in the United Nations. For better or for worse, recruitment policy cannot be based exclusively upon the criterion of the individual's personal qualifications; in the field of international employment, the relevant irrelevancy is not "whom do you know" but "where are you from?" From a strictly administrative point of view, there is some positive value in securing broad nationality

[8] Article 101, paragraph 3.
[9] *Ibid.*

distribution, even at the expense of sheer quality; for some purposes, a slightly incompetent man's nationality may make him more useful than a more expert civil servant of inappropriate nationality. For the most part, however, the Charter principle of geographical distribution is a concession to political necessity. It licenses a kind of international spoils system in which states seek to nourish their national self-esteem by securing an adequate quota of international jobs for their citizens. Ironically, perhaps, because it is politically necessary it is also politically and administratively desirable; what shall it profit an international organization to maintain its administrative purity and lose its own members or their political support?

Both the League and the United Nations have experienced the battle over the distribution of secretariat posts. Typically, member states have pressed for the maximization of their "quotas," and small states collectively have protested against the tendency of the great powers to assert a vested interest in the most important posts. In both cases, these quarrels have subsided, temporarily, with the adoption of the rule of thumb that jobs should be allocated in approximately the same ratio as budgetary contributions of member states, and with the compromising of the claims of small and great powers. In the United Nations, this relative political peace was broken after 1959, when pressures from the Soviet bloc and the growing African segment of the organization led to reconsideration of the flexible formula for geographical distribution. These pressures reflected dissatisfaction with the predominantly Western cast of the secretariat. The underrepresentation of the Communist states was largely the result of their own unwillingness to release nationals for service in the secretariat, particularly for permanent appointment. The effort to accommodate their demands was complicated by their insistence that personnel be treated essentially as governmental officials on short-term assignment to the United Nations, rather than as recruits for an international career service. In the case of African and other new states, the lack of a national surplus of trained and experienced public service personnel made it difficult for the United Nations to secure qualified staff. The urge of these states to place a substantial number of their citizens in United Nations jobs ran counter to their need to retain their most competent people for the national service. Under these circumstances, the United Nations tended to employ citizens of the African states for limited periods, treating this employment in part as a means to provide training for members of national bureaucracies.

The problem of administrative efficiency in the United Nations is also complicated by the quantitative burden and qualitative variety of functions which the secretariat must be equipped to perform. The veteran of Geneva who participates in the hurly-burly of United Nations, New York, must often be tempted to exclaim, "the League was never like this!" The accelerating pace of international life, the expanded functional ambitiousness and structural elaborateness of the United Nations, and the growing paper-work proclivities of all governmental institutions have conspired to magnify and diversify the tasks of the international civil service.

The headquarters buildings of the United Nations are equipped with a conveyor system which "carries fifty thousand pounds of printed matter a week when the General Assembly is sitting and forty thousand pounds a week when it isn't. That works out to Lord knows how many billion words a year, a lot of them worth thinking quite hard about." [10] The secretariat produced more than 306 million pages of records and documents in 1961,[11] as part of its contribution to the functioning of the United Nations as a center for continuous international debate and discussion. In addition to the basic conference-supporting and internal housekeeping functions of the secretariat, its tasks include research in almost every conceivable field, large-scale publishing and other informational activities, liaison and mediatorial functions, and field work ranging from policing armistice arrangements to conducting mass immunization campaigns for children. The United Nations secretariat is a collective jack-of-all-trades, a global mother whose work is never done.

The effective performance of its tasks is impeded by the tendency of governments to assign workloads with their left hands and budgetary resources with their totally uninformed right hands; to paraphrase a prominent American statesman, governments persistently follow the policy of being liberal where the secretariat's work is concerned and conservative where their peoples' money is concerned. The pinch of governmental stinginess is one of the earliest sensations of international organization. Anthony Eden devoted his maiden speech in the League to viewing with anxiety the growth of the organization's budget, which included funds for the International Labor Organization and the World Court, from five million dollars in 1923 to six and one third million in 1931.[12] "Throughout its existence the League suffered from a stupid and unnecessary penury." [13]

International organization is considerably more expensive in the United Nations era. In 1961, the total expenditures of the United Nations system ran to more than $450 million. This total included $72 million for the regular budget of the central organization, $65 million for the regular budgets of the Specialized Agencies, $154 million for special operations in the Middle East and the Congo, and $159 million for programs of the United Nations and the Specialized Agencies which are financed by the voluntary contributions of states.[14] It is tempting to draw conclusions of

---

10 *The New Yorker*, February 26, 1955, p. 22.

11 *New York Times*, October 13, 1962.

12 Walters, *op. cit.*, II, 516.

13 *Ibid.*, I, 130.

14 Data from "Information on the Operations and Financing of the United Nations," Joint Committee Print of the Committee on Foreign Relations, U. S. Senate, and the Committee on Foreign Affairs, U. S. House of Representatives, February 6, 1962 (87th Congress, 2d Session), pp. 69-70.

greater governmental generosity from these figures, which show a dramatic growth in financial support of international institutions since the days of the League.

Nevertheless, the objectives of international organization still are sought at bargain basement prices—a strict regime of penny pinching is imposed upon international secretariats, and hardly a member state, from the richest to the poorest, can refrain from quibbling over the relatively negligible sums required to support the activities of international secretariats. Moreover, as the major financial crisis encountered by the United Nations after the launching of the Congo operation in 1960 demonstrates, the refusal of states to meet their budgetary allotments is a formidable political weapon which opponents of a given United Nations action may wield.[15] The work of the United Nations secretariat is persistently vulnerable to the power of financial deprivation, possessed in some degree by all states and in significant measure by the major states.

THE PROBLEM OF ALLEGIANCE

A second great problem area relating to the international secretariat is bounded by the concepts of international loyalty and independence of national governments on one side, and national loyalty and respect for the security requirements of national governments on the other. If efficiency is the central technical problem, questions of allegiance constitute the central philosophical and normative problem.

Although the Covenant was silent on the subject, Drummond's fundamental decision that the League staff should be *international* in character determined the approach which the Council ratified on May 19, 1920, in its declaration that "the members of the Secretariat, once appointed, are no longer the servants of the country of which they are citizens, but become, for the time being, servants only of the League of Nations. Their duties are not national but international." [16] Beginning in 1932, this concept was formalized by the requirement that members of the secretariat make a declaration of fidelity, in which they subscribed to a revised version of Article 1 of the Staff Regulations, stipulating the pledge "to discharge their functions, and to regulate their conduct with the interests of the League alone in view," and binding them not to "seek or receive instructions from any Government or other authority external to the Secretariat of the League of Nations." [17]

These provisions are indicative of the nature of the problem as it emerged in the League. The crucial task was to define and to secure re-

---

[15] See pp. 296-297, below.

[16] Judith Jackson and Stephen King-Hall, eds., *The League Year-Book, 1932* (New York: Macmillan, 1932), p. 153.

[17] *Ibid.*, p. 156.

spect for the concept of international loyalty. It was generally agreed that the ideal was "not the denationalized loyalty of the man without a country . . . [but] the conviction that the highest interests of one's own country are served best by the promotion of security and welfare everywhere, and the steadfast maintenance of that conviction without regard to changing circumstances." [18] What was sought was not the rootless cosmopolitan, the nationally maladjusted globe-trotter, but the normally patriotic individual who could be regarded as a typical product of his country and yet could be numbered among those enlightened moderns "for whom the common interests of a world society are more than a bare abstract idea, and who value international co-operation above national deification." [19] The classic statement of the concept has been provided by C. Wilfred Jenks:

> A lack of attachment to any one country does not constitute an international outlook. A superior indifference to the emotions and prejudices of those whose world is bounded by the frontiers of a single state does not constitute an international outlook. A blurred indistinctness of attitude toward all questions, proceeding from a freedom of prejudice born of lack of vitality, does not constitute an international outlook. The international outlook required of the international civil servant is an awareness made instinctive by habit of the needs, emotions, and prejudices of the peoples of differently-circumstanced countries, as they are felt and expressed by the peoples concerned, accompanied by a capacity for weighing these frequently imponderable elements in a judicial manner before reaching any decision to which they are relevant.[20]

The League encountered difficulties in establishing the propriety of this rather vague principle in an extremely and increasingly nationalistic world which included numerous articulate groups to whom any subtle manifestation of less than one hundred per cent, my-country-right-or-wrong nationalism smelled of nefarious subversion. However, significant opposition to and defiance of the organization's efforts to realize the ideal of an internationally devoted secretariat were confined mainly to the nationals and governments of Fascist Italy and of Germany, particularly the Germany of the Nazi era.[21]

The League conceived the allegiance problem in the positive terms of securing the independence and international loyalty of the secretariat, and

---

[18] *The International Secretariat of the Future* (London: Royal Institute of International Affairs, 1944), p. 18.

[19] The quotation is from a discussion of Gunnar Myrdal's treatment of this problem, in a note by Laszlo Ledermann, "Psychological Impediments to Effective International Co-operation," *American Journal of International Law,* April 1954, p. 306.

[20] C. Wilfred Jenks, "Some Problems of an International Civil Service," *Public Administration Review,* Spring 1943, p. 95.

[21] Ranshofen-Wertheimer, *op. cit.,* Chapters 16 and 17.

its record was one of substantial, though not unblemished, success in realizing this purpose. The reflections of an outstanding group of League officials confirmed that:

> Experience shows that a spirit of international loyalty among public servants can be maintained in practice. It shows also that maintenance of such a spirit is an essential factor in the activity of an international service, since this alone can ensure to it that confidence without which it cannot function as it ought. . . . National interests must be represented and defended, of course, but representation (in the diplomatic sense) and defence should not be the function of secretariat officials.[22]

The United Nations began with the constitutional incorporation and elaboration of the principle of international independence which the League had adopted in practice. Article 100 of the Charter not only stipulated that members of the staff should act independently of their governments and responsibly to the organization, in terms reminiscent of those used in League regulations, but it also drew a lesson from League experience in imposing upon member states the obligation "to respect the exclusively international character of the responsibilities of the Secretary-General and the staff and not to seek to influence them in the discharge of their responsibilities." Moreover, the General Assembly and the analogous organs of the Specialized Agencies established the requirement that staff members subscribe to this concept in a formal oath of office.[23]

In practice, however, the problem of allegiance has assumed new forms in the workings of the United Nations system. To a considerable degree, emphasis has shifted from the problem of securing adequate commitment of the secretariat to the international interest, to that of assuring the maintenance of sufficient loyalty by its members to their own states. Obviously, these problems are not neatly separable. It could be argued that the issue has simply been changed from that of securing the acceptance of the principle of international loyalty by staff members, unaccustomed to putting themselves in that normative context, to securing the acceptance of that principle by governments, unaccustomed to tolerating deviation from the established norms of patriotism. From this point of view, the loyalty demands of states upon their citizens who serve the United Nations are simply expressions of governmental dissent from the concept of an internationally dedicated secretariat. The problem is the same as that which the League faced; the difference is that the League concentrated on the positive job of building the standard of international loyalty and its successor has been forced to the defensive position of resisting the destruction of that standard.

---

[22] *The International Secretariat of the Future,* pp. 19-20.

[23] F. R. Scott, "The World's Civil Service," *International Conciliation,* No. 496, January 1954, p. 286.

This argument contains something of the truth, but not all of it. There is a distinction between the two problems. The great issue in the United Nations has not been the propriety of international loyalty, but the impropriety of ideological allegiance to a particular movement which is antithetical to national loyalty. The deviations from nationalism which have been primarily at issue are not deviations toward internationalism but deviations toward Communism. The problems have tended to merge in the sense that national efforts to ensure that the secretariats of the United Nations system are not contaminated by members disloyal to their own country have collided with the principle of the independence of the international civil service; but it is clear that this amounts to an incidental violation of the procedural means for obtaining a genuinely international secretariat, rather than a deliberately direct assault upon the substantive concept itself. The United Nations and its sister organizations do have to grapple with the same problem which confronted the League, that of maintaining secretariat independence as a protective shield for the positive work of building a staff wholly dedicated to the international interest; but national pressures have produced the view, implicitly accepted by the international agencies themselves, that the critical problem is that of safeguarding the integrity of the international civil service against the membership of persons who are inadequately loyal to their own states.

This problem has been posed primarily by the United States. As the country in which the United Nations maintains its major headquarters, as the supplier of the largest national group of secretariat members, as the indispensable financial supporter of the organization, and as an extraordinarily influential great power, the United States has been able almost singlehandedly to impose its definition of the problem of allegiance upon the United Nations.

The heart of the American position has been the contention that Americans who are Communists or quasi-Communists should not be considered eligible to obtain or retain secretariat posts. It should be noted that the demand implicit in this view is not that American members of international staffs should serve the interests of the United States, but that they should *not* serve the interests of the Soviet Union. This distinguishes the American position from that of the fascist states, which undertook to *use* their nationals in the League secretariat, and from that which the Communist states are assumed to maintain with respect to their nationals in international posts. This American position is one which the heads of the United Nations secretariat have consistently and heartily espoused as their own.[24]

A major crisis in the development of the international secretariat occurred in 1952 and 1953, when the rampant forces of demagogic anti-Communism in the United States concentrated their fire upon the United

[24] See Lie, *op. cit.*, p. 388.

Nations. A series of inquiries by a Federal Grand Jury and Congressional investigating groups produced a small group of American staff members—about one per cent of the United States citizens employed by the United Nations—who admitted past membership in the Communist Party or resorted to the constitutional privilege of silence when questioned about Communist affiliations. None of these persons was indicted or otherwise seriously charged with specific violations of American law or definite acts of betrayal of American interests. In the supercharged atmosphere of the American political arena, however, these meager findings were magnified into decisive evidence that the United Nations had been infiltrated by "an overwhelmingly large group of disloyal United States citizens," [25] and tremendous pressure was brought upon the Secretary-General to sacrifice his independence as chief officer of an international secretariat in order to appease an American public which had been deliberately aroused by its lunatic fringe; Lie was expected to abdicate control over United Nations personnel policy to vigilantes who convicted American staff members of subversion on slender evidence and by flagrantly unjudicial methods.

The Secretary-General's response to this challenge combined vigorous insistence upon recognition of the principle that he was answerable only to the United Nations for the exercise of his functions, with discreet acceptance of the political necessity of regaining American confidence in the administration of the secretariat. He asserted his unwillingness to compromise the integrity of his international position by accepting dictation from any government or succumbing to pressure from any nation, and denounced the gross exaggeration and distortion of the facts which characterized many public criticisms of the secretariat in the United States. But he also agreed to the thesis that no American Communist should be employed by the United Nations, fired temporary staff members who had excited suspicion by refusing to answer questions put to them by American investigators, and terminated the contracts of permanent employees who had put themselves in the same position, after first obtaining the opinion of a special committee of legal advisers that he was within his rights in so doing.[26] Moreover, he moved to prevent the development of similar crises in the future by endorsing the propriety of a new plan whereby the United States Government would conduct an investigation of all present and future American members of international staffs, agreeing to use the administra-

---

[25] This charge by the Grand Jury was cited by Lie in a statement to the Assembly on March 10, 1953. See *United Nations Bulletin*, March 15, 1953, p. 222.

[26] It was subsequently established that Lie acted upon bad advice. The Administrative Tribunal of the United Nations ruled that eleven permanent members of the staff were entitled to compensation for discharge in violation of their contractual rights. The United States urged the General Assembly to set aside this ruling, but the Assembly voted in 1954 to honor this obligation, after having obtained an Advisory Opinion of the World Court to the effect that it had no legal alternative. See *New York Times*, December 18, 1954.

tive machinery of the United Nations to facilitate the execution of this plan, and committing himself to give serious attention to derogatory evidence against American employees which might be discovered and submitted to him under this system of inquiry.[27]

It is clear that Lie's acceptance of the proposition that the purging of Communistically inclined Americans from the secretariat was a matter of vital urgency rested primarily upon considerations of political necessity. As for its intrinsic merits, the best he could say for this proposition was that "an American Communist is not a representative American citizen"; he asserted that he "had no fear of espionage or sabotage or other threat to the security of the United States by reason of activities of such Communists within the United Nations. There was nothing to spy on in the United Nations . . . the United Nations was about as barren a field for spies as could be imagined." [28] He stated his position regarding American Communists in these terms: "I did not want them there for good policy reasons, but I was not afraid that any who remained would overthrow the United States government and subvert its constitution." [29] In short, he believed that the Communist problem in the secretariat was objectively a molehill, but recognized that it had become a subjective mountain which had to be removed if the United Nations was not to be destroyed by the withdrawal of American public support.

This episode brought little credit to the United States Government. In general terms, the responsible managers of American relations with the United Nations were not guilty of positive disrespect for the principle of the independence of the international secretariat, but they were guilty of failure to give adequate assistance to the Secretary-General in his efforts to withstand the assaults of intemperate American critics. At worst, the government left Lie to fight the battle for the integrity of his staff alone and unaided; at best, it devised a scheme—the system for investigation of American members of international staffs—which would assist him and the administrative heads of the Specialized Agencies in satisfying assailants. The government was hard pressed to save itself, and the constitutional values of the American political system, from the ravages of reactionary attack, and it had little strength to devote to the salvation of the United Nations and the emergent constitutional values of international organization.

The battle has subsided, and it appears that Lie's tactic, that of doing what his American critics insisted that he do but doing it less arbitrarily than they wished and maintaining that he had the right not to do it, was successful; suspected American officials have been eliminated, new ma-

---

[27] For the Secretary-General's version of this episode and of his policy, see Lie, *op. cit.*, Chapter XXI.

[28] *Ibid.*, p. 388.

[29] *Ibid.*, p. 391.

chinery has been set into motion for enabling the United States to give official notice of its attitude toward international employment of its citizens, the Secretary-General has acquired a freer hand in discharging employees whose political loyalties are under suspicion,[30] and the principle of the independence of the secretariat has been formally vindicated and solemnly reaffirmed.

Nevertheless, it is not yet clear that the institution of the international secretariat has escaped vital damage. While the American investigatory system formally respects the principle that a national government can only give information and advice, not dictate the personnel policy of international agencies,[31] the reality is plain that an international chief of staff can decline to accept the advice of the United States Government concerning the fitness of an American citizen for employment only at the peril of precipitating a new crisis. In the fall of 1954, Ambassador Lodge, chief American spokesman in the United Nations, denounced the Director-General of UNESCO for having failed promptly and unquestioningly to dismiss all Americans on his staff who had received unfavorable loyalty reports,[32] thereby indicating that the American conception of the independence of international administrative leaders does not include recognition of their right to reject the "advice" of Washington. Moreover, Mr. Lodge entered public objections to a report prepared by the International Civil Service Advisory Board, in which the basic principle of international loyalty of secretariat officials prescribed in Article 100 of the Charter was restated, and belligerently declared his intention "to do something about it." [33] It may be that the United Nations has survived the barrage of attacks by American extremists only to find itself permanently subjected to the thinly concealed domination of Washington in regard to questions bearing upon the loyalty of United States citizens in the international service.

Additionally, the question of generalizing the concessions made to the United States involves a serious dilemma for international organization. If the headquarters of the United Nations and the Specialized Agencies are to become infested with investigating missions from each member state, and if the presumption is to be admitted that the international employment of any person who fails to meet the standards of political allegiance defined by his particular government is of doubtful propriety, the future of the international civil service is dim indeed. On the other hand, if only the United States is to be permitted to intervene in this fashion, there is no conceivable way of avoiding the development of the impression that the

---

[30] See the text of the resolution passed by the General Assembly on December 9, 1953. *Charter Review Documents*, pp. 245-247.

[31] See the relevant Executive Orders, *ibid.*, pp. 232-238.

[32] *New York Times*, October 17, 1954.

[33] *New York Times*, October 11, 1954.

agencies of the United Nations system are peculiarly under the American thumb.

In short, the problem of allegiance poses difficulties for the institution of the international secretariat for which no solutions are in sight. International loyalty is an anomaly in an intensely nationalistic world, yet it is the indispensable basis for an effective international staff. It is not incompatible with national loyalty, but it is a tender plant which cannot be successfully cultivated in a field where national governments insist upon the right to trample at will. As we shall see, the problem of allegiance is intimately related to the issue of the political function of the secretariat.

THE PROBLEM OF POLITICAL INITIATIVE

A final constitutional issue relating to the secretariat which claims attention is the question of the degree of its political initiative and involvement. This is inherently a relative matter; administration and policy inevitably merge in defiance of analytical dividing lines, and the real question—in international organization as in national government—is never *whether* bureaucrats will influence policy. It is relative also in the sense that interested partisans alternately welcome and deplore the intrusions of administrative officials into the policy field, depending upon their approval or disapproval of the bureaucratic position on specific issues. One welcomes the support of "disinterested experts" and denounces the opposition of "unrepresentative bureaucrats." Nevertheless, there is a meaningful distinction between the concept of an essentially apolitical, primarily administrative international secretariat, associated with the name of Sir Eric Drummond, and the ideal of political leadership by an international staff which was espoused by Albert Thomas.

The San Francisco Conference clearly leaned toward the Thomas conception of the international secretariat. Focusing its attention upon the office of the Secretary-General, it conferred upon the occupant of that position not only the functions of head of the staff and "chief administrative officer of the Organization," [34] but also a political role. In writing Article 99 into the Charter, authorizing the Secretary-General to function as a kind of "twelfth member of the Security Council" [35] by invoking the consideration by that body of matters which he deems relevant to the maintenance of peace and security, the Conference justified the statement that "A root concept of the United Nations is that the Secretary-General is an international statesman." [36] The notion that the Secretary-General should be nothing more than an anonymous, unobtrusive, administrative technician was

[34] Article 97 of the Charter.
[35] Schwebel, *The Secretary-General of the United Nations,* p. 23.
[36] *Ibid.,* p. 17.

discarded in favor of the effort to create the foundations of a new office—that of an international chief executive.[37]

It fell to Trygve Lie, the first Secretary-General of the new organization, to begin the task of filling in the rough sketch of his institutional position which had been provided by the Charter. He proceeded with a keen sense of the challenging potentialities of the office and an equal consciousness of the factors limiting the development of effective international statesmanship in the mid-twentieth century. His political task was fraught with extraordinary perils and pregnant with unprecedented possibilities.

The resources discovered and developed by Lie were varied in nature. They included the capacity to stand before the world as the ideological symbol of international organization and the unique spokesman for the global interest, and to stand before the World Court and to sit in negotiations with states and other international agencies as the head of the United Nations and the official representative of its institutional interests. They included the opportunity to exert powerful influence, both positively and negatively, upon the content of the agenda of all the organs of the United Nations, and to intervene freely in the debates. Lie made his Annual Report a kind of State of the Union message, and sought to realize the potentialities of the power of proposal and evaluation. He found himself the possessor of significant influence through the power to present legal opinions and research studies, to participate in drafting of resolutions, to nominate mediators, investigators, and the like, to prepare budgetary allocations, and to control the day-by-day operations of bodies ranging from armistice supervision teams to technical assistance missions. He became the chief coordinator of the world's newly-elaborated organizational system and a major consultant, liaison man, and conciliator in the world's old system of diplomacy.

These resources have their obviously significant limitations. Superficially, the major point is that they do not include anything resembling a coercive capacity. As Lie himself put it, he was advised to be "more the general than the secretary—but where were his divisions?" [38] This is an important point, but not so important as it looks. Successful political leadership requires physical power at its command as a last resort, but that sort of power is the emergency medication, not the daily bread, of political leadership. Would Calvin Coolidge have been a stronger President than Franklin Roosevelt with twice as many police behind him? The crucial limitation on Trygve Lie's United Nations statesmanship was not his lack of an army to command, but his lack of a party to lead and a body politic to rally behind him. His weakness derived not so much from a lack of mili-

---

[37] See *The United Nations Secretariat,* United Nations Studies 4 (New York: Carnegie Endowment for International Peace, 1950), pp. 19-30.

[38] Lie, *op. cit.,* p. 42.

tary weapons as from an inability to compete effectively with national statesmen in the use of political weapons.

In general, Lie found that his supporters were a fickle crew, staying with him only so long as his definition of the international interest happened to coincide with their national policies. At one time or another, virtually every important member state praised him as the champion of the real interests of the human family, and denounced him as an ally of the forces of evil. In the latter case, disapproval of his substantive position was customarily prefaced by denial of his right, as a mere office boy of sovereign states, to have any position at all. The United Nations bids fair to rival the United States as the institutional homeland of those who prefer argument about constitutional authority to debate about substantive policy.

Operating in a world where clashes of national interest relegated the problem of the international interest to a low spot on the agenda of attention, Lie had to define the international interest primarily in the negative terms of the avoidance of open warfare among the great powers. When he abandoned this mediatorial role in 1950, to espouse the positive international interest in collective security against even an aggression supported by a great power, he soon found himself encumbered by the excessively affectionate embrace of the United States, which would not recognize the right of his term to expire, and the inexorable hostility of the Soviet Union, which would not recognize his continued existence. Maintained in office by an American procedural maneuver of dubious constitutionality, he struggled against overpowering odds until 1953, when he retired in favor of Dag Hammarskjold, who could begin his work with an asset which Lie had irretrievably lost, and which the Charter had clearly intended to be the fundamental equipment of its projected international statesman: the confidence of all the great powers.

Hammarskjold's career as Secretary-General, in the years before his death in 1961, provided even more striking evidence than Lie's of both the potentialities and the limits of that office as a political institution. His exceptional ability and skill in developing a style of operation combined with prevailing political circumstances to give him a diplomatic and executive role of the greatest importance. Stressing at some times his function as sponsor of and participant in "quiet diplomacy" and at other times his capacity to organize and direct peace-keeping operations which he described as ventures in "preventive diplomacy," Hammarskjold attained—or, in some instances, had thrust upon him—a prominence far exceeding that of Lie. By the same token, he finally encountered an even more dramatic political challenge than his predecessor; whereas Lie's activity in the Korean crisis had merely provoked the Soviet Union to oppose his continuance in office, Hammarskjold's position in the Congo case ultimately evoked a Soviet attack upon the very institution of the Secretary-Generalship. Although the "troika" proposal gained little support and was subsequently shelved by the USSR, it expressed, nevertheless, Russia's fundamental disavowal of the concept of the Secretary-General's role which Hammarskjold had both articulated and put into practice, and it represents—even from its position on the shelf—formal notice by the Soviet Union that the latter will not passively tolerate the continued evolution of the office along the lines set by Lie and Hammarskjold. Moreover, in its power to veto the appointment of a new Secretary-General whenever the office becomes vacant, the USSR possesses a formidable weapon, even though it is incapable of imposing its troika concept upon the organization. This power to block the filling of the office, held in abeyance to permit U Thant to step into Hammarskjold's shoes, remains a potent device for hindering the future development of the political functions of the Secretary-General. The crisis produced by the Soviet attack upon Hammarskjold and upon the institutional position which he developed, like that brought about by American reactions to the personnel situation in Lie's time, has merely subsided without being definitely resolved.

The Soviet-made crisis also shares with the earlier one a significant relevance to the problem of allegiance, despite its more ostensible relationship to the issue of the political role of the Secretary-General. Soviet condemnation of Hammarskjold was grounded upon the allegation that his political functions in the conduct of the Congo operation were being exercised in support of Western interests, and in violation of Soviet interests. The accusation was, in short, that the Secretary-General and the officials whom he had made his principal colleagues gave allegiance to an anti-Soviet coalition; they were not, in this view, genuinely impartial servants of the United Nations. What is important at this point is not the question whether this charge was correct, but the fact that it was made. The Soviet Union purported to have lost confidence in the political neutrality of the Secretary-General. In demanding the abolition of the office in favor of a tripartite leadership group, the USSR did not so much deny the ideal of a Secretary-General dedicated to the international interest, as deny that the ideal had been realized and repudiate the expectation that it could be realized. Khrushchev's proposition that "there are no neutral men" purports not to state a preference but to assert a reality. The scheme for placing frankly acknowledged political spokesmen for blocs at the head of the secretariat was represented as a plan for ending hypocrisy and deception, not for supplanting an operative principle of international allegiance. It was described as a device for equalizing the impact of bloc allegiances upon the functioning of the organization, in reaction to a situation allegedly characterized by the predominance of Western allegiance, masquerading as international loyalty.

As this episode clearly indicates, the problems of the political function and the fundamental allegiance of the secretariat, and particularly of the Secretary-General and those whom he associates with himself in the top ranks, are inextricably interwoven. No major power will acquiesce in the playing of a significant political role by an international official who seems to it to be motivated by loyalty to the interests of an opposing state or bloc. The only sound basis for the performance of such a role is the development of a general conviction that genuine international loyalty is possible, a general recognition that it has in fact been achieved within the secretariat, and a general appreciation of the value to all states, including one's own, of the services which a truly international secretariat is uniquely eligible and equipped to render.

The question of the amount of international statesmanship permitted by the realities of world politics can never be answered precisely or permanently. Generalization about the political potential of international secretariats must be tempered by recognition of the differences between international organizations. Sir Eric Drummond and Albert Thomas were not simply distinguished by different backgrounds and temperaments; they were heads of different organizations. In one of the supreme examples of historical casting, Thomas, the dynamic politician, went to the International Labor Organization, and Drummond, the sober civil servant, to the League. As the latter put it, "It is quite, quite certain that Albert Thomas in my job would have been forced to resign. They wouldn't have stood for it. He would have tried—and failed. The 'Chancellor' wouldn't have been successful." [39] The concept of the permanent staff's leading role in policy determination which has proved acceptable and valuable in the International Bank[40] is not necessarily transferable to such a general political organization as the United Nations.

The Secretary-General of the United Nations has a constitutional license to be as big a man as he can. He has a limited body of precedents to guide him. He has a newly-formulated ideal of international statesmanship to serve as a light unto his feet—or to blind him to the hard realities if he permits it to shine in his eyes. He has the difficult task of wending his way between the folly of attempting too much and the ignominy of risking too little. He has a uniquely challenging position, for as Trygve Lie put it: "the political role of the Secretary-General of the United Nations is something new to the world. The concept of a spokesman for the world interest is in many ways far ahead of our times. . . ." [41]

The unsolved problems of the international secretariat, and the unchecked threats to its integrity, are legion, but it nevertheless represents the most valuable product to date of the historical process of international organization; it is, in the words of Pierre Mendes-France, "that

---

[39] Schwebel, *op. cit.*, p. 3.

[40] See John J. McCloy, "The Lesson of the World Bank," *Foreign Affairs*, July 1949, pp. 559-560.

[41] *Op. cit.*, p. 88.

valuable and fragile nucleus of a united world . . . that valiant group of men and women who are more sensitive than any others to the progress and incidents in relations between nations, and to the successes or failures in international cooperation."[42]

SUGGESTED READINGS

Bailey, Sydney D., *The Secretariat of the United Nations,* New York: Carnegie Endowment for International Peace, 1962.

Foote, Wilder, ed., *Dag Hammarskjold: Servant of Peace,* New York: Harper and Row, 1962.

The International Secretariat of the Future, London: Royal Institute of International Affairs, 1944.

Lash, Joseph P., *Dag Hammarskjold: Custodian of the Brushfire Peace,* Garden City, N. Y.: Doubleday, 1961.

Lie, Trygve, *In the Cause of Peace,* New York: Macmillan, 1954.

Loveday, A., *Reflections on International Administration,* London: Oxford University Press, 1956.

Phelan, E. J., *Yes and Albert Thomas,* New York: Columbia University Press, 1949.

Ranshofen-Wertheimer, Egon F., *The International Secretariat: A Great Experiment in International Administration,* Washington: Carnegie Endowment for International Peace, 1945.

Schwebel, Stephen M., *The Secretary-General of the United Nations,* Cambridge: Harvard University Press, 1952.

[42] *New York Times,* November 23, 1954.

Approaches to Peace Through International Organization

CHAPTER II

Peaceful Settlement of Disputes

THE CAUSES OF WAR AND THE CONDITIONS OF PEACE

International organization is fundamentally, even though not exclusively, a reaction to the problem of war. In truth, it would be necessary even if the possibility of armed hostilities should somehow permanently disappear from the modern international scene; in that unlikely event, international organization might become an even more indispensable part of the equipment of world civilization.

This probability is suggested by the example of the American federal system. The central government of the United States is not maintained today as an antidote to the danger of civil war; the essentiality of its role has increased during the last century despite the transformation of the political situation from one in which civil war was first an imminent possibility and then a grim reality to one in which internecine conflict is almost unthinkable. Indeed, it could be argued that the United States Government has grown in importance *because* of that transformation, which has brought with it an intensification of relationships across state lines which increasingly necessitates central policy-making and administrative services.

The point is that government is required not simply because men are in conflict but also because they are in contact—and the less hostile men are toward each other, the more they elaborate the contacts which require the facilitating functions of government. Hobbesian men need government to suppress antisocial belligerence; Lockean men need government for the less strenuous but equally vital function of regulating and lubricating the relationships which stem from their very sociability. Lockean men require a different sort of government than Hobbesian men, but, in the final analysis, they require more, not less, government.

All this applies to the international realm. Objectively, the need for international organization exists, independently of the problem of war. Nevertheless, the fact remains that the main impetus for international organization has derived from the urge to avoid war, and it is doubtful whether the subjective basis for organizational efforts would exist if the danger of war were eliminated. For all practical purposes, international organization must be looked upon as an expression of the quest for world peace.

Given the antiwar orientation of the movement toward international organization, it is clear that collective approaches to peace must rest upon assumptions concerning the nature and causes of war. The phenomenon of war has been regarded in many different ways. It has been viewed as a salutary exercise, contributing usefully to the development of men and of nations. It has been considered as an inescapable reality, deriving inevitably from the nature of individual and collective man. International organization represents a denial of both these contentions; it assumes that war should be, and can be, prevented. Beyond this, there has been very limited agreement among the makers and supporters of international agencies in the analysis of the problem of war. Various approaches to peace through international organization have been advocated, formulated, and attempted, each of them resting upon a distinctive conception of the nature of war and therefore emphasizing a correspondingly distinctive solution for the problem of war.

The assumptions about war which constitute the theoretical underpinnings of organizational enterprises have not always been clearly articulated or even consciously adopted by those who have acted upon them. International organization is the work of pragmatic statesmen engaged in the experimental pursuit of objectives, not of theorists engaged in the systematic construction of institutions upon philosophical foundations. Nevertheless, the underlying assumptions of international agencies have operative significance, and a sophisticated understanding of these foundation stones is essential to the serious study of the process of international organization.

This and succeeding chapters are devoted to an analysis of the various approaches to peace through international organization which have been given expression in the United Nations system. In each case, we shall expose for critical examination the assumption about the nature of war which provides the theoretical rationale for the particular prescription for avoidance of war, and then relate the therapeutic results to the diagnostic premises.

It will be noted that the contemporary system of international organization represents the adoption of a number of approaches to peace, which derive from different conceptions of the nature and causation of war. However dogmatic and monistic certain thinkers may be in explaining the cause of war and the means to peace, the founding fathers of the United Nations have clearly been prepared to try every device which shows promise of contributing to the conditions of peace, and to reject exclusive reliance upon any single device. Our present institutional structure is analogous to a shotgun rather than a rifle, inasmuch as it reflects distrust of the accuracy of anyone's aim at a solution and preference for releasing a shower of shots in the general direction of the problem; we do not know which approach to peace is valid, so we try them all, hoping that not all the shots will be wasted. In view of the world's lack of an analysis of the problem of war which could give the commendation of scientific certitude to a particular method of solution, this organizational eclecticism, this dedication to randomness, has the virtues of common sense.

However, the United Nations system is not quite so casual about marksmanship as this concept would seem to indicate. Its experimentation with a variety of solutions is not simply a confession of ignorance as to which of them may prove to be the correct answer to the problem of war, but also an indication of a sophisticated hunch that war is a complex phenomenon, produced by multiple causes, and susceptible of eradication only by the simultaneous application of a number of carefully interrelated methods. The world today is not engaged in an undiscriminating search for the certain answer to the problem of war, but in a tentative effort to develop adequately complex means for dealing with that complex problem.

PACIFIC SETTLEMENT AS AN APPROACH TO PEACE

Perhaps the oldest and most ubiquitous of the approaches to peace which have been formulated by thinkers about international relations and injected into the stream of international organization is that of the pacific settlement of disputes. One could go back to the civilization of ancient Greece and find city-states registering agreement that "If there be any dispute . . . whether about boundaries or anything else, the matter shall be judicially decided. But if any city of the allies quarrel with another, they shall appeal to some city which both deem to be impartial." [1] Jump-

[1] J. B. Scott, *Law, the State, and the International Community* (New York: Columbia University Press, 1939), II, 264.

ing to modern Europe, we find the powers assembled at Paris in 1856 expressing the wish that "States, between which any serious misunderstanding may arise, should, before appealing to arms, have recourse, as far as circumstances might allow, to the good offices of a friendly Power." [2] Emphasis upon this approach to peace in contemporary international organizations stems directly from the conclusion of Conventions for the Pacific Settlement of International Disputes at the two Hague Conferences.[3]

In essence, this approach rests upon the assumption that war is a technique for the settlement of the disputes which arise among nations. It is not a crime of national leaders or a disease of international society, but simply a traditional method of resolving the quarrels that inevitably arise in international as in all other societies. However, it has always been an inappropriate method, undistinguished for the moral quality of the solutions which it has produced, and unworthy of the character of man; as Cicero put it, "Since there are two methods of settling a difference, the one by argument, the other by force, and since the former is characteristic of men, the latter of beasts, we should have recourse to the second only when it is not permitted to use the first." [4] In modern times, war has become so costly, so destructive, so imprecise in its impact and unpredictable in its results, that its continued use for the settlement of disputes is insupportable.

In terms of this analysis, the problem is to find, develop, institutionalize, and persuade states to use other methods for the solution of their differences. War can be eliminated only by the provision of a functional equivalent. The task of international organization is to make available a variety of peaceful substitutes for the technique of violence, and to encourage—if not to insist upon—their utilization by the parties to disputes.

This has the apparent virtue of being a "head-on" approach to the problem of war, going directly and immediately to the locus of the problem, but it is marked by the superficiality which is all too frequently characteristic of common-sense attitudes. War occurs when states disagree; it is simply a clumsy and now an intolerably dangerous method of resolving disputes; hence, it must be, and can be, supplanted by superior methods for producing settlements. The adequacy of such a simple analysis is surely open to question.

The pacific settlement approach has been characterized by emphasis upon the problem of discouraging resort to war as a means of solving disputes. It appears that war, even though it has been interpreted in functional terms, has been recognized as a problem in itself; the task is not so

---

[2] Scott, *The Reports to the Hague Conferences of 1899 and 1907*, pp. 112-113.

[3] For the texts, see *ibid.*, pp. 32-42, 292-309.

[4] Cited in Frank M. Russell, *Theories of International Relations* (New York: Appleton-Century-Crofts, 1936), p. 157.

much to settle the quarrel as to prevent the adoption of violent means for its settlement. The pacific settlement physician finds himself engaged as seriously in curing the addiction to a false remedy as in curing the original disease. In dealing with this problem, the pacific settlement approach reveals a series of basic assumptions about the nature of war. These may be described as secondary assumptions, in contradistinction to the primary assumption that war is a means for solving disputes.

In the first place, it is assumed that war is chosen as a settlement device because of the passions that are aroused by disputes. War is a kind of national temper tantrum; in the heat of anger, peoples fail to seek and disdain to use the rational means of solution which are available, and, losing their heads, rush rashly into war.

The obvious solution is to impose delay, to institute a "cooling-off" period, so that tempers may subside and temperate judgment may prevail. This has been a favorite tactic of the champions of peaceful settlement. The Hague Conventions carried the recommendation that states postpone hostilities while disinterested mediation or inquiry by a special commission took place; the network of bilateral conciliation treaties negotiated for the United States by Secretary of State Bryan, beginning in 1913, called for a mandatory delay of one year in initiating war; the drafters of the elaborate peaceful settlement provisions of the League Covenant hoped "to enforce on the parties a delay of some months before any war took place, believing that during that period some pacific solution would be found" [5] and the United Nations Charter similarly demands resort to methods and agencies of peaceful settlement whenever disputes become acute.[6]

In each of these cases, the time gained by the moratorium on violence is supposed to be used in the active pursuit of solutions which will make ultimate resort to force unnecessary. However, pacific settlement theory has always relied heavily upon the supposition that delay will prove a good in itself; aside from what is done with the time, the mere passage of time will have a healing effect, and the important thing is to secure an interval upon almost any pretext. As Leonard Woolf put it, one of the reasons for the peace-keeping utility of an international conference is that

> it prevents excitement by being so intolerably dull. When a score of diplomatic gentlemen have been sitting around a green baize table discussing an international question for a fortnight, they have killed all interest in that question for at least a year. The Algeciras Conference killed the Morocco question in this way. Before it met, Germany and France were boiling with excitement; long before it finished its

---

[5] Lord Robert Cecil, *A Great Experiment*, p. 74.
[6] Article 33.

> work, everyone was so bored with it that it was quite impossible to use Morocco as a *casus belli* for five years. . . .[7]

Senator Vandenberg was somewhat less cynical, but equally confident of the curative value of postponement *per se,* when he asserted that the "cooling-off" process prescribed by the Charter "will temper and discourage impetuous wrath which too often flames out of sudden national hysteria. It allows time for rules of reason to reendow our sanities." [8]

A second assumption underlying pacific settlement doctrine is that war is often caused by ignorance and misunderstanding of the facts involved in an international crisis. Rushing into hostilities is the result of jumping to conclusions—about, for instance, who blew up the battleship *Maine,* or what lay behind an assassination at Sarajevo. The great thing is to bring out the facts, to dispel the fear that breeds in darkness, to eliminate the suspicions born of prejudice, to counteract the falsehoods planted by malevolence and cultivated by chauvinism, and thus to prevent governments from leading—deceptively or innocently—their peoples into war over grievances which seem greater than they really are. In keeping with this belief, the advocates of peaceful settlement, from the first Hague Conference to the present, have set great store by the institution of the impartial commission of inquiry. If the investigators can putter around at some length, so much the better; but they can serve the cause of peace not merely by killing time, but also by allaying the misapprehensions and correcting the misconceptions of the disputants.

Thirdly, it is assumed that war results from international quarrels because the pride of governments and peoples becomes too heavily involved in these situations to permit them to seek a more reasonable and less drastic solution. Once a dispute begins, harsh allegations, bitter denunciations, indignant denials, and defiant challenges become the order of the day, and it becomes difficult to back down, to admit error, or to compromise claims. If traditional international law ascribed to war the legal character of a duel, champions of pacific settlement have attributed to it the psychological character of a duel; war comes because there seems to be no honorable alternative for stubborn and prestige-conscious states.

At this point, pacific settlement steps in with face-saving graces. Appealing at a relatively low level, it offers to inject into the dispute a disinterested party, with whom negotiations may be conducted by states which have become too estranged to negotiate with each other, and to whom concessions can be made which either state would refrain, as a point of honor, from making directly to the other. Pitching its appeal somewhat higher, pacific settlement seeks to establish the proposition that

---

[7] *International Government,* p. 134.

[8] Speech in the Senate, June 29, 1945, *Congressional Record,* Vol. 91, Part 5, p. 6893.

what is dishonorable is resort to an avoidable war. The supreme evidence of national manliness is not readiness to engage in international fisticuffs, but demonstration of the national adulthood which expresses itself in a sense of responsibility to the community's interest in international decorum. Whatever a state gives up in order to avoid war becomes, in these terms, less a concession to the opposing disputant than a contribution to the welfare of the larger community. These two appeals are combined when the intervention of a third party distinguished by the symbols of peculiar respectability is suggested, for instance, that of an arbitral tribunal or a court. The supposition is that while states may take a certain muscular pride in willingness to fight, they may value more highly the moral pride which they can derive from exhibition of devotion to the rule of law. Pacific settlement is heavily committed to the proposition that states need help in getting themselves out of psychological dead-end streets.

A further hypothesis is that states frequently go to war for lack of imagination; blinded by their aroused passions and wounded sensitivities, they are unable to conceive honorable schemes of mutual accommodation and consequently blunder into belligerence in a state of intellectual bankruptcy. Again, the concept of the third party becomes relevant. The function of the outsider is to exercise the creative imagination which is the special gift of the dispassionate observer, bringing to the attention of the emotionally distraught participants the reasonable alternatives to a violent resolution of the dispute. Proposals which would never occur to the disputants may receive their concurrence, especially if sober recognition of the grim consequences of modern war can be induced. As Quincy Wright has said, "In modern civilization war springs from 'emotions devoid of ideas and desires devoid of appraisals.' " [9] It may be the peculiar responsibility of intermediaries to supply the ideas and appraisals that are essential for the preservation of peace.

Finally, the traditional doctrine of pacific settlement has rested heavily upon the proposition that war is a product of the irresponsibility of selfish and cynical national leaders. Kant expressed the belief that autocratic rulers were prone to go to war all too readily, since they stood to reap the gains of war without paying the price; "the ruler . . . does not lose a whit by the war, while he goes on enjoying the delights of his table or sport, or of his pleasure palaces and gala days. He can therefore decide on war for the most trifling reasons, as if it were a kind of pleasure party." [10] This notion has been deeply embedded in the international or-

---

[9] *A Study of War* (Chicago: University of Chicago Press, 1942), II, 1117. Copyright, 1942, by the University of Chicago.

[10] *Perpetual Peace,* translated by M. Campbell Smith and edited by A. Robert Caponigri, "The Little Library of Liberal Arts," Oskar Piest, General Editor (New York: The Liberal Arts Press, 1948), p. 12.

ganizational theory of the twentieth century. Kings, dictators, diplomats, militarists, financiers, and arms manufacturers have shared the opprobrium of the accusation that they are the rascals who lead unwitting peoples to the slaughter for their private ends; their accusers range from Marx to Wilson to the Nye Committee.

The most obvious solution to the problem of war, conceived in these conspiratorial terms, is the one that Kant prescribed and Wilson espoused: let the *people* decide questions of war and peace—i.e., establish democratic systems in every state—and we can rest assured that the potential victims of war will "weigh the matter well, before undertaking such a bad business." [11] Additionally, however, pacific settlement doctrine proposes an international contribution to the solution: let international agencies shine the spotlight of publicity upon disputes, exposing the machinations and deceptions of war-minded leaders, and enabling the democratic forces of the countries concerned—and of the world at large—to see the need and grasp the opportunity for insisting upon decent and rational solutions. According to this conception, war is a phenomenon of the proverbial smoke-filled room, and what is required is the ventilation of disputes, permitting the wholesome, commonsense rationality of public opinion to have its effect. This approach to peace has increasingly dominated the international scene ever since Wilson injected into the League his antipathy for secret diplomacy.

A rather blurred conceptual line separates the problem of pacific settlement from the so-called problem of *peaceful change*. The latter is a somewhat specialized concept, referring to the problem of substituting amicable for forcible methods of resolving disputes which arise out of demands for alteration of the legally established status quo. Roughly, pacific settlement is concerned with disputes *within* the legal order, and peaceful change with disputes *about* the legal order; the former seeks solutions in or out of court, and the latter is more appropriately concerned with decisions in or out of a legislature. These are meaningful differences, in so far as the familiar constitutional distinction between judicial and legislative functions is tenable, but for most practical purposes, pacific settlement and peaceful change may be taken as parts of a single international problem: that of securing the abandonment of force and the substitution of other means for the resolution of all manner of conflicts among nations.

The development of the pacific settlement approach to peace upon the theoretical bases which I have outlined has been, first of all, a process of establishing the fundamental proposition that the international community has a stake in the avoidance of war which justifies it in insisting that states attempt to settle their disputes by peaceful means, and in intruding into embittered situations to promote that ideal. In the Hague

---

[11] *Ibid.*, p. 11.

Convention of 1899 for the Pacific Settlement of International Disputes, the signatory states agreed upon the desirability of attempting pacific settlement, pledged themselves "as far as circumstances allow" to make such efforts, and acknowledged the right of third parties to make friendly interventions for the purpose of offering assistance in reaching nonviolent solutions.[12] The League Covenant went further, binding member states to submit dangerous differences to instrumentalities of pacific settlement, imposing upon them a definite period of abstention from fighting while the quest for solution took place, restricting their right to go to war after the conclusion of efforts at pacification, and formalizing the right of outsiders to invoke community action to forestall the collapse of world peace.[13] In consequence of the general recognition that the Covenant's legal barrier against the violent settlement of disputes was marked by "gaps," the League Assembly adopted in 1924 the Geneva Protocol, which purported to close these breaches and to subject any state guilty of attempting to crash through the wall of pacific settlement to the charge and the penalties of aggression.[14] This project failed for want of ratification, but in 1928 most of the states of the world agreed, in the Pact of Paris, to "condemn recourse to war for the solution of international controversies, and renounce it as an instrument of national policy in their relations with one another," and to restrict their efforts to solve conflicts to "pacific means." [15]

This trend culminated in the United Nations Charter, which commits member states (and purports to obligate all other states, in almost equal degree) to seek peaceful solutions and in any case to abjure coercive solutions of disputes, and authorizes outsiders, ranging from uninvolved states to the Secretary-General, to initiate collective action for encouraging peaceful settlement.[16] It has been firmly established that there are no "private" disputes among nations; international controversies are a concern of the world community, which minds its own proper business when it intervenes in the troubled relations of states to ensure the maintenance of peace.

The development of the pacific settlement approach to peace has been, in the second place, a process of institutionalizing and elaborating the means of promoting the discovery and acceptance of suitable terms of settlement. This has meant the creation of synthetic "third parties," the advance mobilization of "strangers" to whatever disputes might arise for the fulfillment of the community's pacificatory responsibilities, and the evolution of techniques for carrying out those responsibilities.

---

[12] Articles 1-3, 9, 16. For citation of the text, see note 3, preceding.
[13] Articles 10-15.
[14] See the text (especially Article 10) in Russell, *op. cit.*, pp. 588-597.
[15] *Ibid.*, pp. 610-612.
[16] Articles 2, 33-38, 52, 99.

Perhaps the most striking aspect of this evolutionary process has been the large-scale development of multilateral diplomacy. For better or for worse, much of the world's diplomatic business has come to be transacted in drafty assembly halls rather than stuffy consultation chambers, in rooms equipped with loudspeakers rather than soundproofing. This trend, anticipated by the development of the nineteenth-century conference system, has reached its climax in the General Assembly of the United Nations.

In ideal terms, the functions of the multilateral assemblage are to dramatize the concern of the community with the quarrels which arise among its members, to impress upon disputants the gravity of their responsibility for maintaining peace and to enable them to assess the general reaction to the positions which they assume, to permit disinterested states to contribute their ideas for possible solutions, and to initiate and supervise the operation of more specialized procedures appropriate to the needs of parties involved in particular disputes. In short, the big conference is at its best in insisting upon, and providing facilities other than its own platform for promotion of, pacific settlement.

Twentieth-century international organization inherited a textbook list of methods for bringing external assistance to states whose own diplomatic resources were inadequate to compose their disputes. These included such devices as good offices, inquiry, mediation, and conciliation—methods which varied in the degree to which they brought strangers into active participation in the substantive discussion of disputed matters, but which were alike in that they all involved the introduction of third parties for the purpose of promoting the voluntary acceptance of politically evolved terms of settlement.

From 1899 to the present, a major task of the builders of international order has been that of perfecting these political techniques and establishing institutional arrangements for their utilization. The first Hague Conference hardly went beyond the recommendations that contending states welcome such mediatorial assistance as might be proffered by neutral bystanders and that they themselves initiate *ad hoc* commissions of inquiry to facilitate their efforts at diplomatic settlement, although it also defined the general rules for the operation of these pacificatory devices. However, this action stimulated a flurry of bilateral treaties designed to regularize resort to "third-partyism" in resolving controversies, and paved the way for the pacific settlement emphasis of the League Covenant.

The League was deeply committed to the idea that international machinery could and should play a significant role in supplementing the political processes of traditional diplomacy. It had no precise blueprint and evolved no rigid procedure for pushing quarreling states to a settlement, but it operated pragmatically, tailoring its methods to the peculiarities of particular situations, and applying creative imagination to the development of its conciliatory potential. This segment of the League's operations fell primarily within the province of the Council, which proceeded energetically to establish "for the first time in history a regular system of mediation . . . [which] is something organic and fundamentally changes the character of international relations . . . [and which] strikes out a new path toward the attainment of peace, a path which had scarcely been thought of before 1919." [17] The Council evolved a flexible mode of procedure, involving stern insistence upon the suspension of acts and threats of violence, careful avoidance of condemnatory finger-shaking which might disrupt the delicate psychological fabric of conciliatory moods, and judicious interweaving of public exhibitions and private negotiations. It invented an important peace-keeping role for its President, acting in the capacity of guardian of the global interest. It undertook mediatorial functions as a body, or entrusted them to smaller committees or to individual delegates who consented to act as rapporteurs for the Council in dealing with specific cases. It developed to a considerable degree the institution of the special commission, assigned to visit troubled areas in order to supervise adherence to provisional arrangements for the suspension of hostilities and withdrawal of armed forces, to investigate the factual basis of disturbances, to sponsor negotiations between disputants, and to formulate proposals for solutions. On the whole, the Council displayed admirable inventiveness and wisdom in developing the organizational structure and techniques required for pacific settlement.[18]

This evolutionary process has been continued under the auspices of the United Nations. Both the Security Council and the General Assembly have figured prominently in the conciliatory work of the new organization, and the principle of flexibility has received renewed emphasis. Parties to disputes are encouraged, under the Charter, to avail themselves of pacificatory devices of their own choice, and to appeal to the United Nations only after they have exhausted other resources. The organization has adopted the basic premise of the League system, that the primary task is to avert or interrupt the use of force, "preventing an aggravation of the dispute and keeping the contenders apart while the processes of international conciliation are set in motion." [19] It has to a large extent simply adapted to its own requirements the techniques developed by the League, playing down the use of the rapporteur, making increased use of field missions, and giving greater prominence to the full-dress debate in the glare of full-scale publicity. It has supplemented the stock of instrumentalities for promoting pacific settlement by developing a cluster of devices under the heading of the United Nations Presence, all of which involve the

---

[17] T. P. Conwell-Evans, *The League Council in Action* (London: Oxford University Press, 1929), pp. 5-6.

[18] For an excellent analysis of this development, see Conwell-Evans, *op. cit.*

[19] Jiménez de Aréchaga, *Voting and the Handling of Disputes in the Security Council,* p. 117.

physical insertion into troubled areas, for varying periods of time, of one or more persons—ranging from the Secretary-General or representatives designated by him, to groups of diplomatic or military personnel supplied by member states—who symbolize the interest and involvement of the United Nations. The concept of the Presence is notably expressed in the form of the United Nations Mediator or Commissioner—the single individual of high prestige, bearing exclusively international responsibility and carrying the full authority of the United Nations, who performs high-level political and administrative functions on behalf of the organization in the locality where troubled international relations exist. The United Nations has experimented in the combination and coordination of the pacifying efforts of the General Assembly, the Security Council, and the Secretary-General, applied simultaneously to a single conflict. It has gone much further than the League in assuming responsibility for peaceful change, asserting quasi-legislative competence in certain situations where the legal order has manifestly dissolved. The development of the political mechanisms of pacific settlement has been a continuous process for half a century, and it may be expected to extend into the indefinite future.

Modern international organization also received from the past a legacy of judicial techniques for the settlement of international controversies. The ancient practice of arbitration, whereby disputants resort to a panel of judges chosen for the occasion by themselves in order to secure a binding judgment based upon existing law, enjoyed a considerable revival in the nineteenth century. The Hague Conferences achieved the codification and rudimentary institutionalization of this practice, and bequeathed to the League the determination to overcome the obstacles to creation of a genuine international tribunal which would be available for the judicial settlement of disputes.

The League succeeded in equipping the world with its first such tribunal, the Permanent Court of International Justice, which has been continued in the United Nations era under the title of the International Court of Justice. Consequently, states desirous of achieving pacific settlement of disputes, and international agencies desirous of promoting peaceful solutions, have had, for the past generation, the legal methods of arbitration and adjudication as available alternatives to political techniques. The political organs of the League and the United Nations have enjoyed the competence to recommend that states submit their differences for judicial settlement, and to a limited degree to obtain judicial advice concerning their own handling of disputes. The Court, in accordance with its Statute, has conscientiously respected the principle that it can consider contentious cases only if both parties have clearly signified their assent, either *ad hoc* or by advance acceptance of conditional compulsory jurisdiction under the Optional Clause of Article 36 of the Statute, and it has been wary of permitting political organs to tempt it to evade that principle by rendering advisory opinions pertaining to contentious cases without the consent of the parties.[20] Nevertheless, the availability of judicial modes of settlement has contributed significantly to the flexibility of procedure which has been a leading characteristic of the pacific settlement systems of the League and the United Nations.

THE RESULTS OF PACIFIC SETTLEMENT DEVICES

It is very difficult to render confident evaluations of the international services rendered by the pacific settlement agencies of the League and the United Nations. The problem is complicated by the relevance of a whole series of unanswerable questions of the historical "what if" variety. No one can say what global catastrophes might have occurred if certain controversies had not been successfully dealt with, or what easy solutions might have been reached even if elaborately institutionalized procedures had not been available.

It is even more difficult to secure fair public appraisal of the record of pacific settlement agencies. We have our historical accounts of the wars that have taken place, but the list of wars that have not occurred is not equally prominent in the public intellectual domain, just as we see headlines about actual murders but are not informed about the murders that do not happen. Everyone knows that the League failed to settle several disputes that paved the way for World War II, but who remembers that "During the first ten years of its life the Council . . . successfully dealt with seventeen cases likely to lead to a rupture, and brought to an immediate end hostilities which had broken out on seven or eight occasions between Members of the League"? [21] There is general awareness of the failures of the United Nations, but less consciousness of its pacificatory successes, and still less recognition of the possibility that it has prevented some controversies from growing big enough to bring it either blame for failing to solve them or credit for success in so doing.

A major limiting factor of the organized pacific settlement system is the essential principle of voluntarism regarding its utilization. The legal starting point is the basic proposition that "no State can, without its con-

---

[20] The PCIJ refused to give its advice in the Eastern Carelia Case (1923), on the ground that the Soviet Union, an interested party, objected to its jurisdiction. (Hudson, *World Court Reports,* I, 190-206.) The ICJ declined to follow this precedent in 1950, when it consented to render an opinion concerning Interpretation of Peace Treaties with Bulgaria, Hungary and Romania, despite the objections of those three states. (*American Journal of International Law,* October 1950, pp. 742-752.) Nevertheless, evidence that the Court is still quite cautious about assuming jurisdiction in the absence of definite consent of the parties is found in its opinions on the Anglo-Iranian Oil Co. Case (Jurisdiction) of 1952 (*ibid.,* October 1952, pp. 737-751), and the Case of the Monetary Gold Removed from Rome in 1943 (Preliminary Question), decided in 1954 (*ibid.,* October 1954, pp. 649-655).

[21] Conwell-Evans, *op. cit.,* p. 254.

sent, be compelled to submit its disputes either to mediation or to arbitration, or to any other kind of pacific settlement." [22] Nevertheless, under the Covenant and the Charter, most states have gone far toward formal acceptance of restrictions upon their sovereign freedom to resort to war and to reject alternative methods of achieving solutions to controversies, and the responsible international agencies have in considerable degree exploited their opportunities for insisting upon universal acceptance of the principle that orderly procedures should be invoked for the preservation of peaceful relations.

It is notable that in the Palestine Case, the General Assembly attempted to establish the legal finality of its decision regarding the terms of settlement, involving the partition of the disputed area; it is equally notable that this legislative pretension was flouted by the states immediately concerned, and that the Security Council, under the influence of the United States, declined to assert the view that it was competent to give executive backing to the Assembly's claim.[23] This episode illustrates one facet of the basic legal situation, which is, in general terms, a situation characterized by the obligation of states to try methods of pacific settlement, and the freedom of states to choose which methods they shall try, to avoid the judicial methods which would produce legally obligatory decisions, and to reject the recommendations for settlement which may be produced by political agencies. Disputants are bound to honor the decisions of arbitrators or the World Court, but free to prevent the rendering of those decisions; they are free to repudiate the proposals of other pacific settlement agencies, but bound to permit the development of those proposals.

The basic political situation is, in some respects, more favorable to pacific settlement. The rise of international organization, occurring in conjunction with increasing recognition of the grave consequences of war, has contributed to the establishment of the normative principle that international violence must be deferred until every conceivable alternative possibility has been exhausted. As is often the case in human affairs, this normative principle is largely derived from and dependent upon prudential considerations. The function of the United Nations has been less to provide the basis for reluctance to engage in violence than to capitalize upon the caution bred by the new military technology and the international power configuration. The organization gives legal and ideological expression to the growing sense of the irrationality of war as an instrument of national policy. Enormous pressures to avoid resort to arms may

---

[22] Reply of the PCIJ to request for advisory opinion on Status of Eastern Carelia, July 23, 1923, Hudson, *op. cit.*, I, 204.

[23] See L. Larry Leonard, "The United Nations and Palestine," *International Conciliation*, No. 454, October 1949, pp. 654-661; Lie, *In the Cause of Peace*, pp. 164-168.

be mobilized on occasion, and it has become a normal expectation of international life that collective agencies will step into a critical situation with preventive measures and insistent proposals for nonviolent solutions. War is still a last resort and ultimate possibility, but the emphasis has shifted to the adjectives, "last" and "ultimate"; it is no longer generally accepted as a proper first resort and routine instrument for resolution of differences.

Despite all this, the nonutilization of agencies of pacific settlement has remained a troublesome problem. Advocates of the exclusive and invariable use of judicial means of settlement have been persistently disappointed. The movement for compulsory arbitration which arose late in the nineteenth century was transformed after the First World War into a drive to establish the compulsory jurisdiction of the World Court, but the latter version has been hardly more successful than the former. The Court has gained a considerable area of guaranteed jurisdiction through ratifications of the Optional Clause and the insertion of appropriate provisions in multilateral treaties, and it has succeeded in resolving a respectable number of contentious cases, but it has not become a major instrument in the management of the conflicting relationships of the family of nations. Its primary contribution has been in developing the principles of international law, not in solving disputes or creating a reliable expectation among states that orderly judicial processes will routinely uphold the rule of law in the international community. Refusal of states to use the Court is still a major barrier to its full usefulness.

Thinkers who stress the vital importance of peaceful change in international relations have similarly been frustrated. The limited potential of the League as an instrument of peaceful change under Article 19 of the Covenant was never realized. The General Assembly of the United Nations, which was endowed with a vague competence to concern itself with issues of peaceful change by Article 14 of the Charter, has been somewhat more active in this field. It legislated a new status for the former colonies of Italy, on the basis of exceptional authority conferred upon it by the great powers,[24] and it exercised something imperfectly resembling legislative authority in the Palestine Case, as a result of Britain's abdication of responsibility in its favor, but it has encountered serious opposition to its pretension to serve more generally as a global parliamentary body for deciding upon changes in the legal status quo, particularly in regard to the liquidation of colonial situations. Organs of the United Nations, including the Assembly, have been significantly involved in the promotion of the process of decolonization, and have doubtless contributed to the relative orderliness of that process, even though the organization has not formally presided over this most drastic revision of the old inter-

---

[24] See Benjamin Rivlin, *Italian Colonies* (New York: Carnegie Endowment for International Peace, 1950).

national order.[25] Adequate institutional means exist for the consideration of demands for basic legal alterations, but states have neither accepted the legal duty nor developed the political disposition to utilize international agencies as the regular decision-makers in such cases.

The road to war is paved with the documentary good intentions of states, which have for a half-century exhibited far greater enthusiasm for formulating treaties and designing institutions of pacific settlement than for utilizing the arrangements thus created. A number of commentators have recently pointed with some cynicism to such facts as the virtually complete nonutilization of the elaborate machinery for arbitration and conciliation created by the United States in almost a hundred treaties during the first three decades of this century.[26] While these critics customarily overlook the significant fact that "Since 1920 approximately 50,000 cases have been decided by . . . [arbitration] tribunals under agreements between many nations," [27] they nevertheless have a valid point: the attempted institutionalization of pacific settlement—and, more generally, the process of international organization—have involved an inordinate amount of wasted effort and stimulated an excessive amount of international self-congratulation over paper achievements which were destined never to be translated into reality.

To some extent, this tendency has affected the two major world organizations created in the first half of the twentieth century. For various reasons, including the failure to achieve the universal membership of the great powers and the widespread skepticism of diplomats and military leaders concerning newfangled international processes, the League did not function consistently as the focal point of global diplomacy which it was intended to be. Similarly, the United Nations has often been relegated to the periphery of world affairs, as nations, uttering pious declarations about the organization's being the very foundation of their foreign policies, have resorted to other agencies, to *ad hoc* international conferences, and to traditional diplomatic methods for the solution of great political issues.

It is not easy to estimate the real significance of the problem of "bypassing" as it affects the United Nations. We hear a great deal of indignant criticism from persons who are wedded to the doctrinaire view that nothing useful ought to be done unless it can be done through the United Nations. This position fails to take into account the fact that the Charter deliberately encourages efforts to settle disputes outside the organization, and contemplates not a centralized system of pacific settlement but a central agency for upholding the principle of pacific settlement and at-

---

[25] Harold K. Jacobson, "The United Nations and Colonialism: A Tentative Appraisal," *International Organization,* Winter 1962, pp. 37-56.

[26] See George F. Kennan, *Realities of American Foreign Policy* (Princeton: Princeton University Press, 1954), pp. 18-19.

[27] Cited in a note by Willard B. Cowles, *American Journal of International Law,* July 1954, p. 460.

tempting to apply that principle when other instrumentalities have proven inadequate for the job. Indeed, the protest has been made more than once in the United Nations that states were guilty of burdening the organization prematurely with issues that should have been subjected first to treatment by other means, and it is at least arguable that the United Nations has been damaged less by arbitrary by-passing than by excessive buck-passing. Governments tend to call upon the United Nations to deal with situations in which they anticipate political disadvantage equally from meeting the requirements of achieving peaceful settlement and from failing to achieve such settlement. The reference to the United Nations of the problem of American military prisoners detained in Red China, at the end of 1954, is perhaps a case in point; the United Nations is in constant peril of being used as a dumping ground for such hot political potatoes. In many cases, the United Nations must breathe an institutional sigh of relief and utter a fervent "more power to them" when statesmen decide to undertake the settlement of disputes outside its arena.

If Dag Hammarskjold's conduct as Secretary-General eventually aroused the implacable animosity of the Soviet Union, this was in part at least the result of the tendency of states to burden him with political responsibilities which they should have carried themselves, and to impose upon him the task of making delicate decisions without the guidance which they should have provided. The political usefulness of the Secretary-General is constantly imperiled by the political vulnerability which he acquires if states shift their responsibilities to him; after all, it is the function of political leaders to be expendable.

However, this does not dispose of the problem of by-passing. It is true that there is great merit in the pragmatic doctrine that disputes should be handled wherever they can best be settled, and that it is unfortunate to force the United Nations to accept controversies less to settle them than to assume the blame for possible failure to settle them, but it is also true that neither the progressive development of international organization nor the cause of world peace is promoted by the arbitrary withholding from the United Nations of the opportunity to deal with the disputes which most urgently require treatment by the techniques of pacific settlement. The United Nations has no dearth of conciliatory work to do, but it must share the anxiety of its institutional ancestors that states will not, in good faith, resort to it for the full exploitation of the possibilities of pacific settlement of the disputes that really count.

If the usefulness of international mediatorial agencies depends upon the disposition of states to use them, it depends also upon their willingness to be used. A persistent deficiency of such agencies has been their reluctance to be concerned, especially in cases involving demands for peaceful change. At least since 1871, when Russia was rewarded for kicking over the traces fastened upon it by the Paris Treaty of 1856 by being relieved of the traces,[28] the object lesson has been clear: states are likely to get what they want if they raise a sufficient fuss, and unlikely to get it if they fail to do so. On the whole, this rule applies today. Under the Charter, the political agencies of the United Nations can work up constitutionally legitimate excitement only about situations which are deemed to involve a genuine threat to the peace.[29]

Egypt learned this lesson the hard way in the United Nations. Bringing its claim for revision of treaty relations with Britain to the Security Council in 1947, it encountered the British argument that the Council should take no action, on the ground that the dispute did not endanger the peace.[30] While the Council did not formally accept the British contention, it failed to adopt any resolution regarding the case, and kept the Egyptian complaint as an inactive item on its agenda. It required a proper rebellion by Egypt against the treaties concerning Suez and the Sudan in 1951 to secure serious consideration of its demands by Britain, and ultimately to precipitate agreement upon new arrangements.

This problem was again illustrated in the debate concerning Tunisia and Morocco in the 1953 session of the General Assembly. The Syrian representative, protesting against the tendency of the Assembly to defer action in these cases, declared that "Popular action in those countries was largely peaceful up to now. Evidently only communism and violence can attract the attention of the powerful in council and war." [31] A French spokesman, arguing the other side of the case, asserted: "More and more numerous among you are those who understand that recourse to violence becomes a form of blackmail to obtain the ear of our Assembly." [32]

The dilemma is obvious: if dissatisfied states or peoples behave themselves, their demands are not considered urgent enough to deserve attention; if they do not, they are accused of blackmail, of trying to shoot their way onto the agenda—whereas, in fact, they are taking what seems to be the only course that leads to serious consideration of their grievances. To insist upon rebelliousness as a prerequisite for satisfaction of demands is a poor way to bring up children or to run a peaceful change system; the United Nations would do well to make itself useful, as a matter of principle, to disgruntled states which do *not* press their demands in such fashion as to engender a threat to the peace.

When everything has been said about the nonutilization of pacific settlement agencies, the fact remains that since 1920 the world has been

---

[28] Cf. P. E. Corbett, *Law and Society in the Relations of States* (New York: Harcourt, Brace, 1951), pp. 83-84.

[29] See Articles 1, 11, 33-38.

[30] See Security Council: Official Records, 2nd Year, No. 70, p. 1768; No. 73, pp. 1873-1874; No. 75, p. 1954.

[31] *United Nations Bulletin,* October 15, 1953, p. 347.

[32] *Ibid.*, p. 349.

equipped with general political organizations which have been put to constant use and have achieved considerable success in the field of pacific settlement. However, the record indicates that the concept of success in pacific settlement must be interpreted in relative terms.

The United Nations has clearly contributed little to establishing the sanctity of the principle of judicial decision. Its political organs have been little inclined to emphasize the legal approach to accommodation, a tendency which I think is sound even though it may not have been motivated by the right reasons. In at least one contentious case, the World Court has made it clear that judicial settlement may be virtually useless because of deficiencies in the law which the Court must apply. Ruling on the Asylum Case involving Colombia and Peru, the tribunal could do little more than state the indecisive conclusions dictated by the relevant international law, and advise the parties that they must look to political processes for a means of escape from the impasse in which they found themselves.[33] More generally, the judicial approach is limited by the fact that, given the fundamental nature of the major disputes that arise in international relations, a judgment does not constitute a settlement. One can admit that the much-disputed line between legal and political questions is purely a subjective phenomenon of the minds and wills of the disputants, but the conclusion still emerges that many issues will be as far from settlement after a judge has said all that a judge can properly say as they were before such pronouncement. Indeed, the authoritative statement of legal rights and wrongs may even impede settlement, by encouraging legally self-righteous rigidity on one side in a controversy which can be settled only by political compromise. The United Nations may not have achieved the ideal balance between legal and political approaches to pacific settlement, but it has been on sound ground in rejecting primary reliance upon the device of adjudication.

Pacific settlement must be judged in qualitative terms. In the final analysis, the value of this approach to peace will depend upon what kind of solutions, rather than how many solutions, it produces. This insight is one of the strong points of the champions of judicial settlement, whose insistence upon a major role for judges is symbolic of concern for the element of justice in international relations. But justice is not the sole value which deserves attention, nor is it exclusively the product of jurists whose professional function is to uphold international legal rules which legitimize alike the just and the unjust aspects of the status quo. The rule of law guarantees justice only if the law incorporates justice, which is all too often not the case in the international sphere. Hence, it is conceivable that the ideals of fairness and decency may be better served by creative

[33] For the excerpted text of this judgment, see *American Journal of International Law*, January 1951, pp. 179-198, and October 1951, pp. 781-788.

political processes than by processes which, in so far as they are genuinely judicial, involve essentially the restatement of established legal rights and duties.

The settlements fostered by the political organs of the United Nations are subject to evaluation not only in terms of their conformity with abstract justice—which is in itself an extraordinarily difficult concept to apply in a world characterized by a minimum of moral consensus and a maximum of situational complexity—but also in terms of their clarity, their prospects for permanence, their political realism, and their basic wisdom. The standing temptations of the United Nations are to prefer any solution to no solution, to confuse a vague verbal formulation which is acceptable only because of its ambiguities with a genuine settlement, and to lend itself to the manipulation of voting blocs whose resolution-passing power bears little relation to the realities of world politics. If there is danger that the organization will sponsor the surrender of the demands of the weak to the interests of the strong, and the forfeiture of justice to order, there is equal danger that it may incur responsibility for settlements which gratify the ideological passions of massive voting blocs but offend against the canons of responsible statesmanship.

The area of pacific settlement offers an ideal proving ground for the general proposition that there is no adequate substitute, whether in legal codes or organizational mechanics, for wise and perceptive statesmanship—and that international organization can only facilitate, not guarantee, the development and application of the kind of political wisdom and decency that achieves the best possible balance between justice and order, power and aspiration, ideal and reality.

Some of the greatest triumphs of United Nations processes are best described as instances of not-quite-pacific settlement and pacific non-settlement.

In a number of cases, including those involving Greece, Indonesia, Palestine, and Kashmir, the world organization was confronted with outbreaks of belligerence rather than mere disputes, and its most urgent preoccupation and greatest ultimate contribution was to bring pressure for the suspension and limitation of hostilities. The handling of these cases has generally been assigned to the credit side of international organization's ledger, but it should be emphasized that the results were "pacific" only in the relative sense; thanks in an uncertain but undeniably significant degree to the intervention of United Nations agencies, violence was briefer, less intensive, and less contagious than might have been the case. In an inflammable world, it is no mean achievement of international organization to serve as a candle snuffer so as to minimize the necessity for relying upon an unreliable fire department.

"Settlement," like "pacific," is a relative term. In some cases, the realistic ideal may be not to achieve the permanent settlement of a dispute, but to persuade the parties to settle down permanently with the dispute. The agendas of the Security Council and the General Assembly are liberally sprinkled with items that are beginning to seem like permanent fixtures, quarrels which the United Nations has managed to subject to peaceful perpetuation rather than peaceful settlement. This is not a cynical comment; many of life's problems are meant to be lived with rather than solved, and the urge to have a showdown, to settle the matter one way or the other, is often an unwise impulse in both personal and international affairs.

The United Nations has operated on the assumption that it is useful to keep currently insoluble problems in the public international eye, attempting to extend indefinitely the validity of provisional pacificatory measures, maintaining surveillance to detect and offset any tendency toward disintegration of tentative arrangements, and recurrently testing the possibilities of moving on to definitive settlement. One of the most valuable techniques which the organization has stumbled upon is that of leaving commissions of investigation, conciliation, and supervision hanging on indefinitely in the field, accomplishing little except for symbolizing the determination of the United Nations that the peace must not be broken, standing ready to inform the organization of changes in the situation, and being available to assist the parties if a conciliatory mood should develop. Kashmir and Palestine are classic examples of the application of the philosophy expressed by Henry Cabot Lodge, Jr., in these terms:

> I see some things that you cannot solve, now. Maybe in 10 years you can, but you can't do it now, and the best thing you can do is to sort of spin it out and drag it along and temporize and pettifog, and that way they don't shoot each other, and that is that much clear gain.[34]

This practice raises some interesting questions regarding the problem of *timing* in the tactics of pacific settlement. The old assumption that the enforced postponement of a showdown is in itself conducive to pacific settlement has been subjected to the critical observation that heating up is a more likely result than cooling off during such an interval.[35] Moreover, there is a cogent argument to the effect that the longer a dispute is permitted to drag on in public, the more rigid and unyielding the positions of the parties become, so that the prospects of reasonable compromise progressively diminish; in short, passions move toward the boiling point while positions move toward the freezing point. This assault upon one of the basic positions of the traditional doctrine of pacific settlement is irresistible, and yet it cannot be denied that some disputes, if properly con-

---

[34] *Charter Review Hearing,* Part 1, p. 59.

[35] See Elmore Jackson, *Meeting of Minds* (New York: McGraw-Hill, 1952), pp. 162-164.

trolled over a period of time, ultimately wither into insignificance or become ripe for settlement. This point has been borne out in postwar international relations by deferred solutions of such matters as the Trieste dispute, the Anglo-Iranian Oil case, the question of an Austrian peace treaty, and the West Irian issue, and it may yet prove that the solvent of time rather than the solutions concocted by statesmen will dispose of such issues as those which have long persisted in regard to Kashmir, Palestine, China, and Germany.

It is probable that there are two periods of golden opportunity for composing an international dispute: the period of incipiency, before the formulation of positions which it would be embarrassing to abandon and the exchange of insults which it would be difficult to expunge; and the period of maturity, after the conflict has become boring rather than adventurous, people have almost forgotten why they were so excited, and awareness of the inconveniences and dangers of perpetual discord has set in. The capacity of the United Nations to display sophistication in the matter of mediatorial timing is limited by the fact that it is unlikely to receive disputes until the former period has already passed. The Charter's emphases upon the criterion of the dangerousness of disputes and the desirability of exhausting alternative means of solution before resorting to the United Nations contribute to the probability that the organization will lose the chance to nip controversies in the bud. In these circumstances, the nursing of disputes to the stage of maturity may well become a specialty of the United Nations as a pacific settlement agency.[36]

The record of the United Nations in this field includes some instances of the exacerbation of disputes and of failure to achieve settlements in cases where a happier result might reasonably have been expected. It is doubtful that the ideal development of pacific settlement techniques has been achieved.

The technical deficiencies of United Nations pacificatory action are intimately related to the political trends which dominate the organization. Its inadequacies may be in some degree traceable to its politically determined deviations from the norm of universality; certainly, it has a better chance to exert pacific influence upon members than upon outside states. The limited applicability of the great power veto to pacific settlement action in the Security Council is something of a handicap, although the transferability of problems to the Assembly and the inherent requirement of consent of the parties for successful pacific settlement suggest that the importance of the veto in this respect is not overwhelming. What damages the Security Council is not so much the technical fact of the veto as the political fact that its major members are so deeply involved in conflict that they transform the Council from an organ of conciliation into an

[36] *Ibid.*, pp. 137, 140.

arena for their own mutual antagonisms. All too often, Security Council consideration of a case

> develops into an argument between the members of the Council and the argument is conducted in a way that gives more attention to the differences between members of the Council than to the differences between the parties to the dispute. In every case up to date the Council discussion has eventually reached a point where there is little hope of composing the dispute or adjusting the situation without first composing the differences of Council members.[37]

A major difficulty in the General Assembly has been the tendency of governments to insist upon using the committees of the whole and the plenary body for full-scale public debate and formal voting upon international disputes. This is virtually equivalent to saying that they reject the whole idea of pacific settlement, for a massive international conference is about as inappropriate a place and a general counting of votes as unpromising a method of achieving pacific settlement as could be devised. In so far as states have renounced the concept of the Assembly as a creator and sponsor of specialized bodies and intimate procedures for mediation, and forced it into the role of loud-speaker for their contentions and registrar of their political victories, they have undermined its usefulness as an instrument of pacific settlement. To a very large extent, the Assembly has become a battlefield rather than a peace conference.

This tendency is well illustrated by the case of India's dispute with South Africa over treatment of the Indian minority in the latter country. It has become a hardy perennial of the Assembly's agenda, and the passing years have brought it no nearer to solution. At best, it has been overshadowed by broader controversies regarding the racial policies of South Africa. The record in this case is dominated by the fact that India brought its problem to the United Nations not to achieve a settlement but to score a victory; it invoked not the conciliatory skill of the organization but its denunciatory capacity.[38]

The problem of collective accusation, of international finger-shaking, is a very serious one for the business of pacific settlement. There are no doubt occasions when condemnation of guilty parties by the United Nations is morally justified, and when it may serve a useful purpose; but it is doubtful if such action can ordinarily serve the purpose of pacific settlement. Indeed, most states recognize this fact except when they are obsessed with the hope of securing political triumphs in cases involving themselves. The same Indian Government demanded that the United Na-

---

[37] Paul Hasluck, *Workshop of Security* (Melbourne, Australia: F. W. Cheshire, 1948), p. 94.

[38] Inis L. Claude, Jr., *National Minorities: An International Problem* (Cambridge: Harvard University Press, 1955), pp. 195-201.

tions condemn South Africa in the case just cited and Pakistan in the Kashmir case, and deplored the stigmatization of Red China as an aggressor in Korea on the ground that this action would impede the achievement of pacific settlement; the same American Government demanded the condemnation of Red China and opposed the assignment of guilt in the Kashmir case on the ground that this action might prejudice the possibility of pacific settlement. The issue poses a real dilemma for the United Nations: how to retain its capacity as an instrument of pacific settlement, without sacrificing its capacity for distinguishing between the more and less guilty parties in the troubled situations with which it deals.

The problem of publicity is an equally delicate one for present-day agencies of peaceful accommodation. In contrast to the traditional assumption that the opening of diplomatic windows would admit the moderating breezes of popular rationality, decency, and peace-mindedness, there is considerable evidence that the publicization of diplomacy has the effect of tempting—or forcing—negotiators to make angry speeches rather than to negotiate. The era of secret diplomacy had its seamy side, but the contemporary revolt against open diplomacy represents less the nostalgia of cynical diplomats for the days of nefarious scheming than the wistfulness of earnest statesmen for an opportunity to seek compromises without exciting clamorous demands to force surrenders instead. As Quincy Wright has written:

> Parliaments are usually more nationalistic and belligerent than executives, and people than parliaments, because they are less aware of the risks. Although the people want peace, that want is abstract and less influential than their insistence that the nation shall be recognized, secure, and victorious.[39]

Given this kind of situation, the function of pacific settlement agencies is not so much to let the people get at the diplomats as to protect the diplomats from the people. This may be done by providing a cozy nook for negotiation, sheltered from the gusts of popular passion, and by providing mediators to shoulder the responsibility for insisting upon compromises which national representatives could hardly risk making on their own initiative.[40]

The management of international affairs in the mid-twentieth century requires both intimate diplomacy and the public processes of multilateral debate, and the United Nations provides opportunities for both kinds of activity. If the world organization tends to fail in striking the balance between privacy and publicity which would be most conducive to

---

[39] *Problems of Stability and Progress in International Relations.*

[40] Cf. Georges Kaeckenbeeck, *The International Experiment of Upper Silesia* (London: Oxford University Press, 1942), pp. 358, 526-527.

successful promotion of pacific settlement, this results from the fact that the choice is controlled by national statesmen intent upon gaining political victories for their countries, rather than international statesmen dedicated to the fullest exploitation of the pacifying possibilites offered by international organization.

However, when all is said and done, the crucial limitation of pacific settlement as an approach to peace is discoverable in the inadequacy and inaccuracy of its original assumptions. War is not simply a dispute-settling mechanism adopted because angry men are too excited and proud to seek another way out, or because scheming militarists monopolize the decision-making process, or because the techniques of the international mediation service are insufficiently developed. The basic analysis of war which I described at the beginning of this chapter is too simple, and the therapeutic doctrines of pacific settlement rely upon excessively rationalistic assumptions concerning the nature of man as a member of a multistate society.

The hard fact of international relations is that "disputes are not always raised for the sole purpose of being settled."[41] The kind of war which challenges most seriously the survival instinct of modern man is not the war which occurs in default of the successful application of skilled techniques of pacific settlement, but the war which represents a deliberate political design, a calculated assault upon the foundations of the existing international order. The issue between those who adopt and those who oppose such plans is not susceptible of formulation in the terms of disputes which can be submitted to peaceful resolution. Their disputes are minor symptoms of a fundamental hostility which is not definable as the sum of the disputes or removable by the solution of the disputes.

The experience of the great international organizations of this century does not reveal the incapacity of collective agencies for the settlement of disputes, but rather the inadequacy of the settlement of disputes as a means to world peace. The crucial antagonisms which brought about World War II and those which threaten the renewed disruption of world order were not and are not matters capable of being dealt with primarily by a transfusion of calm rationality, or by injection of level-headedness and deliberateness into the situation; they were and are eruptions of the deep-seated malignancy of the human situation, outcroppings of forces, manifestations of drives, and symptoms of irrationalities of power politics which are essentially beyond the range of pacific settlement techniques. The lesson of the twentieth century is not so much that the world needs better arrangements and devices for pacific settlement, but that pacific settlement—however well institutionalized—is not a sufficient remedy for what ails the modern world.

This analysis leaves much useful work to be done by pacific settle-

---

[41] *Ibid.*, p. 535.

ment agencies. We need, and we have largely achieved, the development of instrumentalities capable of insisting upon and assisting in the solution of controversies which threaten to produce unnecessary, unwilled, and essentially avoidable wars. In the thermonuclear age, the danger of an inadvertent drift or an irrational plunge into total war has appeared in an unprecedentedly critical form, and we have no assurance that it can or will be wholly eliminated. Nevertheless, the point remains that international organization has produced a variety of devices available for pacificatory use, and is capable of producing new mechanisms more explicitly designed to meet the requirements of the changing technological situation. In so far as the avoidance of unwilled war is dependent upon the availability, actual or potential, of pacific settlement agencies, the problem has been essentially solved. However, it is necessary to recognize the limitations of this approach; for dealing with the gravest threats to world peace and order, "chairs and tables are not enough," [42] nor are Assembly debates, Security Council resolutions, rapporteurs, commissions of investigation and conciliation, or United Nations mediators.

SUGGESTED READINGS

Bloomfield, Lincoln P., *Evolution or Revolution: The United Nations and the Problem of Peaceful Territorial Change,* Cambridge: Harvard University Press, 1957.

Bloomfield, Lincoln P., "Law, Politics and International Disputes," *International Conciliation,* No. 516, January 1958.

Conwell-Evans, T. P., *The League Council in Action,* London: Oxford University Press, 1929.

Garcia-Granados, Jorge, *The Birth of Israel,* New York: Knopf, 1949.

Gordenker, Leon, *The United Nations and the Peaceful Unification of Korea: The Politics of Field Operations, 1947-1950,* The Hague: Nijhoff, 1959.

Jackson, Elmore, *Meeting of Minds,* New York: McGraw-Hill, 1952.

Lissitzyn, Oliver J., *The International Court of Justice,* New York: Carnegie Endowment for International Peace, 1951.

Stone, Julius, "The International Court and World Crisis," *International Conciliation,* No. 536, January 1962.

Taylor, Alastair M., *Indonesian Independence and the United Nations,* Ithaca: Cornell University Press, 1960.

[42] Zimmern, *The League of Nations and the Rule of Law,* p. 77.

CHAPTER

12

Collective Security as an Approach to Peace

If the movement for international organization in the twentieth century can be said to have a preoccupation, a dominant purpose, a supreme ideal, it is clear that the achievement of collective security answers that description. Other objectives have figured prominently in the development of international organization, but the hope of establishing a successful collective security system has been the primary motivating force behind the organizational enterprises of our time. *Security* represents the end; *collective* defines the nature of the means; *system* denotes the institutional component of the effort to make the means serve the end. It is doubtful whether international organization can properly be evaluated exclusively in terms of its success or failure in realizing this ideal, but it is certain that this criterion applies in judging the extent to which the aspirations of its creative spirits have been satisfied.

While collective security has been the central concern of the builders of international agencies, it has not been regarded as an exclusivistic approach to peace. It has, for instance, been intimately related to pacific settlement. Collective security is necessary because pacific settlement cannot always succeed; it is feasible, if at all, only because pacific settlement succeeds most of the time; and its existence increases the probability that pacific settlement will succeed more of the time. Hence, the creators of the League and the United Nations have sought to combine the techniques of moral inducement and coercive threat for the preservation of peace.

Collective security has generally been regarded as a halfway house between the terminal points of international anarchy and world government. Given the assumption that the former has become intolerable and the latter remains, at least for the foreseeable future, unattainable, collective security is conceived as an alternative, far enough from anarchy to be useful and far enough from world government to be feasible. Advocates of collective security have differed as to whether it should be envisaged as a temporary expedient, contributing to the ultimate possibility of world government, or a permanent solution to the problem of order, eliminating the ultimate necessity of world government. But, regardless of their differing expectations concerning the probability that collective security will yield ideal results, they have been united in the belief that its requirements are less revolutionary than those posed by world government, and that it is therefore within the realm of possibility in an age dominated by the basic values of a multistate system.

It should be noted in the beginning that collective security is a specialized concept, a technical term in the vocabulary of international relations. Its definition may be approached by the process of elimination: it represents the means for achieving national security and world order which remain when security through isolation is discarded as an anachronism, security through self-help is abandoned as a practical impossibility, security through alliance is renounced as a snare and a delusion, and security through world government is brushed aside as a dream irrelevant to reality. The concept of collective security may be stated in deceptively simple terms: it is the principle that, in the relations of states, everyone is his brother's keeper; it is an international translation of the slogan, "one for all and all for one";[1] it is the proposition that aggressive and unlawful use of force by any nation against any nation will be met by the combined force of all other nations.

Emphasis upon the specific character of collective security is particularly essential because in recent years the term has been so loosely used that it has virtually lost its original meaning. The kind of semantic debasement which collective security has undergone cannot be prevented, and it may be argued that it should not be resented, in accordance with the precept of tolerance that every man has as good a right as any other to use whatever words he pleases to express whatever meaning he wants to convey. Yet, just as a considerable medical literature would be invalidated if doctors fell into the habit of using the word "penicillin" for

[1] Hans J. Morgenthau, *Politics Among Nations* (1st ed.; New York: Knopf, 1949), p. 331.

what has previously been called "insulin," a substantial body of international thought is confused by the tendency to use "collective security" to refer to concepts alien to its original meaning.

The term, collective security, is now being generally applied to arrangements of virtually any sort which involve the probability of joint military action in a crisis by two or more states. Thus, it has come to be a synonym, used for euphemistic purposes, for the policy of creating alliances to function in a balance of power system. For instance, an editorial in the *New York Times* interpreted the development of NATO as both a necessary return to the system of balance of power and a symbolic recognition by Western nations "that their only salvation lies in standing together in a system of collective security." [2] Senator McMahon defined collective security as "the attempt to weld together a military alliance to keep the peace such as we have attempted to do in the North Atlantic Pact," [3] and General Omar Bradley described that treaty as "our collective-security alliance." [4] An official American publication in 1952 asserted that a treaty of alliance, signed by the United States, Australia, and New Zealand, "pledges these three nations to a program of collective security." [5]

Such statements ignore the fact that collective security was originally set out not only as something different from an alliance system, but as a consciously contrived substitute for such a system, based upon the supposition that the latter was, as Wilson put it, "forever discredited." [6] Wilson, the chief spokesman for the concept of collective security as the fundamental principle of the League of Nations, made it absolutely clear that the new concept was incompatible with, and antithetical to, a policy of alliances.[7]

The predilection of the United States for decorating its alliances with the attractive terminology of collective security was explained, probably inadvertently, by an American spokesman in the First Committee of the General Assembly, on January 2, 1952. Discussing the issue of the relationship between the North Atlantic and Rio (Inter-American) treaties and the ideal of collective security, Benjamin V. Cohen admitted that such arrangements might conceivably "degenerate into mere military al-

---

[2] January 6, 1951.

[3] *Military Situation in the Far East, Hearings before the Committee on Armed Services and the Committee on Foreign Relations, United States Senate, 82nd Congress, 1st Session* (Washington: Government Printing Office, 1951), Part 1, p. 87.

[4] *United States News and World Report,* March 28, 1952, p. 84.

[5] *Our Foreign Policy: 1952,* Department of State Publication 4466, General Foreign Policy Series 56 (Washington: Government Printing Office, 1952), p. 39.

[6] Address to Congress, February 11, 1918, cited in Green H. Hackworth, *Digest of International Law* (Washington: Government Printing Office, 1940), I, 424.

[7] See the quotations from Wilson in Hans J. Morgenthau, *In Defense of the National Interest* (New York: Knopf, 1951), pp. 24-25, 27-28.

liances, employing force or the threat of force for the achievement of narrow purposes inconsistent with the Charter." [8] This remark clearly implies that the United States applies an ideological and subjective definition of collective security; if our government approves of a treaty of alliance, believing that it reflects proper motives and promises results acceptable to the United States, it describes it as a segment of a collective security system; if the United States disapproves of such a treaty, it denounces it as a "mere military alliance." To put it bluntly, the blessing of Wilsonian idealism, which breathed the hope of a new era of collective security, is invoked upon American alliances, and the curse of Wilsonian prejudice against special combinations which "have been the prolific source in the modern world of the plans and passions that produce war" [9] is called down upon the alliances constructed by the Soviet Union. This may be a good propaganda tactic, but it does nothing to facilitate the scientific understanding of the concept of collective security.

Another example of the loose usage of the term may be found in the public expressions of President Eisenhower. In June 1952, the future President declared at a press conference:

> I believe we should not commit ourselves to any geographical line or tie ourselves down any other way. I do not believe we should handcuff ourselves with pre-action statements. We should be ready to act in our own interests when the time comes and in accordance with our own self-interest, enlightened self-interest with respect to the free world.[10]

This was a classic statement of the flat *rejection* of the fundamental principle of collective security. Yet, a few days later, Eisenhower warned against the dire result of a possible turn toward isolationism, and asserted: "But it will not happen if we firmly maintain a high order of collective security." [11] As chief executive, Eisenhower embraced collective security wholeheartedly, saying on June 10, 1953, that "there is no free nation too humble to be forgotten . . . all free nations must stand together, or they shall fall separately." [12] However, the same newspaper which reported that speech also carried a dispatch attributing to the Secretary of Defense the view that no commitment could be made in advance as to whether the United States would join in opposing a Communist assault at some point, such as Indo-China, along the containment perimeter. This represented no disunity in the Administration; it reflected

[8] *Department of State Bulletin,* January 21, 1952, p. 100.

[9] See the citation from Wilson, in Morgenthau, *In Defense of the National Interest,* p. 25.

[10] *New York Times,* June 6, 1952.

[11] *Ibid.,* June 24, 1952.

[12] *Ibid.,* June 11, 1953.

the settled American policy of accepting the terminology of collective security and rejecting the substantive meaning of collective security.

Collective security has gone the way of most other ideal concepts; respectable people insist upon believing in it, but they also insist upon retaining beliefs which are incompatible with it and rejecting beliefs which are fundamental to it. In these circumstances, the problem of evaluating the principle of collective security as an approach to peace requires especial care.

This problem is complicated not only by the loose and inconsistent usage of the term, but also by the warmth of the friendly and hostile emotions which have been aroused by the concept of collective security. No approach to peace espoused by international organization has produced more exaggerated praise or more fervid denunciation. A sound analysis must be characterized by equal wariness against ready acceptance of the assumption that collective security is an infallible formula for world order or that it is a concept which has been conclusively discredited.

THE THEORY OF COLLECTIVE SECURITY

Collective security depends less heavily than pacific settlement upon the precise accuracy of a set of assumptions about the nature and causes of war. By the same token, it purports to be applicable to a wider variety of belligerent situations, assuming that not all wars arise from the same type of causation. It is at once a second line of defense against the wars which pacific settlement should but does not prevent, and a supplementary defense, on the flanks of pacific settlement, against the wars which are not within the range of the latter; thus, it adds to the protective system of world peace the benefits of both defense in depth and defense in breadth.

The necessary assumption of collective security is simply that wars are likely to occur and that they ought to be prevented. The conflicts may be the fruit of unreflective passion or of deliberate planning; they may represent efforts to settle disputes, effects of undefinably broad situations of hostility, or calculated means to realize ambitious designs of conquest. They may be launched by the irresponsible dictate of cynical autocrats or the democratic will of a chauvinistic people—although the champions of collective security have frequently evinced the conviction that most wars are likely to stem from the former type of initiative. The point is that the theory of collective security is not invalidated by the discovery that the causes, functional purposes, and initiatory mechanisms of war are varied.

However, the basic assumption about the problem of war is more precise in certain important respects. Collective security is a specialized instrument of international policy in the sense that it is intended only to forestall the arbitrary and aggressive use of force, not to provide enforcement mechanisms for the whole body of international law; it assumes that, so far as the problem of world order is concerned, the heart of the matter is the restraint of military action rather than the guarantee of respect for all legal obligations. Moreover, it assumes that this ideal may be realized, or at least approximated, by a reformation of international policy, without the institution of a revolution in the structure of the international system.

To some degree, collective security shares with pacific settlement the belief that governments, or the peoples who may be in a position to influence their governments, are amenable to moral appeals against the misuse of force, and it may also be described as a rationalistic approach to peace. But the rational appeal directed by collective security to potential belligerents is not so much a suggestion of a decent and sensible alternative to violence, which characterizes pacific settlement, as a threat of dire consequences if the warning against violence is imprudently ignored. The stock in trade of pacific settlement is investigation, conciliation, arbitration, and the like—equipment for inducing rational decision to follow a morally respectable course; the stock in trade of collective security is diplomatic, economic, and military sanctions—equipment for inducing rational decision to avoid threatened damage to the national self-interest. Pacific settlement assumes, at least for tactical purposes, the moral ambiguity of a situation of conflict; avoiding an initial judgment on the moral merits of the positions held by disputants, it applies pressure equally to the two parties to adopt positive moral attitudes conducive to an agreed solution. Collective security, on the other hand, assumes the moral clarity of a situation, the assignability of guilt for a threat to or breach of the peace; starting by tagging one state as the culpable party, it then discards primary concern with the factor of international morality in favor of the principle of power. Whereas pacific settlement fails if it proves impossible to make states rationally calm enough to behave morally, collective security falls down if either of two assumptions proves invalid: that blame can be confidently assessed for international crises, and that states are rationally calculating enough to behave prudently.

Collective security may be described as resting upon the proposition that war can be prevented by the deterrent effect of overwhelming power upon states which are too rational to invite certain defeat. In this respect, it is fundamentally similar to a balance of power system involving defensive alliances. However, as we shall see, collective security has other essential aspects which are its distinguishing marks, and which validate the Wilsonian claim that collective security is basically different from the system of policy which it was explicitly designed to replace.

However simple the collective security approach may seem upon superficial acquaintance, the truth is that it assumes the satisfaction of an extraordinarily complex network of requirements. The first group of prerequisites includes those of a *subjective* character, related to the general acceptability of the responsibilities of collective security; the second group may be characterized as a category of *objective* requirements, related to the suitability of the global situation to the operation of collective security.

Subjective Requirements of Collective Security. In contrast to pacific settlement, which is mainly concerned to evoke peaceful attitudes from quarreling states, collective security depends upon a positive commitment to the value of world peace by the great mass of states. Its basic requirement is that the premise of the "indivisibility of peace" should be deeply established in the thinking of governments and peoples. Collective security rests upon the assumption that it is true, and that governments and peoples can be expected to act upon the truth, that the fabric of human society has become so tightly woven that a breach anywhere threatens disintegration everywhere. Unchecked aggression in one direction emboldens and helps to empower its perpetrator to penetrate in other directions, or, more abstractly, successful use of lawless force in one situation contributes to the undermining of respect for the principle of order in all situations. The geographical remoteness of aggression is irrelevant; Kant's prophetic insight that "The intercourse . . . which has been everywhere steadily increasing between the nations of the earth, has now extended so enormously that a violation of right in one part of the world is felt all over it," [13] must be universally acknowledged. The world's thinking must undergo the transformation that was exemplified by British Prime Minister Neville Chamberlain, when he switched from sighing, in the fall of 1938, "How horrible, fantastic, incredible it is that we should be digging trenches and trying on gas-masks here, because of a quarrel in a far-away country between people of whom we know nothing," to asserting, one year later, that "If, in spite of all, we find ourselves forced to embark upon a struggle . . . we shall not be fighting for the political future of a far-away city in a foreign land; we shall be fighting for the preservation of those principles, the destruction of which would involve the destruction of all possibility of peace and security for the peoples of the world." [14] Collective security requires rejection of the isolationist ideal of localizing wars, in terms of both its possibility and its desirability, and recommends to all the classic advice proffered by Alfred Nemours, the representative of Haiti, in the League debate concerning Italian aggression against Ethiopia: "Great or small, strong or weak, near or far, white or coloured, let us never forget that one day we may be somebody's Ethiopia." [15]

---

[13] *Perpetual Peace,* p. 21.

[14] Cited in Alan Bullock, *Hitler: A Study in Tyranny* (New York: Harper, 1953), p. 499.

[15] Cited in Walters, *A History of the League of Nations,* II, 653.

In requiring conviction of the indivisibility of peace, collective security demands what is essentially a factual agreement; it then imposes a related normative requirement: loyalty to the world community. The system will work only if the peoples of the world identify their particular interests so closely with the general interest of mankind that they go beyond mere recognition of interdependence to a feeling of involvement in the destiny of all nations. The responsibilities of participation in a collective security system are too onerous to be borne by any but a people actuated by genuine sympathy for any and all victims of aggression, and loyalty to the values of a global system of law and order. The operation of a collective security system must always be precarious unless the conviction that what is good for world peace is necessarily good for the nation is deeply engrained in governments and peoples.

The leaders of nations and their constituents must be prepared to subordinate to the requirements of the collective security system their apparent and immediate national interest—to incur economic loss and run the risk of war, even in situations when the national interest does not seem to be involved, or when this policy seems to conflict with the national interest or to undermine established national policies. This means that states must renounce both pacifism and the right to use war as an instrument of national policy, while standing ready to resort to force for the fulfillment of their international obligations. As Arnold J. Toynbee has put it: "We have got to give up war for all the purposes for which sovereign communities have fought since war has been in existence, but we have still got to be willing to accept the risks and the losses of war for a purpose for which hitherto people have never thought of fighting." [16] It means that states must abandon as illusions any convictions they may have traditionally held that they are peculiarly safe against aggression, overcome the temptation to regard any specific conflict as immaterial to or even favorable to their interests, and dedicate themselves to the performance of duties which may upset the equilibrium of their national life and disrupt relationships which they have laboriously constructed. All this theoretically takes place within a system which assumes the maintenance of the basic multistate character of international society, and demands not that national loyalties be abandoned, but that they merely be harmonized by the enlightened conception that national interests are identifiable with the global interest. What it really requires is that a state adopt this conception once and for all, and thereafter act on the assumption that it is valid, despite contrary appearances that may arise from time to time.

---

[16] Royal Institute of International Affairs, *The Future of the League of Nations*, p. 14. Cf. Werner Levi, *Fundamentals of World Organization* (Minneapolis: University of Minnesota Press, 1950), p. 77; Morgenthau, *Politics Among Nations*, p. 333.

Collective security is a design for providing the certainty of collective action to frustrate aggression—for giving to the potential victim the reassuring knowledge, and conveying to the potential law-breaker the deterring conviction, that the resources of the community will be mobilized against any abuse of national power. This ideal permits no *ifs* or *buts.* If it merely encourages states to hope for collective support in case they are victims of attack, it must fail to stimulate the revisions of state behavior at which it aims and upon which its ultimate success depends; if the hope which it encourages should prove illusory, it stands convicted of contributing to the downfall of states whose security it purported to safeguard. If it merely warns potential aggressors that they may encounter concerted resistance, it fails to achieve full effectiveness in its basic function, that of discouraging resort to violence, and if its warning should be revealed as a bluff, it stimulates the contempt for international order which it is intended to eradicate. The theory of collective security is replete with absolutes, of which none is more basic than the requirement of certainty.

In accordance with this essential of the collective security system, the states which constitute the system must be willing to accept commitments which involve the sacrifice of their freedom of action or inaction in the most crucial of future situations. They must say in advance what they will do; they must agree to dispense with *ad hoc* national judgments, and bind themselves to a pattern of action from which they will not be at liberty to deviate. This pattern may be prescribed, at least in part, by the explicit terms of a multilateral treaty. It may, additionally or alternatively, be determined by the decision of an international agency. What is essential, in either case, is that the states upon which the operation of collective security depends should clearly renounce the right to withhold their support from a collective undertaking against whatever aggressions may arise.

Moreover, the renunciation of national decision-making capacity necessarily includes surrender of discretionary competence to resort to forcible action in the absence of international authorization. Collective security can tolerate the maintenance of a carefully restricted right of self-defense, to be exercised within the bounds of international supervision, but it is a fundamental requirement of a full-fledged system that an international authority should be the master of all situations involving the use of coercive instruments. Basically, the state must abdicate its traditional control over the elements of national power, accepting the responsibility to act or to refrain from acting in accordance with the stipulations of a multilateral agreement and the dictates of an international agency. Thus, the state exposes itself to obligations determined by the community for dealing with situations which may be created by the action and policy of other states.

It is very clear that the acceptance of this kind of commitment is a drastic if not a revolutionary act for a national state. It involves a relinquishment of sovereignty in the most crucial area of policy; "To all intents and purposes a state's right of disposal of its military potential is the most sensitive segment of national sovereignty, and that part which traditionally is impervious to foreign decision or control." [17] For constitutional democracies, it implies a transfer of power to make vital decisions which is likely to collide with established concepts of the distribution of governmental functions and powers, and a rigidification of national policy which is difficult to reconcile with the democratic principle that the people have an inalienable right to change their minds through the continuous operation of the mechanism of majority rule. It requires democratic statesmen, as democrats, to follow policies which their people may not approve in the circumstances, and, as statesmen, to abjure the exercise of the most cherished virtue of statesmanship, that of demonstrating empirical wisdom by making sound decisions in the light of the unique characteristics of a given situation. Thus, the good politician is required to betray the democratic ideal of doing what the people want, the shrewd politician is required to violate his vote-getting instincts, and the wise statesman is required to follow the rule book in a manner befitting an automaton. Finally, it means that governments and peoples must develop an unprecedented degree of confidence in the judgment and good will of foreigners, for the discretionary authority which is subtracted from the competence of the democratic majority and the national leadership is added to that of an international organization. Indeed, it is ultimately transferred to unidentifiable foreign states—those whose policy may be so obtuse that they provoke aggression against themselves, and those whose policy may be so cynical that they deliberately resort to aggression.

The essential commitments of a collective security system necessitate the willingness of nations to fight for the status quo. Collective security is not inherently an attempt to perpetuate an existing state of affairs; it is entirely compatible with a system of peaceful change, and such a system is in fact absolutely necessary for producing the kind of status quo and the kind of attitudes toward the status quo that are required if the ideal of collective security is to be realized. But at any given moment, the function of collective security is to combat assaults upon the currently legitimate pattern of national rights, and the responsibility of participating peoples is to cooperate in that enterprise without regard to any underlying sympathies they may have for claims of frustrated justice that may be enunciated by the assailants. As a general proposition, peace through justice must be the watchword of collective security. However, its provisional rule of action can hardly be any other than peace *over* justice, and the member states of the

---

[17] Karl Loewenstein, "Sovereignty and International Co-operation," *American Journal of International Law,* April 1954, p. 235.

system must be prepared to go to war to preserve the system which keeps the peace, even though this involves injury to innocent people and the squelching of valid objections to the moral legitimacy of the legally established state of things.

A basic requirement of collective security is that it function impartially. It is a design for preserving the integrity of the anonymous victim of attack by the anonymous aggressor; it is no respecter of states, but an instrument to be directed against any aggressor, on behalf of any violated state. This description points to one of the significant differences between a balance of power system and a collective security system: in the former, collaborative activity is directed against *undue power,* as such, while in the latter it is turned against *aggressive policy,* whether that policy be pursued by a giant which threatens to grow to earth-shaking proportions or by a pygmy which has scant prospect of becoming a major factor in world politics.[18]

The demands imposed by the principle of anonymity upon the states which form a collective security system provide further indications of the distinction between the new and the old regimes for the management of international relations. If collective security is to operate impartially, governments and peoples must exhibit a fundamental flexibility of policy and sentiment. France must be as ready to defend Germany as Belgium against aggression, and Britain must be equally willing to join in collective sanctions against the United States or the Soviet Union. In short, collective security recognizes no traditional friendships and no inveterate enmities, and permits no alliances *with* or alliances *against.* It is true that a balance of power system, in the long run, requires similar changes of partners and redefinition of villains, but in the short run, such a system operates through the basic mechanism of alliances. For the purposes of collective security, an alliance is either superfluous—since every state is already committed to the defense of every other state—or it is incompatible with the system—since it implies that its members will defend each other but not outsiders, and raises doubt that they will join in international sanctions as readily against one of their number as against other states. The principle of alliance tends to inject into international relations a concept of the advance identification of friends and enemies that is alien to the basic proposition of collective security: whoever commits aggression is everybody's enemy; whoever resists aggression is everybody's friend.

All of this adds up to the fundamental subjective requirement that all states be willing to entrust their destinies to collective security. Confidence is the quintessential condition of the success of the system; states must be prepared to rely upon its effectiveness and impartiality. If they are so prepared, they are likely to behave in such a way as to maximize

[18] Cf. Wright, *Problems of Stability and Progress in International Relations,* p. 355.

the probability that this confidence will prove justified. If they are not, they are almost certain to resort to policies which undermine the system and make it unworthy of the confidence which they declined to bestow upon it. The familiar dilemma of circularity appears here: collective security cannot work unless the policies of states are inspired by confidence in the system, but it requires an extraordinary act of political faith for states to repose confidence in the system without previous demonstration that collective security works. The stakes are high in the world of power politics, and states do not lightly undertake experiments in the critical field of national security.

This analysis of the subjective requirements of collective security proves nothing if not that the realization of the ideal first institutionally espoused by the League makes singularly stringent demands upon the human beings of the twentieth century. It calls for a moral transformation of political man. It offends the most pacific and the most bellicose of men; it challenges neutralism and isolationism as well as militarism and imperialism; it clashes with the views of the most conservative supporters of national sovereignty and the most liberal proponents of democratic control of foreign policy; it demands alike the dissolution of ancient national hatreds and the willingness to abandon traditional national friendships. Indeed, the question inexorably arises whether the demands imposed upon the human mind and will by collective security are in truth less rigorous than those imposed by the ideal of world government. Is collective security really a halfway house? If human beings were fully prepared to meet the subjective requirements of collective security, would they be already prepared for world government?

Objective Requirements of Collective Security. The prerequisites thus far discussed have to do with the human situation. Collective security also depends upon the satisfaction of a number of basic conditions in the external sphere—in the power situation, the legal situation, and the organizational situation.

The ideal setting for a collective security system is a world characterized by a considerable diffusion of power. The most favorable situation would be one in which all states commanded approximately equal resources, and the least favorable, one marked by the concentration of effective power in a very few major states. The existence of several great powers of roughly equal strength is essential to collective security.

Given a power configuration meeting this minimal requirement, a collective security system next demands substantial universality of membership. It might be argued that potential aggressors might just as well be omitted, since they presumably will dishonor both the negative obligations and the positive responsibilities incumbent upon members, or that they might better be left out, since their absence will facilitate the planning and initiation of collective measures to restrain their misbehavior. This is a plausible view, even though it ignores the value for an organized community of having lawless elements clearly subject to the legal regime—surely, criminals are the last persons who ought to be formally exempted from the bonds of the law. The basic objection to this position is that it misses the point that collective security knows no "probable aggressor" but assumes that *any* state may become an aggressor. In a sense, this is an expression of the *abstractness* which is a leading characteristic of collective security; for better or for worse, collective security is not an expedient for dealing with a concrete threat to world peace, but a design for a system of world order. In another sense, however, this is an implication of the *generality* of collective security. The system is intended to provide security for every state against the particular threat which arouses its national anxiety, and if every potential aggressor, every state which is the source of the misgivings of another state, were excluded, the system would have very sparse membership indeed.

In any event, a workable system of collective security can hardly afford the exclusion or abstention of a major power. It is particularly damaging to have an important commercial and naval power on the outside, for the danger of its refusal to co-operate and to acquiesce in the infringement of its normal rights is sufficient to render improbable the effective application of economic sanctions to an aggressor. The doctrine of collective security relies heavily upon the proposition that nonmilitary measures will normally be adequate to stifle aggression—its military commitments are acceptable only because of the presumption that they will rarely be invoked—but economic sanctions are peculiarly dependent upon universal application for their efficacy.

The basic importance of the objective conditions of power diffusion and organizational comprehensiveness lies in the fact that collective security assumes the possibility of creating such an imbalance of power in favor of the upholders of world order that aggression will be prevented by the certainty of defeat or defeated by the minimal efforts of collective forces. This assumption may be invalidated by the inadequate diffusion of power. If the power configuration is such that no state commands more than, say, ten per cent of the world's strength, the possibility is open for collective security to mobilize up to ninety per cent against it, a very comfortable margin of superiority. If, however, one state controls a very substantial portion of global power resources, forty-five per cent, for instance, the collective matching of its strength is doubtful and the massing of overwhelming power against it is manifestly impossible. The importance of universality is also clarified by this analysis; as a collective security system approaches all-inclusiveness, the possibility of its disposing of sufficient resources to outclass any aggressor grows; as it moves in the opposite direction, that possibility is correspondingly diminished.

The point is that collective security is not a design for organizing coalition warfare in the twentieth-century sense, but a plan for organizing international police action in an unprecedented sense. Its aim is not to sponsor the winning team in a free-for-all, but to eliminate international brawls by forcing aggressive states to forfeit their matches before being decisively beaten. It purports to require of participating states not that they should consent to compulsory involvement in major wars, but that they should accept obligatory service in a system for preventing major wars, and it can expect to retain their loyal support only if it succeeds in reducing, rather than increasing, their exposure to the perils of military involvement. All this is dependent upon the existence of a power situation and the achievement of an organizational situation making the massive overpowering of potential aggressors a feasible objective. The first essential of a police force is that its power should be so considerable, and that of its possible opponents so negligible, that any contest will be virtually won before it has begun; otherwise, its function will be that of conducting warfare, no matter how it may be described.

The intrinsic disadvantages of a collective security force are so great that its margin of superiority is always smaller than any purely objective standard of measurement would reveal. Since it confronts an anonymous aggressor, its capacity for formulating advance plans of action is severely limited. Since it is by definition a coalition force, its strength is very likely to be less than that of the sum of its parts. Its value depends heavily upon its ability to act quickly, so as to forestall threatened aggression, and yet its very inability to concentrate on plans for defeating a specific enemy and its complex structure militate against promptness in the effective mobilization of its potential strength. Collective security can command little confidence if it promises to become effective only after an aggressor has ravaged a country. Given the nature of modern war, a military campaign cannot be organized overnight, and the power of an aggressive state is maximized by preparatory measures. The collaborative force required for the implementation of collective security must be overwhelmingly preponderant in theory if it is to be even somewhat preponderant in practice.

The situation envisaged by collective security is marked not only by the wide distribution of power among states and the possibility of the near-monopolization of power by the community, but also by the general reduction of power, as embodied in military instruments. That is to say, collective security is based upon the assumption of partial disarmament. In strict theoretical terms, the system might work as well at a high level of armament as at a low level, but the intrusion of the subjective factor makes it virtually essential that collective security have a substantially demilitarized world to work in. This is because collective security is fundamentally an attempt to mobilize the world's antiwar forces for the prevention of war by the threat to make war; the ambiguity of the system is underlined by the fact that it relies for its initiation upon recognition that the risk of war is intolerable, and for its operation upon willingness to accept the risk of war. Its army of pacifists is tentatively willing to use force only because it abhors the use of force. Being precariously founded upon this psychological and moral paradox, collective security requires a power situation which permits it to do its job with a minimum of military exertion. If every state is reduced to military weakness, no aggressor will be strong enough to make a catastrophic war out of an encounter with the community's forces, and no member of the enforcement team will be tempted to feel that its joining up has been a jump from the military frying pan into the military fire. Just as the peaceful citizen may be less inclined to volunteer as a policeman if potential criminals are equipped with machine guns rather than mere fists, the willingness of peacefully-inclined states to participate in the venture of collective security is dependent upon the magnitude of the military involvement prospectively required; they are prepared to serve as whistle-blowing and nightstick-wielding policemen, but they reserve decision about becoming full-fledged soldiers.

At this point, we again encounter the troublesome problem of circularity. Collective security cannot work unless states disarm, but states will not disarm until collective security has clearly shown that it merits confidence. The maintenance of national military strength is an indication that states are unwilling to entrust their fate to a community agency, but their armament policy, born of lack of confidence in collective security, prevents the development of an effective collective security system.

Another significant objective requirement might be described as the universality of economic vulnerability. Collective security assumes that the states of the world are as interdependent for their strength as for their peace, and that its restraining function can be exercised in large part by the imposition of isolation, the organization of deprivation, without resort to collective measures of suppression. It envisages a world in which every state is not only susceptible to the impact of organized force, but also vulnerable to the squeeze of organized boycott, and it accordingly regards economic sanctions as its first line of attack. It recognizes the vital importance of holding the military weapon in reserve, but it offers to its participating members the reassuring possibility that they may be able to discharge their responsibilities by the relatively painless and humane method of denying to aggressors the benefits of normal intercourse, rather than by running the risks involved in the resort to arms.

In summary, collective security assumes the existence of a world in which every state is so limited by the distribution of power, the reduction of military power levels by a disarmament program, and the lack of economic self-sufficiency, that any state which may develop aggressive inclinations can be held in check by methods which probably need not include the large-scale use of force. It assumes the possibility of securing the acceptance by states of theoretically formidable responsibilities for enforcing the peace, only because it assumes the improbability that it will be necessary to invoke the performance of the most drastic enforcement duties.

Finally, collective security requires the creation of a legal and structural apparatus capable of giving institutional expression to its basic principles. This involves the legal establishment of the prohibition of aggression, the commitment of states to collaborate in the suppression of aggression, and the endowment of an international organization with authority to determine when and against what state sanctions are to be initiated, to decide upon the nature of the inhibitory measures, to evoke the performance of duties to which states have committed themselves, and to plan and direct the joint action which it deems necessary for the implementation of collective security. The meaningfulness of the system is dependent upon the capacity of the organizational mechanism to exercise these vital functions without obstruction. In specific terms, this means that the decision to set the system into operation against a particular state must not be subject to the veto of an obstinate minority, and that no state can be permitted to nullify its commitment to act on behalf of the community by withholding its assent from a decision to call for the performance of that obligation. The elaboration of an adequate supervisory agency is no less important to collective security than the satisfaction of the subjective requirements and the realization of the prerequisite conditions in the global power situation.

COLLECTIVE SECURITY AND INTERNATIONAL ORGANIZATION

It is obvious that at no time have all or even most of the basic preconditions of collective security been realized, and that collective security has not become the operative system of international relations. Various conclusions have been drawn from this fact. Some people have argued that collective security has demonstrably failed, and deserves to be thrown into the ash heap of discredited ideals. Others have pointed out that it has never been put to a genuine test; it has not failed to work, but men have failed to take the necessary steps for permitting it to be tried. Some have concluded that it can never be tested, because it is impossible in this world to create an experimental model of the system envisaged in the blueprints. Others believe that it is within the capacity of human beings to satisfy the requirements for the establishment of collective security, and that, once established, it will prove a valid and useful approach to peace.

These diverse points of view have been reflected in the history of international organization in the twentieth century. Since the First World War, the nations have been unable to put the issue of collective security out of their minds. It has been the ideal which they have been able neither to repudiate nor to effectuate; it has posed requirements which they have been alternately determined to satisfy and eager to evade. It has stimulated the creative imagination of the states which constitute international organization and offended their sensibilities; it has appealed to their highest aspirations and challenged their deepest preconceptions. The record of general international organization has been one of vacillation around the central point of collective security.

The Practicability of Collective Security. The preliminary question concerning collective security is that of its feasibility: can it be established, and, if so, will it work? The League and the United Nations have been committed to the pragmatic exploration, and not the mere speculative consideration, of this basic problem.

It is perhaps unavoidable that international organizations should focus attention upon the legal, constitutional, and structural aspects of the problem of establishing collective security. In any event, the problem has been discussed primarily in those terms in the League and its successor organization, and scholarship has tended to emphasize the criteria of treaty commitments, institutional authority, and organizational procedures.

The League Covenant represented a great stride toward the formal establishment of the elements of a collective security system. It incorporated, in Article 10, a classic statement of the fundamental legal concepts: the obligation of every state joining the system "to respect and preserve as against external aggression the territorial integrity and existing political independence of all Members of the League." Thus, in one stroke, it accomplished the prohibition of aggression, providing the basis for legal action against defaulting states, and the obligation of assistance to victims of aggression, providing the basis for the mobilization of positive support for the system. In Article 11, it stated the ideological premise of the new regime: the proposition that "Any war or threat of war, whether immediately affecting any of the Members of the League or not, is hereby declared a matter of concern to the whole League. . . ."

This affirmation of the community's involvement in all the "private" conflicts of its members led inexorably to the provisions of Article 16, which spelled out the positive responsibilities of participating states. Members accepted the principle that resort to war by any of their number in violation of legal obligations contained in the pacific settlement sections of the Covenant should be regarded *ipso facto* as an "act of war" against them all. In response to such an act, they undertook to impose immediately a strict embargo on all normal personal, commercial, and financial relations with the offending state, creating a situation which Wilson envisaged in these terms:

> Suppose somebody does not abide by these engagements, then what happens? An absolute isolation, a boycott! The boycott is automatic. There is no 'but' or 'if' about that in the Covenant. . . . No goods can be shipped in or out, no telegraphic messages can be exchanged, except through the elusive wireless perhaps; there should be no communication of any kind between the people of the other nations and the people of that nation. . . . It is the most complete boycott ever conceived in a public document.[19]

Although it was assumed that this weapon of "economic strangulation" was a truly formidable one,[20] and Wilson doubted that any nation could long withstand its effects,[21] Article 16 also provided for the possibility of collective military sanctions, to be initiated upon the recommendation of the Council. Members retained the right to abstain from this phase of the enforcement program, but they repudiated the right to maintain strict neutrality by accepting the obligation to afford special facilities to the joint forces mobilized for upholding the Covenant.

Finally, the Covenant gave formal expression to the conceptual relationship between peaceful change and collective security by authorizing, in Article 19, the consideration by the Assembly of demands for alteration of the legally established status quo.

This scheme for the implementation of collective security was subjected to the most searching critical scrutiny from its very inception. Its flaws were fairly obvious. The "gaps" of the Covenant, which theoretically opened the way for states to resort to the arbitrary use of force without violating the letter of the law and thereby triggering off the enforcement mechanism, were quickly spotlighted. The criticism that the League had no "teeth" was invited by the lack of a positive obligation of states to participate in military sanctions, either in fulfillment of treaty commitment or in obedience to an international decision. The peaceful change provision was hardly more than a gesture, since it permitted at most a mere recommendation by the Assembly that unjust situations be altered. Moreover, the League mechanism was subject at every point to jamming by the monkey wrench of the universal veto.

The Covenant was far from a perfect design for collective security. It imposed inadequate legal restrictions upon potential aggressors and exacted insufficient commitments for enforcement action from member

---

19 Royal Institute of International Affairs, *International Sanctions* (London: Oxford University Press, 1938), p. 2.

20 Sweetser, *The League of Nations at Work,* p. 175.

21 Cf. Levi, *op. cit.,* p. 80.

states. The League which it created was deficient in legal authority and practical competence for making the international decisions required for the management of a collective security system. The Wilsonian ideal had inspired the Covenant, but it had not been translated by the Covenant into a set of definite prescriptions for guaranteeing that the combined resources of the community would be available to frustrate aggression.

The history of the League was a record of constant efforts to strengthen and to weaken the collective security provisions of the Covenant. This was not so much a contest between friends and enemies of the principle of collective security, as a vacillation between the desire to enjoy the benefits and the urge to avoid paying the price of collective security. The League could neither take collective security nor leave it alone.

This process began almost before the ink was dry on the Covenant. Misgivings about the excessive commitments contained in Articles 10 and 16 were expressed in the earliest debates of the League, and, in 1921, the Assembly passed a series of Resolutions Concerning the Economic Weapon[22] which emphasized the right of each state to decide for itself whether the occasion for application of economic sanctions had arrived, and approved the idea that the principle of immediate and absolute boycott should be interpreted to mean gradual and partial boycott. Having succeeded in watering down the strongest section of its collective security provisions, the League now gave its urgent attention to projects for concocting a headier brew; in 1923, the Assembly considered a draft Treaty of Mutual Assistance, and in 1924, it adopted the Geneva Protocol, calling for the strengthening of obligations for enforcing the peace. These were typical episodes in the life of the League. Studies and consultations concerning the sanctions system went forward almost incessantly, but it took a man with exceptional mental power to remember whether on any given day he was expected to be dedicated to strengthening or weakening the provisions of the Covenant.

In 1935, the League powers overcame their misgivings about the burdens of collective security long enough to stigmatize Italian aggression in Ethiopia and to organize economic sanctions against Italy. However, this surprising initiative did not represent a genuine rededication to the principles of collective security enshrined in the Covenant; the spirit of irresolution quickly returned, and the spark of determination to make the League an effective bulwark against aggression sputtered and died. Mussolini was permitted to triumph in contempt of the League, and the first great attempt to create a collective security organization was for all practical purposes terminated.[23] In the final analysis, the members of the League could never bring themselves to adopt in policy the collective

[22] League Document A.14, 1927, v.
[23] For an excellent treatment of this episode, see Walters, *op. cit.*, II, 623-691.

security system which they had ratified in the Covenant. Instead, they sought to find security in the League era through the traditional devices of national policy and diplomacy.

The Charter of the United Nations is in many respects a more satisfactory constitutional basis for a collective security system than the Covenant. It leaves no such convenient gaps in the legal fence for aggressors to crawl through as did the latter; it substitutes for a limited prohibition of war the more comprehensive proscription of the threat or use of force,[24] and it even undertakes to close the gap of fictitious defensive and law-enforcement measures by subjecting all coercive activity to the control and supervision of the Security Council.[25] It incorporates more elaborate and ambitious provisions for sanctions. Instead of requiring states to impose economic penalties if and when they unilaterally recognize the existence of aggression, and permitting them the luxury of voluntary participation in military sanctions, the Charter brings all enforcement activity under the aegis of the Security Council, conferring upon that body the authority to identify the aggressor, to order members to engage in nonmilitary coercion, and itself to put into action the military forces presumably to be placed at its permanent disposal by members of the organization.[26]

Nevertheless, the Charter falls significantly short of providing an ideal institutional system for the realization of collective security. It is an incomplete document, in the sense that it postpones to the future—a future that shows no signs of arriving—the agreed allocation by states of military contingents to function as coercive instruments of the United Nations. It offers no more assurance than did the Covenant that disarmament and peaceful change, basic prerequisites for collective security, will be achieved. Most importantly, it establishes the rule of great power unanimity in the Security Council. The adoption of this provision clearly reflected a deliberate decision not to attempt to institute a system of collective security applicable to the great powers—the very states which possess the greatest capacity to threaten the security of other states. Given the veto power of the Big Five, the Security Council is legitimately subject to the unilateral blocking of any efforts it might make to declare the impropriety of purportedly defensive measures or enforcement action not authorized by itself, to invoke sanctions against an aggressor, or to require states to perform the positive duties enjoined upon them by the principle of collective security. In short, the extensive decision-making competence conferred upon the Security Council is drastically reduced by the extensive decision-blocking competence conferred upon the great powers. This arrangement is wholly incompatible with the requirements of

---

24 Article 2, paragraph 4.

25 Articles 51 and 53.

26 Articles 39-50.

the doctrine of collective security that states should be entitled to rely upon the certain support of the community in resistance to aggression, that aggressors should be subjected to the threat of the certain opposition of the community, and that these circumstances should hold without regard to the identity of the aggressor or the victim.

Like the League, the United Nations has in practice refrained from simply following the pattern laid down in its basic document, and has instead improvised policies related to the general problem of collective security. In the case of the United Nations, however, there has been little evidence of the urge to patch up the legal and structural system to make it conform more closely to the requirements of a full-fledged collective security system. The first reaction of the Western powers to the realization that they needed an arrangement for collective defense against the threat of Soviet aggression was not to reverse the San Francisco decision against relying upon collective security for this kind of job, but to create an extra-United Nations system—the North Atlantic Treaty Organization.

The point should be made clear that NATO is *not* a collective security system, however often statesmen and commentators insist upon calling it that. It does not purport to be an arrangement whereby a community proposes to put down any aggressor that might arise within its ranks; rather, it is a design for joint resistance to possible aggression stemming from a particular power bloc external to the community. NATO is a system of *selective* security, embodying the principle of some for some, whereas collective security is dedicated to the concept of all for all. Far from contributing to the collective security ideal of disarmament, NATO is fundamentally concerned with the rearmament of its members in competition with the Soviet coalition. Aside from its deviations from the substantive policy objectives which lie at the heart of the collective security concept, NATO does not even constitute an advance toward the formal regime required by collective security. Its basic document, the North Atlantic Treaty, leaves it to each party to decide for itself what assistance it should render to an assaulted colleague,[27] whereas collective security envisages ironclad commitments for joint sanctions. Moreover, the NATO Council perpetuates the strict rule of unanimity, whereas collective security demands an agency which can invoke the obligations of member states without the requirement of their individual consent to the decision.

In short, NATO is not a collective security system added as an afterthought to the United Nations, but a new type of alliance. The makers of the Charter abstained from undertaking to institute a system of collective security for dealing with potential Soviet aggression, leaving it to the nations concerned to devise means of coping with that problem, if it

---

[27] Article 5.

should arise. The problem has arisen, and the choice of means has been exercised. The decision has been to try a different method than collective security.

This is not to say that the *wrong* decision was made. There is nothing inherently dishonorable or necessarily unwise about choosing an alternative to collect security. In fact, I think that NATO represents a more practicable and effective approach to the problem of containing Soviet expansiveness than the effort to establish a collective security system would have been.

To assert that the decision was made to refrain from trying to institutionalize collective security is not to admit that the decision failed to reflect creative imagination. NATO does not represent simply a retrogression to the bad old days of competitive alliances. In terms of formally binding commitments, it is *less* than an old-fashioned alliance, but in fundamentally vital respects, it is far *more* than such a grouping.

In organizational terms, NATO is something new under the international sun. It is an alliance which involves the construction of institutional mechanisms, the development of multilateral procedures, and the elaboration of preparatory plans for the conduct of joint military action in future contingencies. It substitutes for the mere promise of improvised collaboration in the event of crisis the developing actuality of planned collaboration in anticipation of a military challenge to its members. It is a coalition consisting not merely of a treaty on file, but also of an organization in being—a Secretary-General and permanent staff, a Council, a network of committees, a military command structure, study groups, and liaison agencies. NATO represents a twentieth-century elaboration of the alliance concept, in contrast to the collective security ideal of obtaining the abandonment and replacement of the alliance concept. In comparative terms, NATO is not an exceptionally advanced form of international organization, and it is by no means self-evident that NATO is destined to become the progenitor of audacious internationalist schemes. Nevertheless, it represents an impressive organizational achievement, in that it applies the principle of multilateral organization to a new area—that of the alliance. This utilization of the concept of international organization for the transformation rather than the supplantation of alliances may prove to be a highly significant precedent.

The organizational factor in NATO clearly has a considerable effect upon the contractual factor. In terms of formal commitment, the North Atlantic Treaty is as inferior to a true alliance as the United Nations Charter is to a true collective security arrangement. Yet, the political reality of the situation is that the members of NATO are more firmly bound together for mutual defense than they have been disposed to state in the explicit clauses of a treaty. Most significantly, the United States has insisted upon maintaining the fiction that it reserves the sovereign right to decide for itself whether it will take military action in defense of its Atlantic allies, but has also promoted and participated in a process of organizational involvement and entanglement which suggests—and is intended to suggest—that it has in fact forfeited that right. NATO has become an organizational web expressing and reinforcing the political determination of the United States to align itself definitively with the free nations of Europe in resistance to Soviet expansionism. Joint military action of the members of NATO is not so much a promise of their treaty as a premise of their organization.

This point is indicative of the major virtue of the decision to choose the NATO alternative to the erection of a collective security system for dealing with the Soviet threat. The North Atlantic Treaty means more than it says, whereas every documentary expression of the collective security principle thus far contrived has meant less than it said. The political realism of the NATO enterprise is evidenced by the fact that the loopholes for sovereign irresponsibility which mar its basic treaty have tended to be constricted rather than expanded in the process of organizational development.

NATO provides no certain answers to the question of how to achieve a satisfactory world order. It is a superior kind of alliance, and it may be able to do what an alliance has always been theoretically capable of doing: preventing the launching of a major war, or winning that war if it occurs. It may be that only an alliance, and only an alliance institutionalized in the unprecedented fashion of NATO, is capable of generating the power and effectuating the policy necessary for dealing with the Soviet threat to peace in the present world situation. Nevertheless, it must be recognized that NATO can do only what an alliance can do; it cannot do what collective security theoretically could do if collective security were a feasible achievement. This is to say, in essence, that NATO offers only a means of dealing with an immediate and specific situation, and not a pattern for a permanent and general system of world order. But there is no occasion for champions of NATO to feel defensive about the fact that it is not a collective security system; it is a feasible project today precisely because it is different from collective security, and it is useful in so far as it offers realizable alternatives to the currently unobtainable benefits of collective security.

The second major reaction of the United Nations to the realization that world peace was urgently threatened by a great power against which no collective security bulwarks had been erected was to adopt the elaborate Uniting for Peace scheme, whereby the General Assembly projected itself into the area of security operations hitherto reserved for the Security Council.

On the face of it, this alteration resembled the patching-up operations which the League periodically undertook for the purpose of strengthening its collective security aspects. It was initiated in response to the realization that collective enforcement of some sort might be organized even against aggressors supported by a great power, provided that the blocking effect of the Security Council veto rule could be circumvented. Specifically, it followed upon the Korean action of 1950; in that case, a fortuitous combination of factors had made the United Nations willing and able to sponsor collective military resistance to an invasion supported if not instigated by the Soviet Union, in contradiction to the implicit assumption of the Charter that the organization should not attempt the collective security function in such circumstances. The Uniting for Peace plan represented an effort to institutionalize the reversal of that assumption, to provide a regularized means for doing what had been done by improvisation in the Korean case. Thus, it might be interpreted as a move to create a system of collective security applicable, as the original Charter system had not been, to aggression by, or under the auspices of, a permanent member of the Security Council.

However, the Uniting for Peace scheme, viewed as an expedient for extending the theoretical range of the United Nations collective security system, is marked by serious deficiencies. Its operative organ, the Assembly, has only recommendatory authority, and is too big, too slow, and too diffuse in political composition to constitute an ideal instrument for collective security; the Assembly's incapacities are different from those of the Security Council, but they are not necessarily less significant. Moreover, the Uniting for Peace system falls seriously short of guaranteeing collective security, in that it involves no firm commitment by any state, and consequently offers no potential victim of attack any real assurance of collective assistance. In short, this system fails to meet the crucial test of *certainty;* states cannot realistically depend upon it to provide the essential measure of security, and they are for that reason unable to abandon the quest for strength through national armament and alliance-building. The continuation of these policies is a definite symptom of the failure to realize the ideal of collective security, and an obstacle to progress toward that ideal. The Uniting for Peace system, like NATO, has its values, but they are not the values that might be attributed to a genuine and full-fledged collective security arrangement.

In terms of political realism, this alteration of the Charter scheme was not intended as a move to institute collective security in a realm left vacant by the statesmen of San Francisco. It was an American initiative, and it was clearly conceived as a device whereby the United States might invoke the moral support of the United Nations for such resorts to force as it might find necessary and desirable in the course of its cold war struggles. In proposing the plan, the United States did not purport to expose itself to new and more rigorous obligations to aid victims of aggression. American postwar policy has consistently failed to reflect any inclination to develop the capacity of international organization to tell the United States that it *must* act militarily, or that it must *not* act; the Uniting for Peace plan was typical of American policy in that it put the United Nations in a position to tell the United States and its allies that they *may* act, to confer its official blessings upon such action as the Western bloc may choose to undertake.

The first use of the Uniting for Peace plan was in relation to the Korean crisis, which had inspired its adoption. Acting under its newly asserted powers, the Assembly undertook to deal with the intrusion of Communist China in the conflict, initially by sponsoring an effort to obtain a cease-fire, and then by characterizing the Chinese intervention as an aggressive act and recommending economic sanctions supplementary to the collective military action already under way.[28] In this instance, the Assembly gave virtually full effect to the Uniting for Peace plan as it had been originally conceived.

Since 1951, the plan has been invoked four times for the convening of Emergency Special Sessions of the Assembly to deal with critical situations in which the Security Council has been immobilized by the use of the veto: the Suez and Hungarian cases of 1956, the Middle Eastern crisis of 1958, and the Congolese situation in 1960. In the two cases which arose in 1956, the Assembly condemned the use of force by Israel, Britain, and France against Egypt, and by the Soviet Union in Hungary. In none of these cases did the Assembly move to the point of attempting to organize sanctions and thus put to the test its capacity to function as the central agency of a collective security system.

This record is inconclusive. It indicates that the Assembly may be expected to make full use of the Uniting for Peace plan as a justification for prompt consideration of political and security matters when the Security Council is prevented, by the rule of unanimity, from acting. The role of the Assembly as an organ of appeal from the Security Council is quite clearly and firmly established. Beyond this, the situation and the trend of development are less clear. The events of 1956 suggested that the Assembly maintained a collective security *orientation*—an orientation which condemned the use of force for unilaterally determined national purposes, without regard to the military importance or political complexion of the offending state. The record does not equally demonstrate that the Assembly has maintained the intent to attempt the operation of a collective security *system*.

While the history of the utilization of the Uniting for Peace scheme provides no clear indication as to the prospect for collective security under

---

[28] General Assembly Resolutions 384 (V), 498 (V), and 500 (V), of December 14, 1950, February 1, 1951, and May 18, 1951. See Leland M. Goodrich, *Korea: A Study of U. S. Policy in the United Nations* (New York: Council on Foreign Relations, 1956), pp. 156-173.

the auspices of the United Nations, a political analysis of the evolution of the General Assembly suggests a negative indication. The failure of members of the United Nations to follow their own advice, incorporated in the Uniting for Peace resolution, to designate military contingents for possible enforcement actions recommended by the Assembly was the initial clue to the diminution of their enthusiasm for the project of building a collective security system. Indeed, the dedication to this project did not survive the vicissitudes of the Korean conflict. The difficulties and dangers ultimately encountered in that case stimulated a return to the view, expressed by the founders in the Charter, that it is neither feasible to carry out nor prudent to undertake collective security action in direct or indirect opposition to a major power.

This retreat from the commitment to collective security has continued. The Soviet Union was opposed to the Uniting for Peace plan from the beginning. In the Suez crisis of 1956, the anxiety of Israel, Britain, and France concerning the possibility that sanctions might be turned against them was matched by American embarrassment at the thought of supporting collective action directed against those states. The United States was unwilling to contemplate collective action along with the Soviet Union in the Middle East, or against the Soviet Union in Hungary. The uncommitted states have gradually moved to the recognition that the collective security implications of the Uniting for Peace plan contradict their urge to stand aside, so far as possible, from the struggles of the cold war. As the Assembly has been progressively expanded by the admission of new recruits for the Afro-Asian bloc, the prospect of mobilizing a two-thirds majority for the condemnation of aggression by a major power or an associated state, and, *a fortiori,* for the involvement of the United Nations in an effort at collective suppression of such an offensive act, has steadily declined.

In short, the Uniting for Peace plan, conceived as a device for giving the United Nations a collective security role in cases involving conflicts of interest among the great powers, appears to be dead. It survives merely as a device for enabling the Assembly to concern itself with such conflicts, and to develop some other role in relation to them.[29]

We have seen that neither of the great world organizations has measured up to the legal and structural requirements of a collective security system. The failure to achieve collective security, however, goes much deeper than inadequacies of formal commitment and imperfections of institutional structure and competence. The truth is that hardly any of the fundamental requirements of collective security has been met in the world of the twentieth century.

---

29 For more elaborate discussion of the rise and fall of commitment to the effectuation of collective security, see Inis L. Claude, Jr., "The United Nations and the Use of Force," *International Conciliation,* No. 532, March 1961, pp. 356-364.

In the objective sphere, the League had the advantage of being born into a world characterized by a considerable diffusion of power. States of great power rank were numerous enough at the end of the First World War, and the concept of universality of economic vulnerability was sufficiently reflected in reality, to provide a setting reasonably well adapted to the operation of collective security, if other conditions had been favorable. But other conditions were not favorable, and the result was that the world lost its chance. Indeed, history may record that the first chance to institute collective security was also the last, for the relatively favorable configuration of power which prevailed when the League was created was not duplicated at the end of World War II, and, given the distinct trend toward the polarization of power, is not likely to occur again in the foreseeable future.

The League's asset of a power distribution appropriate to collective security was offset by the liability of its failure to approximate the objective requirement of universality. In this respect, the critical factor was the abstention of the United States. The ambitious design of the Covenant for collective security postulated the collaboration of the United States, Britain, and France in discouraging or squelching the illegal use of force. When the United States refused to join the team, raising doubt that it would cooperate at all in the frustration of aggression, and stimulating fear that it might actively impede the operation of collective sanctions, it destroyed the objective basis of the League security system before that system was even inaugurated. The collapse of the fundamental premise that the commercial, financial, and naval power of America would be available for restraining would-be aggressors invalidated the assumption that future crises could almost certainly be dealt with by methods more analogous to blockade than to war, and transformed the obligations of League members into much more onerous responsibilities than they had bargained for. Reaction was instantaneous; the states most responsible for the operation of collective security and those most dependent upon its operation recognized that the scheme had been dealt a serious blow. They did not follow what might have been the logical course of formally abandoning the plan, but they shifted to a half-hearted acceptance of the responsibilities and reliance upon the safeguards of collective security, which betrayed an implicit acknowledgment of the fact that the objective conditions of the successful operation of the system had been destroyed. Explicit recognition of the importance of the American decision was contained in a statement by British Prime Minister Stanley Baldwin, in 1934: "Never, so long as I have any responsibility for governing this country, will I sanction the British Navy being used for a naval blockade until I know what the United States of America is going to do." [30]

---

[30] Cited in Royal Institute of International Affairs, *International Sanctions,* p. 153.

When the United States knocked out the objective prop of essential universality, it became almost inevitable that the objective condition of regulated disarmament should fail of realization. Thus, despite the potentiality offered by the global power configuration, the League did not secure the kind of world—a world of substantially disarmed nations, united in virtual unanimity for carrying out the functions of collective security—which was requisite for the experiment in security policy to which it was verbally committed. The League might have failed even if the objective conditions of collective security had been realized, but it could hardly have met any other fate under the circumstances with which it was actually confronted.

The United Nations was spared the crippling at birth which had been inflicted by the United States upon its predecessor, but it had the misfortune of being introduced into a world characterized by a pattern of power distribution wholly out of keeping with the objective requirements of collective security. A less favorable environment than that of the present postwar era, marked by the concentration of effective power in two massive states, each of them able to dispose of resources making it virtually invulnerable to nonmilitary sanctions and rendering illusory the concept of overwhelmingly preponderant force against it, can hardly be conceived. In 1920, a sensible man could envisage the possibility that any state might be seriously hampered by economic sanctions or decisively outclassed by collective forces organized to frustrate aggression; in 1945, no sensible man could believe that this held true in the case of the Soviet Union or the United States. Superpowers of their ilk, possessing or being in a position to control so great a percentage of the world's war-making resources, are not realistically susceptible to the workings of a collective security system. Aggression launched by such a power might be *defeated,* but it could not be *frustrated* in the manner conceived by the theorists of collective security. The failure of the United Nations to bring about the disarmament of the giants only intensifies the situation. The sad fact is that the kind of world in which collective security might be a feasible proposition, assuming that all the requirements other than those relating to objective conditions were satisfied, simply does not exist. History may record that collective security was a conceptual scheme for dealing with an eighteenth- or nineteenth-century kind of world, doomed to irrelevance in the twentieth century because of the disappearance of the multiplicity of great powers in favor of the duality of superpowers.

The final and decisive reason for the failure of the League and the United Nations to achieve a working system of collective security is the unfulfillment of the requisite subjective conditions. Neither peoples nor governments have undergone the transformation of viewpoints, attitudes, and values which collective security demands. Much effort has been expended in singling out the villains who have frustrated the realization of the conditions of peace, as defined by the theory of collective security, but the truth is that the responsibility is widely diffused. Stodgy old diplomats and militarists have sneered at the idealism of collective security, and idealists and pacifists have betrayed its realistic premise that the upholders of peace must be prepared to fight at the drop of a steel helmet. Ruthless dictators like Hitler have defied the law against aggression, and isolationist democracies like pre-World War II America have indulged in the selfish and self-defeating luxury of sovereign irresponsibility. Great powers have insisted upon maintaining a free hand in foreign policy, and minor states have sought to enjoy the status of consumers only, and not producers, of collective security.

In the League era, the United States never went further than assuring the Disarmament Conference that, if it should put into effect a general scheme of disarmament, America would be willing to consult regarding threats to the peace and to pledge itself not to interfere with collective actions directed against aggression, provided it should agree that such actions were justifiable in the given case.[31] Lest this promise that "we probably will refrain from hindering your work" should sound too daringly cooperative, the American spokesman later announced that "The United States will not . . . make any commitment whatever to use its armed forces for the settlement of any dispute anywhere." [32]

In the same era, virtually identical sentiments were being expressed by the leaders of states which had theoretically accepted, rather than rejected, the obligations of collective security. A Canadian spokesman, Senator Dandurand, rationalized his country's reluctance to fulfill collective security commitments by arguing that: "In this association of mutual insurance against fire, the risks assumed by the different states are not equal. We live in a fireproof house, far from inflammable material." [33] France displayed enthusiasm for collective security only in so far as it might operate to promote French security against a German resurgence, and Germany pointed up the problem of creating a genuinely impartial and universal security system in a statement that "The German Government cannot imagine it a practical reality that Germany, one day, should be defended on her own territory by Soviet Russian troops against an attack in the West or by French troops against an attack in the East." [34] British statesmen sounded strangely like representatives of the United States, in such expressions as these:

---

[31] See the citation from a statement made by Norman Davis at Geneva, in May 1933, *ibid.*, pp. 156-157.

[32] Cited in Philip C. Jessup, *International Security* (New York: Council on Foreign Relations, 1935), p. 60.

[33] Cited in Harold Butler, *The Lost Peace* (London: Faber and Faber, n.d.), p. 34.

[34] Cited in Royal Institute of International Affairs, *International Sanctions*, p. 134.

Nations cannot be expected to incur automatic obligations save for areas where their vital interests are concerned. . . .

It is really essential that we should not enter into any extensive general and undefined commitment with the result that, to a large extent, our foreign policy would depend, not on this country, this Parliament and its electors, but on a lot of foreign governments.

I am not prepared to engage this country by new unspecified commitments operating under conditions which cannot be foreseen. . . .[35]

These subjective conditions have not been basically changed in the United Nations era. The world's sense of interdependence has increased, and the community of peril has to some extent been recognized as a community of interest. In many instances, the horizons of national concern have been broadened. A most significant change has occurred in the attitude and policy of the United States, which has largely discarded its isolationist illusions and its fetish of the right to be irresponsible. Nevertheless, the fundamental human alterations which are essential to collective security have by no means been accomplished. Men, by and large, are still unprepared to act as if they believe in the indivisibility of peace; they are not ready to acknowledge the primacy of a global community and to assume the identity of national interests with the universal interest; they are not willing to accept the risks of commitment to defend any victim against any aggressor under unforeseeable circumstances in accordance with the decision of an international agency which is independent of national control; they are not prepared to bet their national life upon the proposition that the international community will faithfully and effectually safeguard their security; they are not confident that they can forego the autonomous pursuit of national strength and the discretionary formulation of national policy for dealing with future contingencies. To cite an important example, the American people have just become psychologically and ideologically fit to participate in a modernized type of alliance, designed to deter or defeat aggression from a specified quarter. This represents progress, but it is a far cry from the mentality of collective security. As things stand today, only a state which is threatened by the possibility of Communist aggression enjoys the reasonable prospect that it may benefit from multilateral assistance resembling in some measure the collaborative aid envisaged by collective security.

The Desirability of Collective Security. The official ideology of in-

---

[35] Citations from Anthony Eden, Sir John Simon, and Neville Chamberlain, in John W. Wheeler-Bennett, *Munich: Prologue to Tragedy* (New York: Duell, Sloan and Pearce, 1948), pp. 33, 355-356, 358.

ternational organization in the twentieth century has tended to treat collective security as an unquestioned ideal. Internationalist reaction to the failure to achieve the ideal has generally involved regretful reflection upon the difficulty of transforming the value systems and behavior patterns of nation-oriented leaders and peoples, and hopeful consideration of the possibility of inducing the human alterations and promoting the changes in objective circumstances which are essential for its attainment. Collective security would be a good thing if it could be established; the problem is to establish it. This rather smug ideological assumption demands a skeptical evaluation.

The challenging of the collective security proposition may well begin with a critical look at the bias toward automatism which pervades the doctrine. Collective security seeks to provide a deterring effect upon potential aggressors and a reassuring effect upon potential victims of aggression; for the achievement of this central purpose, it relies upon the inflexible definition in advance of the policy of the constituent states of the system. Neither friend nor foe of international order must be left in doubt that the illegal use of force will inexorably evoke the collective action of the community.

This concept of foreordained, automatic reaction to aggression is incapable of realization, regardless of the degree to which the conditions of collective security may be fulfilled. In this realm, the quest for absolute certainty is the pursuit of a will-o'-the-wisp. If the commitment to institute sanctions is defined in a treaty rule, as in the case of the League, the finding that appropriate occasion has arisen for carrying out the obligation must be made by the responsible leaders of the participating states, and there can be no guarantee that they will make such a finding; if the responsibility for setting the collective security mechanism into motion is entrusted to an international agency, as in the case of the United Nations, the essential decisions will have to be determined by the votes of governmental representatives, and there can be no guarantee that their votes will reflect the realities of aggression or the ideal of collective security. The point is that the critical decisions must always be made by *men,* and no treaty formulation or institutional blueprint can give assurance that human beings will infallibly produce decisions representing accurate appreciation of the facts and faithful adherence to principle. It is unavoidable that the aggressor should always be able to hope, and the victim be compelled to fear, that the collective security system would not be put into operation. As P. B. Potter has put it:

> no advance definition can remove the necessity for the exercise of some judgment in the premises. And the power to apply or not to apply sanctions must be lodged in some authority of the states, in order to work the system at all. Automatic sanctions in any literal sense

> are figments of the imagination; no legal prescriptions, however complete, which require positive action for their execution, can ever operate without the intervention of some human agency.[36]

There can be no substitute for, or guarantee of, sound judgment and moral integrity.

Aside from the ultimate unattainability of absolute predictability in this sphere, a good case can be made for the undesirability of the kind of automation in foreign policy which collective security postulates. There is undoubted value in making it absolutely clear in advance what the response to aggression will be; it is quite probable that World War II might have been averted, as has so often been suggested, if the Axis dictators had been convinced that they would be confronted with the coalition which was in fact mobilized against them. But this coin has another side. To adopt a rigid formulation of future policy in international relations is to ignore the infinite variety of circumstances, the flux of contingency, the mutability of situations, which characterize that field, and to abdicate the function of applying statesmanlike rationality to problems as they arise. Hans Wehberg recognized the importance of preserving an area for the exercise of discretionary statesmanship when he warned that the concept of automatism might mean that "sanctions would run the League instead of the League running the sanctions." [37] There is something to be said for keeping the potential enemy guessing as well as for informing his expectations, and there is a great deal to be said for preventing his becoming master of the disposition of potential opposing forces by exploiting the possibility of making them rush to points of his own choosing whenever he rings a bell. For example, assuming the existence of a full-fledged collective security system today, there would be a serious danger that the Soviet Union might deliberately pull the triggers that would bring collective forces into Asia, in order to catch the United Nations off balance for a major assault in Europe. This kind of maneuver is always a danger, and the way to guard against it is assuredly not to adopt a policy of automatic response which precludes cautious avoidance of the trap.

In short, it is a counsel of prudence that, in a world which is approaching the development of push-button warfare, there should be no attempt at push-button foreign policy. If the nations have poor statesmen, they had better try to get good ones, rather than try to substitute robotistic collective security operatives. The successful conduct of international affairs requires a more pragmatic approach than is compatible with the essentially doctrinaire theoretical system of collective security.

---

[36] "Sanctions Against a Recalcitrant State," Howard O. Eaton, ed., *Federation—The Coming Structure of World Government* (Norman: University of Oklahoma Press, 1944), p. 107. Copyright, 1944, by the University of Oklahoma Press.

[37] Cited in Payson S. Wild, Jr., *Sanctions and Treaty Enforcement* (Cambridge: Harvard University Press, 1934), p. 149.

From a practical point of view, there are problems in the application of collective security which have not been fully appreciated or dealt with in its theoretical formulation. Collective security is very much like Marxism, in the sense that its theory has reflected excessive preoccupation with the moment of initiation of decisive action. Marxism focuses on the revolution, without adequate concern for what happens later; collective security focuses on the instigation of sanctions, without adequate concern for further developments. In particular, collective security offers no theoretical guide to the problems of concluding collective action, determining the limits of community coercion, and establishing a settlement after the successful squelching of aggression. This was illustrated in the Korean case, imperfect as it was as an instance of collective security in operation.[38] The doctrine calls the upholders of world order into action, but it leaves them unenlightened concerning such vital questions as how far to press their action and how to liquidate the state of quasi-war between the community and the culprit.

The Marxist analogy may also be applied to the closely related problem of leadership. Marxism postulates an automatic outcropping of revolution, but then turns to reliance upon dedicated leaders—without, however, remembering to provide a means for guaranteeing that leaders will not distort the revolution to serve their own ends. Collective security seems to neglect the whole issue of leadership, assuming a kind of spontaneous collective response to the challenge of aggression. As the Korean episode made clear, however, the doctrinal system needs a well-developed concept of leadership. Only the determined initiative of the United States made United Nations intervention in Korea possible, and only a much more elaborate system for controlling and directing the exercise of American leadership could have made the episode a reasonable facsimile of collective security operation. Collective security is both more dependent upon the availability of great power leadership and more needful of means for confining its leaders within the framework of collective responsibility than its theorists have realized.

Aside from these indications that the problems of collective security go beyond the mere difficulties of getting it established and accepted, there are reservations of a moral nature which call into question the very desirability of collective security as an ideal purpose of international organization.

The moral criticism begins with a sophisticated reminder that no highly developed moral consensus exists on the global plane, that no nation's history is free from the taint of immoral international behavior, and that no international conflict is unaffected by moral ambiguity. It may be argued that collective security is the embodiment of an offensive moral

[38] See Leland M. Goodrich, "Korea: Collective Measures Against Aggression," *International Conciliation,* No. 494, October 1953.

pretentiousness, in that it purports to organize the forces of good against the evil-doers, and of a tendency toward enormous moral oversimplification, in that it equates rebelliousness with moral guilt, even though it be rebelliousness against the injustice of a coercively established and maintained status quo.

There is certainly much truth in the observation that moral issues are seldom clear-cut in international affairs. In practice, collective security might either operate on the basis of dubiously valid moral judgments, or be reduced to inactivity by the difficulty of making nice moral distinctions.

Yet, all this is beside the point. Collective security is conceived as a legal, rather than a moral, system, and it has only such moral value as may be attributed to any scheme for obviating the arbitrary use of force. The whole legal enterprise of human society is involved in the penalization of disturbers of the peace, without too much consideration of the factors which make the peace susceptible of disturbance. In moral terms, the justification of law and order, whether it be upheld by governmental or collective security systems, is that it provides a stable context within which the quest for substantive justice may be pursued. It may be doubted whether the "plague on everybody's house" of those whose consciousness of moral relativism makes them unwilling to hazard moral distinctions is normatively superior to the "plague on a particular house" which collective security is supposed to pronounce. Collective security is based upon the proposition not that the international moral spectrum is limited to black and white, but that the differential shadings of gray are more significant than the universality of gray.

The moral objection raised by literal pacifism is not one that can detain us here. Suffice it to say that collective security is at one with every significant concept of national or world government in assuming the necessity and legitimacy of posing the threat of authorized force for the purpose of minimizing the incidence of unauthorized force. The argument that collective security tends to increase the global quantity of violence by universalizing every local war is really directed against the practicability rather than the moral quality of the collective security concept. The design is to prevent local wars by organizing universal opposition to local aggression; this scheme may not work, but it is no less devoted than pacifism to the ideal of eliminating war.

Finally, collective security is subject to the moral criticism that it contemplates the indiscriminate punishment of entire populations for the misdeeds of their governments—in short, that it involves resort to *war* rather than *police action*. This moral problem has long weighed on the hearts of advocates of collective security; it affected the members of a special League body in 1935 so drastically that they brought themselves to suggest, in a report on possible economic sanctions:

> It is possible that a deterrent effect of some importance might be attained without any very serious disturbance of economic life, for example by the withholding of some product such as coffee or codfish, which the population are unwilling to forego, but which, so far as any essential needs are concerned, could easily be dispensed with.[39]

In general, the League suffered from a coffee and codfish mentality which reflected not so much a hopeless stupidity concerning the realities of international politics as a moral sensitivity concerning the implications of starving, or shooting, innocent women and children. Today, this moral dilemma has become largely the property of champions of world government, who use it to dramatize the urgency of establishing a global regime which would improve upon collective security by making the punishment fit the crime and hit the criminal and him alone.

The feasibility of creating such a regime will be discussed in Chapter 18. It is appropriate at this point to remark that collective security action, like ordinary war, entails collective suffering because human beings are organized in political collectivities to which they give their fundamental allegiance. So long as men fight as nations, they must be defeated as nations. "The innocent are involved with the guilty in conflicts between groups, not because of any particular type of coercion used in the conflict but by the very group character of the conflict." [40]

The precise punitive impact of police action is possible only when men have renounced ultimate loyalty to groups within the society, transferring their decisive allegiance to the larger entity. To achieve this kind of political transformation on a global scale is a very big order indeed, far bigger than world federalism has assigned itself. As late as 1860-1865, it had not occurred in the United States; when Americans revolted as members of states, they were put down by war against the states, rather than by police action against individuals. For as long a future as one can dimly envision, the world seems likely to be a pluralistic political society, characterized by the existence of collective units possessing the political capacity for launching organized violence which can be dealt with only by measures having a collective impact.

For our time, the moral choice is not between the destruction of innocents and the punishment of guilty individuals, but between failure and success in preventing the unleashing of all-encompassing destruction upon the human family. No system, be it collective security or world government, which is not prepared to deal with states as such, including if necessary the guiltless civilians of states, can claim relevance to the human crisis of the twentieth century. The theory of collective security has many de-

---

[39] Cited in Royal Institute of International Affairs, *International Sanctions,* p. 203.

[40] Reinhold Niebuhr, *Moral Man and Immoral Society* (New York: Scribner's, 1952), p. 241.

merits, but its insistence that it is states that must be controlled is surely one of its merits.

CONCLUSION

The ideal of establishing collective security has been neither realized nor abandoned. The goal has been pursued more ardently and consistently in words than in deeds, and statesmen have regularly turned to other objectives when confronted with concrete situations of urgency. The world is very far from the satisfaction of the essential requirements for permitting the operation of a collective security system, and such a system, even if feasible, is in fact a less attractive ideal than it has often been considered. Nevertheless, this doctrine has achieved a major ideological significance, and it is probable that international organization will continue to pin its gaze upon the objective of collective security, while vacillating toward and away from it in actual policy.

If the analysis has suggested that the establishment of collective security would be a miracle, but that it would not work miracles if established, this point ought not to be taken too seriously. There are few if any doctrinal systems which can withstand the rigors of a maximalist analysis. Democracy, for instance, fares no better than collective security if subjected to a logic which pushes to the edges of its theoretical foundations. There is a logic of the practicable minimum, according to which systems are imperfectly established, and work moderately well, in defiance of the laws of logical gravity which should bring them tumbling down.

This happy rule of thumb in human affairs applies in the case of collective security. Some approximation of collective security action has been undertaken in two notable cases: the Italian invasion of Ethiopia in 1935, and the Communist assault upon South Korea in 1950. If the League's action in the former case was a failure, it was certainly not an unqualified failure, for it proved if anything the possible effectiveness of collective sanctions under better circumstances rather than the inherent unworkability of such an enterprise. If the action of the United Nations in the latter case was a success, it was certainly not an unqualified success, for it did little to increase the probability that similar action—but action more fully compatible with the concept of collective security—would be forthcoming in future emergencies. Neither theoretical criticism nor practical experience has disposed of the possibility that the principles embodied in the doctrine of collective security may serve as elements contributing to the empirical development by international organization of a more effective approach to world order than has hitherto been realized.

It can be devastatingly demonstrated, as Walter Schiffer has done, that collective security is based upon the inherently contradictory proposition that states are both irresponsible enough to create the urgent problem of war and responsible enough to solve the problem; as Schiffer put it, in a discussion of the League:

> The idea that a special machinery for the prevention of war was necessary implied the pessimistic assumption that the world's condition still was far from being perfect. But without the optimistic assumption that reason and good faith prevailed in the world, it could not be hoped that the new regime would work. It may be said that, as far as the prevention of war was concerned, the League's successful functioning depended on conditions which, if they had existed, would have made the organization unnecessary.[41]

It can be proved that collective security is a circular proposition, demanding the prior satisfaction of requirements which can be satisfied only after collective security has become successfully operative, and purporting to solve problems by means which assume that the problems have already been solved. It can be pointed out that a full-fledged collective security system cannot be achieved at one fell swoop, but that an incomplete and imperfect system may do more harm than good, by inducing states to rely upon it when it is unreliable, and by promoting the universalization of wars when it is in no position to achieve the collective frustration of aggression.

Yet, the point remains that the theory of collective security has inspired the growing recognition that war anywhere is a threat to order everywhere, has contributed to the maintenance of the realistic awareness that it is states which are the effective components of international society and which are consequently the essential objects of a system aiming at the control of international disorder, and has stimulated the rudimentary development of a sense of responsibility to a world community on the part of governments and peoples. As a doctrinaire formula for a global panacea, collective security is a snare as well as a delusion; as a formulation of the reality of global involvements and the ideal of global responsibilities, it may be a vital contribution to the evolutionary development of the conditions of peace through international organization.

SUGGESTED READINGS

Claude, Inis L., Jr., *Power and International Relations,* New York: Random House, 1962.

Goodrich, Leland M., *Korea: A Study of U. S. Policy in the United Nations,* New York: Council on Foreign Relations, 1956.

Goodrich, Leland M., and Anne P. Simons, *The United Nations and the Maintenance of International Peace and Security,* Washington: The Brookings Institution, 1955.

[41] *The Legal Community of Mankind* (New York: Columbia University Press, 1954), p. 199.

Haas, Ernst B., "Types of Collective Security: An Examination of Operational Concepts," *American Political Science Review,* March 1955, pp. 40-62.

Liska, George, *International Equilibrium,* Cambridge: Harvard University Press, 1957.

Martin, Andrew, *Collective Security: A Progress Report,* Paris: UNESCO, 1952.

Royal Institute of International Affairs, *International Sanctions,* London: Oxford University Press, 1938.

Walters, F. P., *A History of the League of Nations,* London: Oxford University Press, 1952, Vol. II, Chap. 53.

Wolfers, Arnold, *Discord and Collaboration,* Baltimore: Johns Hopkins, 1962, Chaps. 11-12.

CHAPTER

13

Disarmament as an Approach to Peace

The concept of disarmament—a term which is used here to include the limitation, control, and reduction of the human and material instrumentalities of warfare as well as their literal abolition—has occupied a prominent place in the thinking of persons concerned with world peace for more than a century and a half. Immanuel Kant included the elimination of standing armies as the third of his "Preliminary Articles of Perpetual Peace Between States," [1] and the nineteenth century was marked by the development in many countries of a considerable body of support for the idea of disarmament. The conclusion of the Rush-Bagot Agreement of 1817, whereby the United States and Britain laid the foundations for the remarkable policy of nonmilitarization of the Canadian-American frontier, signified the intrusion of the idea into the realm of practical statesmanship. On various occasions during the century, governmental leaders expressed interest in disarmament, and the concept achieved an unprecedented degree of official international notice when Czar Nicholas II cited its realization as one of the major objectives of the first Hague Conference, in his celebrated Rescript of August 24, 1898. Thus, disarmament became a part of the stock of ideas bequeathed to the twentieth century by the nineteenth.[2]

---

[1] *Perpetual Peace,* p. 4.

[2] See Merze Tate, *The Disarmament Illusion: The Movement for a Limitation of Armaments to 1907* (New York: Macmillan, 1942).

THE THEORY OF DISARMAMENT

Taken with strict literalness, disarmament appears as an appealingly direct and simple means to peace. Whereas pacific settlement proposes to leave states with nothing to fight about, and collective security proposes to confront aggressors with too much to fight against, disarmament proposes to deprive nations of anything to fight with. It purports to eliminate war in the most straightforward way conceivable—by eliminating the means by which it is possible to wage war. Franklin Roosevelt gave voice to this concept when he defined his "Fourth Freedom" in terms of "a world-wide reduction of armaments to such a point and in such a thorough fashion that no nation will be in a position to commit an act of physical aggression against any neighbor—anywhere in the world." [3] It is a feature of this approach that it renders unnecessary any analysis of the causes of war; no matter what men fight about, or even if they fight simply because they are men, it provides an answer to the problem of belligerence.

Disarmament theory is not always so rigorously simple-minded as this. It has, in fact, contributed its share to the body of thought concerning the causation of war. In its more sophisticated versions, it rests upon the assumption that national military resources do not merely make war physically possible, but that they figure significantly among the factors which make war a political probability.

It may be argued that the sheer possession of vast lethal power imposes an undue strain upon mere human beings. Men are not gods, and when they gather the power of the gods in their hands they come to behave like beasts. The nation which develops inordinate military strength can hardly avoid the ultimate loss of self-restraint, the disposition to gain its ends by coercion, and the repudiation of the values of peaceful accommodation. The corrupting influence of power operates not only in dictatorships, where it stimulates the aggressive instincts of unchecked rulers, but also in democracies, where it debases popular standards of international morality and tends to promote the excessive influence of professional military men. This analysis lays particular emphasis upon the point that great armaments enhance the possibility that a state's foreign policy will be colored by the presumably militaristic views of its officer class.

If military superiority breeds arrogance and ruthlessness, military rivalry breeds mutual fear which is all too easily transformed into hatred and neurotic insecurity. Disarmament theory is really less concerned with the political effects of military preponderance than with the implications of the arms race. Tensions produce armament; armament breeds counter-armament; competitive armament increases tensions. The self-propelling arms race is regarded as an inexorable march to the violent climax of

---

[3] *A Decade of American Foreign Policy,* p. 1.

war. The certainty of the catastrophic conclusion may be explained in various ways. It may be postulated that war will be precipitated by the calculated decision of a party which gains a precarious lead, or which fears that time is on the side of its competitor. It may be anticipated that the stress of the race will produce trigger-happiness on one or both sides, making for explosive reactions to minor provocations. Resort may be had to the argument that taxpayers' weariness will lead to war, as the economic burden of sustaining the competition grows to intolerable proportions.[4] Theorists may introduce the deterministic concept of automatic detonation, suggesting that military establishments have a way of exceeding the bounds of human control, reaching a point of critical mass and thereupon "just going off." The argument may be broached that armaments, having no other utility than for making war, are clearly created for that purpose and will obviously be used for that purpose; who can believe that politicians build up ready military potential except to put it to military use? The prediction of a bloody conclusion may be based upon the alleged lessons of history; have not arms races always culminated in war?

Whether the inevitability of the result be attributed to the frailty of human nature, the rationality or the irrationality of governmental leaders, the inherent combustibility of counter-poised military forces, or the inscrutable workings of history, the point is the same: the theorists of disarmament are convinced that arms races cause wars. On the basis of this assumption, they advance the proposition that the elimination of national armaments, or the limitation of competitive military development so as to keep force levels at a very low point, offers mankind's best hope for a peaceful world.

This general line of reasoning has its strong points. Certainly, the competitive massing of national power tends to exacerbate rather than to diminish frictions, and to heighten the tensions of insecurity. The existence of powerful military establishments may increase the probability of hot-blooded wars; if a quarrel occurs between disarmed nations, an automatic cooling-off period is built into the situation, whereas the instant availability of armaments makes it feasible—and may make it tempting—for rash statesmen to plunge recklessly into war.

However, the disarmament thesis is subject to the fundamental criticism that it confuses germs and symptoms, causes and effects, means and ends. According to this view, armament policy reflects rather than creates the ambitions, antagonisms, and fears which underlie the phenomenon of war; arms races are the product rather than the cause of the intent to make war or the apprehension of the danger of war; in the final analysis, peace is a political problem, and disarmament should be envisaged as the happy result rather than the effective method of its solution. The truth is that this

---

[4] Cf. Kant, *loc. cit.*

is a circular problem, in which causes and effects, policies and instruments of policy, revolve in a cycle of interaction and are blurred into indistinguishability. Nevertheless, there are strong indications that the elimination of war is more dependent upon intervention into the vicious circle at the points of political conflict than at the points of military technology.

Regardless of the primary or secondary nature of the problem of armaments, the transformation of the world into an armed camp is a perilous enterprise. However, sound thinking requires that we avoid the temptation to take too seriously the figurative language that comes so easily to mind when we consider the problem; war material may be made of explosive substances, but it does not follow that an armed world is a powder keg, and it may be misleading to use the terminology of physical explosions—spontaneous combustion, sparks of static electricity, critical mass, etc.—in analyzing the prospects for political explosions. Military establishments are instruments at the disposal of policy makers, and while the possession of vast power may incite governments to go to war, it may equally tend to induce sober constraint. It is not necessarily true that "as a greater part of national life becomes consumed by military preparation, the imagination toward peaceful solutions is dulled." [5] Quite the reverse may be true; rising consciousness of the destructive potential of modern warfare may breed reluctance to resort to force. Operating at a relatively low level of power, statesmen may regard war as a manageable instrument of policy, and decide to use it without serious hesitation. The effect of drastically raising that level may be to destroy the serviceability of war, and to promote a search for alternative means of conducting policy.

This analysis has possible application to the current situation of political hostility and arms competition between the Soviet and the Western blocs. The accumulation of enormous quantities of destructive power may lead not to the spontaneous detonation of hydrogen bombs but to the spontaneous repudiation of war by statesmen; opposing stockpiles may produce mutual cancellation rather than mutual ignition. Indeed, it is conceivable that the nations are on the road to becoming too strong to fight. The phenomenon of the cold war may be a straw in the historical wind. It is less remarkable as an expression of hostility than as an indication of reluctance to use military means for implementing hostile purposes; historically, it may figure as an improvised substitute for war, adopted because the world was too effectively armed to permit the use of force. Similar significance may be attributed to the postwar development of aggression by proxy and fraudulent civil war; the limited military conflicts since World War II have been expressions of the Soviet Union's reluctance to initiate World War III no less than of its inclination to use force to achieve its aims. The great struggle of our time has not been caused by the

---

[5] Clark M. Eichelberger, *UN: The First Ten Years* (New York: Harper, 1955), p. 48.

extraordinary development of lethal weapons, but the disposition to conduct it by primarily nonmilitary means may have been so caused. If it eventuates in global and total war, this may be not so much because of as in spite of the fact that unprecedented armed might has become available to the contestants.

This point of view has been most ably expressed by Sir Winston Churchill, who told the British House of Commons on November 3, 1953, with reference to the new weapons of mass destruction:

> Indeed I have sometimes the odd thought that the annihilating character of these agencies may bring an utterly unforeseeable security to mankind.
>
> When I was a schoolboy I was not good at arithmetic but I have since heard it said that certain mathematical quantities when they pass through infinity change their signs from plus to minus—or the other way round.
>
> It may be that this rule may have a novel application and that when the advance of destructive weapons enables everyone to kill everybody else nobody will want to kill anyone at all.
>
> At any rate, it seems pretty safe to say that a war which begins by both sides suffering what they dread most, and that is undoubtedly the case at present, is less likely to occur than one which dangles the lurid prizes of former ages before ambitious eyes.[6]

The British statesman has been quoted as referring to "the balance of terror" as a possible substitute for the balance of power, and as asserting: "It is to the universality of potential destruction that we may look with hope and even confidence." [7]

Many will feel less than fully reassured by the thesis that the weapons of fission and fusion which are certain to make a new global war infinitely more terrible tend also to make its occurrence less probable. Nevertheless, the indication of this possibility is a useful offset to the dogmatic and somewhat mystical contention of disarmament theorists that the explosiveness of the international situation is a direct and inescapable function of the size of existing stockpiles of military explosives. The Churchillian inversion does not deny the ideal of a disarmed world, but it does challenge the fatalism of those who can find no hope in an armed world. The world has a way of managing to survive less by abolishing dangerous forces than by finding and utilizing countervailing forces and tendencies.

The concept of disarmament is at its theoretical best when it is combined with other approaches to peace. As we have seen, disarmament is integrally related to the theory of collective security; as a theoretical proposition, the drastic limitation of national weapons and the effective

---

[6] *New York Times,* November 4, 1953.

[7] Richard H. Rovere, "Letter from Washington," *The New Yorker,* January 29, 1955, p. 74.

organization of collaborative coercion add up to a hopeful answer to the question of how to assure world order. Similarly, disarmament forms a part of the conceptual complex in most schemes for world federation. Disarmament has assumed an equally prominent place in the development of theoretical approaches to peace through economic and social welfare. In the latter context, the case against competitive armaments is not so much that they may cause war as that they cost money and absorb resources, "threatening the stability of the world's economic structure which is necessary for peaceful existence," [8] and impeding concentration upon the constructive task of improving the lot of mankind. A notable shift toward this emphasis is indicated by the fact that the League Covenant referred simply to the proposition that "the maintenance of peace requires the reduction of national armaments," [9] whereas the major allies of World War II stated the problem in the Moscow Declaration and the Dumbarton Oaks Proposals, and the founding fathers of the United Nations expressed it in the Charter, in terms of the desirability of achieving "the least diversion for armaments of the world's human and economic resources." [10]

Whether or not disarmament *per se* constitutes a valid approach to peace, it is probable that any adequate solution to the problem of world order must include disarmament as one of its elements. The uncontrolled accumulation of military strength by national states is a symbol and a consequence of failure to solve the political problem of world order. It is futile in the sense that it offers states no prospect of meaningful and permanent security. It is dangerous in the sense that it may increase the probability of war, and that even if it has the opposite effect, it nevertheless makes any possible war a more certain catastrophe for human civilization. It is damaging to global society because it consumes economic resources to such an extent that it hampers the achievement of human welfare, thereby facilitating the encroachment of totalitarian tyrannies upon free peoples without the necessity of military conquest, and contributing to the creation of fundamental economic and social evils which render the world more susceptible to war. It is incompatible with the launching and operation of experimental schemes which offer hopeful possibilities of solving the basic problems of world order. If disarmament is no panacea for what ails the world, it is at least a necessary condition for the development of therapeutic methods which give promise of useful results.

---

[8] Eichelberger, *op. cit.*, p. 48.
[9] Article 8, paragraph 1.
[10] United Nations Charter, Article 26.

INTERNATIONAL ORGANIZATION AND THE DISARMAMENT MOVEMENT

The case for disarmament has proved sufficiently attractive to secure a place for the project of arms reduction on the agenda of official international discussion ever since the Hague Conference of 1899. The second Hague Conference tried, not quite successfully, to exclude the issue from its deliberations, but the framers of the League Covenant took pains to ensure that the first general world organization would devote considerable attention to the problem, making disarmament one of the featured aspects of its quest for peace and security.[11] The League was almost continuously occupied with efforts to formulate an acceptable plan for the limitation of military forces, efforts which were supplemented by such extra-League negotiations as those at the Washington Conference of 1921-22 and the London Naval Conference of 1930, and which culminated in the Disarmament Conference convened at Geneva in 1932. The United Nations Charter reaffirmed, albeit with less decisive emphasis than the Covenant, the concern of international organization with the problem of disarmament,[12] and the new organization has continued the League tradition by sponsoring persistent efforts to achieve general agreement upon a solution of the problem.

The disarmament movement has been extraordinarily successful in the sense that its project has been firmly established as a part of the necessary and proper business of international organization; this progress is strikingly illustrated by the contrast between the twenty-five minute brush-off which was accorded the disarmament question at the Hague Conference of 1907,[13] and the interminable discussions to which the question has given rise in the United Nations. The concept of disarmament has achieved such ideological sanctity that international organizations are as little likely to strike it off the agenda of debate as churches are to eliminate prayers from their Sunday services.

This, of course, is very far from saying that substantial progress has been made toward the realization of the disarmament ideal. It is important to avoid confusing long hours of international debate, vast piles of printed documents, and elaborate charts of institutional structure with meaningful accomplishment. Aside from certain limited and ephemeral successes which were achieved outside the League structure in the interwar period, and the conclusion, in 1963, of a multilateral treaty banning certain types of thermonuclear test explosions, the movement for arms reduction and limitation has been as unproductive of results as it has been

---

[11] See Articles 1 (paragraph 2), 8, 9, and 22 (paragraph 5).

[12] Articles 11, 26, and 47. See Inis L. Claude, Jr., "The United Nations and the Use of Force," *International Conciliation,* No. 532, March 1961, pp. 331-333, 340-342.

[13] Tate, *op. cit.,* pp. 340-342.

productive of words. The tremendous display of military fireworks from 1939 to 1945 was only the final and most tragic bit of evidence that the League's efforts had been an abject failure, and the virtual sterility of the work thus far undertaken by the United Nations in this field is one of the most glaring facts of international life. Unprecedented attempts at using multilateral machinery to secure disarmament in the twentieth century have not prevented our witnessing history's greatest war and the competitive accumulation of unprecedented stocks of destructive potential.

The long and wearisome record of multilateral debates concerning disarmament reveals an impressive list of difficulties which must be surmounted before the ideal of global demilitarization can be achieved. The most elementary requirement is that negotiations should be seriously undertaken and honestly motivated. This clearly was not the case at the Hague Conference of 1899, where the powers were extremely reluctant even to talk about disarmament and quite determined to do nothing more than make a gesture in deference to the dignity of Czar Nicholas II, who had initiated the conference, and to the idealism of pacifist elements in their populations.[14] Subsequently, statesmen have developed a much greater readiness, if not eagerness, to engage in international discussions concerning disarmament, but this is not to say that they have consistently exhibited a sincere desire to explore the possibilities of agreement. International organization has become a great promoter of sheer diplomatic loquacity and has provided exceptional opportunities for the exercise of propagandistic skill; disarmament debates provide as good examples as one might seek of speeches for the record only, and proposals formulated with a view to their unacceptability.

Even if statesmen are as interested in disarmament as in public international talks about disarmament, the possibility of achieving general agreement on the subject is severely limited by the intricate relationships between the instruments of power and the fundamental political factors of world affairs.

Military establishments are, in the first instance, related to the problem of the status quo. The function of national power is to uphold or to challenge the existing pattern of relationships, or to influence the establishment of a new one at a time when the world stands between the dissolution of the past and the definition of the future. Power is a relative phenomenon, and it lies in the nature of politics that statesmen should be more profoundly concerned with the ratios of its distribution than the absolute levels of its development. A scheme for the regulation of armaments must involve either the freezing of the configuration of power, at or below existing quantitative levels, or its alteration through the prescrip-

---

[14] *Ibid.*, pp. 267-293, 349.

tion of differential degrees of disarmament. In the former case, the attitudes of governments will be determined by their estimates of the adequacy of their power position for implementing their policies with respect to the status quo; in the latter case, acceptability of the scheme hinges upon the capacity of the disadvantaged states to become convinced that the distribution of national power will be irrelevant to the management of international relations in the era that lies ahead. In either case, the focus of practical statesmanship must lie upon the question of power relationships, in contrast to the preoccupation of disarmament theory with the quantitative aspect of the power situation.

There is no political barrier to the reduction of armaments as such, except in so far as it may have an unwanted impact upon domestic politics. But disarmament projects necessarily evoke political evaluation because any prescribed reduction of forces may be found to alter power ratios, and because a permanent regulation of national military policies in the future—which is essential if disarmament is to do more than end an old and start a new arms race—involves the commitment of states to abandon the autonomous manipulation of power relationships. Thus, the effect of disarmament is to rigidify *some* configuration of power—either the prereduction or the postreduction configuration.

If disarmament is conceived in terms of perpetuating an existing pattern of power distribution at a lower level of armament, it is confronted with the political difficulty that some states are always eager to improve what they consider to be their dangerously inferior position and others are determined to consolidate what they consider to be a precariously superior position. Moreover, satisfaction with a given power configuration is conditioned by attitudes toward the status quo; a literal balance of power is theoretically adequate for upholders of existing arrangements, but a definite preponderance of strength must be the objective of ambitious revisionists. The trouble with disarmament is that it must begin at some point in time, and no time is ever quite right—in the eyes of all the essential participants—for beginning it. Indefinite procrastination, not definitive repudiation, is the political reaction most responsible for the gray hairs of the champions of disarmament.

If a disarmament plan which freezes the status quo by stabilizing the power situation is frustrating to ambitious states, one which promises to undermine the status quo by reversing power relationships is alarming to the beneficiaries of the established order. The urge to avoid the worsening of the national power position is the universal passion of participants in disarmament conferences, far more significant than any enthusiasm for disarmament itself; responsible statesmen may be prepared to consider the forswearing of national ambitions, but never to entertain the idea of reducing the relative strength of the nation.

The prominence of this cautionary attitude is attributable to the direct involvement of the fundamental problem of security. General attitudes toward the global status quo pale into insignificance beside this basic national concern. It is a fact of international life that no nation is likely to believe that it enjoys more than the essential margin of safety, or to admit that its competitors have confined themselves to the military preparations necessary for the defense of legitimate interests; "in the realm of arms, one nation's common sense is another nation's high blood pressure." [15] Statesmen may accept the abstract view that an arms race is inimical to security, but this does not lead to the conclusion that the acceptance of inferiority under a disarmament treaty, any more than the failure to keep pace in an arms race, is conducive to security.

The answer to all these political reservations is presumably that disarmament must be part of a package which includes means for establishing a general settlement of outstanding issues, upholding the status quo, promoting peaceful change, and guaranteeing national security. This is to say that national forces must be rendered superfluous through the provision of alternative means for the performance of their legitimate functions. The moral of this story is that "the problem of disarmament is not the problem of disarmament. It really is the problem of the organization of the world community." [16] Thus, in political terms, disarmament is feasible only within the context of an institutional system which falls somewhere within the range of ambitiousness bounded by the League of Nations and world government.

This is not a prescription which permits the evasion of the problems of priority and circularity. The League represented an effort to create an organized world order in which disarmament would make political sense, but it also relied heavily upon disarmament to establish the conditions in which its system of order could become operative. Its history was a record of incessant wrestling with the problem of priority, but if the conclusive lesson of League experience was that political settlement and collective security must precede disarmament, it was not discovered how these goals could be reached in a world which had not yet subjected arms competition to control. This same dilemma applies in the case of the United Nations.

Despite the development of a sophisticated awareness of the interrelationship between fundamental political arrangements and disarmament, neither of the world organizations of the twentieth century has altogether escaped the notion that the problem of disarmament is the problem of disarmament. Consideration of the question in international agencies has been more heavily influenced by the Litvinov conception that "the way to

---

[15] *Steps to Peace: A Quaker View of United States Foreign Policy* (Philadelphia: American Friends Service Committee, 1951), p. 13.

[16] Salvador de Madariaga, cited in Quincy Wright, *A Study of War,* II, 801.

disarm is to disarm"[17] than by the more appropriate conception which a better Marxist than Litvinov might have expressed as belief in the ultimate "withering away" of armaments, given the requisite change in political circumstances. The long record of futility raises the basic question as to whether the major contribution of international organization to disarmament may not be expected to derive from wide-ranging activities which affect general political conditions, rather than from sponsorship of deliberations about disarmament.

The project of establishing a limitation of armaments is beset by technical as well as political problems. The measurement of power is by no means a precise science, and it is hardly surprising that national politicians should quarrel about quantitative estimates concerning which even disinterested experts would disagree. Yet the measurement of power is precisely the business of those who would formulate disarmament conventions.

The necessary foundation for a disarmament program is an agreed system of calculating the relative weights of the diverse elements which constitute military power. Which adds more to military potential, a submarine or a tank? Is the American industrial plant a greater asset than the Chinese manpower supply? How does a set of missiles measure against a powerful land army? These and a thousand other questions might be used to illustrate the impracticability of achieving precision in the quantitative comparison of existing national forces and the definition of equivalent power reductions.

Disarmament schemes which purport to reproduce a given ratio of power at a lower level of armament tend to encounter political objections because there can be no guarantee of their technical accuracy. Plans based upon the guiding principle of reducing each state to the military strength essential for legitimate defensive purposes fare no better, for they involve the double uncertainties of measuring power requirements and power potentials; pondering the imponderables of future defensive needs is surely as precarious an enterprise as measuring the immeasurables of military might. Projects of qualitative disarmament, aimed at eliminating "offensive" weapons while permitting the retention of "defensive" arms, give rise to insuperable problems of definition; the animals at Madariaga's imaginary conference found that "The lion wanted to eliminate all weapons but claws and jaws, the eagle all but talons and beaks, the bear all but an embracing hug."[18]

It might be argued that the obstacles to disarmament are all, in the final analysis, political ones, and that the technical problems would dis-

---

[17] See comment and texts relating to Soviet disarmament proposals in the League era, in Marina Salvin, "Soviet Policy toward Disarmament," *International Conciliation,* No. 428, February 1947.

[18] Wright, *op. cit.,* II, 806.

integrate if their political foundations were removed. The plausibility of this thesis is established by the complex entanglement of political and technical difficulties which is discernible in abstract analysis and which has been fully demonstrated in disarmament debates since World War I. However, the technical problems are real enough to cause trouble in their own right. Neither an implacably lawless state nor a situation of bitter rivalry is required to frustrate disarmament. Political animosities such as those between France and Germany barred disarmament in the League era, and similar conflicts between the Soviet Union and the United States have blocked agreement under the United Nations, but it does not follow that good will and good faith would pave the way to agreement. Even such inveterate friends as the United States and Britain probably could not agree on a formula of mutual arms limitation. The arms question currently causes no friction between them because they are now interested in the mutual enhancement, rather than the mutual reduction, of their strength; in a different world situation, their established political relationship might well make them indifferent to the question of their comparative power; but if they should set out to agree upon a set formula of permissible armament for each other, based upon the supposition that it was important to maintain a defined ratio between themselves, it is altogether likely that the technical obstacles to agreement would prove formidable. The technical problems of disarmament are exaggerated by political factors, but they also contribute directly to the difficulty of achieving acceptance of plans for regulating national strength.

The proposal of total disarmament might be considered the way out of the impasse which is created by the technical difficulty of reaching agreed estimates of power needs and potentials. But the power to destroy cannot be literally obliterated so long as human beings and their productive capacity exist; deindustrialization and perhaps even depopulation of the globe are the ultimate requirements for making war impossible. The best that human society can realistically aim at is to render arbitrary resort to violence improbable, and this necessarily involves an effort to establish the political control, rather than to accomplish the physical abolition, of the power factor in human affairs. The establishment of community mastery over the potential violators of peaceful order, whether it takes the form of collective security or world government, requires the lodgment of some power in some human hands, and this means that the problem of preventing the abuse of power is one that can never be definitively eliminated but must always be subjected to the precarious processes of political management.

THE PROBLEM OF INTERNATIONAL ATOMIC CONTROL

The complexities of the power problem are well illustrated by the course of the negotiations concerning disarmament, and particularly the control of atomic and hydrogen weapons, which have been conducted under the sponsorship of the United Nations.

The recognition of the new dimensions of the problem of war which are attributable to the dawning of the atomic age prompted the United Nations to assign greater importance to discussions about arms regulation than had been anticipated in the drafting of the Charter. The original effort, begun in 1946, to divorce consideration of atomic weapons from that of conventional weapons was succeeded in 1952 by the adoption of a unified approach to the whole arms question. The Disarmament Commission, enjoying the marked advantage of authority to deal with all types of military weapons, has thus far been no more successful than the previous Atomic Energy Commission and Commission for Conventional Armaments in securing agreement on means for reducing the levels and ending the competitive building of national power structures. Negotiations have been conducted in a variety of bodies, both related and unrelated to the United Nations structure, with monotonously negative results.

It is tempting to assign to one intransigent and ruthlessly expansive state, the Soviet Union, the entire responsibility for blocking the realization of the disarmament ideal in the post-World War II world. The Western powers have exhibited the intellectual comprehension of the requirements of human survival in the new age and the political reasonableness which are essential to the conclusion of civilization-saving agreements; the Communists, on the other hand, have displayed only suspicion, hostility, and bitter determination to pursue the power struggle to the resolutely desired end of world conquest. To assert the inaccuracy of this analysis is not to say that it exaggerates the difficulty of negotiating with the Soviet Union on disarmament questions, but rather that it understates the inherent difficulties of the disarmament approach to the problem of peace.

The original impasse in atomic negotiations was reached during the brief period when the United States enjoyed a temporary monopoly of atomic weapons and of the capacity to produce them. The United States developed the so-called Acheson-Lilienthal plan for the international control of atomic energy, which was presented, with some modifications, by Bernard Baruch as the official American proposal to the Atomic Energy Commission in 1946.[19]

This plan was based upon certain fundamental assumptions of unchallengeable validity: that the American monopoly was a passing phe-

---

[19] See *International Control of Atomic Energy: Growth of a Policy,* Department of State Publication 2702 (Washington: Government Printing Office, n.d.), Chapters V and VI, and Appendix 13.

nomenon, and that the real choice therefore lay not between American monopoly and international control, but between an atomic arms race and international control; that atomic energy promised to make available enormously useful nonmilitary benefits, and that it was therefore neither realistic to assume nor desirable to advocate the abandonment of scientific exploration in the atomic field; and that the avoidance of an atomic arms race required the creation of a continuously operating international control system which could give states assurance that agreed limitations and prohibitions were being universally observed.

The nature of the institutional safeguards against clandestine evasion of commitments was to be determined by the relevant scientific and technological facts. The production of nuclear materials for peaceful uses could not be divorced from the production of potential ingredients for atomic weapons; if states were to be permitted the uncontrolled operation of atomic processes for presumably innocent and constructive purposes, no control system could provide certain detection or prevention of the illegal diversion of fissionable materials to warlike ends. Hence, the system of international control should include ownership and direct operation of the mines and the plants for producing atomic fuel, monopolistic capacity for research in the field of atomic weapons, authority to limit states to licensed activity involving the utilization of nuclear material, and a supplementary power of uninhibited inspection of national scientific and industrial establishments, to ensure detection of illicit operation of processes reserved to the international organ and of misuse of facilities permitted to states under the restrictive international licensing power.

It should be noted that inspection was assigned a very limited, albeit a vital, role in this scheme. It was believed that inspection could produce reliable results only if the area of national atomic operations were drastically restricted by the international monopoly; if states were allowed to engage independently in the full range of activities necessary for the creation of fissionable materials, it would be technically impossible for any inspection system to certify that all such materials were being put to legitimate uses, and it would be politically impossible for international inspectors to secure the freedom of intrusion which would be essential for making a serious effort to provide that certitude. In short, for both technical and political reasons, inspection was regarded as the apex, but not the base, of the proposed control system.

These considerations were incorporated in the American proposal for an Atomic Development Authority, which would use its capacity for ownership, management, research, licensing, and inspection to fulfill its responsibility for ensuring the full exploitation of the peaceful potentialities of atomic energy and for providing states with security against sudden attack by enemies which had secretly violated the prohibition of atomic weapons. This plan has been rightly described as a proposal of limited world government, in the sense that it envisaged an international agency with functions and powers cutting deeply into the traditional preserve of national sovereignty. As Baruch elaborated the scheme in the Atomic Energy Commission, the Atomic Development Authority would have had a capacity for intrusion into national concerns, overriding the principle of domestic jurisdiction, and an authority for determining and acting upon breaches of the disarmament treaty, uninhibited by the veto power of any state.

The American position included a firm insistence upon the evolutionary unfolding of the scheme for international control of atomic energy. The plan was to be put into effect by stages, and the crucial requirement was that the control mechanism should become fully established and should demonstrate its capacity for effective operation, before the United States would undertake to carry out the obligation, which would be stated in the basic treaty, to dispose of its atomic weapons, accept the prohibition of the manufacture or use of such weapons, and turn over to the new agency its full stock of scientific and technological knowledge concerning the utilization of atomic energy. Control must come first; atomic disarmament would follow.

The response of the Soviet Union to the initiative of the United States was to propose instead a scheme which would involve the preliminary abandonment by the United States of its monopolistic position in atomic energy.[20] Existing stocks of nuclear weapons should be destroyed, and a legal prohibition of the manufacture or use of such weapons should be established; thereupon, a system for the international supervision of these commitments should be established and put into operation. Not only did the USSR demand the reversal of the pattern of priorities put forward by the United States, but it also rejected the comprehensive list of control mechanisms envisaged in the American plan. The international agency suggested by the Soviet Union would lack the authority to own, operate, and license atomic facilities, would have only a vaguely defined and apparently quite limited competence to inspect national atomic establishments, and would function in definite subordination to the Security Council, where the rule of great power unanimity would prevail in respect to all decisions of substantive importance.

The confrontation of these two fundamentally different proposals soon produced an impasse which destroyed all hope of achieving the timely establishment of international regulation in the new field of atomic energy, and of avoiding the development of an arms race of unprecedented dimensions. A modified version of the American proposal was accepted by the Atomic Energy Commission, and approved by the General Assembly on November 4, 1948, but the bitter dissent of the Soviet

---

[20] *Ibid.*, Appendix 22.

Union prevented progress toward the realization of the ambitious scheme for the international control of atomic energy which had been formulated in the United Nations on the basis of the American initiative.

This deadlock, formally acknowledged in 1948, has not been broken. Circumstances have changed in important respects; American monopoly has given way to intensive American-Soviet competition, and the dreaded expansion of the "nuclear club" has begun; fusion has become a more terrible word than fission, with hydrogen bombs towering over atomic bombs as mountains over molehills; diversified arsenals of thermonuclear weapons have been developed; and recurrent revolution in the means for delivering such weapons has become the norm. Against this changing military backdrop, disarmament discussions have continued in a variety of institutional settings. The United States has dropped its insistence upon international ownership of materials and facilities for production of the weapons of the new era, and has concentrated its emphasis upon the inspection phase of a possible control system. The Soviet Union has made, or purported to be willing to make, a number of concessions, including modification of its insistence upon the priority of atomic prohibition over atomic control, and enlargement of the supervisory authority of an international control agency. The combining of negotiations concerning conventional and mass-destruction armaments has led to the elaboration of new patterns in disarmament proposals. Finally, in 1963, the partial test-ban agreement was negotiated and promptly accepted by the great majority of states. These developments may ultimately prove to have contained the wedges for cracking the stubborn problem of disarmament, but the record of negotiations does not encourage an optimistic evaluation of this possibility. Despite the changes in circumstances and shifts in announced policies which have occurred since the atomic impasse was reached, it would appear that the fundamental gulf between American and Soviet positions has not been decisively narrowed.

An analysis of the unproductive quest for disarmament, which has characterized the United Nations almost since its inception, yields conclusions which are significant for the considered judgment of disarmament as a function of international organization.

First, the record does not support the contention that the erection of obstacles to arms agreements is peculiarly a habit or disposition of totalitarian regimes, or aggressive dictators, or Communist ideologues. The Soviet positions which Americans have considered most reprehensibly unreasonable have not been the products of a special Communist brand of political cynicism, but rather, in many cases, copies of positions not long abandoned by the United States. If the Soviet Union has played down the importance of an authoritative and elaborately equipped international agency for supervising disarmament, it has only adopted the view, officially stated in 1926 by the United States, that "any limitation of armaments must rest primarily upon international good faith and respect for treaties";[21] if it has exhibited suspicion of international surveillance, it has merely reproduced the unwillingness to admit foreign inspection of armaments which was adamantly expressed by the United States, among other Western powers, in 1919 and 1927.[22] The Soviet scheme for applying a standard reduction of one-third to the forces of the major powers, regularly advanced until 1955 and denounced with equal regularity as an evil Communist plot, was simply a replica of the formula suggested by the United States at the League Disarmament Conference.[23]

Indeed, the exchange of positions on disarmament and other matters has been so prominent a feature of Soviet-American relations that the historians of a future era may find it difficult to accept the notion, so confidently asserted in our time, that the conflict between the two powers is rooted in fundamental ideological differences which dictate contradictory lines of policy. The attitudes which have made the USSR resist the effectuation of ambitious organizational schemes for international regulation of armaments since World War II are clearly not derivatives of a Communist doctrine which other states have not accepted, but of the obsession with national sovereignty which other states have in some degree transcended. In short, the Soviet intransigence in disarmament debates is a reflection of the reactionary rather than the revolutionary character of the USSR.

The second major point concerning the disarmament debate in the United Nations is that no means has been discovered for evading the requirement that states participating in an arms regulation system be imbued with mutual trust. It has often been alleged that the original American plan for control of atomic energy had precisely the merit that it eliminated dependence upon the good faith of states by providing a reliable instrumentality for the enforcement of obligations. In an act of unparalleled generosity and creative statesmanship, the United States offered to relinquish its potential for mastering the world, giving other states certainty against an American atomic assault in exchange for reciprocal acceptance of institutional restraints. In matters of atomic life and death, nations cannot be expected to place their faith in paper promises; when the Soviet Union rejected the American plan, it refused an arrangement, based squarely upon the technical facts of atomic enterprise, which would have safeguarded the USSR against American perfidy just as it would have protected the United States against the danger of Soviet unscrupulousness. Confidence was to be bestowed upon a foolproof system, not upon states.

This proposition does not stand up. The Acheson-Lilienthal-Baruch

---

21 Sir Alfred Zimmern, *The American Road to World Peace* (New York: Dutton, 1953), p. 164.

22 Walters, *A History of the League of Nations,* I, 62, 366.

23 Andrew Martin, *Collective Security* (Paris: UNESCO, 1952), pp. 51-52.

proposal seemed to be in conformity with the requirements of technical reality, but it did not adequately reflect the conditions of political reality. States distrusted each other, with or without good cause, and the plan did not offer a solid basis for discarding the fears born of mutual apprehensiveness.

In particular, it demanded a considerable measure of Soviet confidence in the good faith of the United States. Communist leaders were expected to believe that the United States would in fact proceed to the carrying out of the final stages of atomic disarmament after the initial stage of establishing a control mechanism had been completed. They were to rely upon the honesty of the United States when it should announce that it had faithfully fulfilled its obligation to destroy or hand over to the Atomic Development Authority all its stock of nuclear weapons and ingredients—for there existed no technically reliable means of detecting carefully concealed supplies of fissionable material. American insistence that nothing less than direct international control of processing from mine to bomb would suffice to give security under the operation of the plan constituted an admission that nothing less than Soviet belief in American trustworthiness would suffice to give confidence that the United States did not hold out some lethal material when it purported to hand over the product of its early atomic monopoly to international authority. Moreover, even if America did not cheat at this stage, it would remain under the operation of the system as the only state which possessed the full range of knowledge and experience requisite for constructing atomic weapons; the USSR was asked to abandon atomic arms research and technological experiment under circumstances which would leave it inferior to the United States in scientific capacity to produce nuclear weapons in the event of a breakdown of the control system.

The Soviet-American struggle over priorities provides a clear indication of the underlying suspicions which becloud relations between the two great powers. By common agreement, prohibition of the manufacture, possession, and use of weapons of mass destruction and a control system to enforce this prohibition are the essential elements of an atomic disarmament program. The United States began by regarding prohibition as the element more costly to itself, while the Soviet Union considered control as the more onerous burden for itself. Hence, the United States insisted upon the priority of control, for fear that the USSR would never permit the realization of control if it first succeeded in imposing prohibition upon its rival; the American plan postponed the American sacrifice until the Soviet sacrifice should have been made. Contrariwise, the Soviet Union demanded that prohibition should come first, for fear that the United States would never actually move to the prohibition stage if it first succeeded in securing the development of a control system; the Soviet plan delayed the Soviet sacrifice until the American sacrifice should have been made. In short, the basic American plan did not obviate the necessity of relying upon the assumption of American good faith, and it is reasonable to assume that this was at least one of the reasons for its unacceptability to the USSR.

Soviet rejection of the American plan also reflected skepticism of the political impartiality of United Nations agencies. The Baruch proposal, as approved by the Atomic Energy Commission and the General Assembly, vested highly significant discretionary authority in the projected Atomic Development Authority. From the standpoint of the USSR, this was not the equivalent of a guarantee that Soviet interests would automatically be protected against the hostile policies of other states. Rather, to Soviet leaders, it seemed to involve turning over vital concerns to the tender mercies of "a majority on whose benevolent attitude toward the Soviet Union the Soviet people cannot count." [24] Given the propensity of United Nations organs to register majority decisions regularly opposed to Soviet policies, the USSR had as little reason to feel reassured by aspects of the atomic control scheme which purported to lodge authority in an international agency as by those which demanded confidence in the good faith of the United States.

The atomic impasse was in part at least the result of the fact that neither of the basic plans proposed by the chief rivals eliminated the necessity of mutual trust. The Soviet plan was even more defective from this point of view than the American plan; no scheme has yet been invented, and it is doubtful that any scheme could be devised, which would afford absolute security against evasion, flagrant violation, or abusive domination of the atomic control system by one of the major parties. In a matter so vital, the assumption of good faith is not enough, but it is indispensable.

Finally, it must be emphasized that the abortive American control plan was not a magic formula for abolishing the perils of the atomic age, even from the standpoint of the United States. It is tempting, but misleading, to assume that if the Soviets had accepted it and permitted its implementation, the specter of atomic warfare would have been banished from the earth.

The American plan was designed to place atomic materials behind a reliable burglar alarm, not within a burglarproof vault. At best, it offered the prospect of preventing atomic Pearl Harbors, not of abolishing the possibility of atomic wars; it provided safeguards against wars' beginning with atomic bombs, but not against wars' ending with atomic bombs. The validity of this point becomes clear when it is realized that the scheme did not purport to place at the disposal of the United Nations a power poten-

---

[24] Statement by Gromyko, cited in *International Control of Atomic Energy: Policy at the Crossroads,* Department of State Publication 3161, General Policy Series 3 (Washington: Government Printing Office, 1948), p. 80.

tial adequate to resist efforts by an aggressive state to seize atomic facilities and materials and turn them immediately to the production of nuclear weapons. Envisaging this dire possibility, the formulators of the plan offered as a solution the principle of strategic balance in the distribution of plants and stockpiles under the jurisdiction of the Atomic Development Authority. If this principle were put into effect, the seizure of facilities within its geographical grasp by one power would sound the alarm bell of impending aggression; if the violator persisted, other states would be in a position to take over atomic facilities of equivalent value in their vicinities; thus, the system would have broken down and atomic war would be in the offing, but surprise atomic attack would have been made impossible, and a rough balance of atomic potential would have been assured by the dispersal of facilities.[25]

Seen in this light, the Baruch plan was a scheme for preventing clandestine preparations for atomic assault, postponing to a moment of crisis the development of a nuclear arms race, and establishing moral restraints upon the tendency of states to resort to the threat of massive destruction for gaining their ends. These were notably useful objectives, but they did not include the purpose of making atomic war impossible. In the final analysis, the plan offered no substitute for the fear of retaliation and the sense of moral obligation as limiting factors in the conduct of international affairs. Thus, it was by no means a foolproof solution to the problem of the atomic age.

The intrinsic political difficulties of the project advanced by the United States were clearly not confined to those which presumably entered into the Soviet evaluation of the plan. The risks which would have been entailed for the United States were considerable ones. If the application of the principle of strategic balance had not been seriously undertaken, the suspicions of the Soviet Union would have been confirmed; yet, the application of that principle in good faith would have involved the construction, under international auspices and inevitably at some cost to the United States, of an atomic scientific and industrial complex within the territorial grasp of the Soviet Union comparable to that which had been erected in the United States. The carrying out of the plan would have required the removal from the American military establishment of the new weapon which had suddenly become the major American instrument for counterbalancing the Soviet manpower potential. It would have involved the ultimate development of an internationally owned and operated system of industrial energy which might dwarf the controversial public power enterprises operated by the United States Government. It would have entailed the reduction of American sovereignty to an unprecedented degree. To

---

[25] See the exposition of this concept, *ibid.*, pp. 93, 100-101, 134-135, 213.

list these drastic implications of the Baruch plan is surely to raise the question whether it would have been sound international policy for the United States to put the plan into effect, as well as the question whether domestic political considerations would have permitted the actual implementation of the plan.

All this points to the conclusion that the unreasonable intransigence of the Soviet Union was *not* the sole factor preventing the world from achieving, in the early postwar years, a foolproof solution to the problem of perpetuating civilization in the atomic age. The USSR was certainly unyielding and uncooperative, but the plan which it blocked was far from a perfect solution. It was a genuinely revolutionary scheme in some respects, but not in the sense of providing an adequate substitute for the fundamental requirement of mutual confidence among states, or of supplanting the fear of retaliation and the commitment to humane values as the precarious restraints upon the war-making propensities of nations.

If the concept of internationally regulated and supervised atomic disarmament never offered a meaningful possibility of emancipating mankind from the peril of nuclear catastrophe even in the brief period of American atomic monopoly, its potential as a world-saving principle is still more limited in the present era of competitive production of weapons of mass destruction.

The day has passed when a thermonuclear disarmament arrangement can be legitimately presented to any nation as a technically foolproof scheme. The United States now shares the position which the Soviet Union occupied without American company from 1945 to 1949: the adoption of any conceivable international control system would have to be supplemented by faith that no nation would be unscrupulous enough to conceal a supply of material for conversion into atomic or hydrogen weapons. As explained by Eugene Rabinowitch, editor of the *Bulletin of the Atomic Scientists*, this situation has arisen:

> [The] technical feasibility of atomic disarmament depends now on a reliable *inventory* of existing stocks of fissionable materials. Considering the extremely small bulk of these materials, and the absence of penetrating radiations emanating from them, . . . the only possibility of inventorying them is for the agents of the U.N. control body to be led to the stockpiles by national officials who know where they are located. Neither the West nor the USSR can be expected to base their own atomic disarmament on the faith that the other side has not concealed a substantial part of its stockpile. . . . If this conclusion is true, then we may have to add, to the appalling knowledge of the material and biological damage of an atomic war, the recognition that time for an effectively controlled atomic disarmament has irretrievably passed, and that attempts to find a compromise solution . . .

> are therefore bound to remain futile. . . . Mankind will have to live, from now on, with unlimited and unchecked stockpiles of atomic and thermonuclear explosives piling up, first in America and the Soviet Union, then in Great Britain, and later in other countries as well.[26]

Given this situation, it seems unreasonable to suppose that, as Clark Eichelberger has asserted, "The nations can agree upon a foolproof system of disarmament if a political agreement or series of political agreements clears the way." [27] Political agreements can only clear the way to a disarmament system which is *not* technically foolproof. The fundamental requirement of a universal sense of security has now become the development of a mutuality of confidence and a sense of political harmony so deep and pervasive that peoples of the world will find it irrelevant that no system of inspection can possibly unearth all that might be hidden. The urge for an unattainable foolproofness is itself evidence that the world is still far from the political point of being able to dispense with foolproofness. A happy marriage begins when husband and wife learn not to care in the least that it is impossible for them to devise a foolproof system for checking up on each other; the political units of international society have not achieved this state of bliss, but it would appear that their best hope lies in the ultimate development of relationships which will make the state of uncertainty concerning the configuration of power a tolerable condition.

The passage of the years since the atomic impasse developed has not only reduced the technical feasibility of a fully reliable control system to the vanishing point; it has also brought additional political complications to impede agreement in this field. Suspicions and animosities between the major power blocs have run deeper as the cold war has progressed. Commitments to massive armament programs have become more firmly established; rearmament has ceased to be regarded as a temporary expedient pending initiation of a multilateral disarmament program, and disarmament talks have become peripheral activities of states whose serious business is the building of national strength. Most significantly, weapons of mass destruction have tended to become increasingly indispensable elements of the military capacity which the Western bloc, under American leadership, has laboriously constructed to counter the threat of Soviet expansionism. The political prospects of atomic disarmament are best revealed by the recognition that the United States, the most vigorous proponent of an international atomic control system, would stand in a position perilously close to military nakedness if anything resembling its own original plan were accepted and put into effect. The answer might be found in a scheme involving the simultaneous reduction of conventional and unconventional components of military strength, such as the Soviet Union agreed

[26] "Living With H-Bombs," *Bulletin of the Atomic Scientists,* January 1955, p. 6.
[27] *Op. cit.,* p. 51.

to consider in 1955. But even if that were accepted, the continued existence of the huge population resources of the Soviet bloc would make the maintenance of atomic potential a vital concern of the Western powers. The survival of the human race is increasingly imperiled by the development of the destructive potential which might be unleashed in time of war, but the survival of what Western man has learned to live for and to live by has become increasingly dependent upon the possession of the new varieties of power by the United States and its allies.

For better or for worse, international organization lends itself to the stimulation of disarmament negotiations, and provides a framework of facilities within which such negotiations may take place. So far as the direct approach to disarmament is concerned, international organization can do little more. Disarmament is a field in which states are peculiarly on their own. They may use such an institution as the United Nations for the dissemination of propaganda speeches as well as for the organization of serious deliberations, and they may choose to exploit its voting machinery for the registration of majority positions. But the necessary basis of disarmament is agreement, and this is a function of diplomacy, not of organizational mechanisms. At most, the United Nations may facilitate a disarmament agreement among the powers by providing the institutional context within which an arms control agency might function.

If the concept of disarmament as a direct approach to peace be abandoned in favor of the proposition that the reduction of military establishments is dependent upon the progressive development of the conditions of international stability and order, then the role of international organization in bringing about disarmament may be significant. The history of the League and the United Nations provides little support for the thesis that international organization can contribute decisively to the prevention of war by sponsoring disarmament conferences and consultations; the future of the United Nations holds the possibility that international organization can contribute to the prevention of excessive armament burdens by sponsoring collaborative efforts to get at the heart of the problem of war. What the United Nations can do for disarmament will be determined in the whole range of its organizational apparatus, not merely and not even primarily in the narrow confines of its Disarmament Commission and related bodies.

SUGGESTED READINGS

Bechhoefer, Bernhard G., *Postwar Negotiations for Arms Control,* Washington: The Brookings Institution, 1961.

Bolté, Charles G., *The Price of Peace: A Plan for Disarmament,* Boston: Beacon Press, 1956.

Brennan, Donald G., ed., *Arms Control, Disarmament, and National Security,* New York: George Braziller, 1961.

Finkelstein, Lawrence S., "The United Nations and Organizations for the Control of Armaments," *International Organization,* Winter 1962, pp. 1-19.

Nogee, Joseph L., "The Diplomacy of Disarmament," *International Conciliation,* No. 526, January 1960.

Spanier, John W., and Joseph L. Nogee, *The Politics of Disarmament,* New York: Praeger, 1962.

Tate, Merze, *The Disarmament Illusion: The Movement for Limitation of Armaments to 1907,* New York: Macmillan, 1942.

Tate, Merze, *The United States and Armaments,* Cambridge: Harvard University Press, 1948.

CHAPTER

14

Preventive Diplomacy as an Approach to Peace

If the United Nations has contributed anything new to the list of direct approaches to the problem of peace, it is in the development of the theory and practice of preventive diplomacy. While it would be misleading to treat this phenomenon as an instance of pure innovation, it is nonetheless true that the concept of preventive diplomacy, which is not to be found in the theoretical substructure of the Charter, has emerged from the operating experience of the United Nations to join peaceful settlement, collective security, and disarmament as a major approach to peace through international organization.

This concept is irrevocably associated with the name of the late Dag Hammarskjold, as collective security is tied to that of Woodrow Wilson. It derives from the practice of international statesmanship by the second Secretary-General of the United Nations, and from his theoretical interpretation of the role which he conceived the organization as playing, actually and potentially, in the cold war era. Preventive diplomacy, so labeled by Hammarskjold, represents his answer to the question of how the United

Nations can be made directly relevant to the crucial struggle between East and West.

In his major exposition of the concept of preventive diplomacy,[1] Hammarskjold defined it as United Nations intervention in an area of conflict outside of, or marginal to, the sphere dominated by cold war struggles, designed to forestall the competitive intrusion of the rival power blocs into that area. He began with the acknowledgment that "it is extremely difficult for the United Nations to exercise an influence on problems which are clearly and definitely within the orbit of present day conflicts between power blocs." Having thus conceded that the organization could not effectively intervene in the central arena of the cold war, he turned his attention to the periphery, asserting that "the areas which are not committed in the major conflicts are still considerable." These areas, he suggested, provided "the main field of useful activity of the United Nations, in its efforts to prevent conflicts or to solve conflicts." He described this activity as the filling of vacuums by the United Nations, or the localization of conflicts in the no-man's-land of the cold war, with the relatively uncommitted members of the organization serving as its agents for this purpose. By undertaking such activity, he believed, the United Nations might prevent the extension and the exacerbation of the cold war. Preventive diplomacy, in short, was conceived by Hammarskjold as an international version of the policy of containment, designed not to restrict the expansion of one bloc or the other, but to restrict the expansion of the zone permeated by bloc conflicts; it was put forward as a means for containment of the cold war.

In stating the concept of preventive diplomacy, Hammarskjold was not indulging in armchair speculation. He explicitly related his analysis to a series of cases, including the Middle Eastern crises of 1956 and 1958, the Laos case of 1959, and the Congo crisis of 1960, in which the United Nations had "moved so as to forestall developments which might draw the specific conflict, openly or actively, into the sphere of power bloc differences." Essentially, his theoretical essay was a set of reflections upon recent and continuing experience, and a projection into the future of the role which the United Nations had begun to evolve under his imaginative leadership.

In citing these cases, the Secretary-General stressed the flexibility of the requirements and the variety of the means for United Nations intervention in particular situations. In some instances, largely symbolic manifestations of the United Nations Presence had sufficed—as in Jordan, in 1958, and in Laos, in 1959. The Lebanese crisis in 1958, involving allegations of external intrusion into an unstable domestic situation, had brought about the creation of the United Nations Observation Group in Lebanon (UNOGIL),

---

[1] *Introduction to the Annual Report of the Secretary-General on the Work of the Organization, 16 June 1959—15 June 1960,* General Assembly, Official Records: Fifteenth Session, Supplement No. 1 A (A/4390/Add. 1).

a substantial body of military personnel provided by more than a score of member states, which undertook for several months to discourage infiltration and illegal arms shipments into that troubled country.

The Middle Eastern and Congo crises of 1956 and 1960 had involved the United Nations in much more elaborate forms of intervention. These two cases were the major elements in the background of experience which inspired Hammarskjold's formulation of the concept of preventive diplomacy. United Nations activities in the other cases could be construed as variants of well established international methods for dealing with dangerous disputes, modified forms of pacific settlement technique, fitting into a line of evolution which could be traced back through such institutions as the United Nations Truce Supervision Organization in the Palestine area and the United Nations Military Observer Group in India and Pakistan, to the commissions of inquiry and conciliation which the League had utilized. The two major cases, however, called forth United Nations operations which were sufficiently different in scope and nature from other international ventures to be treated as innovations—the first episodes in the development of a new political and military role for the organization. These cases may be regarded as the prototypes of preventive diplomacy.

When Israel, Britain, and France invaded Egypt in 1956, precipitating the Suez crisis, the Uniting for Peace plan was invoked to enable the General Assembly to take over the case from the Security Council, which was hamstrung by British and French use of the veto power. In this tense situation, the Assembly appealed for a cease-fire and withdrawal of forces. Sensing the need and the opportunity to reinforce the disposition of the invading states to comply, Lester B. Pearson, as spokesman for Canada, introduced the idea of a United Nations Emergency Force (UNEF), to be stationed in the area of conflict on the basis of agreement among the contending states, to supervise the implementation of cease-fire and withdrawal arrangements, ensure the pacification of the borders, and stabilize the situation until the bases of a more durable settlement could be established. The Assembly accepted this proposal and commissioned the Secretary-General to improvise its effectuation. In a remarkable display of political and administrative initiative, Hammarskjold promptly produced a concrete plan which the Assembly endorsed, obtained contributions of troops from several states, carried out delicate negotiations with Egypt on a number of crucial points, and put UNEF into the field. Within a very short time, twenty-five states offered to contribute contingents, and a force of approximately 6,000 men, drawn from ten of those states, was assembled under Major General E. L. M. Burns, who had been chief of staff of the United Nations Truce Supervision Organization in Palestine. The Secretary-General, working in conjunction with an Advisory Committee composed largely of representatives of states contributing troops, assumed political control over UNEF on behalf of the Assembly. He also carried out the assignment of arranging for the clearance of the Suez Canal, which had been blocked by ships sunk in the course of hostilities. At this writing, UNEF remains in place and in operation, contributing to the stability of a region where genuine settlement of basic political conflicts continues to elude the grasp of statesmen.

The Congo crisis erupted in July 1960, when the newly established republic was wracked by mutiny and disorder, and Belgium reintroduced troops into the territory so recently freed from its colonial rule. Faced with a chaotic situation, the Congo government appealed in rapid succession for American military intervention and, at American urging, for United Nations military assistance—and indicated the possibility of a similar appeal to the Bandung Treaty states and to the Soviet Union. The Secretary-General, resorting to his authority under Article 99, called the Security Council into urgent session for consideration of the crisis, requested and received a mandate to organize a United Nations program of assistance, and promptly put into the field both military and civilian elements of a United Nations Operation in the Congo (generally known as ONUC, in reference to its French title). The military force was gradually built up to a maximum strength of approximately 20,000 men, with personnel from more than thirty states participating at one time or another. The Civilian Operations branch of ONUC mobilized the existing machinery of the United Nations and the Specialized Agencies for the recruitment and supervision of an unprecedentedly large and varied team of experts which undertook literally to keep the Congo a viable society by performing critical services in such fields as transport and communications, health, agriculture, education, public administration, and finance. As in the case of UNEF, ONUC continues its work as these lines are written.

It is not my purpose to present elaborate case histories of the operations conducted by the United Nations in the Middle East and the Congo, but rather to treat UNEF and ONUC as initial developments in the exercise of preventive diplomacy, illustrative of the purposes, principles, difficulties, and limitations of that approach to international peace-keeping activity. These cases are marked by basic similarities and differences, all of them significant for an understanding of preventive diplomacy.

PREVENTIVE DIPLOMACY AND PEACEFUL SETTLEMENT

While I have suggested that preventive diplomacy represents the development of a role for international organization that can and should be distinguished from that of promoting peaceful settlement, these cases indicate that the former role is an outgrowth of the latter and that no absolute line of separation can be postulated. UNEF stands closer than ONUC to the peaceful settlement approach, for its initial task consisted in large part of facilitating the reestablishment and maintenance of peaceful relations, however tense and precarious, between Israel, Britain, and France on the one hand, and Egypt on the other. By way of contrast, it should be noted that the problem of Belgian-Congolese relations has from the beginning figured less prominently in the dominant conception of ONUC's responsibility; the *local* task of ONUC has been predominantly that of helping to curb and reverse the tendencies toward internal political disruption and social and economic disintegration within the Congo—an enormous task made doubly difficult by the ambiguity implicit in ONUC's mandate to intervene without interfering, to uphold order without enforcing orderliness, to assist the government without taking sides in controversies regarding the location of governmental authority, and to prevent civil war without becoming involved in efforts to suppress dissident and secessionist movements. ONUC's mission has been both more complex and less susceptible of definition in the standard terms of international organizational experience than that of UNEF.

Nevertheless, both UNEF and ONUC are identifiable as instruments of preventive diplomacy, in that they were conceived and have operated largely as devices for putting the United Nations into trouble zones so as to obviate the competitive intrusion of the major powers. They are not primarily means for promoting the peaceful settlement of existing disputes, but for preventing the development of contests for power in their zones of operation by the leaders of the cold war blocs. UNEF and ONUC reflect a concern with local situations which is related to an overshadowing anxiety about the possible extension and exacerbation of the broader struggle between East and West.

This characterization is less easy to establish in the case of UNEF than in that of ONUC, for the doctrine of preventive diplomacy was fully articulated only after the United Nations had responded to the Congo crisis—and with primary reference to the latter case. It might be suggested that the creation of UNEF represented a largely unconscious groping for a new kind of political role for the organization; certainly, most of the language that has been used in description of UNEF's function fits the familiar category of peaceful settlement. However, there is much in the record to support the idea that the establishment of UNEF marked the beginning of a distinctive approach to international peace-keeping action. The deliberate exclusion of personnel from the major powers indicated an awareness that it was important for the United Nations to fill the Middle Eastern vacuum in such a way as to prevent, not promote, the intrusion of the cold war competitors; Britain and France were to move out, and the Soviet Union and the United States were to stay out. As William R. Frye has put it: "The primary reason for excluding the great powers was to make clear that Britain and France were not to be deputized as UN policemen; a secondary, but scarcely less important, reason, was to keep Soviet troops out of the Middle East." [2] The negative reaction of the United States to the British and French attack upon Egypt had been, in part, a reflection of concern that the attack might precipitate Soviet entry into the region, and a major preoccupation of American policy was to liquidate the crisis without direct Soviet penetration into the Middle East.[3] While the Soviet Union indulged in talk about introducing troops for the defense of Egypt and formally gave UNEF only grudging and critical acquiescence, it is conceivable that Soviet leaders actually welcomed UNEF as a device for forestalling a dangerous confrontation with the Western powers in that area. This was clearly the mood of the West; the exclusion of the major powers was regarded as essential, less because it would facilitate the peaceful settlement of the local dispute than because it would discourage the importation into the region of the general rivalry between East and West. The value of UNEF lies more in its preventive than in its therapeutic action. As an American spokesman expressed it, "Here we have a record of strong, swift action which, without doubt in my mind, headed off a third world war. If the United Nations had done only this one thing in its short life, it would have more than justified its existence." [4]

The rationalization and interpretation of ONUC's mission has been cast predominantly in the new terminology of preventive diplomacy. Hammarskjold was repeatedly explicit in his description of the Congo operation as a means of filling a vacuum that would otherwise invite the introduction of the extraneous conflicts of the great global competitors. American officials have played many variations on the theme that "The only way to keep the cold war out of the Congo is to keep the United Nations in the Congo," [5] always stressing the danger to the whole world of great power confrontations. Prime Minister Harold Macmillan stated the British version of ONUC's contribution to preventive diplomacy in a speech to the General Assembly on September 29, 1960:

> The present division in the world exists and in this situation the interposition of the United Nations is often the only way to prevent the spread of these rivalries into areas where they may be a source not merely of local disturbance but of world danger. For that reason the United Kingdom Government feels that what the United Nations has done in the Congo was timely and should continue. . . . it would

[2] *A United Nations Peace Force* (New York: Oceana, for the Carnegie Endowment for International Peace, 1957), p. 12.

[3] See Robert C. Good, "The United States and the Colonial Debate," in Arnold Wolfers, ed., *Alliance Policy in the Cold War* (Baltimore: Johns Hopkins, 1959), pp. 257-258.

[4] Ambassador James J. Wadsworth, July 15, 1957, *Department of State Bulletin,* August 5, 1957, p. 238, as cited in Lincoln P. Bloomfield, *The United Nations and U.S. Foreign Policy* (Boston: Little, Brown, 1960), p. 157.

[5] The quotation is from Ambassador Adlai Stevenson. See Security Council, Official Records: 16th Year, 934th Meeting, February 15, 1961, p. 9.

be a tragedy if the Congo were to become the arena for the contest between the two great groups of Powers.[6]

All this is not to say that preventive diplomacy is utterly different from peaceful settlement. The two approaches are alike in depending upon the consent of the states immediately involved in troubled situations for the introduction of international mechanisms; UNEF and ONUC, no less than the agencies of conventional peaceful settlement, are based upon this principle. They share the objective of contributing to the improvement or stabilization of relationships among parties directly involved in antagonism. The distinctiveness of preventive diplomacy lies in its substitution of global for local emphasis, its preoccupation with avoidance of the spread of the cold war into areas affected by disputes, rather than with settlement of the disputes *per se*. What it promises is not the solution of cold war disputes, but the restriction of the cold war arena.

PREVENTIVE DIPLOMACY AND COLLECTIVE SECURITY

The line between preventive diplomacy and collective security may not be obvious to the casual observer, for operations representing the former approach, like those associated with the latter, are likely to involve the formation and utilization of an international military force of more than negligible size, composed—in the absence of a standing force—of units made available from national military establishments. Thus, both UNEF and ONUC may be characterized as collective forces, and, consequently, may readily be mistaken for instrumentalities of collective security—although neither of them approaches the level of size and strength that would be required for any significant collective security operation. Indeed, further experience may confirm the impression derived from UNEF and ONUC that an international military operation designed for preventive diplomacy can be identified as one intermediate in size: too large for the requirements of conventional peaceful settlement, but too small for those of collective security.

Size, however, is chiefly important as a clue to *function;* preventive diplomacy is ultimately differentiated from collective security by the mission assigned to the military forces assembled under international auspices. A collective security force is designed for combat with the military arm of an aggressive state. Its function is to defeat and repel aggression. The tasks of a preventive diplomacy force may be varied—and, as in the case of ONUC, ill-defined—but they emphatically do *not* include that of fighting to frustrate a deliberate and systematically organized campaign of aggression. The contrast may be illustrated by comparing the Korean action of the United Nations with operations in the Middle East and the Congo.

[6] General Assembly, Official Records: Fifteenth Session, 877th Plenary Meeting, p. 224.

The Korean operation—which may be roughly described as a collective security venture undertaken in the absence of a collective security system—involved the use of collective forces to combat a determined aggressor. UNEF and ONUC, on the other hand, moved into the crises for which they were improvised, with the acquiescence or consent of all the states involved in those situations, and without the intent or the assignment of doing battle with any of them. To be sure, forces engaged in preventive diplomacy may encounter a variety of coercive tasks, as vividly illustrated by the vicissitudes of the Congo operation; there can be no guarantee that they will be able to function entirely without gunfire and bloodshed. Nevertheless, armed combat is at most a peripheral aspect of their mission, not its primary element as in the case of a force dispatched to effectuate collective security.

The central objective of preventive diplomacy is to abort the development of situations where the need for the operation of collective security might arise—that is, to prevent the extension of great power confrontations that might produce violent conflict. The emphasis here is not on the frustration of a would-be aggressor, but on the avoidance of intensified rivalry. The aim is not to threaten an expansionist state with defeat, but to offer the promise of assistance to competing states or blocs in limiting the scope of their competition. Helping all states to avoid war, rather than helping some states to resist attack, is the theme of preventive diplomacy.

This is not to say that the *preventive* motif is a monopoly of preventive diplomacy. Collective security, too, aims at preventing war; it is a scheme for deterring aggression. However, the two approaches represent different preventive strategies. Collective security focuses upon aggressive intent, while preventive diplomacy concerns itself with dangerous confrontation. The former assumes a situation in which one power may be tempted to strike, and uses the threat of overwhelming resistance to prevent such action. The latter undertakes preventive measures at an earlier stage, and of a different sort; it represents an attempt to aid both parties engaged in rivalry by inhibiting the development of situations conducive to an explosive showdown, deliberately or inadvertently precipitated. A collective security force in action aims to separate an aggressor, forcibly, from his victim. A preventive diplomacy force in action aims to keep competitive powers, by mutual agreement, separated from each other.

The launching and conduct of the United Nations operation in the Congo provides important evidence that the contrast of preventive diplomacy and collective security is not simply a matter of theoretical distinction, but of political choice as well. When the Security Council first considered the Congo crisis, on July 13 and 14, 1960, a number of states—including the Soviet Union—regarded it as a case of Belgian aggression and insisted that the military forces to be assembled under the United Nations flag be used "to take effective action to halt the aggression." [7] From this point of view, ONUC was to be a collective security operation. The majority, however, led by the United States, held that the crucial problem was the chaotic situation in the Congo which had prompted emergency intervention by Belgium, and that the task of the organization was to remedy that situation so as to eliminate the need and minimize the temptation for states to intervene. This position clearly reflected an urge to exculpate Belgium; moreover, it expressed concern about Belgium's action, not on the ground that such intervention represented the international sin of aggression but that it might stimulate intervention by other states. The objective was not to make the Congo another Korea, but to prevent it from producing a new version of the Spanish Civil War of the 1930's. From this viewpoint, ONUC was to serve the purpose of preventive diplomacy.

Both in words and in action, the Secretary-General gave evidence from the beginning of the Congo operation that he agreed with the conception of its mission that had been stated by the United States and other Western powers. Hammarskjold made this explicit in the document, signed on August 31, 1960, containing his basic statement of the doctrine of preventive diplomacy:

> The view expressed here as to the special possibilities and responsibilities of the Organization in situations of a vacuum has reached an unusually clear expression in the case of the Congo. There, the main argument presented for United Nations intervention was the breakdown of law and order, the rejection of the attempt to maintain order by foreign troops, and the introduction of the United Nations Force so as to create the basis for the withdrawal of the foreign troops and for the forestalling of initiatives to introduce any other foreign troops into the territory with the obvious risks for widening international conflict which would ensue.[8]

The USSR's bitter repudiation of ONUC in the fall of 1960 stemmed in part from the realization that the operation had not acquired the charater of a collective security action against Belgium, but had, as an exercise in preventive diplomacy, tended to inhibit Communist moves to transform the Congo into a new arena of the cold war. The ultimate clash of political views as to the purpose of ONUC had been implicit in the original debate in the Security Council as to whether the task should be defined in terms of collective security or of preventive diplomacy.

---

[7] See Security Council, Official Records: 15th Year, 873rd Meeting. The quotation is from a statement by the Soviet representative, p. 21.

[8] *Introduction to the Annual Report of the Secretary-General on the Work of the Organization, 16 June 1959—15 June 1960,* General Assembly, Official Records: Fifteenth Session, Supplement No. 1 A, pp. 4-5.

PREVENTIVE DIPLOMACY AND DISARMAMENT

The contrast between preventive diplomacy and the more conventional approaches to peace through international organization is sharpest in the case of disarmament. Preventive diplomacy is compatible with the latter, in that it raises no obstacles to the elimination, reduction, or control of national armaments. On the other hand, disarmament is incompatible with preventive diplomacy, in that the achievement of the former would undermine the basis for the latter. Preventive diplomacy is a phenomenon arising out of the arms race, a response to the emergence of a situation of mutual deterrence. Since the advent of the atomic age, the USSR and the United States have moved inexorably toward the point of decisive mutual vulnerability, where neither can rationally afford to precipitate a showdown with the other. The approach to this point has bred a mood of prudential pacifism—an urge to avoid total war which is rooted fundamentally in good sense rather than in good will, in calculations of the national interest in survival rather than in idealistic aspirations. The cold war is a form of struggle between powers which are not, in Wilsonian terms, too proud to fight, but in terms of present-day reality, too prudent to fight in all-out encounter; a fight to the finish has become too literally possible for rational men to contemplate it as a deliberate policy choice.

This is the setting within which the possibility of United Nations action to implement preventive diplomacy has arisen. Preventive diplomacy is dependent upon the willingness of the major powers to have the United Nations seal off trouble spots, excluding these areas from their competitive intrusion. This willingness is a function of prudential pacifism; the opportunity to exercise preventive diplomacy occurs only when, and to the extent that, each of the primary contestants dreads the implications of a showdown more than it values the possibilities of winning an engagement in the cold war. Clearly, the essential backdrop for this situation is the thermonuclear arms race; without it, the reluctance of the great contenders to risk decisive confrontation would be deprived of much of its strength.

These observations may explain some of the ambiguities in Soviet policy regarding ONUC. As we noted above, the USSR supported the initiation of the Congo operation with the stated intention and apparent expectation that it would be a device for expelling Belgian forces, which it regarded as having committed aggression in the Congo, but turned sharply against the operation when it became evident that ONUC was being used primarily as an instrument of preventive diplomacy. The Soviet polemic against the operation and its executive director, Secretary-General Hammarskjold, was extraordinarily vigorous for a number of months, beginning in the fall of 1960, and raised a grave threat to the successful continuation of the operation and the survival of the United Nations. Subsequently, the virulence of the attack gradually subsided, and the Soviet position was reduced to one of passive opposition to ONUC. A number of factors may have contributed to this moderation of Soviet opposition—including the death of Hammarskjold and the adoption of limited concessions to Soviet demands—but it is possible that the USSR was ultimately restrained from pressing its attack by an appreciation, however vehemently disavowed in public, of the value of preventive diplomacy, or, to put it differently, of the peril of entering into a confrontation that might eventuate in thermonuclear conflict.

The arms race has not only given the great powers a strong incentive for keeping the cold war cold, and accepting assistance to that end, but, in establishing the context for the cold war, it has also stimulated the emergence of a substantial group of uncommitted states, thereby providing a source of supply for the indispensable operators of preventive diplomacy, the agents of the United Nations in its efforts to promote the containment of the cold war. Whereas collective security in action postulates a "two world" situation—an aggressive camp and an overwhelmingly powerful set of defenders of the established order—preventive diplomacy requires a "three world" system—two groups of antagonists and an in-between world which both serves as the locale for the operation of preventive diplomacy and provides the personnel for that operation. In the present era, the power struggle between East and West has produced just this sort of tripartitism; the bipolar contest makes preventive diplomacy necessary, while the existence of an uncommitted sector makes it possible.

CONDITIONS AND LIMITS OF PREVENTIVE DIPLOMACY

In establishing UNEF, the United Nations was groping for a significant role which it might be able to play in the politics of a world torn asunder by the cold war and threatened by thermonuclear catastrophe. Half-consciously at best, the organization invented preventive diplomacy. In the relatively easy success of the Middle Eastern operation, the Secretary-General and many national statesmen came to recognize the possibilities of this kind of international action. Thus began the transformation of preventive diplomacy from an improvisation to a theory, a conception of the role which the United Nations might perform in future crises.

The Congo operation, which began as a second major exploration of the potentialities of preventive diplomacy, soon became an exercise notable in large part for its contributions to an understanding of the difficulties and limitations of preventive diplomacy. In that it did not fail, it tended to confirm the promise of UNEF that preventive diplomacy could serve as a valuable function of the United Nations. In that it did not readily succeed, and that it precipitated a grave crisis within the organization, it provided the basis for a cautious reexamination of expectations regarding preventive diplomacy. Future events may not prove that the Congo had the same negative effect upon the prospects for preventive diplomacy that Korea had upon collective security, but enthusiasm in the United Nations for the launching of future operations under this rubric will certainly be tempered by the memory of the problems encountered in the Congo case.

The Congo experience has involved a succession of extraordinarily complex difficulties; in attempting to cope with these, ONUC has at one time or another stimulated the displeasure of every faction within the Congo, of the Soviet bloc, of the major and minor Western powers, and of the Afro-Asian states. Many of the difficulties have stemmed from the confusion and instability inherent in the domestic situation of the Congo, others from the defectiveness of the policy-making process and administrative structure of the United Nations, and still others from the ambitions, sensitivities, and animosities of member states both adjacent to and remote from the Congo.

Among these difficulties, two are outstanding in that they represent fundamental challenges to the development and continuation of the organization's role as an agency of preventive diplomacy: the financial problem, and the Soviet attack upon the person and the office of the Secretary-General.

The Congo operation, an extremely expensive undertaking by United Nations standards since it costs substantially more each year than the regular budget of the organization, has put the United Nations on the verge of bankruptcy. UNEF, too, has produced troublesome deficits, but it required the addition of substantial deficits attributable to ONUC to precipitate a genuinely critical budgetary situation by the end of 1961. The failure of large numbers of states to pay their assessments, as voted by the General Assembly, for the support of one or both of these peace-keeping operations has called into question the viability of the organization. As of late 1963, the General Assembly has, with the support of an advisory opinion rendered by the International Court in 1962, reiterated its insistence that its allocations of expenses for these operations are binding upon members, and the United Nations has gained temporary financial relief from the sale of a special issue of bonds to governments, but no real solution of the problem has appeared on the horizon.[9]

The financial delinquencies of members, which have produced this crisis, are not all to be interpreted in the same way. Some members have simply been unable to pay. Others have denied the obligatory character of assessments for these special programs, and have, in refraining from payment, expressed their unwillingness to undertake significant responsibilities in the exercise of preventive diplomacy. Still others have used the weapon

---

[9] For a detailed analysis of the financial difficulties of the United Nations, see the forthcoming study, *Financing the United Nations System,* sponsored by The Brookings Institution and produced under the primary authorship of John G. Stoessinger.

of financial deprivation in direct attack upon ONUC, and, in lesser degree, upon UNEF. This last category includes, on the one hand, members of the Soviet bloc, and, on the other, such states as France, Belgium, and South Africa—two groups of states which, for essentially opposite reasons, are opposed to the Congo operation. In fact, the greater part of the deficit is attributable to states which are unwilling, not unable, to pay; that is, the financial crisis is, at bottom, really a political problem. Particularly in the case of the Soviet Union, refusal to share in meeting the expenses of ONUC is a deliberate expression of hostility to the operation, a dramatization of dissent.

Soviet objection to the Congo operation was even more vividly expressed in the campaign of vituperation waged for a time against Secretary-General Hammarskjold, and the accompanying demand for abolition of his office in favor of a directorate composed of political representatives of the East, the West, and the uncommitted states. Financial boycott is essentially an instrument of passive opposition, since it leaves open the possibility that other states may sustain the operation. The USSR's more vigorous attacks appeared to be directed at closing that possibility.

The crisis-ridden history of the Congo operation illustrates how essential is the consent of the major cold war antagonists to the conduct of preventive diplomacy by the United Nations, and points up the political complexities of this central problem of consent. It shows how tenuous the agreement of the major powers to the organization's playing this kind of role may be, and indicates, in particular, the dangerous confusion and uncertainty which may arise if a major power *withdraws* consent once given to an operation—as the Soviet Union did in the case of ONUC. The USSR's turning against the Congo operation posed the question as to whether the United Nations could successfully and safely continue that enterprise. In the event, the action was carried on through intense difficulties to what could be described in 1963 as the verge of success, and this persistence was accompanied by the moderation, not the exacerbation, of Soviet opposition. The conclusion to be drawn from this tentative outcome may be that the dissolution of the consensual foundation for a United Nations operation need not and should not be taken automatically as a signal for abandonment of the operation. In retrospect, it does not appear that ONUC should have been rejected from the beginning because of the obviously ambiguous nature of Soviet support, or that it should have been discontinued when the USSR proclaimed its unequivocal opposition. However, it must be noted that the price of the continuation of the operation in the face of Soviet hostility included the precipitation of a grave financial crisis in the United Nations, and the provocation of a fundamental political challenge to the developing role of the Secretary-General. It is not too much to say that this episode involved a high risk of the destruction of the organization. Hence, the conclusion to be drawn from it should include the recognition that the exercise of preventive diplomacy is extremely precarious business in the absence of sustained support or acquiescence of both sides in the cold war. If the case does not indicate that preventive diplomacy should be abandoned whenever a major power withdraws its consent, neither does it suggest that the problem of bilateral consent can be prudently ignored, or that the United Nations can be realistically expected to move smoothly along the path of "operationalism" in the political-security field without heeding the impediment of Soviet opposition to this trend. While the Congo case shows that something may be accomplished in a particular instance despite Soviet disapproval, it equally shows that the systematic development of a role in preventive diplomacy by the United Nations requires the consent of both the major power blocs.

This requirement, which in its essence refers to the need for Soviet-American acceptance of preventive diplomacy, involves first of all the condition that both powers attach such great value to the avoidance of general war that they be disposed to welcome the neutralization of potential breeding grounds of such war in the zones outside their blocs. The record suggests that the fulfillment of this condition is less clear and complete in the case of the Soviet Union than of the United States. Considerable evidence shows that both leading powers are strongly motivated to avoid a showdown, but the tactics of the USSR have generally been less cautious, and Soviet leaders have appeared less reluctant, in both the Middle Eastern and the Congo case, to expand the realm of competitive confrontation. While Americans and their allies have praised the ideal of keeping the cold war out of the Congo, the Soviets have worked to defeat that ideal. This limitation of the possibilities of preventive diplomacy is fundamentally a problem for the Western deterrent system; the degree of Soviet enthusiasm for preventive diplomacy is a direct function of Western success in inspiring Soviet reluctance to undertake the risks of a major military confrontation.

The second basic condition for the realization of the requirement of consensus is the acceptance of the United Nations as an agency for achieving neutralization of trouble spots along the cold war periphery. Assuming that both the Soviet Union and the United States are keenly aware of their separate but parallel interests in this achievement, there remains the problem of their agreement on the instrumentality for bringing it about. In the aftermath of the political struggle over the use of the United Nations in the Congo, two different versions of this problem are discernible.

The American version raises the issue of the appropriateness of the organization's being "reduced" to playing a neutral role in the cold war setting. American reception of and reaction to neutralism in the postwar era has been both mixed and alterable, but it can be said with some confidence that the United States has consistently preferred that the United Nations influence the neutralist states toward alignment against Soviet expansionism, rather than that those states impress a neutral character upon the United Nations. The American ideology of the United Nations has stressed the ideal of the organization's serving as a bulwark of world order, standing clearly and resolutely in support of Western efforts to stem the tide of Communist aggressiveness. In this view, a neutral United Nations would represent an ignoble betrayal of the principles of the Charter. Moreover, the American experience with the United Nations has stimulated the expectation that the organization can be used in support of the Western cause. Pro-Western action by the United Nations is, in American eyes, as normal as it is proper; ideology and experience have combined to produce a conception of the organization which emphasizes its anti-Communist character. In the court of domestic public opinion and political controversy, official American spokesmen have persistently justified this country's membership in and contributions to the organization by stressing Western success in controlling and using the United Nations. Given this background, it is doubtful that either the political leaders or the general public of the United States can be expected to show much enthusiasm for the organization's assuming a neutral character or playing a neutralizing role in the cold war struggle.

Official American commentary on the Congo operation has revealed the tension between the tendencies to value the neutralizing function of the United Nations in the Congo and to encourage the American public to value the organization as an unneutral—that is, pro-Western—force in world affairs. The major theme has been that ONUC has served the interests of the whole world by helping the major powers avoid a collision in the Congo. But a significant counter-theme has been woven into the composition: that United Nations action in the Congo has given the West a victory over the Soviet bloc that it might not have been able to win for itself. Thus, in a public address on June 5, 1961, the United States Ambassador to the United Nations, Adlai E. Stevenson, spoke of the need of the new nations for the organization to serve as "an impartial instrument with which to keep themselves out of the perils of great power rivalry," but then went on to present this analysis of the Congo case:

> The Belgian withdrawal was followed by anarchy with which on the one hand the Belgians stepped back and on the other the Russians began to step in. In these circumstances, any direct invervention by the West would have been interpreted as an attempt to reimpose colonialism. Local opinion would have swung over to support the Communists, and the West would have been left in the impossible position of fighting a guerrilla war against a background of implacable local hostility. . . . direct Western interventions tend of their very nature to produce a revulsion of local feeling which threatens the effectiveness of the intervention. . . . The result is that in situations such as the Congo, the Western World would be almost powerless if there were no United Nations force available to restore order, [and] check a

> takeover by an outside power. . . . Direct Western action would only hasten a Communist takeover. By putting the whole task of restoring order onto an international basis, favoring neither East nor West, there is at least a chance of avoiding first a Western defeat and secondly the risk of spiralling war. In short, while nations cannot intervene in the internal affairs of other nations, the United Nations can.
>
> It is surely significant that it is since the United Nations frustrated the Communists' plans of rapid infiltration in the Congo that Mr. Khrushchev has been trying to extend his veto to the whole Organization and make sure that neither the Secretary-General nor any other organ of the United Nations shall be free to act or intervene. We by the same token must support and back with all our influence the only instrument by which the end of the Western system of colonialism can be prevented from opening the doors to the new imperialism of the East.[10]

It should be noted that Ambassador Stevenson emphasized, for an American audience, not the impartial but the pro-Western role of ONUC. He credited the United Nations not so much with preventing a battle between East and West as with averting a Communist victory, and a Western defeat, in the Congo. As another American spokesman in the United Nations subsequently put it, "The Congo operation is a notable example of a situation where the policy and actions of the United Nations have been generally in accord with our thinking, while the Soviet view has been consistently overridden." [11] Such an analysis of the Congo case, accurate or not, obviously offers no confirmation of the proposition that the United States is prepared to concede that the United Nations *should,* in exercising preventive diplomacy, play an essentially neutral role between the blocs.

By way of contrast, the Soviet version of the problem of neutralization stresses the issue of the possibility of the world organization's playing a genuinely neutral role. If Americans find it difficult to concede that the United Nations *should* do so, Soviet leaders find it equally difficult to conceive that the United Nations *can* do so. Whereas Americans are doubtful of the propriety of "reducing" the organization to a neutralizing function, the Soviets are skeptical of the possibility of "advancing" it to such a height of impartiality. Both the ideology and the experience of the Soviet Union in the United Nations contribute to this skepticism. Viewing the organization from its position as a minority leader, the USSR has habitually regarded the United Nations as a mechanism which can only with the greatest difficulty be restrained from serving Western interests.

The central theme of the Soviet attack upon ONUC was the claim

---

10 "The United Nations, First Step Toward a World Under Law," *Department of State Bulletin,* July 10, 1961, p. 70.

11 Jonathan B. Bingham, "One Nation, One Vote—and One U.N.," *New York Times Magazine,* September 16, 1962, p. 86.

that it was dominated by Western personnel, purporting to serve the United Nations but actually turning the organization to the service of the Western powers. The Soviet allegation against Hammarskjold was not that he functioned as an international statesman, but that he used his international position as a cover for pro-Western activity. Khrushchev's position appears to have been misrepresented by Hammarskjold in the Introduction to his final report;[12] the Soviet leader did not argue that there *should* be no neutral men, but that there *could* be no neutral men. The troika proposal reflected a Soviet denial of the claim that the Secretary-General was in fact impartial as between East and West, and a repudiation of the expectation that such an impartial chief of the United Nations mechanism might be found. In advancing this proposal, the Soviets purported to believe that they were advocating the abandonment of the pretense, not the destruction of the reality, of an impartial secretariat, and the substitution of a balance for an imbalance of political partisanship in the administrative leadership of the United Nations.

One cannot know whether the Soviet leaders genuinely believed that Hammarskjold deliberately served as a lackey of the West in his conduct of the Congo operation. It is clear, however, that from its beginning the operation has tended to produce results favorable to Western interests, and that the Secretary-General invited Soviet suspicion by including Westerners along with nationals of uncommitted states in the group of United Nations officials presiding over the operation. In short, it is plausible that the USSR really viewed ONUC as an instrument of Western policy rather than of preventive diplomacy. If the chief American spokesman in the United Nations, Ambassador Stevenson, could believe that the Congo operation served to frustrate Soviet ambitions and thereby to present the West with a major political triumph, it is easy to conceive that Soviet leaders, inveterately suspicious of the United Nations, might interpret the action in the same way—and difficult to understand how, under these circumstances, Americans could have thought it reasonable to expect the Soviets to approve ONUC and give it financial backing. The tactic of presenting the United Nations to the American public as a reliably pro-Western instrument while insisting that the Soviets should regard it as an impartial agency of the international community is conducive neither to American acceptance of the propriety nor to Soviet confidence in the possibility of the organization's playing the neutral role envisaged in the theory of preventive diplomacy. The future development of this approach to peace-keeping is heavily dependent upon the conviction of both cold war contestants that the United Nations is capable of rendering impartial service, and that this represents its greatest potential contribution to their political and security in-

[12] *Introduction to the Annual Report of the Secretary-General on the Work of the Organization, 16 June 1960–15 June 1961,* General Assembly, Official Records: Sixteenth Session, Supplement No. 1 A (A/4800/Add. 1).

terests. The Congo case provides a vivid illustration of the limitations of preventive diplomacy when this basic condition is imperfectly realized.

Finally, preventive diplomacy requires not only that the great powers consent to be served, but also that the uncommitted states consent to serve. The conception of a United Nations operating to assist the major powers in avoiding mortal conflict by neutralizing conflict zones in which they might otherwise become embroiled is one which places primary operating responsibility upon the states least committed to the cold war blocs. It presents these states with an opportunity and a challenge to give their neutralism a positive, constructive meaning, to translate their rhetorical urge for global peace and order into responsible action. This conception completes the reversal of the principle written into the Charter, according to which the great powers were to carry the burden of responsibility for United Nations action in the security sphere; preventive diplomacy transfers this burden to the lesser members of the organization.

The record thus far suggests an encouraging willingness on the part of the uncommitted states to undertake the delicate responsibilities and onerous burdens of preventive diplomacy, under the indispensable leadership and direction of the Secretary-General and his staff. India, for instance, has fulfilled its role as a leading neutralist state by providing the largest contingents for both UNEF and ONUC. Nevertheless, the Congo case is indicative of the difficulties in this regard that threaten the development of preventive diplomacy. Some of the states contributing forces to ONUC have revealed the intent of grinding their own political axes, and withdrawals and threats of withdrawals of contingents have plagued the conduct of the operation. Moreover, the intrusion of bitter East-West controversies into the political debates concerning the Congo case may provide the basis for hesitant reaction by uncommitted states whenever appeals are made for contributions to similar operations in the future. In this respect as in others, ONUC serves both as a demonstration of the potentiality of preventive diplomacy and as a warning of its difficulties and limitations.

Thus, preventive diplomacy stands as a creative innovation in the list of peace-keeping techniques available to international organization. Developed in response to the complex realities of the political world in which the United Nations operates and in conformity with the organizational resources which are incorporated in the United Nations, this approach to the stabilization of the precarious international order appears to offer the organization its greatest opportunity to render significant political service in the cold war era. As we have noted, difficulties and uncertainties cloud the prospect for the continued exercise and further development of preventive diplomacy, but it nonetheless represents the opening up of a major new possibility for useful action by international institutions.

SUGGESTED READINGS

Burns, Arthur L., and Nina Heathcote, *Peace-Keeping By UN Forces,* New York: Praeger, 1962.

Claude, Inis L., Jr., "The United Nations and the Use of Force," *International Conciliation,* No. 532, March 1961.

Claude, Inis L., Jr., "The Containment and Resolution of Disputes," Chap. 5 in Francis O. Wilcox and H. Field Haviland, Jr., eds., *The United States and the United Nations,* Baltimore: Johns Hopkins, 1961.

Draper, Theodore, "Ordeal of the UN," *The New Leader,* November 7, 1960.

Frye, William R., *A United Nations Peace Force,* New York: Oceana Publications, for the Carnegie Endowment for International Peace, 1957.

Good, Robert C., "The Congo Crisis: A Study of Postcolonial Politics," in Lawrence W. Martin, ed., *Neutralism and Nonalignment,* New York: Praeger, 1962.

Goodrich, Leland M., and Gabriella E. Rosner, "The United Nations Emergency Force," *International Organization,* Summer 1957, pp. 413-430.

Gordon, King, *The United Nations in the Congo,* New York: Carnegie Endowment for International Peace, 1962.

Hoffmann, Stanley, "Sisyphus and the Avalanche: The United Nations, Egypt and Hungary," *International Organization,* Summer 1957, pp. 446-469.

Rosner, Gabriella E., *The United Nations Emergency Force,* New York: Columbia University Press, 1963.

CHAPTER

15

The Grand Debate Approach to Peace

The efforts of the League and the United Nations to come directly to grips with the political issues of international relations are not wholly reducible to the categories of pacific settlement, collective security, disarmament, and preventive diplomacy. These relatively specific approaches to a solution of the world's political difficulties have been supplemented by a more general type of institutional function in the political area: the sponsorship of a more or less continuous "grand debate" among the representatives of the constituent units of international society. Whatever else international organization may be, it is a platform and an auditorium, an organized colloquy, a talk-shop. The parade of speakers across the stage of the Assembly hall during the general debate which opens each session is no less symbolic of the political role espoused by the United Nations than the figure of the mediator standing between hostile statesmen, the vision of a conglomerate army carrying an international flag in battle against an aggressor, or the spectacle of military experts huddled over a statistical chart of the global armaments situation. The political significance of international organization may depend as much upon its public rostrum as upon its private round tables and its operational apparatus.

THE VALUES OF THE GRAND DEBATE

The utility of international speech-making is very difficult to evaluate with confidence. It may be that the assignment of a forum function to international organization is simply an extension to a new realm of the faith in talk which is fundamental to the liberal democratic tradition. It is no mere semantic accident that democracy has long been associated with *parliamentary* methods; the conviction that conversation is a distinctively civilized mode of behavior underlies the conception of democracy as "government by discussion." This democratic bias toward verbal interchange as an instrument of politics is reflected in the proposition that it is better for statesmen to argue than to fight, and in the hope, embedded in the foundations of international organization, that debate may eliminate the need and the will to fight. Alternatively, it might be suggested that the verbalism of international organization is a characteristic inflicted upon it by the statesmen who are responsible for their countries' foreign relations; not for nothing are they called national "spokesmen," and their urge to speak upon an international stage may derive less from the conviction that world order will be promoted by multilateral discussion than from the belief that national interest may be promoted by their forensic efforts. In any event, the grand debate is an established tradition of international organization.

There can be little doubt that such a forum as the League Assembly or the General Assembly of the United Nations fills an essential role in the world of the twentieth century. The congregation of national representatives does more than symbolize the roundness and the shrinking circumference of the globe. It provides a composite picture of the state of the world. It promotes awareness of the forces and factors, the ambitions and anxieties, the changes and rigidities, the ideals and interests, which constitute the international problems of the time and foreshadow the great issues of the future. In short, it formulates the agenda of statesmanship.

History may well record that the greatest political contribution made by the United Nations in its early years lay not in the settlement of specific disputes or the exploratory development of particular mechanisms, but rather in such matters as the elucidation of the great power conflict, the definition of the issues between states administering dependent territories and the anticolonial bloc, and the revelation of the breadth and depth of the incipient revolutionary movement of the world's underprivileged peoples. General debate has served to dramatize the peril of atomic war, to point up the threat of Soviet expansionism, to reveal the growing strength of neutralism, to demonstrate the sensitivities of newly emergent states, and to indicate the dynamism of nationalist movements among colonial peoples. Under the auspices of the United Nations, the world is laying out its problems as never before, and is learning, if not to solve them, at least to apprehend their scope and the complexity of their interrelationship.

The global "town meeting" may also be conceived as a rudimentary institutional setting for the formulation of the basic principles and the working policies of an international approach to the problems of international life. There is no magic in a multilateral assembly which inexorably expunges nationalistic concerns from the minds of governmental representatives and brings the concept of global interest to the forefront of attention. For that matter, there is no magic in the convocation of representatives of peoples rather than governments which assures the creation of a general will of humanity, animated by single-minded devotion to the global interest. The political compartmentalization of the world corresponds to a subjective parochialism which lies deep in the political reality of our time, and it is not remarkable that an international gathering, whether its participants be designated by executive appointment or popular election, should exhibit a diversity of outlook and a complex of conflicting national purposes.

However, there is another aspect of contemporary political reality which expresses itself in a tentative exploration of the bases of human unity and an emergent sense of the necessity for developing a community of approach to the issues which are determinants of mankind's common destiny. This is not the dominant feature of present-day political mentality, and it therefore cannot be the dominant factor in the approach of the United Nations. Nevertheless, the international forum does serve for the expression of such sentiments of solidarity and the formulation of such principles of order as the political state of human society permits. The deliberation of statesmen in the League and the United Nations has invested the concept of international public policy with some slight meaning; the notion of moral responsibility has acquired a currency which indicates that it has become lodged, however precariously, in political reality; the principle of international accountability has become sufficiently well established to make it a normal expectation that statesmen will submit to the requirement of explaining and justifying their policies before the world. In this respect, the mantle of sovereignty has become very much like the emperor's famous clothes—visible to the determined theorist, but invisible to the literal-minded little boy.

The grand debate has yielded a not inconsiderable list of generally agreed international standards: prohibition of aggressive warfare, avoidance of forcible intervention except under extreme provocation, respect for a minimum standard of human rights, recognition of the legitimacy of aspirations for self-government and economic development, etc. Clearly, these standards are so imprecise that their verbal acceptance represents something less than the achievement of a practically meaningful consensus; equally clearly, they are subject to violation with a cynicism which is provided by the nature of states and an impunity which is permitted by the nature of the international community. But these realistic reservations do not relegate the evolving body of international standards to insignificance any more than the observation that Christians disagree on doctrinal matters and fail to live up to their ideals demonstrates the meaninglessness of the whole Christian tradition, or than the imperfect realization of the promises embodied in the bill of rights convicts American constitutional democracy of being a preposterous sham. It is a sobering fact for Americans to ponder that no nation violates the rights of its neighbors, as defined by the rudimentary international consensus, more consistently than many American states have violated the rights of Negroes, as defined by the United States Constitution; moreover, the agencies of the rudimentary international community certainly do not display an exceptionally uncritical attitude toward violators of international standards, as compared with the tenderness exhibited until very recently by the American Supreme Court toward states intent upon denying Negroes their constitutional rights.

The realization of the ideal of an elaborate body of normatively advanced standards of political behavior, reflecting general agreement upon operative principles and not merely upon verbal formulations, and carrying the guarantee of reliable enforcement in cases of aberrant behavior, is a singularly rare phenomenon in any human society, be it national or international. This ideal has clearly not been realized in the international community, but more than negligible progress toward its realization has been produced by the multilateral consideration of the world's problems and requirements which has been sponsored by the League and the United Nations. In so far as there is, at the present time, validity in the concept of the climate of world opinion and efficacy in the concept of international moral restraint and compulsion, that validity and efficacy are largely attributable to the functioning of the newly-institutionalized international forum. As for the future, it is a good bet that such an interchange among statesmen as is promoted by the General Assembly may be the effective means of developing, registering, and putting into application new standards and principles of international relations as they enter into the sphere of political feasibility. The grand debate holds open the possibility of the progressive development of world policies for dealing with world problems.

The ultimate significance of the international talk-shop may lie in its provision of a sweeping look at the state of the world and an opportunity for the formulation and expression of a world point of view. However, its more immediate functional role has less to do with a nascent global entity than with existing national entities. Regular and extensive multilateral political debate is presently most important for its impact upon national foreign policies. The measurement and evaluation of that impact is a hazardous undertaking which only an inexcusably brash fellow would claim to be able to carry out with precision and certainty. No one can know just how much difference and exactly what kind of difference the practice of general deliberation in established international assemblies has made in the diplomatic history of the world since 1920. Yet, it is indisputable that the habit of dropping foreign policies into an international pot before serving them is a matter of some importance.

The educational value of the international forum may well be one of its most significant attributes. A foreign policy can be only as good as the informational basis upon which it is formulated. A sound foreign policy is designed to promote a purpose, which may be unilaterally determined within the national privacy of a state; but it must also be made with reference to a situation, viewed in the context of other and possibly conflicting policies within which it must operate, and shaped in accordance with an estimate of the probable reactions which it will engender among other states. For meeting these latter requirements, the facilities provided by a global assembly are serviceable if not indispensable; indeed, even the purposive element may properly be subjected to refinement on the basis of the evaluation of needs and possibilities which the grand debate may promote.

The United Nations offers to statesmen the means of identifying the central problems of international life with which foreign policy ought to be concerned. It affords the opportunity of learning much of what needs to be known about the intentions of other states, and of judging the strengths and weaknesses of the policy positions assumed by other states. It provides a laboratory for testing the acceptability and effectiveness of a proposed line of policy. What are the conditions to be dealt with, the obstacles to be overcome, the dangers to be avoided? What are the competitive policies to be defeated, the demands to be resisted, the appeals to be countered? What can a state get away with? What are the requirements for evoking cooperation? What are the sensitivities to be respected, the misconceptions to be rectified, the ambitions to be taken into account? The quality of a state's foreign policy depends heavily upon the discovery of accurate answers to such questions as these, and the institutions of multilateral diplomacy are admirably suited to facilitate that discovery.

The present era is one in which it is peculiarly important that national foreign policies should be subjected to the educational influences of a continuous international political round table. The stakes of diplomacy have been enormously increased; viewed from the standpoint of either the global interest or the interests of particular nations, the price of failure to develop wise and realistic national foreign policies has become well nigh intolerable. The leading roles in world politics have been taken over by two colossi which are relatively inexperienced in the ways of diplomacy.

One of them, the Soviet Union, is deeply committed to an ideological orthodoxy which may tempt it to cling with disastrous tenacity to goals that cannot be reached without pulling down the temple of civilization upon the heads of all nations, itself included, and which may so distort the Soviet view of the rest of the world as to prevent Soviet policy from conforming to the requirements of political reality. The other major power, the United States, having only recently emerged from its moated castle of isolationism, is confronted with the supreme challenge of developing the capacity for responsible and effective leadership while still struggling to cast off the habits and emancipate itself from the viewpoints which derive from its anchoritic heritage. The international stage is becoming increasingly cluttered with new players, each of them with much to learn about the conduct of international affairs, and each of them injecting new uncertainties into the political situation with which foreign policy must deal. The complexities of world politics are growing by leaps and bounds, and the difficulties of adjusting foreign policy to the shifting realities of the political situation are as burdensome as the failure to achieve that adjustment is perilous.

In this situation, the existence of an organized international forum is of vital significance. From the American point of view, it is important that all nations, including the United States, should learn as much about the intentions, the pretensions, the expectations, and the apprehensions of the Soviet Union as can be gleaned from Soviet participation in the grand debate. Conversely, it is important to American as well as to global interests that the Soviet Union should do some serious listening, imbibing awareness of the facts of international life, learning to appreciate the dangers of pressing too hard against the sensitive area of national determination to remain free, and confronting realistically the political evidence of the defensive solidarity of the Western bloc. In so far as the Soviet Union exhibits ruthless contempt for the standards of civilized order, it damns itself with infinitely greater effectiveness than American propaganda could develop; in so far as it demonstrates a capacity to influence and attract other states, it clarifies for American policy-makers the nature of the challenge with which they are confronted; in so far as the USSR comes to recognize the challenge with which it is confronted, its policy is exposed to the potentiality of sober restraint.

It might be remarked that all this applies equally to the case of Communist China. It is an unhappy possibility that the most convincing demonstration of the utility of setting hostile powers into the midst of a multilateral debate may be provided by the failure to carry out that policy with respect to the new rulers of the Chinese mainland. Whatever may be the merits of the American insistence upon excluding Red China from the United Nations, it is clear that this policy deprives the United States and its fellow members of a significant opportunity for learning about Chinese purposes and policies and for teaching Red China about Western purposes and policies—a deprivation for which roundabout and backdoor American contacts with Red China cannot provide adequate compensation.

The significance of the grand debate does not lie entirely in the facilities which it provides for knowing the enemy and ensuring that the enemy knows what he ought to know. The international forum is equally important as a testing ground for policies which are intended to elicit the cooperation of other states. In the present stage of international relations, it can hardly be the primary function of the United Nations to promote either the formulation of a global policy or the harmonization of American-Soviet policies; the practicable objective is the more modest one of invoking the realistic considerations which may serve to induce restraint in great power behavior, and facilitating the development of such areas of harmony and cooperation in the relations of states as are possible in a profoundly divided world. If we can resist the temptation to adopt the characteristic fallacy of our time, the proposition that because the United Nations cannot heal the breach between the USSR and the West it cannot do anything of genuine political importance, it will become evident that these areas are by no means insignificant.

From the American point of view, the impact of multilateral debate upon United States foreign policy is of critical importance for the achievement of all international political values short of the elimination of the danger of global war. The United States has much to learn about its friends, and about the tentatively uncommitted and the determinedly neutralistic nations, as well as about its antagonists in the cold war. It also has much to learn *from* its non-Communist colleagues in the United Nations. The give and take of international political debate is admirably suited to reveal the disagreements, the suspicions, the anxieties, the sensitivities, and the aspirations which American policy cannot afford to ignore if it is to be a policy of successful leadership. The subjection of American policy to criticism in the United Nations is the inescapable means of equipping American officials to contrive a policy which can command maximum support in the non-Communist world. The critics may not always be right, but it is always right that the United States should know about the criticism which its policy engenders. By supplying pressure for fuller explanation, mutual reassurance, concession to urgent demands for modification, and consideration of alternatives, United Nations debate contributes to the refinement of American foreign policy and thereby to the possibility of successful American leadership in the non-Communist world. Submission to the multilateral sandpapering of national policy is not an altogether pleasant experience for the United States, but it is good for American policy.

To a limited extent, the process goes beyond that and involves collective carpentry of a different order, including the joint development of basic designs and the cooperative hammering together of a policy structure for the non-Communist nations. This sort of enterprise cannot be ordained by the United Nations, but its execution, once determined by the development of the political basis for genuine international partnership, can be vastly facilitated by the setting which the United Nations provides. It may be that the building of a military refuge against aggression can best be undertaken in the relative privacy of NATO, but the construction of a political shelter for the free world may be pursued most advantageously in the United Nations, where the constant huffing and puffing of the big bad Soviet wolf may serve to underline the urgency of the project and his immediate presence may offer the builders the opportunity of recurrently checking their handiwork against the size and shape of the threat against which it is built.

The political forum of the United Nations is a supplement rather than a substitute for the ordinary processes of diplomacy. It does not provide governments with all they need to know for the successful conduct of international relations, nor does it relieve them of the responsibility for refusing to believe all that it enables them to hear. It is certainly not a global parliament, capable of adopting an authoritative and effective world policy to supersede the tangle of national foreign policies, nor does it provide a super-conciliator, able to step into the midst of the cold war, knock American and Soviet heads together, and set the giants to doing the world's work in harmonious collaboration. But it does provide a setting within which national foreign policies may be measured against such rudimentary general standards as governments are capable of formulating in agreed terms, subjected to the realities of the political forces which they are destined to confront, exposed to the demands of states whose acquiescence or support is desired, and consolidated in the degree that states are prepared to abdicate their unilateral roles in international affairs.

When the United Nations is evaluated in these terms, it is no abject confession to say that member states seek to use the organization for the promotion of their national interests rather than the global interest. Of course they do; whatever promise the United Nations holds for a brighter political future derives from the fact that when states attempt to promote national policies through the United Nations, they subject themselves to a process which increases the probability that their policies will at least fall within the lower limits of international tolerability and at most conform to the higher requirements of international acceptability. The national urge to use the United Nations is the essential basis of the possibility that it can be of some international use. The improvement of foreign policies is a more modest enterprise than the abolition of foreign policies, but it may be for that reason a more significant one.

Looking somewhat beyond the immediate situation, we may find that the general political processes of international organization have a potential function which is considerably less modest than the one described. Assuming the success of multilateral and other efforts to induce moderation and restraint in Soviet behavior, and to inject political wisdom into the exercise of leadership in the non-Communist world by the United States, it is conceivable that a situation of roughly equivalent strength may be developed which will provide the foundation for a genuine attempt at accommodation between the two sides in the cold war. In this eventuality, the availability of the United Nations as a meeting-ground and of its forum as a place for the registration of willingness to negotiate a *modus vivendi* may be of vital importance. Great powers do not easily repudiate their mutual animosities, and they may be heavily dependent upon the United Nations to provide the context within which fruitful discussions may be possible, and to serve as a quasi-neutral agency to which points of disagreement may be referred for multilateral decision. The contribution of the United Nations to future amelioration of great power relations may lie partly in its institutional readiness to undertake projects analogous to the League's administration of such contested areas as the Saar and Danzig, the abortive project of Security Council supervision over the Trieste Territory, and the accomplished feat of General Assembly legislation concerning the disposition of former Italian colonies. In short, the United Nations may provide acceptable substitutes for substantive agreement on specific issues and for concessions to each other by the major antagonists, as well as encouragement for the working out of agreements and compromises.

Additionally, the world organization may have the essential function of preventing possible great power negotiations from degenerating into a cynical carving up of the world to suit the interests of the giants—of upholding the proposition that "The cold war is no private show of the great powers. The whole world is involved, and no settlement will ever be possible which does not take account of world interests." [1] The negative task of preventing the wrong kind of settlement may be as important as the positive task of facilitating some kind of settlement.

In order to be ready to play this potentially vital role in the process of accommodation to which the course of the cold war may conceivably lead, the United Nations must do more than simply continue to exist. It must maintain its international quality, so as to provide a reasonable basis for the conception that it is an agency of the larger community which envelops both East and West. Considering the reserve function of the organization, Sir Gladwyn Jebb observed that "it would be tragic if the United Nations were rendered incapable of playing this great role either because it had been broken up by the departure of a significant group of Members, or by being discredited with either party through being identified

[1] A. H. Feller, *United Nations and World Community* (Boston: Little, Brown, 1952), p. 122.

too closely with one or the other side in the major conflicts of our time."[2]

From this standpoint, the primary validity of the criticism of efforts to make the United Nations subserve national interests is not that such efforts represent present neglect of the global interest, but that they threaten to undermine the capacity of the organization to grasp future opportunities for promoting accommodation of great power interests. American leaders, in particular, have the delicate task of using the United Nations to assist in the development of situations of Western strength, without at the same time destroying its usefulness for promoting the successful outcome of the negotiations for which the situations of strength are designed to create the political basis.

It may be that the most significant political task of the United Nations is to remain in reserve, keeping its institutional resources in readiness for the day that may or may not come, when the conflicts of the cold war shall have become ripe for political adjustment.

THE DANGERS OF THE GRAND DEBATE

Thus far the values, actual and potential, of the general political forum which is provided by the United Nations have been stressed. It remains to be noted that the grand debate has its definite demerits as well as its limited but significant merits as a contribution of international organization to the conduct of global diplomacy.

In the first place, multilateral assembly halls tend almost inexorably to become huge wind tunnels, channels for the release of enormous supplies of international hot air. Sheer talkiness is one of the leading characteristics of delegates to international conferences. As André Maurois described proceedings in the League,

> Every year . . . a great and sacred orator . . . preaches before the Assembly of Nations a solemn sermon on the text of the Covenant. Then the Congregation sings its favourite psalms: Psalm 159, Disarmament-Security; Psalm 137, Must Politics, Gentlemen, have precedence over Economics? It is an excellent thing for the disbeliever to undergo Church discipline, for ceremonial of any kind lulls to sleep and calms the passions. . . . At Geneva the art of saying nothing has almost reached perfection.[3]

The United Nations has certainly not effected drastic changes in this regard.

Concerning mere diplomatic verbosity, it is seemly that all men who live under national governments, and particularly those who live under

---

[2] "The Role of the United Nations," *International Organization*, November 1952, p. 519.

[3] Cited in David Thomson, *Democracy in France* (London: Oxford University Press, 1946), p. 204.

democratic governments, should adopt a philosophic and tolerant attitude; the United Nations does not compare unfavorably in this respect with, for instance, the United States Congress. The wasting of human breath in the international forum is not exceptional, and it is at worst an occasion for impatience, not alarm.

Nevertheless, this phenomenon does have its dangers. The verbiage of the grand debate tends to be heavily freighted with pious protestations, and it is essential that a high discount rate be applied by those who listen to it. Surely, the governments of the world are not so uniformly devoted to international peace, welfare, and justice as their official speech-makers in the United Nations would have us believe. Allowing for the operation of both natural and acquired skepticism, there is still the possibility that statesmen and the publics whose opinion cannot be flouted by statesmen may be unduly influenced by the fair words which all too often reflect the propagandistic skill rather than the real policy of governments. International organization has developed its stock of conventional themes, and national spokesmen are likely to say what they are expected to say rather than what their governments can be realistically expected to do. This means that the critical faculties must be kept in order, not only to spot the aggressive intent which lurks behind pacific proclamations, but also to discover the insistence upon sovereign autonomy which lies behind declarations of international solidarity, the obsession with national interest which is cloaked in globalistic phrases, and the unwillingness to act which is obscured by calls for ambitious international programs. The grand debate can easily become an instrument for the fostering of illusions about the state of the world and the policies of the nations.

The United Nations is not only a speech-making organization; it is also a resolution-passing organization. There is a very real danger that a congregation of delegates will prefer the formulation of resolutions to the grappling for a solution of problems, and that external observers may mistake the former for the latter. This is not to deny the significance of recommendatory action and hortatory injunction, which are all too often dismissed with contempt by critics who bring to the study of international organization an oddly doctrinaire conviction that nothing counts in political matters except a legal fiat. But it is essential to be on guard against the fallacious equating of formal admonitions with definitive resolution of issues. Given the tradition of unrealism which has marked American conceptions of international relations, it is perhaps especially important that Americans should linger on the thought that a speech is not a policy, and a resolution is not a settlement.

It is hard to know whether the attractive verbiage of pious speeches and hopeful resolutions or the ugly phraseology of vituperative exchanges constitutes the more damaging output of the international forum. It seems unfair to damn the United Nations impartially if it does, and if it does not, reflect the bitterness of cold war conflicts, as the *Wall Street Journal* seemed to do in 1949, when it alleged that the organization had "degenerated from a useless debating forum to a mutual vilification society." [4] Yet, it is true that high-flown oratory can be misleading and low-down billingsgate can be exacerbating; if the former discourages looking problems in the eye, the latter is equivalent to spitting disputants in the eye.

The practice of unrestrained denunciation which has gained currency in United Nations debates may be defended on the ground that diplomatic candor is better than the stilted hypocrisy of traditional diplomatic niceties. Some of the bitter charges are true, and in any event it is better that feelings of profound hostility and distrust should be exposed than concealed. Moreover, some comfort may be derived from the observation that states have developed a capacity for accepting insults without feeling honor-bound to respond by fighting; whatever else international organization may have done to sovereignty, it has certainly made it less thin-skinned than in days gone by. Mutual vilification, if it stops with that, is surely preferable to mutual bombardment.

On the other hand, the combination of excessively laudatory descriptions of a state's own policy and extravagantly denunciatory comments on the policy of rival states does not add up to a demonstration of candor. This tactic can hardly do otherwise than feed the tendency toward "monumental self-righteousness" [5] which exists in all nations, and stimulate holier-than-thou attitudes which are not conducive to political adjustment. The open diplomacy of international organization, with its open invitation to self-praise and other-condemnation, has undoubtedly contributed to the artificial moralization of the issues of world politics and the mounting of moralistic high-horses by governments and their publics. Many contemporary problems would quite probably yield more readily to negotiation in the realistic terms of competing national interests than to debate in the idealistic terms of international moral principle.

The United Nations cannot be held responsible for the existence of bitter conflicts or the degradation of the language of diplomacy. But it does offer facilities and opportunities for statesmen to exploit which may possibly contribute more to the aggravation of conflicts and the rigidification of positions than to the creation of a climate of accommodation. The Wilsonian ideal of ventilating problems with the fresh air of world public opinion is constantly challenged by the reality of statesmen venting their spleen in the international assembly hall.

Finally, the grand debate is subject to the danger of degenerating into an exhibition of international nosiness. This is the reverse side of the

---

[4] Cited in John Maclaurin, *The United Nations and Power Politics* (London: George Allen and Unwin, 1951), p. 1.

[5] *Ibid.*, p. 26.

coin of responsibility to the international community. The establishment of the principle that the collectivity of nations is legitimately concerned with all that affects the common destiny of mankind represents real advance toward the ideal of world order, but this cannot be said of the tendency of governments to convert the United Nations into a cover for their irresponsible meddling in the affairs of other states, or to lead it into the futility of action designed to embarrass their opponents rather than promote settlement of issues. The political usefulness of international organization depends upon the willingness of statesmen to respect the fine distinction between the ideal of permitting multilateral agencies to get their hands on the issues that count, and the abuse of forcing them to stick their noses into matters that had better be left alone.

When all is said and done, the conclusion emerges that the fostering of the collective consideration of the state of the world and the collective discussion of the politics of international relations are a major contribution of international organization to the cause of world order. The grand debate is no panacea. It does not alter the fact that the ultimate responsibility for determining the course of world affairs is vested in a multitude of states, and particularly in two great powers. Nevertheless, it has a significance which cannot be gainsaid. As Werner Levi has put it,

> social order is largely created by developing the habit of adjustment and compromise in many informal ways as well as by the establishment of a legislature and a police force. The importance of diplomacy by conference, bilaterally or multilaterally, cannot be exaggerated. Indeed the sponsoring of constant communication between nations is the most useful mission a world organization can perform in a sovereign nation-state system.[6]

Debate alone will not eliminate disorder. But human experience suggests that the kind of order for which decent men yearn cannot be established and maintained except by means which involve the processes of deliberation.

SUGGESTED READINGS

Bailey, Sydney D., *The General Assembly of the United Nations,* London: Stevens, 1960.

Bloomfield, Lincoln P., "The New Diplomacy in the United Nations," Chap. 3 in Francis O. Wilcox and H. Field Haviland, Jr., eds., *The United States and the United Nations,* Baltimore: Johns Hopkins, 1961.

Bloomfield, Lincoln P., *The United Nations and U.S. Foreign Policy,* Boston: Little, Brown, 1960.

[6] *Fundamentals of World Organization,* p. 53. Coypright, 1950, by the University of Minnesota.

Burton, Margaret E., *The Assembly of the League of Nations,* Chicago: University of Chicago Press, 1941.

Dallin, Alexander, *The Soviet Union at the United Nations,* New York: Praeger, 1962.

Evatt, Herbert V., *The Task of Nations,* New York: Duell, Sloan and Pearce, 1949.

CHAPTER 16

Trusteeship as an Approach to Peace

International organization in the twentieth century has become progressively involved in the development and expression of a new approach to the ordering of relationships between established sovereign powers and dependent peoples, as the traditional system of European colonialism has lost its unchallenged position in the sphere of international relations and been subjected to the processes of political change. *Trusteeship* is the term adopted here as the all-inclusive symbol of the movement to utilize international organization as an instrument for the modification, transformation, or elimination of colonialism.

THE THEORY OF TRUSTEESHIP

This phase of the work of international organization is based in large part upon the assumption that colonialism is one of the factors making for war in the modern world; hence, trusteeship is justified in terms of the general war-prevention function of international organization. This concept was formally stated when the drafters of the United Nations Charter listed the furtherance of international peace and security as the first of the "basic objectives" of the special trusteeship system to be created under the auspices of the new organization.[1] The association between colonialism and war, and between the modification of colonialism and the promotion of peace, may be analyzed in several different fashions.

It may be argued that war is the outcome of rivalry among imperialist powers, the product of maldistribution of colonies, and of conflicting ambitions to stabilize and to upset the balance of colonial holdings. This thesis has become a significant feature of the twentieth-century version of Marxism, although it was not invented by—and has never been the exclusive property of—Marxists. From a proper Marxist point of view, imperialist rivalry is the organic product of the capitalist system, and the abolition of war therefore awaits the destruction of capitalism. The concept of trusteeship, on the other hand, deals with the fact rather than the causation of competition among colonial powers; it postulates the diminution of conflict over colonies not by transforming the economic and political foundations of the powers, but by establishing such international controls over the exploitation and administration of colonies as to make colonial holdings less attractive to the national self-interest of states and to render "ownership" of colonies essentially irrelevant to the international power struggle. Presumably, states will be less interested in grabbing up bits of empire if colonial possession is transformed from a privilege to be exploited into a responsibility to be shouldered.

Alternatively, the danger of war-stemming-from-colonialism may be ascribed to the tendency of subjugated peoples and their sympathizers to develop a revolutionary reaction against their rulers. Imperialism breeds colonial nationalism; dependent peoples learn to hate their oppressors; bloody rebellion, possibly turning into a bitter struggle of the whole colored world against the smugly imperious European community, is the ultimate prospect. Acceptance of this version of the colonial problem is reflected in the concern of trusteeship for remedying the abuses and lessening the exploitative aspects of alien rule. Dependency is to be made tolerable, so as not to stimulate revolt, and it is to be made terminable through processes of peaceful development, so as to provide hope rather than frustration for aspiring peoples.

Still another form of analysis is one which emphasizes neither the possibility of war among rival imperialists nor the danger of conflict between the possessors and the possessed, but views colonialism as both a symptom and a cause of an unhealthy situation in the global body politic. In this analysis, war is traced not so much to conflicts as to conditions; it is treated as an outgrowth of circumstances rather than an act of policy. Peace is a function of a good society, in which all component groups enjoy justice, share in a mutuality of respect, participate in the values of economic and social progress, and move toward political maturity. This

[1] Article 76.

ideal cannot be reached so long as the system of colonial overlordship keeps the map spotted with blighted areas, inhabited by peoples which are denied both the advantages and the responsibilities of full citizenship in the human commonwealth. Hence, the task of trusteeship is to help make the world fit for peace by launching a kind of international slum clearance project, and promoting the progressive development of peoples which have been left behind and pushed to the rear.

The approach of international organization to the colonial question has rested in some degree upon each of these versions of the relationship between colonialism and war. The reasoning has seldom been made explicit, but the operations of the League and the United Nations have been animated by the conviction that international delving into the colonial field is a means of getting at some of the roots of the problem of war.

It must be added, however, that there is a growing sentiment that international intervention to promote the amelioration of colonial evils and the opening up of a full range of opportunities for dependent peoples is a good thing in itself, to be justified by its intrinsic values rather than its efficacy as a means to peace. The most devoted champions of trusteeship would probably not suffer an appreciable loss of enthusiasm if it could be incontrovertibly established that international action in this field is wholly irrelevant to the problem of war. It seems to be the case that any project requiring the instrumentality of international organization, however worthy it may be, must be put forward as a contribution to world peace; and it hardly stretches the point to say that any scheme for international action which is presented in those terms, however far-fetched its relationship to the problem of war may be, is likely to attract considerable support among statesmen whose business it is to determine the functional concerns of international organization. Given the respectability of the notion that the causes of war must be varied and complex, and the lack of scientific certitude as to the exact list of causes which contribute to war, the way is open for anyone with the barest minimum of theoretical ingenuity to develop a plausible case for the peace-creating potentialities of virtually any pet project.

In any case, whether because of genuine conviction that it offers a useful approach to the creation of the conditions of peace or because of considerations only verbally linked to that legitimizing concept, the formulators of the terms of reference of international organization have progressively brought the trusteeship idea into the official international program.

Basically, the concept of trusteeship involves denial of the right of sovereign irresponsibility and the legitimacy of unmitigated self-interest as the guiding principle of the policy of possessor states in their dealings with dependent peoples. It is an assertion of the claim of the international community to determine relations between imperial powers and their colonies in accordance with collective judgment as to what is best for the peoples of non-self-governing areas and for the world at large. Trusteeship represents an attempt to transform colonies from bits of private property subject to exploitation by their owners to parts of the public domain subject to development in the general interest. It aims at making dependent peoples temporary wards and their rulers responsible agents of world society.

Both in theory and in practice, trusteeship reflects a fundamental dualism of origin and motivation. It is, on the one hand, a culmination of liberal humanitarian trends which extend far back into the era of European colonialism. In its insistence on the moral imperative to protect native peoples of subjugated areas against mistreatment and to promote their welfare by positive action, it derives from such various roots as Vitoria's admonition that the sixteenth-century conquests by his country, Spain, could be justified only by government "for the welfare and in the interests of the Indians and not merely for the profit of the Spaniards";[2] Burke's recognition of Britain's ethical responsibility in the government of colonial peoples; the upsurge of humanitarian reformism among nineteenth-century churchmen and secularists, liberals and socialists, romanticists and rationalists; the Wilsonian dedication to the precept of national self-determination; and the Rooseveltian vision of a New Deal for the world's underprivileged. In large measure, the effort to promote the development of humane and enlightened policies toward colonial peoples is a constructive response to criticism and rebelliousness, a product of interaction between the high ideals and the bad conscience of the West.

But trusteeship is a political device as well as a moral crusade. To say this is not merely to admit what is clearly true—that in practice its humanitarian idealism is diluted by the infusion of liberal quantities of political interests, so that international morality tends to become simply a kind of insubstantial film, floating on the deep waters of the politics of colonialism. Certainly, trusteeship lends itself to hypocrisy as well as to reformism, and to the ideological decoration as well as to the genuine mitigation of colonial rule; as Salvador de Madariaga characterized its impact in the League era, "the old hag of colonization puts on a fig leaf and calls itself mandate." [3] But the intrusion of political factors is not simply an instance of the contamination of a pure moral concept which should set idealistic heads shaking regretfully and realistic heads wagging knowingly. The political derivation and coloration of trusteeship are integral to its nature.

---

[2] Scott, *Law, the State, and the International Community,* II, 277-278.
[3] *The World's Design* (London: George Allen and Unwin, 1938), p. 7.

Trusteeship is, in the terminology of H. Duncan Hall, a phenomenon of the "international frontier,"[4] a new and more sophisticated form of the device which, in a variety of models, ranging from buffer states to areas under international administration, has served as the instrument by which the powers have sought to establish stability in the zones where their interests converge. It is, in these terms, a scheme for protecting the world's interest in peace by padding the points of potential conflict among the great powers. Additionally, trusteeship may be regarded as a project for compromising the old claims of the European world-rulers and the new demands of young states and emergent peoples, eager and impatient to undo the Europeanization of world politics. In its essential nature, trusteeship is a concept of political adjustment quite as much as an ideal of humanitarian advance.

TRUSTEESHIP AND THE LEAGUE

As I have indicated, both the moral and the political aspects of the idea of trusteeship are deeply rooted in the European tradition. During the nineteenth century, the colonial powers of Europe took the first halting steps toward giving that concept a place among the operative principles of international politics. On occasions ranging from the Congress of Vienna in 1815 to the Berlin Conference in 1885 and the Brussels Conference in 1890, they exchanged declarations and undertook commitments relating to the exploitation of Africa, in which they developed a joint approach to the suppression of the slave trade and a collective recognition of their responsibility for maintaining some semblance of civilized standards in their dealings with both colonial rivals and colonial victims. This series of diplomatic developments did little more than project onto the twentieth-century stage the idea of institutionalizing international concern with the conduct of competitive colonialism. It did not in any fundamental way alter the fact that such sense of moral responsibility as a European state might have for behaving as if its overseas holdings constituted a "sacred trust" was a product of its own national conscience, and an obligation for the performance of which the state was answerable almost exclusively to that same national conscience.[5]

The establishment of the Mandate System by the League of Nations marked the effective beginning of systematic international intrusion into the workings of colonialism. The incorporation of Article 22 in the Covenant constituted the first explicit declaration of the authority and responsibility of the international community for safeguarding and promoting

---

[4] See *Mandates, Dependencies and Trusteeship* (Washington: Carnegie Endowment for International Peace, 1948), pp. 3-26.

[5] Cf. Georg Schwarzenberger, *Power Politics* (2nd ed.; New York: Praeger, 1951), pp. 648-652.

the welfare of "peoples not yet able to stand by themselves under the strenuous conditions of the modern world," and provided the broad outlines of a working arrangement whereby "advanced nations" would exercise "tutelage" over such peoples "on behalf of the League," and the Council, supported by an advisory Permanent Mandates Commission, would give institutional expression to the League's interest in the faithful performance of the duties entrusted to its national agents.

This set of headlines concerning the establishment of the Mandate System must be read in conjunction with a very different and equally valid set of headlines: the victorious powers of World War I followed the customary practice of stripping the defeated states of their colonies; they distributed those confiscated possessions among themselves, substantially in accordance with the pattern which they had agreed upon in secret treaties during the war and with the realities of military occupation which prevailed at the end of the war;[6] they gave to the League the shadow of supervisory authority over their administration of the newly-acquired colonies, while retaining for themselves the substance of sovereign control; they ostensibly became agents of the League, albeit self-appointed agents, but in fact they created the League as an instrument of their purposes and, in particular, designed it to serve as an agency for bestowing ideological legitimacy upon their colonial conquests.

Much of the commentary inspired by the League Mandate System has consisted of editorialization upon the basis of one or another of these two highly selective groups of headlines. Article 22 has been regarded as either the foundation of an incomplete but to-be-completed international structure for implementing the ideal of trusteeship, or the basis of an imposing moral façade for hiding the ugly realities of colonialism.

The divergence of these interpretations is indicative not only of the conflicting biases of observers, but also of the dual nature of the trusteeship concept and the ambiguity of its expression in the League system. The colonial settlement worked out after World War I reflected the humanitarian revulsion of decent men, expressed by such spokesmen as Smuts, Wilson, G. L. Beer, and Lloyd George,[7] against the evils of uncontrolled colonial exploitation, as well as the political urge, equally basic to the trusteeship concept, to establish safeguards against the dangers of unrestricted colonial competition.

The scope of the experiment in trusteeship was defined negatively by the political capacity of undefeated powers to withhold their possessions, and positively by the political necessity of the Allies to respect their war-

---

[6] See Ernst B. Haas, "The Reconciliation of Conflicting Colonial Policy Aims: Acceptance of the League of Nations Mandate System," *International Organization,* November 1952, pp. 525-531.

[7] *Ibid.,* pp. 522-525, 532-535; Russell, *Theories of International Relations,* pp. 415-419.

time no-annexation pledges and to defer to the anti-imperialist public opinion within their own ranks; thus, the Mandate System was applied exclusively to territories wrenched from the defeated empires. The magnitude of the authority conferred upon the international organs of the system was determined by the interaction among devotion to the principle of international responsibility for the guardianship of the community's wards, skepticism as to the practicability of direct international administration, sensitivity of colonial powers to aspersions upon their trustworthiness as bearers of the white man's burden, and resistance on their part to the excessive development of the anomaly that sovereign states should be ordered about by an international agency. The upshot of this interaction was that the administration of the mandated areas was undertaken by members of the triumphant coalition, on terms formulated by agreement among themselves, and that the League was conceded a supervisory competence which was limited to the powers of interrogation, recommendation, and criticism.

At worst, the Mandate System was an international disguise for the surreptitious continuation of colonialism;[8] even if this damning judgment be accepted, the fact that the powers found it necessary to camouflage the annexation and subjection of colonies to their sovereign control is indicative of the rising significance of the trusteeship idea. An intermediate interpretation would suggest that it was a compromise between traditional imperialism and futuristic trusteeship, permitting the victors to keep the spoils but denying them the clear title of ownership which would legitimize their spurning all efforts to hold them responsible for conforming to standards of colonial policy established by the League. At best, the system was the small-scale beginning of a revolutionary transformation of the status of dependent peoples in the modern world, the first installment of the victory of trusteeship.

In an important sense, each of these views has been confirmed by the subsequent development of the issue of colonialism in relation to international organization, and particularly by the trends which have been manifested in the United Nations. It has become increasingly necessary to mask the conquest and control of foreign territories and peoples, and the acceptance of a mandate—or, in the new terminology, a trusteeship arrangement—has continued to serve that purpose. For instance, the United States Government was able to reach internal agreement on the project of negotiating a United Nations trusteeship for the Pacific Islands formerly under Japanese mandate only by convincing officials of the military services and departments that such an arrangement would give the United States, as administering authority, rights of sovereign control fully equivalent to those which might be gained by forthright annexation. In fact,

---

[8] Cf. Georg Schwarzenberger, *A Manual of International Law* (2nd ed.; London: Stevens, 1950), p. 134.

mandate or trusteeship arrangements have come to be regarded as rather too thin cloaks for the concealment of naked hegemony in the mid-twentieth century; the various ingenuities of satellitism have produced a more popular stock of synthetic fabrics for meeting the requirements of modesty among imperial overlords.

On the other hand, there is abundant evidence of the reality of the compromise between colonialism and trusteeship which has characterized the international situation since the inauguration of the League Mandate System. Winston Churchill provided a splendid sample of this evidence at the Yalta Conference, when he reacted to a proposal for creating a trusteeship system to supersede the Mandate System by asserting hotly "that he did not agree with one single word of this report on trusteeships. . . . He said that under no circumstances would he ever consent to forty or fifty nations thrusting interfering fingers into the life's existence of the British Empire. As long as he was Minister, he would never yield one scrap of their heritage. . . ." The British Prime Minister was reassured by Secretary Stettinius' statement that the projected machinery was to be designed for dealing with territories taken from the enemy, not with British possessions, and he then said that Britain "had no objection if the question of trusteeship was to be considered in relation to enemy territory." [9]

Here, in a nutshell, is proof that insistence upon the unrestricted right to maintain unilateral control of colonies was not dead in 1945, that observation of the Mandate System's operations for a quarter-century had not convinced so realistic a statesman as Churchill that international supervision of colonial rule was either a convenient fraud or an innocuous fiction, and that the major Western powers were still unprepared to let the principle of trusteeship usurp more than a small corner of the colonial field. If trusteeship had been proved an ideological disguise capable of facilitating the perpetuation of colonialism, the colonial powers should have jumped at the chance to apply it to all their possessions; if it had been proved a bit of pious nonsense which changed nothing, Churchill should not have been so sensitive to the danger that it might be applied to the British Empire; if it had been proved a great blessing to dependent peoples, statesmen who were prepared to espouse the principle that the uplift of human underdogs was a sacred responsibility of the international community should not have been insistent upon confining its beneficent impact to a few peoples which were fortunate enough to have been parts of the losing side in global wars. The conclusion must be that the old colonial spirit maintained its vitality throughout the League experiment, that the Mandate System invested the trusteeship idea with significant meaning, and that dedication to the ideal of equipping the civilized world to do its duty by the backward peoples was heavily qualified

[9] *Foreign Relations of the United States, Diplomatic Papers: The Conferences at Malta and Yalta, 1945* (Washington: Government Printing Office, 1955), p. 844.

by political considerations. In short, colonialism and trusteeship were coexistent realities in the period from the League's beginning to its demise.

Finally, the optimistic view that the Mandate System was a genuine beginning, albeit a very limited realization, of the application of trusteeship has been confirmed by the steady development of the essential principles and the necessary mechanisms of international supervision in the colonial field. Whatever its limitations, the League's enterprise in this area did initiate the *internationalization* of the trusteeship idea. It accepted the concept of the Dual Mandate, whereby a colonial power is considered a trustee of the interests of both the colonial peoples and the world at large in the exercise of its governing functions, and sought to give this concept decisive meaning by providing a world agency to which accountability should be rendered and through which responsibility should be made effective. This was, in essence, a denial of the adequacy of national trusteeship and an assertion of the principle that if a state is to be responsible *for* interests other than its own it must be held responsible *to* entities other than itself. The League system initiated the *institutionalization* of trusteeship, casting moral obligations into the form of legal commitments, and developing regularized means by which the performance of obligations should be subjected to scrutiny and supervision.

These innovations constituted what have proved to be the foundations of a rising structure of trusteeship. In the course of League history, they were solidified and elaborated, and even when the League collapsed, they remained intact as the bases upon which building should start anew. The final evidence of the meaningfulness of the League's approach to the implementation of trusteeship lies in the fact that it served as the starting point for the much more ambitious approach of the United Nations.

TRUSTEESHIP AND THE UNITED NATIONS

When the new structure of world organization was designed at San Francisco, a formal Trusteeship System was projected as a rechristened and somewhat revised version of the Mandate System.[10] The basic points of similarity were obvious. The range of the system was to be restricted in much the same manner as that of its predecessor; it should, in principle, apply to territories previously held under mandate and yet not independent, territories wrested from the Axis powers as a result of the war, and such other territories as might be handed over to it by their possessors. The overriding principle, as in the case of the Mandate System, was that the operators of the international laboratory should be dependent upon the will of colonial powers, singly or jointly expressed, for the provision of materials upon which to perform their experimental work.

---

10 See the United Nations Charter, Articles 75-91.

In practice, the map of the Trusteeship System became a new edition, revised but not drastically altered, of the Mandate map. The Middle Eastern sector was eliminated, through the rise to independence of Iraq, Syria, Lebanon, Jordan, and Israel; the Union of South Africa stubbornly asserted its legal right to withhold its former mandate, South-West Africa, from the new system; the United States replaced Japan as the responsible administrator in the Pacific Islands north of the equator; and Italian Somaliland was added for a stated period of ten years as a trusteeship area under Italian administration. Otherwise, the picture remained the same, with Britain, France, and Belgium continuing in charge of six African areas, and Australia and New Zealand maintaining their mandatory positions in three island areas of the South Pacific. The political obstacles to the extension of trusteeship to territories firmly established in colonial empires and not recently affected by changes of sovereignty have remained insuperable. The Trusteeship System represents, as did its predecessor, the very limited willingness of the colonial powers to superimpose a formal trusteeship structure upon their administration of dependent areas.

The pattern of the Mandate System was also generally followed by the designers of the Trusteeship System in respect to provisions for the administration and the exercise of the supervisory function in areas subject to its operation. The Charter stated the possibility that the United Nations might itself undertake to serve as the governing authority in particular territories, but it preserved the normal working principle, so far uniformly observed, that the actual administration of trusteeship areas should be entrusted to the government of a state. In practice, this has meant that, under the United Nations as under the League, states which have had sufficient claim to or hold upon dependent territories to rank as the parties whose consent is necessary for placing those territories under the international system have been accepted as the self-designated administering authorities. The one exception arose in the case of Italian Somaliland, when the General Assembly, exercising a legislative competence delegated to it by the great powers which had destroyed Italy's sovereignty over its former colonies, made a discretionary choice of Italy as the governing authority for that territory.

The principle that supervision of the management of mandated areas should be carried out by international organs, through techniques not involving the assertion of legal competence to command or coercive capacity to enforce, was transferred from the League to the United Nations. The League Council and its auxiliary Permanent Mandates Commission were replaced by the General Assembly and its subordinate Trusteeship Council. The latter Council was designed as a body of governmental representatives in contrast to the independent expert membership of the Mandates Commission, and it was assigned a somewhat more elevated status in the organizational hierarchy than its prototype had enjoyed. It was endowed with formal capacity to consider petitions relating to trusteeship affairs, a function which the Mandates Commission had evolved without explicit constitutional warrant, and with a new instrument of supervision, the authority to dispatch visiting missions for on-the-spot investigation of conditions in territories under its surveillance. These revisions added up to a potentially significant augmentation of the capacity of international organization for exercising effective supervision, but they did not modify the principle that international *influence,* rather than *control,* should be the distinctive mark of trusteeship.

These points of essential resemblance between the Mandate and Trusteeship Systems are only a part of the story. The creators of the United Nations did more than reproduce, with some technical improvements, the League's arrangements for dealing with the colonial problem. They also effected some fundamental changes, which can be explained and understood only in terms of the contrast between the political and ideological context within which they worked and that which had enveloped the drafters of the Covenant.

The League was designed and built in what was still very much a European world. Its makers operated on the basis of the general assumption that the colonial system would and should endure, and they were not confronted with a politically effective challenge to the existence of that system. They exhibited only the slightest interest in matters pertaining to colonialism in general; concerning that issue, they were content to include in Article 23 of the Covenant a vague commitment that member states would "undertake to secure just treatment of the native inhabitants of territories under their control."

The formulation of mandate provisions was essentially an effort to settle the disposition of a particular group of colonies, taken from defeated enemies, in accordance with requirements posed by political viewpoints prevailing within the white man's world. European conflicts over colonies ought to be eliminated in the future; hence, Allied nonannexation pledges should be respected, so as to avoid providing a pretext for a new war to reconquer lost colonies, and to establish the precedent that war should not be used as an instrument of colonial rivalry. The "A" mandates, Middle Eastern territories severed from the Turkish Empire and presumed to be nearly ready for independence, were distributed between Britain and France in such a way as to register an adjustment of the conflicting ambitions of those two states. Those of the "B" category, which included all the African mandates except South-West Africa, were subjected to the rule of the commercial open door, in the interest of avoiding economic clashes among European powers. The latter group and the remaining territories, which were customarily referred to as "C" mandates, were excluded from fortification and militarization, again for the primary purpose of guarding against their conversion into focal points for the development of rivalries among the states of Europe.

In all these matters, it is clear that the political considerations affecting the construction of the Mandate System were factors relating to the internal issues of that part of the world which accepted and practiced colonialism. So far as the interests of dependent peoples were concerned, the primary objective of the system was the prevention of abusive exploitation and misrule, and this purpose too was set in response to politically effective demands which had arisen within the white man's world.[11] In political terms, the peoples on the receiving end of colonialism constituted a passive object, unable to generate pressures significantly affecting the formulation of the League's approach.

The critical difference between the political context of 1945 and that of the early League era lies in the facts that a widespread attack upon the very existence of the colonial system had gathered momentum by the end of World War II, and that the nonwhite world had found its voice and begun to assert its interests. At San Francisco, the representatives of European and European-derived nations could not proceed upon the assumption that the colonial problem was simply *their* problem, to be dealt with in such a way as to promote harmony among themselves and to satisfy the humanitarian instincts of their more morally sensitive elements; they could not even assume with confidence that the issue was definable in terms of reforming the colonial system. Colonialism had become a global question, and the political arena within which it was discussed had been enlarged to include active and vociferous participants from both sides of the colonial fence. The League approach had been determined by compromises among statesmen of the continental and extra-continental European world, including those who had troubled consciences or troublesome constituents with troubled consciences, those who had unsatisfied colonial ambitions, and those who had peace-preserving aspirations. This kind of compromise was still relevant at San Francisco, but it was no longer the central issue; the United Nations approach had to be preeminently the product of compromise between the possessing and the possessed halves of the old colonial world. The position of the former was weakened by its war-debilitated condition, its internal dissensions, and its own gnawing doubts about the legitimacy of colonialism. The other half was on the political and ideological upswing, although it was handicapped by diplomatic immaturity and the incomplete development of the elements of political power. The stage was set in 1945 for a complicated process of negotiation over the future of the colonial system.

The emergent political strength of the non-European and essentially anticolonial world was primarily responsible for the distinctive features of

[11] Haas, *op. cit.*, pp. 521-536.

the United Nations approach to trusteeship questions. The Charter provision for constituting the Trusteeship Council as a body equally balanced between states administering trust territories and members not having such responsibilities was a clear recognition of the new pattern of political forces bearing on colonialism. The decided shift from negative emphasis upon preventing abuse of dependent peoples to positive stress upon the goal of promoting their economic, social, and political advance was in large part a registration of the political potency of the newly articulate peoples. Whereas the relevant part of the Covenant had been a self-denying ordinance of the colonial powers, setting limits to the privileges of ownership, the corresponding section of the Charter was more nearly a negotiated contract between rulers and ruled, asserting the rights and aspirations of the latter as well as the authority of the former. The spokesmen for colonial peoples were successful in making the Charter reflect their determination that the white man's burden should be more burdensome than the mere exercise of decent self-restraint.

The most striking innovation of the United Nations approach to colonial matters was the incorporation in the Charter of Chapter XI, in which members ruling non-self-governing territories committed themselves to the proposition that *all* colonial possessions constituted a sacred trust, accepted a codification of international standards to which colonial policy should conform, and agreed to the obligation of reporting to the United Nations on the performance of their developmental responsibilities. This declaration of responsibility constituted an imperfect universalization of the principle of international trusteeship. While it provided only the vaguest hint of measures for the institutionalization of international accountability, it nevertheless ratified the doctrine that all colonies, whether subjected to the formal authority of the Trusteeship System or not, are minor wards of the human family to be brought to self-respecting and self-reliant adulthood, rather than chattels to be ruled and used at the pleasure of their owners.

The actual formulation of Chapter XI at San Francisco was based upon proposals initially put forward by Britain and Australia, and it has sometimes been suggested that it was a unilateral declaration by the colonial powers, "an act of generosity" on their part.[12] However, the evidence is clear that the adoption of this unprecedented document was a concession to the political effectiveness of the demands posed by representatives of that area which had long been on the wrong side of the colonial tracks. Its provisions, like those of the two following Chapters which laid out the constitutional basis of the Trusteeship System, reflected the interplay of colonial and anticolonial forces. Its major segment,

---

12 Charles Chaumont, "A French View on Security through International Organization," *International Organization,* May 1950, p. 240.

Article 73, represented the outcome of the clash between colonial conservatism and the radical demand for positive measures to end colonialism by advancing its subjects beyond colonial status; Article 74, representing the old-style agreement of colonial powers not to be nasty to each other, was stuck on as a mere appendage.

The significance of the transformation of the colonial debate from a conversation among statesmen of the European tradition to an argument between them and spokesmen of the non-European world is even more evident in the operation and development of the United Nations than in the drafting of its Charter. Since the inception of the world organization, the anticolonial forces have increased in relative numerical strength through the admission of new members, achieved the fuller mobilization of resentments, sensitivities, and aspirations, developed a corps of leaders and spokesmen, and learned new skills of diplomatic bargaining and international parliamentary maneuvering. In short, an increasingly effective anticolonial bloc has emerged as a major factor in the political processes of the United Nations.

Life would be simpler for the analyst if he could describe the political situation regarding colonial issues in the United Nations in terms of a clear-cut division between colored peoples and white men, present and past victims of colonialism and present and past masters, underdogs demanding elementary justice and topdogs insisting upon the perpetuation of their superior status and special privileges. However, this will not do. The anticolonial bloc has a solid membership core which offers some justification for calling it an Afro-Asian grouping. It gains a variable amount of support from the ranks of Latin American states. It enjoys the mixed blessing of the usual support of the Soviet bloc; that support is sometimes more embarrassing than helpful in promoting the mobilization of necessary majorities, and it poses the delicate problem of avoiding the danger of the bloc's becoming a tail wagged by the Communist dog. The anticolonial cause arouses strong sympathies within the Western community, and is capable of attracting votes from that sector.

The colonial bloc, on the other hand, consists essentially of the states which administer or have recently administered colonies or trust territories —Britain, France, Belgium, the Netherlands, Portugal, Spain, Australia, New Zealand, and the United States—along with states particularly subject to their influence, states sharing a fundamentally pro-European outlook, and one formally noncolonial state—South Africa—which is more colonialist than the colonial powers. The solidarity of this group is reduced by persistent defections, representing grudging concessions to pressure, constructive efforts to deal affirmatively with the trend toward the obsolescence of colonialism, and calculated attempts to counter Communist propaganda. Its centrifugal pulls are somewhat offset, however, by the recognition of the need for avoiding the alienation or weakening of the colonialist members of the anti-Soviet front, and the fear that the anticolonial game may emancipate dependent peoples right into the hands of new Communist masters. For instance, the United States, a basically anticolonial colonial power, seems constantly torn by the competing demands of its colonial interests, anticolonial sentiments, European alliances, and plans for extirpating the global roots of Communist expansionist capacity.

However complex may be the relevant political considerations and however shifting may be the alignments, the fact remains that the development of the United Nations approach to the colonial problem has been a function of the interplay of two blocs, one generally representative of the rebelliousness of the victims of the colonial system, and the other broadly representative of the vested interests of colonial masters.

The effect of this confrontation may be described in the first place as a series of victories for the anticolonial movement. This has been achieved in part by outflanking the Trusteeship System, in which colonial conservatism has particular strength because of the constitutional principles that its coverage is limited by the willingness of states to convert their colonies into trust territories and that its managing body, the Trusteeship Council, must consist of administering and nonadministering members in equal numbers.

The anticolonial bloc has worked vigorously at expanding the trusteeship implications of Chapter XI, and has succeeded in establishing the principle that the administration of all non-self-governing territories should be subjected to international examination and criticism in somewhat the same manner as the administration of trust areas. A special committee for the consideration of reports from dependencies, the Committee on Information from Non-Self-Governing Territories, has become a standing feature of the organizational structure of the General Assembly; constituted on the same principle of balanced membership as the Trusteeship Council, it has gone far toward assimilating the status of all non-self-governing territories to that of the select few with which the Council deals.

Beyond this, the major strategy of the anticolonial bloc has been to convert the General Assembly, the organ in which its relative voting power is greatest and has steadily increased, into a forum for the consideration of all issues relating to colonialism, whether they are specifically concerned with the Trusteeship System, the Declaration Regarding Non-Self-Governing Territories, or demands for national self-determination. An aggressive and broadly successful campaign has been waged to override claims of domestic jurisdiction, restrictive interpretations of the commitments in Chapter XI, and demands that the General Assembly respect the delegation of functions to its subordinate Trusteeship Council and Committee on Information. Serving as the instrument of anticolonial voting majorities, the Assembly has asserted the claim of competence to determine what territories fall within the provisions of Chapter XI, and to evaluate the validity of constitutional changes which purport to remove territories from the non-self-governing category. It has created numerous special committees for dealing with issues relating to particular territories or groups of territories, as well as one designed to promote the general objective of completing the process of decolonization, as envisaged in its Resolution 1514 (XV), the Declaration on the Granting of Independence to Colonial Countries and Peoples, passed on December 14, 1960. The Assembly has lent itself to the endorsement of the general thesis that all peoples have a right of national self-determination which transcends the legal sovereignty of colonial possessors, and it has to a very considerable extent functioned as the institutional vehicle for the elaboration and application of the principle that international organization has a broad mandate to intercede on behalf of dependent peoples whenever they or their vigorous champions find themselves at odds with colonial powers. In brief, the Assembly has become the means for nullifying the provisions of the Charter which seemed to guarantee that the United Nations would not adopt a radical attitude toward colonialism, in much the same degree that it has become the instrument for canceling the Charter agreement that the United Nations would not serve in basic political matters as an agency of international opposition to the policy of one of the Big Five.

One way of interpreting the history of the colonial issue in the United Nations is to focus on *results,* stressing the contrast between the scope and status of the colonial system in 1945 and in the early 1960's. From this perspective, this era appears as one of rapid decolonization. All but three of the trust territories—Nauru, the Pacific Islands under American administration, and the portion of New Guinea under Australian administration—have achieved independence, either separately or in association with other territories; thus, the Trusteeship System has been virtually liquidated. Numerous other dependencies have reached the same status, as the drastic enlargement of the United Nations membership list indicates, while still others are clearly moving rapidly toward political emancipation. The colonial system has been reduced to a few remnants, some of which pose troublesome problems for anticolonial clean-up squads, and the virtual completion of its dismantlement seems to be in prospect. Looking at the record in this way, one may interpret it as a chronicle of steady and remarkably rapid triumph for the forces of anticolonialism. The progressive liquidation of European empires is certainly not to be attributed wholly or perhaps even mainly to the existence or the operation of the United Nations, but the organization has evidently served as an important agency in bringing about this result.

From another viewpoint, the most interesting thing about the colonial issue in the United Nations is not the outcome but the *process* by which it has been reached, not the victory of anticolonialism but the battle between contending forces. Adopting this focus, we see decolonization not simply as a sweeping historical trend, but as the subject of intensive political debate and complex maneuvering. To use football terms, the play has been much closer than the score indicates, and the confident prediction of further touchdowns for the anticolonial team should not be taken to mean that the defensive line is exhausted. The play-by-play account of the game shows an impressive and ultimately decisive list of successful drives by anticolonial forces, but it also shows numerous instances of effective blocking by their adversaries. The colonial powers have had the significant advantages of legal authority, administrative control, and physical possession of dependent territories; hence, the passage of Assembly resolutions favorable to the cause of subject peoples, or the adoption of reports critical of administering powers, has not been in itself decisive action against their position. Moreover, the forces opposing the anticolonial drive have demonstrated, on many occasions, the political strength necessary to force the dilution or the abandonment of even such purely verbal challenges to themselves. To a considerable extent, the decolonization campaign in the United Nations has been dependent upon the possibility of securing the collaboration of colonial possessors in the dismantlement of their own empires, since it has not had at its disposal the means for forcing their withdrawal. The fundamental basis for the decisive breakthrough of anticolonialism which occurred at about the beginning of the 1960's was an ideological triumph, the acceptance by an overwhelming majority of states of the proposition that colonial possession on a continuing basis is no longer to be regarded as legitimate. This view, which derives ultimately from the formal statements of the concept of trusteeship incorporated in the League Covenant and the United Nations Charter, was gradually built up by the ideological deposit of innumerable debates, reports, and resolutions on colonial matters, and received its definitive expression in the Assembly's Resolution 1514 (XV), on December 14, 1960. It was stated in extreme form as a justification for India's invasion of Goa in 1961; the anticolonial doctrine was alleged to have invalidated the long-established authority of Portugal over that territory. This powerful solvent of sovereignty is not, of course, universally approved, but it has become effective throughout the colonial realm. The new ideology of legitimacy has undermined the legal claim of sovereignty over dependent territories, thereby preparing the way for the final stage of the disintegration of the European colonial system.

In broad perspective, it is probable that the most significant thing to be said about the course of the United Nations in this area is not that the world organization has become the registrar and instrument of the triumphant surge of dynamic anticolonialism, but rather that it has become the scene of conflict, the field upon which the battle over the future of colonialism has been fought.

To say this is to declare that the original United Nations approach to the colonial issue has been proved a failure, in an important respect. The relevant sections of the Charter represented a design to bring about the harmonious cooperation of all concerned in a collective effort to enhance the welfare and promote the political maturation of peoples who had fallen behind or been held back in the march of progress. The United Nations was envisaged as a community workshop, not a marshaling ground for opposing forces. The ideal of the Charter was to register a basic agreement between groups on the two sides of the colonial fence. Dominant powers renounced the right of irresponsible domineering over subject peoples, accepted the ultimate objective of liquidating the colonial system through the graduation of its wards to autonomous status, and agreed to become accountable administrative agents in the operation of this global enterprise. Spokesmen of the discontents of the non-European world reciprocated by accepting the principle that dependent peoples required preparation for autonomy rather than sheer emancipation, acknowledging the propriety of entrusting the major role in the developmental process to the states which had both a legal foothold in colonial areas and a treasury of experience in the administration of those areas, and promising loyal cooperation in carrying out the constructive tasks that lay ahead. Thus, the conflict between imperialism and emancipatory nationalism was to be transformed from a bitter struggle between irreconcilable antagonists, a confrontation endangering the future peace of the world, into a rational discussion among statesmen who shared, and felt that they shared, a common dedication to the aim of promoting the evolution of new societies able to play a full role in the international relations of the future. There would be debate and disagreement, but it would reflect the different views of collaborators imbued with mutual trust and respect, not the animosities of colonialists convinced that their critics were traitorous rebels and irresponsible fomenters of rebellion, and of anticolonialists committed to the proposition that they had to combat tyrannical oppressors whose only concern was to perpetuate the system which they dominated.

This hopeful image of trustful collaboration in the colonial sphere has proved as illusory as that of great power solidarity in the security sphere. The actual gap between the substantive positions of the colonial and anticolonial blocs is perhaps not so great as it might appear; the former, by and large, is prepared to recognize the collapse of the colonial system and to participate in its orderly dismantlement; the latter, on the whole, is willing that the white man should carry his burden a little longer, provided that he really carries a burden instead of running off with booty, and that he admits the obligation to lay it down when ordered to do so by the United Nations.

But the subjective gap is wide indeed. States administering non-self-governing and trust territories have tended to develop a deep sense of grievance; they graciously accepted commitments at San Francisco which the anticolonial bloc has insisted upon stretching beyond all recognition; they are busily engaged in projects of colonial uplift for which they are rewarded only by accusations of imperialism; they apply their unique expertness and wisdom to the administration of backward regions only to be handicapped by the intrusive ignorance of bumptious amateurs. Feeling themselves unappreciated and maligned, as well as double-crossed by those who have read rabid anticolonialism between the lines of the Charter, they have reacted by falling back upon a very strict interpretation of their legal obligations and of the world organization's constitutional competence to intervene in colonial matters, nourishing an excessive sensitivity to criticism and admonition, and exhibiting a stubborn intransigence in international discussions of issues relating to the trusteeship ideal. Thus, for instance, an Australian spokesman told the Assembly in 1954:

> We in Australia have no objection to constructive criticism, but we resent the sort of criticism and insinuations to which we have been subjected and which we regard as unfounded and captious. Please let me say, with respect to our critics, that the United Nations Trusteeship System does not mean that the United Nations is in charge of our Trust Territories. We are in charge of them and we are footing the bill, and we are meeting our obligations toward the Trust Territories with all the energy and sympathy and expert experience that we can bring to it.[13]

Regarding the question of non-self-governing territories in general, the colonial powers have taken the broad view that Chapter XI of the Charter is merely a unilateral declaration of their enlightened policy which in no way reduces their sovereign right of control or authorizes international meddlesomeness. This position was vigorously defended by a Belgian delegate to the Assembly in 1954, when he explained his government's abstention from participation in recent sessions of the Committee on Information as an act of resistance to efforts to whittle down Belgium's control over the Congo. He asserted that his country's sovereignty over that territory had not been impaired by the acceptance of Chapter XI, and claimed that "it was for Belgium, and not, as some representatives believed, for the General Assembly, to solve the territory's problems"; moreover, he interpreted Belgium's obligation under that chapter as merely a duty to submit technical information—"not a report"—on matters other than political conditions to the Secretary-General—"not to the General Assembly"—for informational purposes—"not for examination or discussion in any organ of the Assembly." [14]

On the whole, the colonial powers have been willing to devote con-

[13] *United Nations Review,* November 1954, pp. 82-83.
[14] *Ibid.,* December 1954, p. 34.

siderable effort to the improvement of conditions in dependencies and even to the furtherance of political trends leading to the termination of their dominance over subject peoples. However, they have offered bitter resistance to the idea that they are, or ought to be, under an obligation to permit international control of their colonial policy, and have insisted that the world should simply sit trustfully, secure in the knowledge that dependent peoples are in good hands, gaze admiringly as expert administrators make sound judgments concerning the proper methods and possible tempo of development, and nod approvingly as the work of civilization is progressively accomplished.

The anticolonial powers, on the other hand, have tended to regard themselves as crusaders, doing battle against the forces of entrenched privilege and oppressive exploitation. They are not much impressed by the claims of benevolent paternalism put forward by their opposite numbers; looking back at the history of imperialism, with its record of positive abuses and negative failures to promote the development of subject peoples, and observing the reluctance of administering powers to countenance the evolution of effective international supervision and direction of their activities, they conclude that the progressive liquidation of colonialism depends upon the exertion of unremitting pressure. They are distrustful of European good intentions, and insistent upon the establishment of firm commitments. They are dissatisfied with devices for the nominal international supervision of colonial policy, and determined to create effectual instrumentalities of international control. They are impatient with slow and uncertain advance, and eager to force the pace toward precisely defined goals. In particular, they are insistent that it should be clearly understood and universally admitted that the whole business of the government and development of dependent territories is very much the affair of the international community; as Dr. Trujillo of Ecuador put it, "We can no more speak of the sovereignty of the Administering Authority over a Non-Self-Governing Territory than we can speak of the ownership by the guardian of the goods of the pupil." [15]

Convinced that the sovereign rights of colonial powers in dependent territories have been virtually annulled, they focus their attention upon the international responsibilities which those powers have assumed; a Brazilian representative said in 1950 that "the only justification for colonialism at the present time was the ability of certain highly-developed countries to promote through their own resources the development of areas where the people were not yet sufficiently developed to manage their own affairs." [16] Impressed by such facts as that three hundred years of Dutch rule left Indonesia with only 1000 physicians, 300 lawyers, 8 engineers, and 10 economists in a

[15] *Ibid.*, November 1954, p. 82.
[16] *United Nations Bulletin,* December 1, 1950, p. 635.

population of 80 million,[17] and that the Italian colonial regime bequeathed to Libya a single native lawyer and no Libyan physicians at all,[18] anticolonialists consider that it is practically necessary as well as legally proper for them to engage in the vigorous prodding of colonial powers.

This is the setting of the persistent and frequently bitter conflict over colonial issues in the United Nations. Mutual recrimination is more characteristic of the situation than mutual consultation. In retrospect, it is clear that what was achieved at San Francisco was not a compromise between colonial conservatism and anticolonial radicalism, providing the basis for a collaborative approach to the tasks of trusteeship, but the creation of an arena within which the struggle of these two forces might be conducted. In the operation of the system, the colonial powers have been less willing to accept the broad application of the principle of international trusteeship than they seemed in 1945, and the anticolonial bloc has been less willing to tolerate an evolutionary transformation of the colonial domain, carried out by colonial powers under a loose system of international supervision, than it appeared at San Francisco. The Charter provisions concerning non-self-governing and trust territories proved to involve more external interference than the administering powers were able to stomach, and to leave more of the elements of sovereign control in the hands of the latter than the anticolonial states were willing to countenance.

Nothing seems more certain than that the colonial system is now in the final stages of liquidation; at the same time, nothing seems more clear than that the formulations of San Francisco failed to initiate a program of harmonious cooperation among all concerned, looking toward the orderly dismantlement of the old system and the gradual development of national freedom and welfare for colonial peoples. This failure means that the United Nations has been unable to contribute to the conditions of peace by forestalling the development of profound antagonisms between those states and peoples which lie on opposite sides of the colonial fence. The struggle over colonialism is not an unmitigated evil, for it furnishes the political fuel for the operation of the legal and institutional mechanism which the United Nations has established in this area. It is significant that the struggle has been largely brought within the confines of an organizational arena, and thus subjected to a set of rules of moderation and the authority of an umpire. Nevertheless, the point remains that the Charter represented a futile effort to compose basic differences and make collaboration rather than conflict the characteristic feature of international relations in the colonial field.

Another failure must be chalked up to the Trusteeship System of the

[17] S. Takdir Alisjahbana, "Tensions in Indonesian Life and Culture," *Confluence*, March 1953, p. 14.

[18] *United Nations Bulletin*, January 1, 1954, p. 44.

United Nations: it has failed to promote the meaningful establishment of the principle that a trust territory is an international zone in which no state can hope for anything more advantageous to its national interest than the privilege of bearing a heavy burden of responsibility. If the basic terms of the system, stated in Article 76 of the Charter, are taken seriously, the administration of a trust area is not the limited enjoyment of special privilege, but the solemn assumption of special responsibility; the qualification for appointment as an administering power is not a claim of legal right or political desert, or even a negative disposition to refrain from abusive treatment of dependent peoples, but a positive willingness and ability to assist in and contribute to the development of a relatively backward people and country.

In fact, nothing can be clearer than that the management of a trust territory is still regarded as a right to be demanded or a privilege to be sought, rather than an onerous duty to be sacrificially performed. The urge to undertake the administration of a trust territory stems mainly from the fact that this involves enjoyment of the perquisites of national ownership at least as much as endurance of the burdens of international responsibility. At the Potsdam Conference, Stalin made a bid for a trust territory by saying that the USSR "would like some territory of the defeated states," [19] thereby indicating a distinctly cynical view of the Trusteeship System. The United States became the administering authority in the Pacific Islands formerly under Japanese mandate in circumstances which made it obvious that this was the act of a conqueror, insisting upon the retention of territories deemed militarily valuable, rather than the generous gesture of an advanced state, consenting to do a difficult job on behalf of the international community. The decision of the General Assembly in 1949 to designate Italy as the administering power in its former colony of Somaliland was quite clearly a victory for a group of states which considered it appropriate and desirable to do something for Italy, rather than a considered judgment that Italy was the state best equipped to do something for the people of Somaliland. The evidence is decisive that managing a trust territory is regarded as having a politically and strategically useful hegemony over that territory; trusteeship modifies colonial possession, but it does not transform it into disinterested international service.

The corollary of the fact that the right to govern a dependent area is still attractive in terms of national interest, even when that right is circumscribed by the restrictions of the Trusteeship System, is that trusteeship has not genuinely become a device for internationalizing a given territory. Ideally, trusteeship should serve as a means of effecting the political neutralization of a colony, contributing to the resolution of conflicts

---

[19] Byrnes, *Speaking Frankly,* p. 76.

among colonial powers and promoting concentration upon the interests of colonial inhabitants by removing the territory from the sphere of political competition. Designation as a trust territory should establish the status of an area as an international zone, off-limits to rival imperialists; it should give assurance to the indigenous population that it is no longer to be treated as a pawn in the chess game of power politics. Only if trusteeship comes to have these implications can it serve the political purpose of diminishing frictions among the owners and would-be owners of international real estate and between that group and the anticolonial bloc, or the humanitarian purpose of mobilizing support for the uplift of subject peoples.

Trusteeship has failed to acquire this meaning. The Mandate System approached it by prohibiting the militarization of territories in the "B" and "C" categories, but the United Nations system has reversed that provision and has gone even further by setting up a special type of arrangement, tailor-made for the United States, which enables the Pacific Islands to be at once a trust territory and an integral segment of the American system of military bases; these islands indeed constitute a "sacred trust" of the United States, but they are sacred primarily to the strategic interests of the administering power. The Soviet Union acquiesced in this arrangement, evidently because it realized that the only alternative was the establishment of unfettered American sovereignty over the area and possibly because it nourished the vain hope that it might become the beneficiary of a similar arrangement, but it is inconceivable that the USSR should have considered the acceptance of American trusteeship as tantamount to the neutralization of the islands.

The Charter contains the seed from which genuine internationalization of trust territories might grow, in its provision that the United Nations itself might serve as an administering authority.[20] This seed has thus far not been permitted to germinate. States which have found themselves in possession and control of dependent areas have not been willing to abdicate in favor of an international regime. Significantly, the one instance in which international administration has been seriously considered was that of Jerusalem, a political no-man's-land so far as the major powers were concerned; even there, trusteeship as a neutralizing device was rendered infeasible by the competitive ambitions of Israel and Jordan. The case in which the nearest approach to genuine international control was made was that of Italian Somaliland[21]—a case in which no power was in a po-

---

[20] Article 81.

[21] The Trusteeship Agreement for this territory contained provisions establishing an international Advisory Council to assist in the administration, setting a time limit of ten years for the achievement of independence by the territory, and requiring adherence by Italy to an annexed Declaration of Constitutional Principles containing the explicit statement that "The sovereignty of the Territory is vested in

sition to dictate the terms of settlement. The United Nations served briefly in 1962-1963 as administrative caretaker of West New Guinea (otherwise known as West Irian), to facilitate the agreed transfer of the territory from the Netherlands to Indonesia, but this temporary arrangement fell outside the confines of the Trusteeship System. Clearly, trusteeship has not become a means for taking colonies out of the arena within which conflicts of national interest operate.

An unfortunate result of this failure is that trusteeship has not been a politically acceptable device for providing a transitional period of tutelage between colonial status and national independence, in the many cases where such an interim arrangement might have been appropriate. The postwar anticolonial movement has not been attracted by the Trusteeship System; consequently, that system has progressively withered away, while new states have been created without serious consideration of their readiness "to stand by themselves under the strenuous conditions of the modern world." Trusteeship has not contributed significantly to the rational and orderly liquidation of colonialism in the sense of obviating the problem of premature independence.

The positive achievements of the experimental application of the trusteeship idea which has occupied international organization since the First World War are difficult to measure, but they are nonetheless real and significant. There can be little doubt that the safeguards provided by the League and the United Nations have contributed to the reduction of colonial evils and abuses, and that the pressures mobilized by international institutions have accelerated the process of economic, social, and political development in colonial areas.

The agencies concerned with the colonial problem in the League and the United Nations have played a varied role. They have provided fig leaves for unregenerate colonialists, and have served as amiable back-patters for administering authorities who deserved sterner treatment; they have been used for inordinate snooping and carping criticism, and have provided a commodious back seat for drivers whose sense of irresponsibility has been matched only by their ignorance of the real problems and possibilities of colonial development. In the final analysis, however, they have also facilitated the expression of the developing concept of the international public interest in the progressive rebuilding of the slums of the global political system, given some substantive meaning to the concept of international guardianship over subject peoples, and made some progress toward turning colonial powers and anticolonial states into workhorses and gadflies.

In institutional terms, the development of trusteeship has been re-

---

its people. . . ." See the text, in *International Organization,* May 1950, pp. 347-356. The territory became the independent state of Somalia in 1960.

markable. One can very nearly exhaust the League's approach to colonialism by analyzing the Mandate System, but a full understanding of the approach undertaken by the United Nations necessitates going beyond the formal limits of the Trusteeship System and the mechanism for implementing the Declaration Regarding Non-Self-Governing Territories. The United Nations has assumed the role of a midwife, assisting at the birth of new states from the matrix of colonialism. It has functioned as a Bureau of Vital Statistics, issuing international birth certificates to new claimants for membership in the world community. It has undertaken to exercise a tutelary function for newly independent states, helping them to develop the resources and master the arts which are essential for the meaningful enjoyment of national autonomy, and to acquire the habits and attitudes which are requisite for responsible participation in the affairs of an increasingly interdependent world. This latter aspect of the organization's work provides a compensatory mechanism for offsetting the effects of politically-induced premature birth of independent states. In the prevailing political climate, the United Nations has greater opportunity to promote the positive values of the concept of trusteeship in the post-natal period than in the pre-natal period of states. The ultimate record may show that the major contribution of the organization to the solution of the problems of colonialism lay in programs of assistance not explicitly related to the mechanism for dealing with dependent peoples.

The United Nations approach to the colonial problem is marked by many shortcomings and inadequacies, but, when all is said and done, it constitutes the most ambitious effort yet made to deal comprehensively, positively, and constructively with the issues that have spilled over from the age of imperialism. In the breadth and depth of its concern with those issues, the United Nations reveals itself as a very rare phenomenon in the field of international relations: an international organization trying to deal with a situation *before,* rather than *after,* it has reached the crisis stage. In a very real sense, the activities of the United Nations in the colonial field may be regarded as an effort to prevent not a possible World War III but a hypothetical World War IV, by preventing the development of an irreparable breach between the European and the non-European worlds.

If the organized effort to tackle the issues of colonialism is commendably forehanded, it is nevertheless clear that it is already almost too late to lay the foundations for mutual respect and confidence between the peoples of Asia and Africa and those of the far-flung European family. The United Nations represents not only the first concerted campaign but quite possibly also the last chance for European civilization to make up for its shady past in dealing with non-European peoples. This opportunity may not have been deserved, but it has been presented. An enlarged version of the old "Yellow Peril" concept has acquired significance in the mid-twentieth century, and it may be that the most important function of the United Nations is to stimulate a response to that challenge which will involve not the solidification of European peoples for the purpose of stifling the rise of non-European peoples, but the unification of all peoples in a collaborative effort to promote the successful achievement of non-European aspirations, and to lay the groundwork for peaceful and cooperative relations between the former masters and the former subjects of the colonial system.

SUGGESTED READINGS

Coleman, James S., "Togoland," *International Conciliation,* No. 509, September 1956.

Good, Robert C., "The United States and the Colonial Debate," Chap. 9 in Arnold Wolfers, ed., *Alliance Policy in the Cold War,* Baltimore: Johns Hopkins, 1959.

Haas, Ernst B., "The Attempt to Terminate Colonialism: Acceptance of the United Nations Trusteeship System," *International Organization,* February 1953, pp. 1-21.

Haas, Ernst B., "The Reconciliation of Conflicting Colonial Policy Aims: Acceptance of the League of Nations Mandate System," *International Organization,* November 1952, pp. 521-536.

Hall, H. Duncan, *Mandates, Dependencies and Trusteeship,* Washington: Carnegie Endowment for International Peace, 1948.

Jacobson, Harold Karan, "The United Nations and Colonialism: A Tentative Appraisal," *International Organization,* Winter 1962, pp. 37-56.

Maclaurin, John, *The United Nations and Power Politics,* London: George Allen and Unwin, 1951, Chap. IX.

Murray, James N., Jr., *The United Nations Trusteeship System,* Urbana: University of Illinois Press, 1957.

Rivlin, Benjamin, *Italian Colonies,* New York: Carnegie Endowment for International Peace, 1950.

Sady, Emil J., "The United Nations and Dependent Peoples," Part IV in Robert E. Asher, et al., *The United Nations and Promotion of the General Welfare,* Washington: The Brookings Institution, 1957.

CHAPTER

17

The Functional Approach to Peace

The "functional" sector of international organization is that part of the mass of organized international activities which relates directly to economic, social, technical, and humanitarian matters—that is, to problems which may be tentatively described as non-political. Functional activities are immediately and explicitly concerned with such values as prosperity, welfare, social justice, and the "good life," rather than the prevention of war and elimination of national insecurity.

In a sense, the development of this type of activity, which had its beginning in the public international unions of the nineteenth century and is now flourishing luxuriantly under the auspices of the United Nations and the Specialized Agencies, represents the deviation of international organization from its single-minded concern with the problem of war. It can be argued that war is not the only nut that international organization has to crack, and that the promotion of human welfare is as legitimate an objective of collaborative arrangements among governments as the abolition of human welfare. Occasionally, this thesis has been frankly stated; for instance, Sir Muhammad Zafrulla Khan of Pakistan has written:

> The paramount aim of the United Nations is the promotion of social progress and better standards of life in larger freedom. . . . Even the maintenance of international peace and saving mankind from the

> scourge of war is but an essential preliminary. Though essential, peace is only a means, a condition precedent, a *sine qua non* toward the ultimate objective.[1]

David A. Morse, the Director-General of the International Labor Organization, once defined the "over-riding consideration" of his agency's work as that of improving the status and welfare of working people,[2] despite the fact that the Constitution under which it operates makes the promotion of peace the formally dominant concern of the ILO, and treats the amelioration of the conditions of labor as a means to that end, or at most a coordinate objective.

However strong may be the tendency of particular statesmen or international officials candidly or otherwise to elevate functional activities to the rank of ends in themselves, the official doctrine is that those activities are undertaken for the sake of the indirect contributions which they make to solving the problems of peace and security. If they are useful in themselves, so much the better; but the day has not yet arrived when governments feel inclined to launch—or feel assured of getting the essential support of their legislatures and peoples for launching—either multilateral or unilateral programs for doing good to foreigners simply for the sake of doing good. International organization clearly reflects, and stimulates, the development of a global social consciousness, "an international ethic of mutual aid," which is a striking innovation of the twentieth century,[3] but it is a curious commentary on our times that the work of international agencies, even though it may be directed toward meeting the most elementary human needs, requires justification in political terms.

THE THEORY OF FUNCTIONALISM

The theory of functionalism, which is essentially an assertion and defense of the proposition that the development of international economic and social cooperation is a major prerequisite for the ultimate solution of political conflicts and elimination of war, has been most elaborately developed and persuasively stated by David Mitrany.[4]

In Mitrany's terms, "the problem of our time is not how to keep the nations peacefully apart but how to bring them actively together." [5] He would not approach the problem of peace directly, by organizing around

---

1 *United Nations Bulletin,* December 1, 1952, p. 511.

2 *Ibid.,* January 1, 1951, p. 28.

3 See the Introduction to the Preliminary Report on the World Social Situation by the United Nations Department of Social Affairs, *ibid.,* May 15, 1952, p. 382.

4 See *The Progress of International Government* (New Haven: Yale University Press, 1933); "Functional Federalism," *Common Cause,* November 1950, pp. 196-199; and, particularly, *A Working Peace System* (London and New York: Royal Institute of International Affairs, 1946).

5 *A Working Peace System,* p. 7.

the points of national conflict, but indirectly, by seeking out the area of mutuality, and "binding together those interests which are common, where they are common, and to the extent to which they are common." [6] Mitrany abjures the effort to devise a comprehensive blueprint for the organization of international relations, preferring instead to rely upon the pragmatic development of special-purpose organizations, which he thinks will tend to evolve their own distinctive structural patterns, procedural systems, and areas of competence in accordance with the inherent requirements of their functional missions.[7] This method is recommended as one which "seeks, by linking authority to a specific activity, to break away from the traditional link between authority and a definite territory. . . ." [8] It is a *horizontal* approach, shifting attention away from the vertical divisions of human society which are symbolized by the sovereignty of states, toward the various strata of social need which cut across national dividing lines. It stresses the question of what contributions are essential to the creative work of solving common problems rather than that of what sacrifices are required for the negative task of reconciling conflicting interests.

Mitrany explicitly links functionalism to the ultimate prevention of war and development of authoritative world political institutions. He sees the ideal of peace in terms of national coactivity rather than national coexistence; he puts his faith "not in a protected peace but in a working peace," [9] and believes that a peaceful world society is "more likely to grow through doing things together in workshop and market place rather than by signing pacts in chancelleries." [10] He states his thesis as follows:

> Sovereignty cannot in fact be transferred effectively through a formula, only through a function. By entrusting an authority with a certain task, carrying with it command over the requisite powers and means, a slice of sovereignty is transferred from the old authority to the new; and the accumulation of such partial transfers in time brings about a translation of the true seat of authority.
>
> [Functionalism is a method] which would . . . overlay political divisions with a spreading web of international activities and agencies, in which and through which the interests and life of all the nations would be gradually integrated.[11]

Mitrany hypothesizes the development of successive layers of functional collaboration, creating "increasingly deep and wide strata of peace —not the stand-offish peace of an alliance, but one that would suffuse the

[6] *Ibid.*, p. 40.
[7] *Ibid.*, pp. 41, 43.
[8] *Ibid.*, p. 6.
[9] *Ibid.*, p. 59.
[10] *Ibid.*, p. 5.
[11] *Ibid.*, pp. 9, 14.

world with a fertile mingling of common endeavour and achievement."[12] This gradual evolution constitutes what Mitrany calls a process of "federation by instalments,"[13] or, in Frederick L. Schuman's felicitous phrase, "peace by pieces."[14]

The functional theory rests upon a very complex conception of the nature and causes of war, and promises a correspondingly elaborate set of results bearing upon the establishment and maintenance of peace. The basic assumptions and prescriptions of functionalism in regard to the problem of peace may be divided into three broad segments.

In the first place, war is regarded as the product of the objective conditions of human society. It is the result neither of man's native instinct nor of his acquired sinfulness, neither of the state's inherent nature nor of its irrational policy; war is a disease of global society, caused by grave deficiencies in the economic and social circumstances of mankind. Poverty, misery, ill-health, illiteracy, economic insecurity, social injustice, exploitation, discrimination—these are the factors which create the desperation, apathy, frustration, fear, cupidity, and hatred which make the world susceptible to war. This diagnosis owes much to the Marxian insistence upon the significance of material determinants for political conditions, but its popularity has not been confined to representatives of any particular school of thought. The notion that war is traceable to deep-seated causes in the economic and social realm has become part of the standard intellectual currency of the twentieth century.

Given this assumption, functionalism sets out to treat the basic ailments of mankind. It proposes to elevate living standards in backward areas, reduce the interference of national frontiers with the working of the complex global economy, minimize the factors that make for economic instability, and promote the attainment of higher levels of health, literacy, culture, and social justice. This is not merely a program for aiding the poor by enlisting the altruistic, or the enlightened selfish, assistance of the rich; much of the business of functionalism relates to the solution of problems which affect the most highly developed sector of the world, precisely because it is highly developed. Functionalism undertakes to grapple with the effects of both the excessive primitiveness of underdeveloped regions and the excessive intricacy of economic and social relationships in the intensely industrialized parts of the world. Thus, it hopes to extirpate the roots of war.

In the second place, functionalism attributes the phenomenon of war to the institutional inadequacy of the national state system. The state is at fault, not because it is intrinsically a fighting organism, as the power poli-

---

[12] *Ibid.*, p. 63.
[13] *Ibid.*, p. 51.
[14] *The Commonwealth of Man*, p. 314.

tician would have it, but because it is increasingly an inappropriate and ineffectual agency for doing what has to be done in order to promote the economic and social health of the human family. The state system imposes an arbitrary and rigid pattern of vertical divisions upon global society, disrupting the organic unity of the whole, and carving the world into segments whose separateness is jealously guarded by sovereignties which are neither able to solve the fundamental problems nor willing to permit them to be solved by other authorities. Peace requires solutions of economic and social problems which can be achieved only by problem-solving agencies coterminous in territorial competence with the problem areas. The appropriate administrative unit varies with the nature of the problem, but it only accidentally corresponds to the boundaries established by the state system; more and more, the problems which are crucial to the fitness of human society for sustaining a peaceful regime are becoming bigger in scope than national states. Hence, the mission of funcionalism is to make peace possible by organizing particular layers of human social life in accordance with their particular requirements, breaking down the artificialities of the zoning arrangements associated with the principle of sovereignty.

Beyond this, functional theory purports to provide an indispensable laboratory for the experimental development of organizational patterns and techniques which may serve as models for the ultimately necessary machinery of internationalism on the highest political levels. In the long run, the world requires a replacement for the state system. The essential process of institutional invention can be expected to gain momentum by being put into operation first in the areas of recognized common interest.

Finally, functionalism envisages its task in terms of the alteration of the subjective conditions of mankind. War is caused by the attitudes, habits of thought and feeling, and allegiances which are fostered by the state system. Functional organizations may, by focusing attention upon areas of common interest, build habits of cooperation which will equip human beings for the conduct of a system of international relations in which the expectation of constructive collaboration will replace that of sterile conflict as the dominant motif. Working international agencies will create a system of mutual advantages which will assume too great a value in the eyes of its beneficiaries for them to contemplate disrupting it by permitting resort to war. Men will recognize international organization as the giver of good gifts which their states are no longer able to provide; they will cease to regard the derogation of sovereignty as a dubiously permissible national sacrifice, and come to think of it as a transfer of authority which is essential to the attainment of desirable results, a profitable investment in the good life. Thus, fundamental loyalties will be increasingly shared by the state and the agencies of the world community, the sentiment of human solidarity will be deepened, and the subjective basis will be prepared for progressively broader and more effective cooperation among the peoples of the world.

This concept involves not only the notion of transforming the international outlook of particular human beings, but also that of transferring competence from one set of human beings to another. So far as the traditional ruling classes of international affairs, the diplomats and the military men, are concerned, functionalism is perhaps a project for *evasion* as much as for *conversion.*

For all its emphasis upon the underlying economic and social roots of war, it does not altogether avoid the concoction of a devil theory; its villains are those gentlemen—perhaps more properly described as inveterate sinners in the national interest than as genuine devils—who have long held something approaching a monopolistic control of the conduct of relations among states. Functionalism comes very close to regarding these officials as incorrigible. Long habituated to the treatment of international affairs as an area of conflict and competition, they are unlikely to be swayed by the new mode of thought. Hence, functionalism envisages a process of circumvention, described hopefully by H. G. Wells as the evolution of "a comprehensive world control in the presence of which Foreign Offices would fade out, since, by reason of the conditions of their development, they are themselves incapable of establishing peace,"[15] and sarcastically by Georg Schwarzenberger as a project by which the "vicious dragons" who are presumed to inhabit Foreign Offices are to be "cleverly outwitted by gallant reforming knights."[16]

More seriously, the expectation of functionalism is in line with the concept of multilevel interpenetration of governments which was brilliantly formulated by J. A. Salter after World War I.[17] The development of specialized international agencies dealing with problems outside the scope of traditional diplomacy will result in making virtually every department of government a kind of Foreign Office, and bring into the active conduct of international relations a host of national officials whose professional training and interests give them a predisposition to concentrate upon the pragmatic issues of how to solve common problems for the common advantage, rather than to focus upon questions of national prestige and sovereign authority. Internationalism will well up from the collaborative international contacts of officials in labor, health, agriculture, commerce, and related departments, eventually endangering the citadels in which diplomatic and military officials sit peering competitively and combatively at the world outside the state.

In summary, functionalism proposes to promote peace by eliminat-

---

[15] Royal Institute of International Affairs, *The Future of the League of Nations,* p. 122.

[16] *A Manual of International Law,* p. 148.

[17] *Allied Shipping Control* (Oxford: Clarendon Press, 1921).

ing objective conditions which are deemed conducive to war, introducing new patterns of organization which may transform the global institutional system, and initiating the development of subjective trends which may cause the "erosion" of sovereignty, thereby assisting "states to work together and so gradually develop a sense of community which will make it psychologically more difficult to press the claims of sovereignty in ways that are anti-social." [18]

The analysis of the theoretical structure of functionalism may be approached in yet another way, this time giving emphasis not to the general propositions concerning the nature of the causes of war and the conditions of peace, but rather to the sequential steps in the logic according to which functional theory envisages the ultimate production of a world capable of sustaining peaceful relationships.

The first of these is what I should call the "separability-priority" thesis. It involves the assumption that human affairs can be sliced into layers, that the concerns of man are so stratified that economic and social problems can, in a preliminary fashion, be separated from political problems and from each other. Having adopted this assumption, functionalism then proceeds on the theory that the treatment of economic and social matters should take priority.

The next step in the logic of functionalism is the assertion of a thesis which may be variously described as a doctrine of transferability, expansibility, ramification, or accumulation. Some have argued that men, having learned the arts of fruitful international cooperation at the level of technical or economic problems, will transfer their new skills and habits of mind to the development of collaborative solutions at the highest political levels. Writing before the First World War, Paul S. Reinsch adumbrated a "concentric circles" concept of international organization, according to which the idea of multilateral attack upon world problems will function like a pebble dropped into the international pond, giving rise to a series of circles of cooperation which will expand from the limited area of technical agencies to the vast circumference of a global political and security organization.[19] Paul G. Hoffman has suggested that "The good thing about the spirit of unity is that it ramifies out; when you cultivate habits of unity in the economic sphere, they naturally spread over to the political sphere and even to the military sphere when the need arises." [20] Others have intimated, rather vaguely, that the accumulated agenda of constructive work under functional organizations will produce such a preoccupation that men will abandon war in a fit of absentmindedness; they

---

[18] Brierly, "The Covenant and the Charter," *British Yearbook of International Law,* 1946, p. 93.

[19] *Public International Unions* (Boston: Ginn, 1911).

[20] *Peace Can Be Won* (New York: Doubleday, 1951), p. 62. Copyright, 1951, by the Great Books Foundation.

will forget to fight because they will be "too busy with things that matter." [21]

In all these cases, the point is the same, however it may be expressed: the separability of economic and social problems from political problems is only provisional, and they are ultimately inseparable. International action at one level affects the other level, and leads to comparable action at the other level. This assumption of the effective connecting link lies at the heart of functional theory.

It should be noted that the functionalist promise to transform the political mentality and allegiance of human beings rests upon a logic which emphasizes both the irrational and the rational aspects of human nature. On the one hand, functionalism assumes that political unity must be built, pearl-wise, around a central irritant; it offers a new type of common enemy—such as poverty, pestilence, or ignorance—to serve as the focal point around which men may unite. It similarly stresses the irrational side of human behavior when it suggests that men are such creatures of habit that they will forget to clash in political matters once they have become accustomed to cooperating in other areas. Finally, however, functionalism postulates a transfer of loyalties to the international community in response to the growing usefulness of functional agencies. This notion that men can be expected to distribute their allegiances on the basis of a utilitarian calculation implies a significant concept of the rationality of the human loyalty structure. At bottom, the logic which expects a sense of world community to derive from the operation of functional agencies is rigorously rationalistic.

EVALUATION OF FUNCTIONAL THEORY

The concept of functionalism as an approach to peace is an extraordinarily attractive doctrine in many ways and for many reasons. It may appear to be an easy way out of the dilemma which confronts modern civilization. Men who have come to regard the directly political approaches as nothing better than prescriptions for humanity's beating its bloody head against the stone wall which guards national sovereignty may be heartened by the notion that there are poorly watched backdoors through which access may be gained. Functionalism may be regarded as a device for sneaking up on sovereignty, full of hopeful possibilities for establishing the groundwork of international community.

It has the great merit of appealing both to humanitarian idealism and to national self-interest. Pacifists may see functionalism as an admirably nonmilitary approach to peace and security, and they may be joined by other men of exceptional good will and moral sensitivity in noting with

---

[21] Maclaurin, *The United Nations and Power Politics,* p. 306.

approval the contrast between its positive, constructive aspects and the negative, restrictive, preventive character of other approaches to peace. There is a widespread urge to agree with Salvador de Madariaga that "Peace is no policy. . . . The only way to secure peace is to stop bothering about it and begin to work together to carry out together the business of the world." [22] There is much to be done to convert the world into a good society, and it is reassuring to be told that the doing of it is a major contribution to peace—not to mention that it is convenient to have governments persuaded that it is a legitimate and necessary part of their business to support and subsidize the doing of it.

Here the element of national self-interest begins to obtrude, and a major strength of the appeal of functionalism begins to emerge. Functionalism proposes not to squelch but to utilize national selfishness; it asks governments not to give up the sovereignty which belongs to their peoples but to acquire benefits for their peoples which were hitherto unavailable, not to reduce their power to defend their citizens but to expand their competence to serve them. The realist who repudiates the expectation that altruism can become a major factor in international politics may find much to hope for in a system of organization which invites states to the common pursuit of common interests.

Moreover, functionalism is capable of striking a responsive chord in both conservative and liberal hearts. To the conservative, it may appear as an organic, naturalistic, evolutionary approach to world organization. Mitrany's formulation of the theory is empirically oriented in the best tradition of British conservatism. Functionalism eschews the rigidity of a formula and the neatness of a blueprint; it projects the growth of international organization as needed and in accordance with needs. It is flexible and opportunist; it makes an appeal to common sense for the discovery of practicable solutions to definite problems, rather than to the radical urge of doctrinaires to devise an ingenious scheme for the comprehensive reform of international arrangements.[23] At the same time, the liberal may regard functionalism as a distinctively modern, progressive concept. Mitrany writes like a social democrat, and he finds his great inspiration in the New Deal's notable invention, the TVA.[24] Functionalism represents the application of the welfare state philosophy to the international sphere, emphasizing the responsibility of international agencies for rendering services rather than merely enforcing controls, and for extending their concern into areas hitherto falling within the private entrepreneurial domain of the national state.

Lastly, functionalism has all the earmarks of a profound and so-

---

22 Cited in Wright, *A Study of War,* II, 1092.

23 Cf. the citation from Robert Boothby, in de Rusett, *Strengthening the Framework of Peace,* pp. 194-195.

24 "Functional Federalism," *Common Cause,* November 1950, p. 198.

phisticated approach to the problem of war. To those who are weary of superficial approaches, it justifies itself by burrowing deep under the surface of reality to find the roots of the problem. To those whose skepticism is excited by panaceas, it offers the appeal of a system which prescribes specific treatment for the primary ills from which war derives, instead of a cheap patent remedy for the secondary symptoms of human society's malaise. Functionalism seems to emerge from the diagnostic clinic, not the drug counter, of the internationalist movement.

On the other hand, the student of international organization will do well to keep his critical wits about him when he is confronted with the functional answer to the problem of world order. The impressiveness of the theory and attractiveness of the program of functionalism are not in themselves evidence of either the theoretical validity or the practical adequacy of this approach to peace. The testing of functionalism may well begin with the posing of some fundamental questions in regard to its basic assumptions.

The central thesis that war is a product of unsatisfactory economic and social conditions in the global community should arouse a bit of skeptical eyebrow-arching. Charles Malik of Lebanon has stated the challenge to the cliché: "The poor, the sick, the dispossessed, must certainly be done justice to. But to suppose that there will be peace when everybody is materially happy and comfortable, is absolute nonsense." [25] Hans Kelsen has insisted upon reversing the functionalist proposition: "It is not true that war is the consequence of unsatisfactory economic conditions; on the contrary, the unsatisfactory situation of world economy is the consequence of war." [26] The recent history of the world clearly fails to confirm the existence of a direct correlation between national economic backwardness and aggressiveness; it was advanced Germans, not primitive Africans, who shattered world peace in 1939. The debate concerning the role of economic factors and motivations in world politics is an involved and quite possibly an interminable one, certainly not one to be settled here. The point is that the analysis of the causes of war and the conditions of peace falls into the category of unfinished business, and that the assumptions which underpin the functional approach should be regarded as hypotheses, not established verities.

The logical apparatus of functionalism, involving the concepts of the preliminary separability of the economic and social strata from the political, the essential priority of action in nonpolitical layers, and the ultimate impact of results achieved there upon the problems of the political stratum, requires cautious evaluation. Is it in fact possible to segregate a group of problems and subject them to treatment in an international

---

[25] *United Nations Bulletin,* May 1, 1951, p. 459.

[26] *Peace Through Law* (Chapel Hill: University of North Carolina Press, 1944), p. 16.

workshop where the nations shed their conflicts at the door and busy themselves only with the cooperative use of the tools of mutual interest? Does not this assumption fly in the face of the evidence that a trend toward the politicization of all issues is operative in the twentieth century? Considering only the problems which may most appropriately be styled economic and social, it is possible that the horizontal slicing in which functionalism engages may be quite as unfavorable for their proper administrative treatment as the vertical segmentation imposed by the national state pattern; excessive stratification is no more helpful than excessive compartmentalization. As Gerhard Bebr has warned, "the artificial dissection of organic economic ties into separate economic organizations under independent authorities endangers their viability." [27]

Assuming the feasibility of marking off a distinctively nonpolitical sector of human affairs, it is not self-evident that work in this area should or can be assigned first place on the international schedule. In objective terms, it may be that "the elements of order are the prerequisite of economic and social progress," and that "to forward the world's material welfare and human rights the peoples must first be freed from the scourge of modern war." [28] Reverting to the subjective sphere, we may ask whether states can in fact be induced to join hands in functional endeavor before they have settled the outstanding political and security issues which divide them. Functionalism's insistence upon putting first things first does not settle the matter of what things are first.

If it be granted that the assumptions and prescriptions of functionalism are valid up to this point, it remains necessary to raise questions concerning the efficacy of the functional process as preparation for a solution of the ultimate problems of world order. If economic and social organization is indeed the horse, can it in fact pull the political cart? This is again an area of legitimate doubt.

The concentric circle theory is subject to the criticism that it begs some very big questions in assuming that the dropping of the functional pebble produces a steady progression of everwidening circles of cooperation, reaching out without limit to encompass finally the whole area of the international pond. This metaphorical concept makes sense only if it can be assumed that the global waters offer a placid surface for the rippling-out process; in fact, the lashing winds and roaring waves of world politics are always likely to play havoc with the developing pattern of functional circles. The problem of the recurrent setback, the interruption and disruption by war of the projects of functionalism for the eventual elimination of war, poses a critical dilemma. Moreover, it is not lightly to be assumed that the expansibility of the concentric circle pattern is un-

---

[27] "The European Coal and Steel Community: A Political and Legal Innovation," *Yale Law Journal,* November 1953, p. 42.

[28] Grenville Clark, *A Plan for Peace* (New York: Harper, 1950), pp. 47, 48.

limited. There may be barriers to the encirclement of vital political areas which the momentum of functional development cannot cross. Functionalism cannot guarantee that one thing leads inexorably and interminably to another in international relations.

The assumption of the rational transference of human loyalties is also a fit subject for skeptical scrutiny. How malleable is human allegiance? Do men actually shift their emotional bonds so as always to keep them connected with the entities from which their real blessings flow? Can functional agencies do enough, fast enough, conspicuously enough, to capture the imagination of peoples and elicit from them the rational recognition of, and consequent emotional dedication to, the values of an organized international community? Functional activities are likely to be helpful, but unlikely to be stirring and sensational; international agencies are likely to find themselves stimulating and facilitating the provision of services and solution of problems by national states, with the credit redounding to the states rather than being entered to the account of internationalism. If this were not so, governments could be expected to arrange that it should become so, since the responsible agents of national states are not likely to wax enthusiastic about the sponsorship and subsidization of projects for undermining the normative foundations of the state system. There is room for doubt that functionalists have found the key which infallibly opens the doors that keep human loyalties piled up in sovereign warehouses, thereby permitting those loyalties to spill out into the receptacles of internationalism.

Finally, it must be noted that functionalism is not in a hurry, and its claim to offer hope to the world is implicitly based upon the supposition that a long period is both necessary and available for working out solutions to the problems of the world. How much time does man have at his disposal for building the foundations of peace? The honest answer probably is that no one can say, and the urgent insistence of doctrinaires that the sand is running out and that quick solutions are certainly possible because they are obviously necessary is no more worthy of uncritical acceptance than the smug assumption of functionalists that there is a long run and their stodgy insistence that there is no satisfactory substitute for the methods of gradualism. Nevertheless, there is ample justification in the atomic age for giving serious thought to the question of time limits; as Carlos Romulo suggested at the tenth anniversary meeting of the United Nations,

> Our clients are the next generation . . . but there may be no next generation unless we do today what has to be done for the two billion clients who are now alive.
>
> What makes our age unique, I suppose, is that the immediate questions and the ultimate questions are locked together.[29]

[29] *New York Times,* June 27, 1955.

THE PRACTICE OF FUNCTIONALISM

Functionalism is not merely a recipe to be studied, but also a pudding to be tasted; the twentieth century has seen the transfer of functionalism from the cookbooks and experimental kitchens to the serving tables of international organization. Hence, the major business of evaluation must be related to an examination of the actual dish.

The founders of the League were in disagreement as to the emphasis which should be placed upon nonpolitical matters. Wilson was inclined to minimize this aspect of the work of international organization, and his attitude comported with the tendency of the United States toward hasty withdrawal from the apparatus of economic collaboration in which it had participated during hostilities. However, British influence and particularly the eloquent insistence of General Smuts[30] brought about the inclusion of Articles 23-25 in the Covenant. These established a rather vague mandate for League excursions into the functional area. The creation of the International Labor Organization provided the only real basis for the expectation that a significant experiment in the application of functionalism was to be launched.

In operation, the League bestowed constantly growing emphasis upon the development of functional aspects of international organization. It established technical organizations and committees in various fields, sponsored international conferences for dealing with particular problems, carried out pioneering enterprises in international technical assistance, and gradually emerged as an active center for stimulating and coordinating multilateral efforts to cope with the complexities of modern economic and social problems.[31] Whether because of increasing awareness of needs, clearer recognition of opportunities, or the urgent necessity for finding new uses for the League machinery to compensate for its failures in the political realm, the members of the League turned the organization into the functionalist path.

Except for the recognition of the autonomy of the ILO, the League system was formally committed to the principle of the central control and direction of the machinery of international cooperation by the Council.[32] This arrangement had the advantage of giving members of the Council constructive work to manage and experience in the pursuit of common interests, which may have kept them in better psychological tone than a steady diet of quarrels and conflicts,[33] but it also doomed the nonpolitical activities of the League to less attentive and less expert treatment than

[30] See Walters, *A History of the League of Nations,* I, 59.

[31] *The Aims, Methods and Activity of the League of Nations* (Revised edition; Geneva: Secretariat of the League of Nations, 1938), pp. 64-76, 122-173.

[32] Covenant, Article 24.

[33] Cf. Murray, *From the League to U.N.,* p. 81.

they might otherwise have received, as well as to involvement in the hy-perpolitical atmosphere of the Council. Hence, the recommendations of the Bruce Committee for a thoroughgoing revision of the system, including the transfer of the directive function to a special body without the political orientation of the Council and the concentration of greater emphasis upon the development of economic and social agencies,[34] reflected a conscious urge to achieve the fuller application of the doctrines of functionalism. This report came too late to influence the further development of the League, but it contributed significantly to the formulation of the United Nations Charter.

In retrospect, the successes scored by its functional agencies seem to be the main redeeming features of the record of the League, and its demonstration of the potentialities of international cooperation in areas furthest removed from the vital issues of power politics may be regarded as the League's most enduring contribution to the modern world. It is curious that Wilson, who was so enamored of the idea that economic cooperation could provide an effective sanction for collective security, was so cool to the doctrine of functionalism. The record of the League suggests that he should have reversed these attitudes; the League did not discover the key to peace, but it pointed to the tentative conclusion that functionalism reflects a sounder view than Wilson's as to the relationship between economic and social matters and the problem of world order.

The designers of the world's new organizational system after World War II assigned major importance to the creation of machinery for international collaboration in economic and social fields. Pre-existing special-purpose agencies were retained, remodeled, or replaced, and new ones were instituted to round out the battery of functional institutions which became affiliated with the United Nations as Specialized Agencies.[35] The central organization was equipped with an Economic and Social Council, subordinate to the General Assembly, which in turn created an elaborate apparatus and set itself to the tasks of supplementing and coordinating the functional activities of the Specialized Agencies. Unlike the League, the United Nations system was, in its original conception, a full-fledged experiment in the application of the functional theory to international

---

[34] Special Supplement to the *Monthly Summary of the League of Nations,* August 1939.

[35] International Labor Organization, Food and Agriculture Organization, United Nations Educational, Scientific, and Cultural Organization, International Civil Aviation Organization, International Bank for Reconstruction and Development, International Monetary Fund, International Finance Corporation, International Development Association, World Health Organization, Universal Postal Union, International Telecommunication Union, World Meteorological Organization, and Inter-Governmental Maritime Consultative Organization.

An additional organization, the International Atomic Energy Agency, has a distinctive formal status but may be considered as essentially a member of the Specialized Agency group.

affairs. The ambitiousness of its scope and the decentralized character of its administrative pattern were both largely the products of American initiative and insistence.[36]

A major feature of the United Nations system in operation has been the steady enlargement and diversification of its functional program. The central organization itself and most of the Specialized Agencies have devoted particular attention to the promotion of economic and social progress in the underdeveloped areas, and the leading components of the organizational system have combined their efforts most notably in the Expanded Technical Assistance Program and the collateral operations of the Special Fund. This development has doubtless been in some measure a compensatory reaction, like that of the League, to the frustration of organizational endeavors in the most sensitive political fields. It has been stimulated by the conversion of the first Secretary-General, and of many other international officials and national leaders, to the view that "poverty remains mankind's chief enemy," [37] when confronted with the reality that misery, disease, and ignorance are the chief facts of life for more than half of the world's population. It has been facilitated by the fortuitous circumstance that the American conception of how best to combat the spread of Communism has largely coincided with the functionalist conception of how best to build the foundations of a peaceful world society; as a result of this contingency, the critical portion of the financial support for the developing program has been provided by a government which is much more deeply committed to anti-Communism than to functionalism. Its political dynamics have been supplied primarily by the newly emergent peoples of the non-European world, whose conception of what is needed to achieve the goals of national advance has tended to coincide with functionalism's doctrine of what is needed to achieve the purpose of international order; thus, the effective political demand for expansion of the program has emanated mainly from states which are more deeply committed to specific national interests than to the general propositions of functional theory.

The development of the United Nations system has inspired such comments as these:

> The world is now looking at its problem in the round. It is no longer content with sporadic attempts at settlement of sporadic disputes. It has learned that the problem of war is only a part of the international problem, and that it must tackle the underlying causes of conflict and the consequences of strife. It has also learned that there is a continuing agenda of routine business, each item of which is a minute part of the structure of a world society.[38]

---

[36] Stettinius, *Roosevelt and the Russians,* p. 17; Hull, *The Memoirs of Cordell Hull,* II, 1643.

[37] Lie, *In the Cause of Peace,* p. 142.

[38] Feller, *The United Nations and World Community,* p. 119.

> Never in the history of mankind has an attack on the first causes of war been launched on so many fronts and with the mobilization of comparable scientific resources.[39]

It is conceivable that, in the perspective of history, the mid-twentieth century will be primarily regarded, not as an era of cold war and deep divisive conflict, but as the time when the world began actively to grow together.

The functional experiment of the United Nations is full-scale in terms of the number of international agencies and the diversity of the technical, economic, social, and humanitarian problems which are placed within their range. But to say that the agencies are competent to *deal* with problems is not to say that they are equipped to *solve* them. The experiment is decidedly less than full-scale in terms of the conferment upon functional agencies of authority to make decisions, to order compliance, to command resources, and to initiate and conduct activities.

To a limited extent, organs of the United Nations system have acquired powers of a legislative and executive nature in regard to their special substantive areas, including the responsibility for framing technical regulations and the right of following up the passage of resolutions by methods considerably more meaningful than the mere expression of hope for faithful implementation by states. Some advance has also been made toward development of actual operational competence by international agencies; the temporary International Refugee Organization, set up to deal with the massive human displacement of the immediate postwar period, and the participating agencies of the technical assistance program are striking examples of international bodies which have directly administered and managed field programs, doing jobs through their own personnel and with their own budgetary resources.

However, the primary functions of United Nations machinery have been of a more modest nature. They have included fact-finding, research into the nature and magnitude of problems, idea-sharing, sponsorship of consultation among experts and responsible officials of national governments, and encouragement of the standardization and harmonization of national programs and policies. In short, international agencies have been largely confined to the work of helping governments to help themselves and encouraging governments to help each other. What the former Director-General of the World Health Organization wrote concerning his organization applies generally to the whole system:

> WHO is not a supra-national health administration. It cannot act in place of and for the national health authorities in any area of public health. Its only role is to use all possible means of international co-operation in order to provide certain essential elements which those

---

[39] Martin, *Collective Security*, p. 22.

authorities need to promote the health of their peoples. The rest is up to each individual nation itself.[40]

EVALUATION OF FUNCTIONAL PRACTICE

The evaluation of functionalism in operation may well begin with an examination of the problem of coordinating the instruments of international collaboration. Since World War II, there has been such a proliferation of multilateral mechanisms that it has seemed that the world was in danger of being overwhelmed by the sheer complexity of its apparatus. The difficulty of creating and maintaining order in the United Nations workshop, so as to avoid wasteful duplication of effort and loss of efficiency through the friction of agencies working at cross-purposes, is compounded by the fact that the Specialized Agencies have an autonomous status based upon their own constitutional documents, nonidentical membership lists, and widely scattered headquarters.

The San Francisco Conference evolved no clear conception of the pattern of relationships which should prevail in the decentralized organizational system of the postwar era, but contented itself with providing in the Charter that the special-purpose organizations should negotiate agreements with the United Nations,[41] which would define the extent to which and the means by which they would be welded into a coordinated system by the Economic and Social Council. The negotiations which were undertaken in pursuance of that basic policy decision revealed the development of an interesting and potentially significant new factor in international relations: the "sovereignty consciousness" of international agencies. For instance, the spokesmen for the International Labor Organization displayed a keen sense of institutional self-importance, expressed in the remark that they proposed "to seek cooperation with the UN as partners. To this end they might have to make some sacrifices of their sovereignty, but they did not intend to act in a subordinate capacity." [42] Evidence is growing that international agencies are fully capable of developing vested interests and "empire-building" tendencies; indeed, it may not be merely idle speculation to suggest that the world of the future, having finally conquered the assertiveness of sovereign states, may be confronted with the nasty problem of knocking together the heads of sovereign international organizations. The pacts concluded between the central organization and the Specialized Agencies are, in large measure, agreements to agree.

The problem of coordination has been further complicated by the

---

40 Brock Chisholm, in *United Nations Bulletin*, December 1, 1951, p. 446.
41 Articles 57, 63.
42 United Nations Document E/NSA/13, June 10, 1946.

tendency of the Economic and Social Council to generate its own quota of institutional offspring, new units requiring controls to prevent their overlapping and conflicting with each other as well as with established agencies outside the United Nations proper. This has posed the question of who is to coordinate the coordinators. Moreover, the member states of the United Nations have given free rein to their instinct of institutional procreativity, siring regional and other limited-membership agencies with something approaching abandon. The result of all this activity is that the world is so filled with a chaotic jumble of specialized instrumentalities of multilateral cooperation, within the United Nations, attached to the United Nations, and divorced from the United Nations, that governmental chiefs can hardly be expected to remember to what organizations their states belong, much less to develop consistent national policies toward and within those organizations. If conflict is the major problem of international political organization, confusion is an equally serious problem in the functional sphere.

The record of the United Nations is not entirely unimpressive in dealing with this problem. One of the earliest tasks of the Economic and Social Council was to serve as a kind of "Hoover Commission" for the international community, and it achieved a considerable rationalization of the world's haphazard institutional pattern, even though it has not subsequently been able to curb tendencies to re-create confusion and duplication. The Administrative Committee on Coordination, with representation of the United Nations and the Specialized Agencies at the highest secretariat level, has made important contributions to the effective meshing of the parts of the complex system. Most importantly, the cooperative conduct of the work of technical assistance has produced both formal and informal arrangements for coordination; teamwork has been stimulated by the challenge of concrete problems far more effectively than by the abstract desire to realize the ideal of institutional tidiness. In carrying out this program, the United Nations has acquired a hold on the strings of the international purse which is used for support of technical assistance projects, thereby gaining a potential power to direct the activities of Specialized Agencies which is analogous to the coordinative effect of the "grant-in-aid" technique used by the Federal Government in its relations with American states.

In the final analysis, the profusion of international agencies may be evidence of the vitality of the idea of international community, and the confusion may simply prove that the multilateral institutions, like national ones, are owned and operated by human beings; after all, the tangle is no worse in the global system than in Washington or other national capitals. In an era of big government and big international organization, a certain amount of confusion and inefficiency is inevitable, and it may even be salutary. The problem of coordination in the United Nations system will never be solved, and ought never to be abolished, but it seems likely that it can be managed.

A closely related problem of functionalism in operation is that of maintaining a reasonably clear and restricted focus of international activities and a keen sense of discrimination in determining the allocation of limited resources. The tendency toward excessive proliferation is matched by the tendency toward undisciplined scattering of organizational efforts. Functionalism is dedicated to the proposition that there are many roads to peace, but it does not envisage the exploration of every back street and country lane that any member of the party finds fascinating.

Postwar functional agencies have experienced difficulty in concentrating on important matters, rejecting trivial proposals, and abjuring interesting diversions. They stand in constant peril of being treated as hobbyhorses to be ridden off in all directions at once. Pressures for indulgence in irrelevancies emanate in part from governmental representatives, who in many cases find it as difficult to vote against any proposal requiring the staff to conduct a special study, as to vote for any measure increasing the budgetary responsibility of their states. Such pressures also derive from secretariat officials in agencies which are to a large degree the property of their staffs and special constituencies, and in which governments are practically confined to the tasks of paying the bills and exercising sporadic and ineffectual policy control.

As in the case of the coordination problem, the steadily growing emphasis upon programs designed to promote economic development has contributed to the mitigation of this tendency. By providing a generally accepted focal aim for functional endeavor—dramatized by the designation of the 1960's as the "United Nations Development Decade" in Assembly Resolution 1710 (XVI), of December 19, 1961—this emphasis has countered the pressures for frittering away the limited resources of international institutions on a miscellany of unintegrated or even trivial projects.

The most basic questions to be faced in evaluating the working experiment in functionalism which is being conducted under the auspices of the United Nations are political questions. Functional theory invites this kind of examination, since its emphasis upon economic and social matters is explicitly justified in terms of ultimate political impact; functional experience demands it, since the intrusion of political factors is almost invariably one of the earliest facts of life brought to bear upon a fledgling agency for international cooperation in any field whatever.

The clearest lesson of United Nations experience is that functionalism's assumption of the preliminary separability of political and nonpolitical matters does not hold true—not in this generation, at any rate. We are not vouchsafed the privilege of warming up the motors of international collaboration in a sheltered area of concordant interests, getting off to an easy start and building up momentum for crashing the barriers of conflicting interests that interpose between us and the ideal of world order. The dilemma of functionalism is that its ultimate impact upon politics may never be tested because of the immediate impact of politics upon functionalism.

This point has been increasingly recognized. In 1950, the leading professional officials of the Specialized Agencies were torn between asserting the doctrine, enshrined in the constitutional documents of the agencies, that functional activities would bring an end to political conflict, and warning that political conflict would put an end to functional activities; they ended up by stressing the latter point.[43] The Director-General of the World Health Organization, for instance, expressed the view that peace was a prerequisite for the successful working of the Specialized Agencies, thus implicitly adopting the position that the preamble to the constitution of his own agency should be altered to read, not "The health of all peoples is fundamental to the attainment of peace and security," but rather "The health of all peoples is dependent upon the attainment of peace and security." The actual order of priorities, as distinguished from the order assumed by functionalism, dictates the preliminary analysis of the influence of politics upon organized economic and social cooperation.

The two great political struggles which have developed in the United Nations, the cold war between the Soviet Communist bloc and the anti-Communist bloc led by the United States, and the separate but closely intertwined conflict between the non-European attackers of colonialism and the heirs of the colonial system, have both impinged sharply upon functional operations. Separately and in combination, they have decisively affected the answers to basic questions of national participation, of the uses to which the machinery of collaboration can and should be put, and of the scope and distribution of the functional effort. In general, they have decreed that the United States should lead and direct the enterprise, making it primarily an element of the anti-Communist program and secondarily a device for alleviating the tensions of the struggle over colonialism. The Soviet Union has shifted from an initial policy of virtually complete abstention to one of general, but yet relatively small-scale, participation in functional activities. The underdeveloped states, a group which largely coincides with the anticolonial bloc, has tended to resent the anti-Communist orientation determined by the United States, and to demand the appropriation of a greater share of a much larger functional budget to meet the needs of their aspiring peoples.

The crucial political fact of the United Nations functional system is

---

[43] See *United Nations Bulletin,* October 15, 1950, pp. 343-346, and *Annual Report of the Secretary-General on the Work of the Organization,* July 1, 1949-June 30, 1950, United Nations General Assembly: Official Records, 5th Session, Supplement No. 1, p. 88.

the dominant position assumed by the United States, for reasons which include the unrivaled economic stature and the general political importance of this country as well as the disinclination of the Soviet Union to compete for the role of leadership in this realm. This fact carries with it a tendency for the agencies of economic and social action to become excessively reliant upon the support, and particularly the financial support, of the United States. Such heavy dependence upon a single power inevitably minimizes the international flavor of the functional program. Stated differently, the unique position held by the United States serves as the basis for excessive American control. This control is in the first instance negative; the United States has a financial veto power which it has used to accomplish such purposes as the termination of the United Nations Relief and Rehabilitation Administration and the International Refugee Organization, and the blocking of efforts to establish "SUNFED," the Special United Nations Fund for Economic Development so avidly and persistently advocated by spokesmen for the less developed states. It extends also to the positive direction of policy. As Paul G. Hoffman innocently put it in Congressional testimony, he maintained such personal relations with the successive Presidents of the International Bank for Reconstruction and Development during his service as head of the Marshall Plan administration that

> we had no problem, because we discussed all these loans they were thinking of making and they were always good enough to come to us and say, "What about the impact of this loan to Turkey? Do you think we ought to go ahead with it?" That was informal and that is one of the best ways of control. . . .[44]

American predominance not only has the effect of permitting the harnessing of international cooperative mechanisms to the objectives of United States foreign policy, but it also exposes them to the internal political peculiarities of the American scene.

The self-assertiveness of Congress, a defensive reaction to expansion of the significance of the executive branch in the American constitutional system, is expressed in insistence upon keeping functional agencies tied tightly to the purse strings which Congress holds, occasional attempts to extend Congressional patronage privileges to international organs, and such flagrant outbursts as Senator Capehart's objection to American participation in the proposed International Finance Corporation on the ground that it appeared likely that the agency would, quite improperly in his view, be beyond the reach of Congressional authority to subpoena its records

---

[44] *The Mutual Security Program, Hearings before the Committee on Foreign Affairs, House of Representatives, 82nd Congress, 1st Session* (Washington: Government Printing Office, 1951), p. 339. Cited in Guy J. Pauker, *Obstacles to Progress in Underdeveloped Countries: Some Political Considerations* (Harvard University: unpublished doctoral dissertation, 1952), pp. 382-383.

and collar its officials for investigative purposes.[45] The Congressional urge to control does not stop at the boundary lines of the American governmental system.

The political issues of states' rights and untrammeled free enterprise are also transmitted by American predominance to the international functional system, where they have significant impact. International cooperation in economic and social fields requires the participation of national governments which have sufficient domestic authority in those fields to be able to cooperate. This is precisely the status which jealous champions of states' rights and defenders of pre-New Deal free enterprise wish to deny to the Federal Government of the United States. Hence, the functional program of the United Nations is subjected to the leadership of a government which either does not have, or frequently thinks it impolitic to assert, the domestic competence to accept and carry out extensive commitments relative to economic and social policy, and which therefore tends to oppose the development of international policy standards. This American tendency was most marked under the Eisenhower Administration, but it did not originate with the Republican assumption of power in Washington. The United States stands aloof from the Genocide Convention, rejects most conventions formulated by the International Labor Organization, registers its rejection in advance of conventions in the human rights field, and generally proposes to abstain from further participation in the international legislative development of global standards of economic and social policy.

Given the various bases of hostility toward the functional enterprise which exist in the United States, including the reaction against the political mentality which was epitomized by the New Deal, it is perhaps surprising that the United States should be a major participant. Indeed, it is probably accurate to qualify the assertion that this country is the leader of the functional system by saying that the United States supports international programs designed to produce effects in other countries which are compatible with American purposes—and which the United States does not opt to produce by alternative methods more fully subject to its own control—but that it tends to be an abstainer, rather than a leader, in regard to functional projects which might have an impact upon its own domestic affairs.

Hardly less important than the fact that American foreign policy and domestic political tendencies impinge upon the work of the functional agencies is the fact that the Soviet bloc has played only a minor role in the cooperative system. During the formative stage of the United Nations, the Soviet Union exhibited very little interest in the establishment of the functional elements of the system; once the economic and social agencies were created, it refrained from all but the most spotty and limited participation. This general policy may appear strange for a state which professes adher-

---

[45] *New York Times,* June 7, 1955.

ence to Marxism, a doctrinal system which stresses the fundamental importance of economic problems and the secondary character of political phenomena. But the Soviet Union's position was in fact basically consistent with its ideological professions. Orthodox Marxism does not permit the assumption that cooperation among states which are predominantly capitalistic can do for the world what Marx said only a global series of Communist revolutions can do. One who views reality through the peculiar spectacles of Marxism cannot be expected to believe that capitalist states will cooperate in good faith with Communist powers, or that the Communist fatherland can properly join in the promotion of such nefarious projects of world capitalism as an International Bank, or in the spreading of such noxious doctrines as the proposition of UNESCO that wars begin in the minds of men rather than in the rotten structures of capitalist economies.

For whatever reasons—and they certainly include others than the ideological one—the Soviet Union originally restricted its role to normal membership in the most strictly technical organizations and to the occupancy of the seat of the scornful in the Economic and Social Council and its subsidiary units, whence it poured out denunciations of "American imperialism." More recently, the USSR and its satellites have moved toward fuller participation in the system, relaxing the Communist boycott of the technical assistance program and most of the Specialized Agencies. It is not clear whether this change represents more than an effort to acquire additional vantage points for issuing fulminations against the American management of the system.

What is clear is that the political animosity between the opponents in the cold war has thus far denied functionalism the opportunity to test its capacity for weaving pacifying webs between them. The major antagonists have either refrained from joint participation in functional agencies, thereby eliminating the possibility that they might be joined by the subtle threads of functional activity, or they have made their common membership an occasion for the raucous proclamation of conflicting political interests rather than the cooperative pursuit of common economic and social interests. In terms of functional theory, the knitting of economic and social bonds between the United States and the Soviet Union is the critical peace-building task of our time; yet, this is precisely the job that functionalism cannot even begin to perform until *after* some sort of political peace has been established between the two great powers. The politics of the cold war shows no susceptibility to being transformed by functional programs; rather, it shows every indication of being able to transform functional workshops into political arenas.

The failure of functionalism under United Nations auspices to demonstrate its validity as a means of achieving the immediate or even of initiating the ultimate reduction of political tension between the United States and the Soviet Union does not mean that the functional approach to international organization has been entirely discredited. The agencies of international economic and social cooperation have displayed a notable gift of institutional inventiveness; such of their creations as the international expert, the comprehensive survey mission, and the special-purpose international working team may prove to be major contributions to the future development of human civilization. In substantive terms, they have hardly been able to keep up with the job of making the world a livable place; the gap between the living standards of developed and underdeveloped countries is steadily widening, and many of the latter countries are swimming against a demographic current which forces them to push forward with great speed in order simply to remain in the same place. Nevertheless, the situation of mankind is less unsatisfactory then it would have been without the strenuous international efforts of the last decade.

The functional experiment of the United Nations represents the laying of the groundwork for the first systematic global attack upon basic economic and social problems, the beginning of the definition of the assignment which devolves upon the organized international community, and the initiation of the process of learning how to tackle the job. The actual achievements thus far are substantial and significant, even though not spectacular, world-shaking, or world-saving. Above all, the record to date indicates that functional activity is, at least in the short run, more dependent upon the political weather than determinative of the political weather. In the long run, however, it may be that the economic and social work of international organization will prove to be one of the means of developing a system whereby man can control his political climate.

SUGGESTED READINGS

Asher, Robert E., et al., *The United Nations and Promotion of the General Welfare,* Washington: The Brookings Institution, 1957.

Davis, Harriet E., ed., *Pioneers in World Order,* New York: Columbia University Press, 1944.

Hyde, L. K., Jr., *The United States and the United Nations: Promoting the Public Welfare,* New York: Manhattan, for the Carnegie Endowment for International Peace, 1960.

Jacobson, Harold K., *The USSR and the UN's Economic and Social Activities,* Notre Dame, Indiana: University of Notre Dame Press, 1963.

Laves, Walter H. C., and Charles A. Thomson, *UNESCO: Purpose, Progress, Prospects,* Bloomington: Indiana University Press, 1957.

Lie, Trygve, *In the Cause of Peace,* New York: Macmillan, 1954, Chap. IX.

Matecki, B. E., *Establishment of the International Finance Corporation and United States Policy,* New York: Praeger, 1957.

Mitrany, David, *A Working Peace System,* London and New York: Royal Institute of International Affairs, 1946.

Myrdal, Gunnar, *An International Economy,* New York: Harper, 1956.

Sharp, Walter R., *Field Administration in the United Nations System,* New York: Praeger, for the Carnegie Endowment for International Peace, 1961.

Sweetser, Arthur, "The Non-Political Achievements of the League," *Foreign Affairs,* October 1940, pp. 179-192.

Yates, P. L., *So Bold an Aim: Ten Years of International Cooperation Toward Freedom From Want,* Rome: FAO, 1955.

The Future of World Order

CHAPTER 18

World Government and World Order

The vision of a unified world, freed from the anarchy of tribalistic strife among organized fragments of the human race and possessed of a government able to dispense justice and maintain order among all men, has long captured the prophetic imagination of a few philosophers and poets. A much more mundane version of the One World concept has actuated a procession of conquerors and would-be conquerors, who have been dedicated to the ambition of ruling the world rather than to the ideal that the world should be ruled, and who have sought to extend their power over all men rather than to provide a just and stable peace for all men. The noble ideal, as distinguished from the demonic drive, has not entered significantly into the picture of world political reality in times past.

THE MOVEMENT FOR WORLD GOVERNMENT

Since World War II, the concept of a world government achieved by consent and directed toward the supreme moral purposes of aspiring humanity has ceased to be the exclusive property of dreamy theorists. It has become a cause rather than a mere vision, a project rather than a mere ideal. Organizations for the promotion of world government, usually conceived in terms of a more or less limited federation of a selected group, as large a number as possible, or the total list of the nations of the world, have enlisted the support or active participation of prominent leaders in many fields, and have carried on vigorous campaigns of advocacy which have generated substantial popular support. This is primarily a phenomenon of the Western European and English-speaking world. The success of the movement for selling the idea of world government should not be exaggerated; its gains are tentative, subject to wide fluctuations as the pattern of events changes from day to day, and much of its support is undoubtedly purely verbalistic and abstract, representing something less than deep commitment and firm acceptance of the practical implications of world government. The strength of the movement in the United States is probably not so great as is assumed or asserted either by its opponents, many of whom are neurotic conservatives given to depicting themselves as a heroic remnant defending the last redoubts of Americanism against a multifarious horde of subversives, or by its champions, who tend to share with the bulk of the prophetic profession an aversion to the idea that they are doomed to crying in the wilderness. Nevertheless, the world government approach to world order has now achieved a sufficiently articulate and influential body of support to justify the demand that it be taken seriously and studied critically.

In strict theory, world government offers a distinctive approach to the central problem of peace and security. It sees war as a necessary, natural, and inescapable product of the multistate system; consequently, it proposes to abolish and replace the system, rather than to tinker with it. The problem of modern man is not to correct minor flaws in the operation of the international system, or to equip the system with improved apparatus, or to remove wicked and foolish men from its managerial board, or to prevent troublesome states from disrupting it, but to recognize its inherent defectiveness and take the drastic step of dismantling "the absurd architecture of the present world." [1]

In contrast, the various approaches to peace which have been adopted by international organization involve working within the national state system to achieve the redemption of man from the evils of anarchy. The United Nations undertakes to improve the techniques and machinery of the system, to improve the states which are its constitutent units, and to improve the people who are its ultimate components. Its objectives are these: to prevail upon governments to settle their quarrels peacefully, persuade them to behave reasonably, and debar them from acting aggressively; to promote the abandonment of old areas of controversy and the anticipatory resolution of problems that threaten to become sources of discord; to facilitate the development of national societies characterized by such economic

---

[1] *The City of Man, A Declaration on World Democracy* (New York: Viking, 1941), p. 27.

and social well-being, respect for human rights, and political maturity that they will produce decent, cooperative, responsible governments; and to educate human beings to renounce nationalistic arrogance and ideological intolerance, helping them to become spiritually and morally fit for participation in the collaborative enterprises of a world community of separate but interdependent states. By such means, international organization purports to offer hope of making the multistate system work reasonably well. The movement for world government, on the other hand, is animated by the conviction that this hope is a snare and a delusion, and that a revolutionary transformation of the global political system offers the only meaningful prospect for achieving world order.

Actually, however, the distinctiveness of the advocacy of world government has definite limits. Many thinkers who are outside the fold accept the fundamental end of world government, while insisting upon means which are associated with international organization. For instance, functionalists or supporters of the UNESCO concept of international cooperation for changing the minds of men may look forward to the ultimate development of global institutions which will be more governmental than organizational in nature. Others may find themselves in substantial agreement with world governmentalists while preserving differences in regard to terminology and form; there is not necessarily a wide gulf between the proponent of a limited world government and the advocate of a strengthened United Nations. Indeed, it can be argued with some merit that the major distinction of the world government movement is that it insists upon using the word "government."

Moreover, there are variations within the movement which make it difficult to characterize the advocacy of world government as a distinctive approach to world problems. One finds such assorted bedfellows as regionalists and universalists, proponents of full-fledged and of narrowly limited international government, contemptuous critics and interim supporters of international organization, patient gradualists and eager "one-fell-swoopists." Some sincerely believe that world government is attainable in the near future, while others believe merely that agitation for the ideal will produce salutary effects on human political development in the longer run, and still others appear to be mainly motivated by the idea that American sponsorship and Soviet rejection of a sweeping proposal for establishing peace would redound to the advantage of the United States in the propaganda war with the USSR. Some seem to be disinterested spokesmen for the interests of mankind, but others give the impression of wishing to annex the world to the United States, thereby achieving the institutionalization of the American Century concept; not all human beings would be reassured by the notion that America has an inevitable mission to serve as a Platonic ruler of mankind, a proposition that led a group of prominent

Americans to conclude in 1940 that "the United States must be the Uniting States. No number is prescribed to the stars on its flag." [2]

When these diversities are taken into account, it is possible to arrive at this limited generalization: the contemporary movement for world government regards the establishment of international federal institutions as the necessary basis of a peaceful world, looks upon international organization as at best a step toward the creation of such institutions, and assumes that it is useful at the present time to engage in vigorous advocacy of the drastic alteration of the global political pattern.

Since the federal form of government is so overwhelmingly the choice of those who pursue this line, let us treat world federalism as synonymous with the advocacy of world government. Additionally, we shall adopt the terms "internationalism" and "internationalists" to designate the doctrine and the proponents of the doctrine that international organization rather than world government provides the most hopeful approach to a solution of the world's fundamental problems of peace and security.

THE QUESTION OF PRACTICAL ATTAINABILITY

The first critical questions to be raised concerning the world government approach to world order relate to the attainability of its ideal and the suitability of the means used for promoting the ideal. Is world government feasible in the foreseeable future? Does persistent agitation for its achievement serve a useful purpose?

There is a strong tendency among its proponents to assume that world federalism is possible because it is believed to be necessary. Internationalism grimly reminds man that he must do what he can; world federalism more sanguinely asserts that man can do what he must. There are no insoluble problems or unanswerable questions; history has no dead-end streets. Taken literally, this is a declaration of faith at which the unbeliever may scoff, but which he cannot disprove. He may insist upon pointing out that mankind has solved few of its basic problems, but has at best managed to muddle along from one partial solution to another. Confronted with the retort that humanity has never before the atomic age come face to face with absolute necessity and final destiny, he may agree, and yet find himself unable to share the conviction that all things are possible for those who stand in the shadow of the mushroom clouds that overhang human civilization. How literally this credo should be taken is another question. Conviction is often a buttress for fearful uncertainty and desperate hope, and in this case the declaration of possibility may be a kind of self-administered pep-talk for those who are most deeply convinced that world government is urgently necessary.

[2] *Ibid.*, pp. 63-73. The quotation is from p. 72.

The literature of world government contains the recurrent theme that the basic requisite for achievement is the circumvention of the obstacles raised by the stodginess and vested interests of national governments. Let the people speak and act, over the heads of their governments; call a special People's Convention, brushing aside unimaginative politicians and selfish officials who cannot see beyond the nose of old-fashioned national interest. As Stringfellow Barr puts it, his ambitious proposals are "based on the assumption that if the men and women in the world wait until national governments act, they will never get the common government which the world clearly needs." [3] Presumably there exists a universal sense of human solidarity which is concealed and distorted by existing governments and which requires only a new set of institutions to give it expression.

This is a very big assumption. It would be considerably more credible if it could be demonstrated that the American State Department had been continuously assailed for being too narrowly nationalistic rather than for being too soft toward foreigners, that Congress had been more consistently inclined toward international commitment and cooperation than the Executive, and that American taxpayers had established a record of deploring the paucity rather than the magnitude of expenditures on behalf of other peoples. In fact, the record makes it difficult to deny the assertion of P. E. Corbett:

> Most massive of all the checks on world organization . . . is the inert multitude. . . . The great majority of even relatively enlightened populations pay little attention to foreign affairs. This is not the reservoir of world brotherhood, waiting to be channeled into peaceful and universal co-operation, which it is represented to be by the champions of world-federation. It can perhaps be persuaded to sound the slogans, so long as it does not understand their bearing on its ingrained habits of thought, speech, and action. But hostility to the out-group in this section of the population does not have to wait for stimulation by the leadership. To assert its general willingness to share what privileges it has with aliens of all breeds and manners of life is to indulge in fantasy.[4]

Moreover, this world federalist position reveals some curious attitudes toward democracy. In so far as it rests upon evidence, it looks to the results of public opinion polls, thereby betraying the conviction that the democratic will is more reliably expressed through those devices than through the normal electoral processes. The notion that majority rule can be exercised through appointive officials responsible to elected repre-

---

[3] *Citizens of the World* (Garden City: Doubleday, 1953), p. 160. Copyright, 1952, by Stringfellow Barr.

[4] *Law and Society in the Relations of States* (New York: Harcourt, Brace, 1951), p. 289.

sentatives is quite generally repudiated by champions of world government; the people will be truly represented only by spokesmen chosen by direct election. In Barr's terms, what is necessary is "an international agency as independent as possible of all governments and as dependent as possible on the men and women who dwell together on this steadily shrinking planet." [5] This general evaluation of democracy is a strangely pessimistic one for advocates of the establishment of a presumably democratic world federation. If democracy works so badly in the United States that the American people, desiring world government or at least a vigorously affirmative approach to international cooperation, find themselves regularly represented by legislators and officials who exhibit instead a considerable stickiness about sovereignty, how can it be expected to work satisfactorily in a global political unit?

In fact, the belief that the peoples of the world are ready and eager to make the federalist plunge, if only they can push their unresponsive governments aside or ahead, is not the controlling factor in the movement for world government, for that movement is pre-eminently a campaign to persuade human beings to accept and support the federalist solution. As such, it tends to rely heavily upon the persuasive potency of three major themes: the imminent peril of atomic destruction, the utter inadequacy and essential futility of international organization, and the availability of salvation through the transformation of international anarchy into international government.

There is no room for doubt that mankind stands in unprecedented danger, although civilization records a long line of premature obituaries which proved to be such less because humanity possessed ingenious therapists than because it had fallible diagnosticians. In any event, there is substantial room for doubt that the vivid display of the dangers of atomic hell will necessarily produce popular willingness to adopt world federation; when the peoples of the world become desperately afraid and insecure, those who hope for moderation, reasonableness, and constructiveness in international relations may have less rather than more reason for optimism.

The instinct of the salesman to belittle the merits of inferior substitutes poses another problem. Not all proponents of world government regarded the incipient United Nations with such utter contempt as did Emery Reves, who wrote that "The San Francisco Charter is a multilateral treaty. That and nothing else," and denied with dogmatic finality that it was or could be even a useful first step toward world order.[6] As the history of revolutionary movements bears out, however, advocates of

---

[5] *Op. cit.*, p. 245.

[6] *The Anatomy of Peace* (New York: Pocket Books, 1946), p. 87. This paperbound edition is a revised version of the original book, published in 1945 by Harper and Brothers.

drastic change can hardly avoid the conviction that reform is worse than useless, since it offers palliatives which reduce the sense of revolutionary urgency without actually affecting the ultimate necessity for revolution. World governmentalists have proved sensitive to the charge of impeding the development of maximum effectiveness by the United Nations, and have largely turned from their initial emphasis upon the stupidity of expecting anything good to come from international organization to affirmative support of the international institutions which, however imperfect they may be, have the important virtue of being in existence. In the nature of the case, however, this support is highly tentative and dubiously effective; it is not much good telling people that, on the one hand, they ought to support the United Nations, and, on the other hand, the United Nations is doomed to futility because it represents a fundamentally unsound approach to the problem of world order. For those who take this skeptical view of the United Nations, its virtue lies not in its existing nature but in the possibility that it may provide a framework for the establishment of an institution of fundamentally different character. Given the basic assumption that nothing short of world government will do, there is obvious merit in the proposition that it is the hopeful transformation, not the hopeless operation, of international organization that is most deserving of support.

Aside from questions relating to the tactics used in the campaign to sell the idea of world government, there are more fundamental issues bearing upon the validity of the persuasion technique itself. It is questionable whether the campaign can be successful in the foreseeable future, considering, among other factors, the strength of the competitive propaganda which the advocacy of world government generates, and the fact that the campaign is clearly debarred from operating at all in major sectors of the world, including most prominently the territory of the USSR. If the need is urgent and the time is short, the project of establishing a global federation by persuading peoples all over the world to support the idea and relying upon them to make their newly formulated demands politically effective—which involves, in many cases, the overthrow of dictatorial systems which thrive on the suppression of the popular will—seems doomed to utter ineffectuality. World federalists are men in a hurry, but they have chosen a long, long road.

Beyond the questions of whether people can be persuaded and whether they can, if persuaded, do anything about it on a global scale, the basic issue arises: is the real task that of *persuading* people to accept or initiate drastic institutional change, or is it rather that of *preparing* people, changing them, making them fit for world government? The latter formulation would seem to characterize the problem much better. What is required is the profound alteration of attitudes, loyalties, attachments, and values, which in turn involves an attack upon the basic conditions of human society that provide the context within which men are shaped. This is clearly not an overnight process, and it is clearly not to be conducted like a propaganda campaign. In fact, it is precisely the kind of work which the United Nations system, particularly in its functional agencies, is carrying on. It is quite possible that an ounce of international organizational service and experience is worth a pound of world governmental sermons pointing out the inadequacy of international organization.

World federalism suffers from a much too literal acceptance of the social contract theory. Finding the nations in a state of nature which has become intolerable, it prescribes an apocalyptic leap out of anarchy into social order. It is an excessively mechanistic and rationalistic doctrine, relying upon the ingenious invention, rationally conceived, contrived, and accepted; in pseudo-Lockian fashion, it postulates a flash of creativity which carries mankind into the era of order. This is a dramatic and challenging conception, but its accuracy bears some examination.

In the first place, it is not good Lockian doctrine. Although the contract theorists of the sixteenth and seventeenth centuries seemed to attribute political community to a deliberate and determinate act of establishment, they actually assumed a pre-existing community. As Frederick Watkins has pointed out: "Although men like Locke might postulate a social contract as the basis of community, they used it primarily as a device to determine the proper limits of government and made little effort to investigate the process whereby men actually acquire the capacity for effective group action." [7]

Opposed to this conception of sudden solidarity, achieved in reaction to a vivid awareness of need and in response to a convincing description of potentiality, is an organic, evolutionary conception of the slow growth of the foundations of community feeling, the development of social tissue, the enlargement of psychic and moral horizons, and the emergence of common patterns of feeling and action.

This brings us again to the recurrent problem of circularity, this time involving the relationship between community and government. There is evidently some truth in both the propositions that community creates government and that government creates community. Yet, there remains a large area of uncertainty. What is the minimum degree of community feeling that must be achieved before the establishment of community institutions is feasible and their successful operation is probable? How can it be measured? How can it be created? Can world government be relied upon to deposit its own foundations, or can an evolving world community be expected to throw up its own appropriate institutional superstructure in the fullness of time?

---

[7] *The Political Tradition of the West* (Cambridge: Harvard University Press, 1948), p. 90.

These questions add up to the ultimate mystery of the social sciences, which any mere man ought to approach with agnostic humility. It is, in fact, a "flower in the crannied wall" kind of enigma; we do not even know how a nation comes into being, much less possess the key to contriving a we-group encompassing all of mankind. Kenneth Boulding has posed the problem, without purporting to solve it:

> The person I cannot get out of my mind these days is the young man who dropped the first atomic bomb. . . . If he had been ordered to go and drop it on Milwaukee, he almost certainly would have refused. . . . Because he was asked to drop it on Hiroshima, he not only consented but he became something of a hero for it. . . . Of course, I don't quite see the distinction between dropping it on Milwaukee and dropping it on Hiroshima. The difference is a "we" difference. The people in Milwaukee, though we don't know any of them, are "we," and the people in Hiroshima are "they," and the great psychological problem is how to make everybody "we," at least in some small degree. The degree need be only extremely small. . . . All that is necessary to create the psychological foundations of a world society is that people in Maine should feel the same degree of responsibility toward the people of Japan or Chile or Indo-China as they feel toward California. That is pretty small, really, but it is apparently enough to create the United States.[8]

There is an unmistakable tinge of brashness in the pretension to certainty that man can, in a magnificent spasm of resolve, catapult himself from a perilously divided and anarchical state into a situation of political unity capable of sustaining the essential instrumentalities of peace and order.

The maintenance of a decent respect for the bounds of our own ignorance is compatible with the observation that it is illogical to cite the relative failure of the United Nations as evidence of the need for world government and to fail to cite it as evidence of the improbability that mankind is now capable of creating and sustaining a more ambitious institutional structure. The dilemma of the world federalist is that there is no necessary correlation between human need and human capacity. If the United Nations had worked exceedingly well in its early years, the campaigner for world government would have a weaker argument for the urgency of his project but a vastly stronger one for its feasibility; since the United Nations has had very limited success, it is easy to argue that much more drastic measures are necessary but difficult to prove that they are possible. There is little in the record to indicate that the Charter sets the standards too low, that there are reservoirs of international solidarity which the United Nations leaves untapped, that the peoples of the world are straining to exceed the narrow bounds of collective commitment and

[8] Quincy Wright, ed., *The World Community* (Chicago: University of Chicago Press, 1948), pp. 101-102. Copyright, 1948, by the University of Chicago.

action which the Charter sets, and that the nations are ready and able to achieve a greater pooling of sovereignty and acceptance of obligation and responsibility than is possible within the flexible limits of international organization. On the contrary, the weakness of the organization derives largely from the fact that commitments are unfulfilled, onerous responsibilities are evaded, and opportunities for collaboration are neglected. The evidence suggests that the world organization is too primitive for the requirements of mankind in this dangerous age, but too advanced for the present political capacities of mankind. And all this indicates the pertinence of the question: is the world's most urgent need the erection of a heavier and more imposing institutional superstructure, as the world federalist would have it, or the creation of stronger foundations for such structural apparatus as already exists? There is basis for more than a suspicion that we now have, in the United Nations system, at least as ambitious a structure as the community can support.

THE QUESTION OF THEORETICAL VALIDITY

The world government movement may have slight prospects for conquering the world, but it bids fair to conquer the internationalists. There is a strong tendency among supporters of international organization to concede ultimate theoretical superiority to world federalism. While maintaining the view that it cannot now be accomplished, and that it is futile and perhaps even unfortunate to press too hard for it at the present time, they are inclined to admit that world government is obviously the one and only real and definitive solution to the problem of war, and that the future, if there is one, belongs to the courageous prophets of that doctrine. This statement of surrender is often tinged with self-deprecation and grudging admiration for the victor; internationalists are disposed to be a bit apologetic for lacking the moral courage to break away from the patterns of traditionalism, to admit the bankruptcy of the old system, and to emulate the adventurousness of world federalists in pursuing the vision of what is eternally right. There is nothing very heroic or inspiring about timid realism, as compared with passionate idealism; the world will ultimately pay tribute to the visionaries who were not afraid to be men ahead of their time, and consign to historical oblivion the little men who grasped at straws, resorted to halfway measures, tried to patch up the doomed edifice of international relations, and evaded the clear call of destiny. This is the verdict which internationalists are inclined to render, as they ponder the truth that "Where there is no vision, the people perish," and upbraid themselves for being men of little faith.

This deference of internationalists is in large part the product of disappointment with the record so far achieved by international organization. The League collapsed ignominiously, and the United Nations has assuredly not given grounds for confidence that it can save the world. International organization has proved useful, but mere usefulness is not enough when the world stands on the brink of irretrievable disaster. Moreover, internationalists are not even equipped with an emotionally compelling and logically impregnable theory; not since the early days of the League have substantial numbers of them believed that they possessed the key that would infallibly open the doors to a brave new world. They have had to say, "Maybe this will help," rather than "Here is a certain solution to the world's problems," and to recommend measures as worth trying rather than as worthy of confidence.

Their approaches to peace are vulnerable to a theoretical attack, as Walter Schiffer brilliantly demonstrated, which reveals them as self-contradictory and illogical. Shiffer played a bit unfairly, by stuffing the creators and supporters of international organization with ideological straw of his own gathering, and he attributed to them a sublime confidence that their loose associations constitute the ideal approach to world order[9] which even the most casual reader of the record ought to realize is not characteristic of their tribe. He nevertheless scored heavily as he drove home the point that it is a curious logic which acknowledges the necessity for coercive government over individual men but entertains the idea that such human groups as states may contrive to live in peaceful coexistence without government, and the point that international organization is either unworkable or unnecessary, since it sets out to solve problems resulting from the irresponsible behavior of states by methods which will work only if states behave responsibly, and relies for its success upon the existence of conditions which, if they existed, would make international organization superfluous.[10]

Internationalists may not be guilty of cherishing "the idea that everything could be obtained for nothing," [11] but they are painfully aware of the fact that their hope that something may be obtained for a price less than the surrender of the most vital segments of national sovereignty to a world government is a slender reed rather than a tower of strength for mankind in a time of desperate need. When pushed into a corner by the demonstration that international organization neither actually provides nor theoretically promises anything approaching a certain remedy for the basic ills of the world, internationalists can hardly avoid the confession that world federalists are right, even though they may never have the opportunity to provide tangible proof of their correctness, in insisting that the acceptance and establishment of world government is the price of peace.

In my opinion, this victory is undeserved, and this surrender is ill-advised. The case for world government must rest upon something more

---

[9] *The Legal Community of Mankind,* pp. 285, 288.
[10] *Ibid.,* pp. 199, 209, 232, 282-283.
[11] *Ibid.,* p. 301.

than a grim reminder that civilization is in danger, a citation of the fact that the United Nations has failed to exorcise that danger, a doctrinaire assertion that international organization, not being government, offers the world no significant hope, and a glib assumption that world federation, being government, provides the exclusive and sufficient means to a solution of the problem of war. The case has not been proved. The imperfection of alternative solutions may just as well point to the unavailability of a perfect solution as to the perfection of the federal solution; there is nothing self-evident about the proposition that world government, if it could be instituted, would guarantee world order. This is not to say that the idea of world government is unworthy of being put to the test, if and when that becomes possible. But the campaign for world government has been so nearly exclusively an enterprise in impassioned salesmanship that its sponors have been more concerned to avoid damaging the marketability of their product than to encourage and participate in a searching examination of its theoretical merits. Before conceding that world government is the obviously ideal approach to peace, we would do well to perform a critical analysis of its substantive promise in addition to speculating about its prospects for adoption.

In one sense, the thesis that world government would produce world order is a truism. If government be defined as a set of effective means for preventing disorder, then this is clearly what the world requires, and there is no occasion for further argument. But definitive solutions achieved by definition are not very helpful. To say that we will have world order when we adopt adequate methods for guaranteeing world order leaves us where we started. Yet, this is the only sense in which the validity of the thesis is obvious.

The essential starting point of an objective analysis of the promise of world government is the recognition that *government* has never served as a magic wand to banish problems of disorder in any human society. It is sheer nonsense to assert, as does Emery Reves, that law has always succeeded in producing peace, wherever and whenever it has been tried, and that conflict between social units has always been eliminated when their sovereignties were merged in the creation of a superior governmental authority.[12] As Quincy Wright has pointed out, deaths resultant from military action were more numerous within the governed United States than in the anarchical continent of Europe during the century preceding the First World War.[13] There is no gainsaying the fact that "Civil war, revolution, mob violence are more frequent manifestations of man's unruly and still savage will than are wars between states." [14]

---

[12] *Op. cit.*, pp. 46, 79, 87.

[13] *Problems of Stability and Progress in International Relations*, p. 169.

[14] Philip C. Jessup, *A Modern Law of Nations* (New York: Macmillan, 1949), p. 189.

The problem of civil war and revolution cannot be dismissed, as Reves attempts to do, by asserting that it is the result of "badly functioning government, of a collapse of legal order, of an incompletely established system of law." [15] The admission that government *may* fail is crucial. This admission defeats the thesis that world government is the clear answer to the problem of peace, and reduces it to a suggestion that consideration should be given to the possibility that the creation of authoritative global institutions might be helpful. This is an eminently reasonable suggestion, but it is a horse of a very different color from that which world federalists customarily undertake to market.

The literature of world government is not all so dogmatic as Reves' exposition, but it is thoroughly suffused with an idealization of government *per se* which is tenable only if one ignores the checkered history of ruling institutions and the unsatisfactory performance of many contemporary governments as peace-keeping agencies, and concentrates an admiring gaze upon the history of a few Western nations, with their civil wars and revolutions expurgated, which have achieved exceptional success in the art of government. The most that can be said for government—and this is saying a great deal—is that it sometimes contributes greatly to the stability of a society and the security of its members, and that, more rarely, it may even promote order without doing violence to the values that many men place above order. Given the right social conditions and the right kind of regime, government may work reasonably well. This is a far cry from the proposition that the establishment of a government is anything like a certain means of solving the most critical problems that beset any human group, including the largest possible human group. The world might be better served by a frank exploration of the limits and difficulties of government on a global scale than by a campaign of persuasion which presents a glorified picture of government.

In more specific terms, world governmentalists offer *federalism* as the brand of political unity which promises twentieth-century man surcease from his gravest troubles. There is merit in this, since the acceptance of federal linkage requires a less drastic revision of political attitudes than acquiescence in the complete fusion of states, and the maintenance of diversity within a pattern of unity is a particularly significant value for the world community.

Nevertheless, there is no justification for the uncritical view of federalism which characterizes the movement for world government. The analysis which is customarily presented is on about the level of the schoolboy's understanding of the great American experiment: the states gave up just enough authority to create a strong nation and kept all the rest, and this ingenious system has worked very well indeed. The sober truth is

[15] *Op. cit.*, p. 77.

that peoples do not just federate and live happily ever after. American history has not been so simple as all that; it includes much wrangling over the division of powers, crises of federal authority, a bloody civil war and a bitter aftermath, the frustration of essential governmental action by anachronistic and rigid jurisdictional boundaries, the gradual breaking down of many of the barriers posed by federalism to effective government, and the resurgence of demands for the raising anew of federal fences. Ultimately, the schoolboy is right: American federalism has, on the whole, worked very well, although there is room for argument as to whether the United States has become a great nation because of or in spite of its federal system, and whether its deviation from or its respect for the pattern prescribed by the Founding Fathers has contributed most notably to its successful development.

The point is that federalism is an extremely complicated form of government which makes extraordinary demands upon the political wisdom and moderation of its participants. Many peoples have no experience in operating a complex federal system, some others have political traditions opposed to the kind of legalistic logic-chopping and governmental pulling and hauling which such a system involves, and few peoples have been able to manage federalism with great success. It requires great audacity to suggest that the lumping together of all these peoples would produce a body politic capable of keeping a global federal system in smooth operation. Federalism has great merits, but the question of its appropriateness as the future pattern of organization for the world is one to be determined by serious study of its problems and implications, not one to be settled by assumption and assertion.

The proponents of world federation make much of the claim that only a "limited" world government is necessary. It may be that they have chosen federalism not so much because they have watched its operation in national situations and concluded that it can be successfully transplanted to the global field, as because the term "federalism" serves to symbolize the limited price which they ask the world to pay for peace. Perhaps the internationalist need not have such a sharp sense of moral inferiority after all; as prophets, his federalist brethren have the courage to demand sweeping change in the global system, but as salesmen they have the prudence to emphasize the limited character of the change. *Government* is the big, brave word; *federalism* is the little, cautious word. In a book advocating world federation, Vernon Nash busied himself so with reassuring timorous souls that he fell into the trap of asserting that the central regime would have little intimate impact upon either national governments or private citizens,[16] thus converting his proposal into a beguil-

---

[16] *The World Must Be Governed* (New York: Harper, 1949), pp. 71-72.

ing picture of happy anarchy rather than a rigorous demand for creation of governmental institutions adequate to cope with global disorder.

In fact, the project of endowing a world federation with powers adequate to prevent war may be big enough to render its description as a program of "limited world government" a trifle incongruous. It is usually taken to involve the concentration of authority to enforce disarmament, require peaceful settlement of disputes, and suppress violence, with a few ancillary powers. But a sophisticated analysis of the problem of war may reveal that much more than the capacity to control the armaments situation is essential. The American industrial plant, for instance, may be as frightening to a potential enemy as the standing army of the USSR, and the problem of peaceful change may loom as large in the causative picture of war as the problem of uncontrolled national navies. How limited a world government can be if it is given unlimited competence to do what is necessary to remove the threat of war is a matter of conjecture. How successful it can be in fulfilling the expectations cultivated by its proponents if it is not granted such broad competence is equally uncertain.

Aside from the factor of the objective requirements for creating a peaceful world society, the factor of political pressures which cannot be wholly anticipated enters into the determination of the limits of federal authority in a hypothetical world government. When the world federalist tells the wary nationalist that his project is safe, because it involves the delegation of clearly defined powers to a global regime and the careful reservation of residual powers to the national state, he is talking through his hat. Whatever American experience proves about federalism, it emphatically does *not* prove that federalism provides a neat, clean line of division between jurisdictional areas, a line which stays put except when it is shifted by constitutional amendment, and which leaves federal and state governments with nothing to do except to tend to their own business. A federal system may be torn apart by centrifugal political forces, or it may be subjected to centripetal pressures which gradually break down the federalistic qualifications of its unity; its most unlikely prospect is that of perpetuating a static equilibrium between the whole and the parts. A federal formula for the distribution of powers and functions is merely a starting point. It is quite possibly true that the gradual transformation of a federal into a unitary system is the only course of development compatible with its survival; in this case, federalism is either an abortive attempt at unity, doomed to end in dissolution, or an interim step toward centralization, destined to be transcended.

No one can predict with absolute certainty the pattern of evolution which would characterize a global federation. What is certain is that changes would take place and that they would not be determined by the preferences of those who had agitated for establishment of the federation.

Campaign promises are difficult to keep even when one is elected to a position of authority; they are impossible to keep when one's victory consists in the adoption of a constitution and the creation of political institutions. All this does not prove that the world should reject federalism, but it does suggest that the experiment should not be launched in the expectation that any given federal arrangement will prove to be definitive.

A world federation would pose particularly difficult problems for existing federal states. A two-level system, involving the working division of governmental powers and functions between national and state regimes, is complex enough; the addition of a third level would compound the difficulties of adjustment. It is already apparent that participation in international organization by the United States creates significant problems for the American federal system, and there is every reason to believe that these problems would be increased, not eliminated, by American membership in a world federation. What would be the pattern of relationships among a World Federal Government, the United States Government, and the Government of Mississippi or Texas? How effectively could government function if its powers and jurisdiction were divided among three units, each jealously competing for its share of sovereignty? Would American federalism have to be abandoned, or would it break down completely, in such a situation? The irony is that the consideration of such questions as these has been left largely to the proponents of the Bricker Amendment, whose bias runs toward insulating the United States from the impact of external involvements, so as to facilitate a reversal of centralizing trends in the American federal system. What needs to be established is the fact that world federalism is a set of problems to be studied, not simply a cause to be preached. These problems are not necessarily insoluble, but they will not be solved by glib assurances that federalism offers a neat formula for escaping the perils of global anarchy.

The case for world federation appears most plausible when one sets aside all the troublesome problems of federalism and simply fixes attention on the telling contrast between the situation of the nations, floundering desperately to keep their heads above water as they cling to the primitive raft called the United Nations, and that of the fifty American states, blithely sailing onward in the proud and sturdy ship, the federal union of the United States. Is it not clear that federation is superior to loose association, and that the United Nations will become worthy of confidence only as, and in so far as, it models itself after the United States? The answer is not so simply affirmative as it might at first appear.

In some respects at least, the organizational form of the United Nations is more appropriate for the facilitation of coordinate relations among separate political entities than is the federal system of the United States. For all its merits, the American system makes only the scantiest provision for the ordering of relationships among its constituent states and between them and the central government. There is no officially established means for the regular consultation of states with each other or with the federal superior. The United Nations is far better equipped to promote the standardization of such matters as road signs or the discussion of general policy questions between France and Italy than the United States is in regard to Ohio and Pennsylvania. Within limits, Washington can impose common standards and policies upon the states, but there remain significant areas of public concern which are less subject to systematic coordination in the United States than in the United Nations. Considerable progress has recently been made toward filling this gap in the American system, particularly through the development of the extra-constitutional Council of State Governments and the utilization of the device of interstate agreements.[17] But the Council is vastly inferior to the United Nations as a coordinating center—for instance, its "General Assembly," the Conference of Governors, functions under the rule that no resolution can be passed except by a unanimous vote—and interstate agreements have by no means achieved functional significance comparable to that of treaties in the international sphere. When the Commission on Intergovernmental Relations recommended in 1955 that formal machinery should be established for the systematic exchange of information between governmental units and the consideration of problems of interlevel relationships,[18] it was in effect suggesting that the United States might profitably emulate the United Nations.

In short, there is significant evidence that the ordering of relationships in a world which is administratively and politically pluralistic is not to be accomplished by the slavish copying of American or any other federal institutions. The theory and practice of federalism doubtless have much to contribute to an ideal pattern of world institutions, but it is altogether possible that the devices which international organization has evolved for dealing with world problems will prove to be at least equally effectual. It is far from clear that the international "adoption of federalism" is the final answer.

The point remains that the federated states of the American union enjoy an infinitely more advantageous interrelationship than the unfederated states which constitute the world community. How can any objection be regarded as valid in the face of the obvious desirability of creating international relationships analogous to the interstate relationships of the United States? One rhetorical question deserves another: how can

---

[17] See Leonard D. White, *The States and the Nation* (Baton Rouge: Louisiana State University Press, 1953).

[18] See the Commission's *Report to the President for Transmittal to the Congress* (June 1955), pp. 61, 79, 86-89.

any man presume to say that world government would produce beneficent effects upon world society comparable to the effects produced upon American society by our central government?

The case for world government rests heavily upon elaborate assurances as to the nature of the proposed regime. Many blueprinters experience no difficulty in predicting offhand what kind of government the world will get if it makes the plunge; it will be, for instance, a democratic regime, dealing fairly and impartially with all states, respecting its constitutional limitations, and sticking closely to its business of keeping the world safe from war. Some even find it possible to explain in considerable detail the policy which it will pursue without describing the basic constitutional structure—representation, voting arrangements, executive establishment, etc.—which they assume it will have. There seems to be full agreement that it will be a "good" government.

The nature of a governmental system does not depend primarily upon the intentions of its advocates or of its actual founders, or even upon the constitutional document which gives it birth, but upon the nature of the community upon which it rests. The exercise of the basic peace-keeping function is particularly conditioned by the essential attributes of the community.

The international community is, and seems likely for the indefinite future to be, characterized by a very precarious unity, a minimal consensus, sharp conflicts, and profound disharmonies. Given this circumstance, it appears that the project of establishing a world government capable of exercising forcible restraint over any and all potential violators of the peace would entail the concentration of really formidable power in the central agencies of the community. In Reinhold Niebuhr's words, "the less a community is held together by cohesive forces in the texture of its life the more it must be held together by power." [19]

Hobbes was right; when a community is so poorly developed that its pregovernmental condition is one of intolerable warfare, and its urge to establish government rests on no other foundation than a desperate desire to escape the perils of anarchy, the only theoretically adequate government is a Leviathan, an omnipotent dictatorship. Locke, too, was right; when a community is held together by strong bonds of agreement concerning what is right and just, and its common life is reasonably satisfactory, a limited and mild kind of government, based mainly upon consent, may suffice to supply its needs. World governmentalists describe the world's situation in Hobbesian terms, with a view to emphasizing the urgent need for a global social contract, but they depict the resultant government in Lockian terms, with a view to making the social contract

---

[19] *The Children of Light and the Children of Darkness* (New York: Scribner's, 1950), p. 168.

palatable. It would be better to recognize that in so far as this is a Hobbesian world, it is likely to require a Hobbesian government.

The problem of power looms large with respect to any governmental system adequate to cope with the elements of disorder and discord in the international community. If a global regime is to have sufficient power to fulfill its task, questions of profound gravity arise: who will exercise and control the force of the community, in accordance with what conception of justice, within what constitutional limits, with what guarantees that the limits will be observed? These are not questions that can be readily answered, but they are crucial—for the threat of global tyranny lurks in unsatisfactory answers. In terms of Western liberalism, the problem is not to get just *any kind* of world government—Hitler and Stalin were only the most recent of a long series of leaders who would have been glad to provide that—but to get a system of world order which is compatible with the political ideals of the democratic heritage. Perhaps this is wrong. It is conceivable that Hobbes' Leviathan is preferable in the atomic age to a Hobbesian state of nature, but such a choice ought to be made advisedly, if at all. The problem of controlling a world government powerful enough to control the situation in an essentially unintegrated world community is not one to be taken lightly.

The point of all this is that the kind of world we have, not the kind of blueprints world governmentalists draw up, is the decisive factor in determining the kind of world government we would get if we got one, and the kind of political problems we would face in trying to preserve the values of Western liberal civilization while undertaking to eliminate the threat of war. This analysis does not disprove the desirability of world government, but it indicates the need to think about government in terms of its relationship to community, rather than assuming that institution-making can safely be divorced from analysis of the community within which institutions have to operate.

One of the most persistent themes in the literature of world government is the concept that world law must be directly applicable to and enforceable upon individuals. Various reasons may be suggested for the assignment of such significance to this idea, including bias against the old devil, the sovereign state, belief that such a concept is inherent in the idea of government, and acceptance of the Hamiltonian thesis that states are intrinsically uncoercible.[20] There is strong reason to suspect that this theme represents primarily an urge to evade the harsh reality that the effective war-making entities of the world are powerful national states and that those are the entities which must be controlled if peace is to reign. It would be comforting if the central problem of international relations

[20] See Inis L. Claude, Jr., "Individuals and World Law," *Harvard Studies in International Affairs,* June 1952, pp. 10-12.

could be reduced to the task of restraining mere individuals rather than confronting the armed might of such a collectivity as the Soviet Union, but the grim fact is that such collective units have a meaningful existence and are not susceptible of being dissolved into insignificance by the touch of a magic wand and the utterance of the formula, "Henceforward, peace will be assured by the application of world law to individuals." In this regard, the kudos for moral courage go to the internationalists, who, in contrast to world governmentalists, have unflinchingly accepted the necessity that states be brought under control. They have not achieved the goal, but neither have they dodged the issue.

This is not to deny the enormous long-range importance of developing close and direct relationships between international institutions and human persons; it is essential that individuals be restrained, protected, served, and converted into loyal and responsible citizens of the republic of mankind.[21] But for the purpose of preventing war, world institutions—be they organizational or governmental in nature—have to deal with the problem presented by the reality of states, and the theorist who is sufficiently aware of that reality to propose a federal system under which the identity and to a large extent the competence of states would be preserved ought to be the first to recognize this necessity.

Ultimately, the world federalist does not succeed even in convincing himself that the tough job of controlling states can be exchanged for the presumably easy task of regulating individual behavior; he is forced to grapple with the problem of upholding world authority against rebellious states and to contemplate federal resort to war against such entities rather than mere arrest and imprisonment of perverse individuals. Moreover, he is compelled to acknowledge, implicitly at least, that the doctrine of individual subjection to world law does not emancipate a hypothetical world government from dependence upon the cooperation of states for the success of its operations. The most impressive scheme for world federation yet developed, that fashioned by Grenville Clark and Louis B. Sohn, envisages individual citizenship of the global state but is permeated by the assumption that national states will collaborate or can be required to collaborate in making the federal system work; for instance, the authors of the plan suggest that the instrumentalities of national governments should be relied upon to collect the taxes required for the support of the world federation, and to assist in the process of enforcing global law upon individual offenders.[22]

However deeply one might wish that the world could be governed by policemen wielding night sticks, the realities are such that a valid concept of world government must define the problem as it has been defined by

---

[21] *Ibid.*, pp. 15-20.

[22] *World Peace Through World Law* (Cambridge: Harvard University Press, 1958), pp. xxv, 40-41, 333.

international organization: how to cope with a multiplicity of national states. Once this is accepted, it becomes evident that there is no magic in the formal supplantation of international organization by world government, but that proposed methods of managing a pluralistic society must be judged on their merits, rather than on the basis of their being labeled "organizational" or "governmental."

Many of the difficulties which have been suggested for world government have been removed by its proponents by the convenient device of assuming them into oblivion. Thus, there is no serious problem of power in a global system because states will disarm and relieve the central regime of the necessity of maintaining huge forces which might pose the threat of world tyranny. The Clark and Sohn scheme is built upon the assumption of a preliminary general settlement of the basic issues between East and West, and relies heavily upon the probability that states can be induced, largely without coercion, to fulfill their obligations for making the federal system function satisfactorily.

This is all very well, but at this point it becomes clear that Schiffer could just as properly have turned his devastating attack upon the logic of world government as upon that of international organization. Does world government, any less than international organization, base its prospects for success upon the prior solution of problems which it is supposed to solve? Is the former less guilty than the latter of assuming the existence of conditions which, if they existed, would make it unnecessary, and which, if they did not exist, would make it unworkable? If, indeed, we can safely assume the end of the cold war, the voluntary elimination of major armaments, and the dependable performance of significant international responsibilities by states, there is every prospect that the United Nations will work quite well. If we cannot make these assumptions, world government and international organization alike fail to measure up to the ideal standards of a mechanism for giving mankind the assurance of a just and lasting peace.

The rejection of the thesis that world government is a theoretically ideal or a practically attainable approach to peace does not imply either a smug assurance that the world does not need to be governed or a pessimistic conviction that the world cannot be raised above the level of anarchy. The concluding chapter will deal with the progress and prospects of efforts to make world order a dependable reality.

SUGGESTED READINGS

Clark, Grenville, *A Plan for Peace,* New York: Harper, 1950.

Clark, Grenville, and Louis B. Sohn, *World Peace Through World Law,* Cambridge: Harvard University Press, 1958, 1960.

Claude, Inis L., Jr., *Power and International Relations,* New York: Random House, 1962.
Cousins, Norman, *In Place of Folly,* New York: Harper, 1961.
Mangone, Gerard J., *The Idea and Practice of World Government,* New York: Columbia University Press, 1951.
Meyer, Cord, *Peace or Anarchy,* Boston: Little, Brown, 1947.
Schuman, Frederick L., *The Commonwealth of Man,* New York: Knopf, 1952.
Wheare, K. C., *Federal Government,* New York: Oxford University Press, 1947.
White, E. B., *The Wild Flag,* Boston: Houghton Mifflin, n.d.

CHAPTER

19

International Organization and World Order

World federalists and champions of international organization can agree that the world needs techniques and institutions capable of preventing war and mobilizing human and material resources in a vast effort to create a good society which encompasses the whole earth. The fundamental difference between them is that the former think in terms of *governmental institutions* as the indispensable means for the realization of these purposes, whereas the latter emphasize the ideal of obtaining *governmental results* by whatever methods may be tried and found useful. To say that the world needs to be governed is not the same as saying that a world government must be erected.

The world requires methods and agencies adequate for performing reasonably well on a global scale the functions which governments have undertaken to perform and have occasionally managed to perform with great success in independent states; yet world government is not the only conceivable or necessarily the best possible means for meeting that requirement. To put it differently, the benefits which governments ideally and sometimes actually confer upon the societies in which they operate are desperately needed by the global society, but it is not certain that those advantages are most likely to be provided by institutions patterned after or closely analogous to the so-called "governmental" institutions of states. The instrumentalities appropriate to the solution of the world's problems may or may not constitute a system which looks like government, sounds like government, or acts like government. The test is functional performance, not institutional resemblance.

THE PROGRESS OF INTERNATIONAL ORGANIZATION

In functional terms, the process of international organization has brought greater progress toward a governed world than has been generally recognized, and certainly more than is acknowledged by those who adhere to the doctrinaire view that government and anarchy are the two halves of an absolute either-or formula.

The last century, and particularly the last generation, has been an era of continuous development of patterns and techniques for managing the business of the international community. The old story of the sociological lag emphasizes the important truth that mankind has far to go, but it tends to obscure the fact that we are living in a period of adventurous experiment and flourishing inventiveness in the field of international relations. The creation of such institutional innovations as the general international organization, the international secretariat, the international conference of the parliamentary type, the international field commission for investigation and supervision, the preventive diplomacy force, the international technical assistance mission, the multilateral defense machinery of the NATO type, and the supranational functional agency of the kind recently developed in the European Community testifies to the significance of that fact. Moreover, fruitful improvisation is being increasingly supplemented by more systematic activities. The invention of invention is not exclusively a phenomenon of the scientific world; the international community is now equipped as never before with the analytical tools, professional staff, and organizational framework for designing and instituting new instruments to meet its needs.

The achievements of international organization include notable gains in the field of noncoercive regulatory devices. The agencies of the United Nations system exercise substantial influence and control—in short, *power* —over the behavior of states through the exploitation of a variety of methods: consultation and advice; inquiry, debate, and criticism of both public and private varieties; examination of reports and conduct of inspections; granting and withdrawal of subsidies and other forms of assistance; and recommendation followed by evaluation of response to this sort of pressure and possibly by insistent reiteration.

International organization has made no such significant progress, nor has it demonstrated great promise, in the realm of coercive control of state behavior. True, the League engaged in a half-hearted effort to suppress Italian aggression in Ethiopia, and the United Nations sponsored the mobilization of collective resistance to Communist attack upon South Korea, with successful if not satisfactory results. And at the regional level, the Organization of American States has displayed some slight potentiality for organized enforcement action. Nevertheless, international coercion of states determined to pursue their objectives by force has not become, in any general sense, a meaningful possibility. The United Nations has offered to states no substitute for the policies of building national strength and entering into alliances as methods for deterring or defending against external attack. The strength of the global organization lies not in a capacity to frustrate aggression but in its capacity to encourage and facilitate mutual self-restraint on the part of states involved, actually or potentially, in disputes or other precarious relationships.

The primary resources for regulation of state behavior which have been discovered by the League and the United Nations fall into the category of persuasion and influence rather than edict and compulsion. The question of the implications to be drawn from this factual situation is of central importance for the evaluation of international organization.

The simplest and perhaps the most tempting response is to conclude that international organization offers no real antidote to global disorder. To say that it relies primarily upon regulatory devices which are noncoercive in character is to admit that it is doomed to ineffectuality. Hence, no reasonable man can avoid making a choice between two conclusions: either that statesmen should give up the illusion that a governed world is possible, and settle down to the serious business of power politics, or that leaders and peoples should recognize the imperativeness of making the jump to a genuine world federation. What is not tenable is the assumption that international organization makes sense for a world in which power is the fundamental reality. The only meaningful alternatives are the mobilization of power behind national interest, or the concentration of power in support of the law of a global government.

This response reveals a curiously narrow conception of the means by which government performs regulatory functions, and, in its world federalist version, an extraordinarily broad view of the regulatory potency of the coercive instruments which are associated with governments. The truth is that all governments rely heavily—and that the most desirable and durable governments rely predominantly—upon noncoercive methods for producing and maintaining social order. To say that international organization has distinguished itself most notably by creating a record of persistence, flexibility, and ingenuity in the development and exploitation of devices for inducing compliance by consent rather than compulsion is not to say that it has proved absolutely either the impossibility or the indispensability of creating a world government. Rather, it is to say that some of the basic means for governing the world have been evolved and are being utilized with increasing effectiveness by agencies which do not conform to theoretical models of governmental institutions. It is surprising how many estimable people, who would recoil with horror at the thought of a purely coercive government in the United States and insist with intelligent understanding that a decent political order in the nation must rest upon processes of inducement and adjustment rather than upon sheer force, seem to picture government solely in terms of a policeman beating criminals into submission when they shift their attention to the international scene. People are being governed at other times than when they cower before a policeman or languish in prison cells. Nations are being governed at other times than when they are being prohibited, restrained, and compelled.

The obvious answer is that noncoercive techniques of social regulation are not enough, either within a nation or among the nations; a system of international organization which must rely almost wholly upon an ability to induce compliance, unsupported by a reserve capacity to command and compel obedience, is not simply an incompletely equipped agency of world order but a fatally defective one.

This observation applies equally to a system which possesses the power to enforce without the capacity to persuade. The experience of governments makes it clear that recognition of the indispensability of force must be qualified by awareness both of its inherent inadequacy and of its limited attainability. Power is not enough, and there cannot in fact be enough power to guarantee against breaches of the peace. The project of endowing a world government with sufficient power to prevent disorder is not only dangerous, but it is ultimately infeasible. Only in a thoroughly atomistic society is there a real possibility that threats to order can be put down by coercion without results which amount to a disruption of social order. Such societies exist only in the minds of theorists and in the objectives of totalitarian dictators. In the real world, national societies are characterized by a pluralism which can never be entirely ground down even by the most determined dictator, and the international society exhibits a pluralistic nature which is so striking that virtually all world governmentalists defer to it by advancing proposals for global federation rather than unitary government. To admit this is in fact to concede that governmental coercion cannot keep the civil peace; it can at best win the civil war.

The American system of government, so often cited as evidence of the desirability of global federalism, serves as an instructive illustration of this point. The creation of federal government in the United States has not produced a situation in which Washington can maintain order by coercing the states which have handed over vital portions of their sovereignty to the union.

> The experience of the Civil War illustrates the fact that in a federal system where state loyalty is strong, the federal government and the state governments must act with constant vigilance to avoid forcing any deep dividing issue to the point where armed resistance comes into view. And if that point is reached no constitutional provisions about the control of the armed forces can prevent armed resistance and a conflict of loyalties for those in the forces of the general government.[1]

The United States Government maintains order among the component groups of its richly pluralistic national society, not by the distinctively governmental method of coercion, a method which is unavailable to the United Nations so long as it remains a mere international organization, but by techniques of persuasion, compromise, and inducement—precisely the sort of method which international organization has developed and is developing for the regulation of the affairs of nations. The truth is that it has no practicable alternative; major segments of American society—be they states, organized labor, the business community, religious bodies, or professional groups—are not so much subject to restraint by the threat of coercion as they are capable of forcing the initiation of a process of political adjustment by raising the threat of collective defiance of governmental authority. For practical purposes, there is no more possibility that Washington will forcibly impose its will upon the segregationist South, or the farm organizations, or the Catholic Church than that the United Nations will resort to compulsion against defiant and disorderly states. In opposition to this view, one might cite the fact that the United States Government has, in recent years, resorted to the use of troops in Little Rock, Arkansas, and in Oxford, Mississippi, to overcome resistance to the desegregation of educational facilities. However, it should be noted that the use of the military arm in these instances was regarded by all concerned as an exceptional expedient, not as a normal expression of Federal authority in dealing with recalcitrant state officials and local population groups. Before these cases arose, the prediction could not have been confidently made that even such limited resort to military pressure would occur; and since these cases have arisen, no thoughtful person has concluded that the problems posed by the racial segregation issue will or should be disposed of by massive military coercion, exercised by the Federal Government. Indeed, in 1963, President John F. Kennedy rebuffed the suggestion, advanced by the United States Commission on Civil Rights, that Washington use the weapon of financial deprivation to compel

[1] K. C. Wheare, *Federal Government* (New York: Oxford University Press, 1947), p. 204.

Mississippi to modify its policy in racial matters.[2] In rejecting the notion that he had, or should have, the authority to invoke even the relatively mild sanction of economic pressure against a defiant state, the President implicitly denied the general relevance of the stronger sanction, military coercion, to the problem of ordering relationships within the pluralism of American society. The facts of life in the United States are that the Federal Government will compromise with a recalcitrant state, not threaten to bomb its cities; it will consult with labor leaders and revise a controversial legislative policy, not send the army into pitched battle against the nationwide membership of aroused labor unions. And if, in some dire emergency, it *does* resort to coercion against a major segment of the national population or a regional bloc of states, this will symbolize not the majestic operation of the governmental principle in preserving social order, but the tragic failure of government to prevent the disruption of social order; the Federal Government will not be presiding over the peace, but conducting war.

It is striking how much *can* and *must*—even in a system of federal government—be done without the pressure of legal dictate and coercive threat. There are vital differences between the United States and the United Nations, but the contrast is not meaningfully stated by saying that the federation can rule by holding the threat of force over the major groups constituting the society which it governs, while the association is dependent upon the effectiveness of noncoercive methods in dealing with analogous entities within its domain. If a bitter conflict should arise between the groups of states east and west of the Mississippi River, the United States Government would be in very much the same position as the United Nations in the period of cold war, and its response to such a situation would be essentially the same; it would rely upon political methods for resolving the issues, just as the United Nations does, and if these methods failed, American society would dissolve into war, just as might happen in the case of global society. The evidence of American federalism does not support the thesis that the critical deficiency of the United Nations is its lack of power to coerce such states as the Soviet Union and that its transformation into a federation would, by remedying that lack, emancipate it from dependence upon methods of persuasion, discussion, and conciliation for maintaining world order. In relying upon such methods, the United Nations, which is not a government, is behaving as a government would have to behave in analogous circumstances.

This argument is only partially met by the thesis that it *is* coercion, but coercion applied against individuals rather than collective entities, which serves federal regimes as the ultimate safeguard of the peace. According to this view, the key to the achievement of international order is

---

[2] *New York Times,* April 20, 1963.

the shift from organizational reliance upon influencing states, to governmental dependence upon enforcing the law against individuals.

American experience lends only limited credibility to this view. It is true that Washington customarily checks collective entities—when they are willing to be checked—by holding their leaders legally responsible; but when a significant element of society exhibits a solidarity of disaffection, the government undertakes to negotiate with its leaders, not to hold the law over their heads, and to placate the group, not to treat it as a mass of individual law-breakers. No reasonable man would contend that the fiasco of the Eighteenth Amendment proved the capacity of government to uphold the law by applying it on an individual basis to a mass of determined violators, and it is doubtful that federal enforcement of desegregation in Southern schools against the wishes of states is rendered feasible by the fact that Washington has the theoretical capacity to imprison all state governors, legislators, and local school officials who defy its will. Governmental authority and power to deal with individuals is important, but it does not suffice to cope with either disobedience by an amorphous mass or resistance by an organized major segment of society in the United States.

Applying this lesson to the international scene, we may well look with skepticism upon the notion that the United Nations could prevent war if only it had the power to enforce its law upon individual citizens or leaders of member states. Governmental coercion of individuals is an effective instrument against scattered criminality and against the recalcitrance of groups which are not prepared to press the issue, but it is not a means of dissolving the solidarity of organized entities which are determined to insist upon the protection and advancement of their vital corporate interests as they conceive them. When such an entity presses its claims, the community has the choice of maintaining order by initiating a process of political compromise and adjustment, or of accepting the collapse of order and submitting the issue to the arbitrament of arms. The choice lies between war against a collective entity and political settlement with a collective entity; the alternative of pretending that the collective entity is a mere fiction and that relations with it can be dissolved into a series of relations between the massive community and the lonely individual does not realistically exist.

In the final analysis, the decisive difference between the United States and the United Nations as systems of order is to be discovered in the fact that the United States is, and the United Nations is not, a society in which the significance of constituent groups has been so reduced that they are unlikely to press their claims to the point of disrupting the social fabric. The difference lies in the nature of the communities. The United States enjoys a degree of stability far superior to that of the international community because its states, regions, interest groups, and other component parts require neither the threat nor the use of federal force to restrain them from launching civil war or revolution; they are amenable to the political settlement of most of the issues which affect them, and there is general agreement within the community that the tough residue of disputed issues will not be forced to a showdown. In contrast, the international community is composed of states which have not, to such a degree, lost the disposition to challenge the order of the community, by force if necessary. Something has happened to Texas that has not happened to the Soviet Union. It is not so much that Texas, unlike the Soviet Union, has been overshadowed by a coercive institutional superstructure, but that Texas, unlike the Soviet Union, has been incorporated in the consensual foundations of a larger community.

If this analysis is correct, then the key to a well governed world is not the endowment of the United Nations with plenary coercive capacity but the reproduction on a global scale of the conditions which have made the pluralistic society of the United States a community in which group conflicts do not normally pose the threat of violent upheavals. The difficulty is that no one can quite say how the United States got that way, but two major considerations may be suggested. One is that the dividing lines of American society have become so numerous and intertangled, the pluralism has become so complex, that no clean-cut divisions of loyalty and interest can be found; the community has not been thoroughly unified, but its divisions have been confused by a process of multiplication. Thus, Texas cannot pose the threat of civil war because there is no one who is wholly a Texan, and labor unions cannot launch a revolution because there is no one who is fully a unionist. The second consideration is that individual loyalties have not only been scattered among a variety of groups, but that some of them—including in most cases the ultimately decisive loyalties—have been detached from smaller entities and lodged in the national community itself. Texas cannot revolt against the United States because its people are more fundamentally Americans than they are Texans. These are perhaps the basic conditions which make the maintenance of order possible in the United States, and which must be reproduced in the international community if stable world order is to become a reality.

The development of these conditions in American society has occurred in large part independently of the influence of government and without conscious social direction and control. Nevertheless, it is clear that government has figured indispensably in the process of creating the foundations of the community upon which it rests. The world governmentalist is right in his rejection of the notion that nothing should or can be done about institutions until a full-fledged world community has somehow sprung into being. He is right, too, in his insistence that the relationship of the individual to the community is a factor of crucial importance. But the governmental contribution to the evolution of the American community has not been produced primarily by the coercive methods which the world governmentalist is so eager to place at the disposal of the United Nations. The United States Government has promoted the development of its social underpinnings by serving the people of the nation in a thousand ways, protecting their rights, welfare, and safety, facilitating mobility, communication, and free association among them, mobilizing them in common enterprises of war and peace, and cultivating a nationalist ideology. These methods have been more significant and effective in "making Americans" than the method of enforcing federal law against private citizens throughout the length and breadth of the land. The helping hand of federal service is a more impressive argument for national allegiance than the long arm of federal justice.

The conclusion to be drawn from this is that what the United Nations most needs for the purpose of helping to create a meaningful world community is not new instruments of coercion, but precisely the variety of tools for doing useful work in the world which it has been busily shaping. In these terms, a world which has recently devoted itself to creating and setting into operation an unprecedentedly elaborate system of international service agencies is to be credited with making an intelligent approach to peace. It is conceivable that the development of a public service corps is a more essential contribution to the creation of a community fit for law and order than the establishment of a police force.

In short, the conception of government as an agency which maintains order simply by commanding and compelling, prohibiting and punishing, has little relevance to a pluralistic national society and still less to a global society which is chiefly characterized by the depth of its divisions, the simplicity of its pluralistic pattern, and the underdevelopment of its capacity to superimpose a universal allegiance upon national loyalties. Given this kind of international community, the realization of the theoretical ideal of subjecting the world to unchallengeable authority would require the creation of an inordinately powerful world government; the fulfillment of the practical task of maintaining order in such a world involves the assiduous application of methods of compromise and adjustment. Here is a real paradox: the international community is so deficient in consensual foundations that it must theoretically be held together more by force than by consent, but it is marked by such decentralization of the resources of political and physical power that it must in practice be managed by agencies, whether they be called instruments of international organization or of world federation, which operate more by persuasion than by coercion. In the world as it is, there is no real alternative to efforts to achieve regulation of state behavior by noncoercive methods, and no more appropriate collective task than the provision of international services which may ultimately prove conducive to the breaking down of those features of the community structure which make reliance upon consent rather than coercion at once so necessary and so precarious. The regulatory methods and functional emphases of international organization may not conform to the image of government concocted by those who are impatient to abolish the problem of war by creating an entity which can, by definition, knock any and all national heads together, but they do correspond closely to the actual approach to the problem of maintaining order in a pluralistic society which the Federal Government of the United States has found essential. It is less significant that international organization is not a federal world government than that it is engaged in the effort to do the sort of thing that must be done, by the sort of method that can be used, to produce the sort of community than can, with proper management, sustain a peaceful existence. In this sense, the experiment of governing the world is now in operation, and the task of making the world governable is already being undertaken.

International organization has not been unaffected by the urge to solve the problem of world order by developing potentialities of coercion; recurrent expressions of interest in collective security and in the concept of an international military force testify to this point. Nevertheless, in actual operation, international organization reveals a fundamental commitment to the proposition that the nature of international society makes the preservation of peace dependent upon the stimulation of voluntary cooperation, the mobilization of moral restraint, the enlightenment of national self-interest, and the development of mutual understanding. The most urgent question of our time is not how to escape from the necessity of relying upon such methods as these, but how to make that necessity more tolerable. It is doubtful that the cause of world order is better served by agitated obsession with the danger that the essential consent of states to accept restraint and responsibility may not be forthcoming, than by constructive devotion to the task of developing more effective means for inducing that consent.

THE PROSPECTS OF INTERNATIONAL ORGANIZATION

To say that international organization does not represent a fundamentally mistaken approach to the problem of world order is not to assert that it is destined to succeed. The tough reality of the national divisions of world society makes the quest for agreed solutions of international problems a necessary enterprise, but the conflicting interests and purposes of national entities also make that quest a difficult one. Mankind is blessed by no cosmic guarantee that all its problems are soluble and all its dangers are avoidable.

The danger of imminent conflict between states possessing vast power is the overwhelming reality of our time. Only the coldest of comfort is to be derived from the observation that the existence of this danger is attributable to the nature of the international community rather than to the nature of the international architecture which was contrived in 1945. In this situation, it is all too clear that the United Nations can offer no guarantee of peace and security; at best, it can facilitate the balancing of power against power, and mobilize the resources of political adjustment. In the long run, international organization may transform the working of the multistate system. In the short run, it is inevitably more affected by the circumstances of international relations than effective in altering those circumstances.

There can be no guarantee that international machinery will in fact be utilized for the high purposes to which it may be formally dedicated. The establishment of an international organization does not involve the creation of an autonomous will, inexorably set upon the pursuit of the ideal of peace in a prescribed manner. Rather, it involves the creation of a mechanism to be placed at the disposal of states, which may use it for whatever purposes their agreements or their disagreements dictate. In practice, international organization may serve as the institutional framework for the joint exploration of approaches to peace, but it is also capable of serving as an arena for the conduct of international political warfare, or as an instrument for the advancement of the political objectives of a particular state or group of states.

International organization does not emancipate the world from dependence upon the quality of its statesmanship. Structural apparatus cannot generate its own supply of political decency, discretion, wisdom, and moderation. In the final analysis, both the possibilities and the limitations of international organization are set by political forces operative within and among member states. The deficiencies of the United Nations indicate a greater need for review and revision of national policies than of the Charter itself.

The most casual observer of the international scene can see that the problem of world order has not been solved. The most careful student of international organization can see that no world-saving miracles have been wrought, no infallible formula for solution of fundamental problems has been drafted, and no glorious certainty of a brave new world has been projected before the troubled eyes of modern man. But there is more to be seen than unsolved problems, unresolved conflicts, and unparalleled dangers of chaos and destruction. Fallibility is not the same as futility; limited achievement is not the same as unlimited failure; danger is not the same as doom.

The development of international organization represents both a realistic response to the requirements of doing national business in an increasingly complex international setting and an idealistic attempt to modify the operation of the multistate system so as to make civilized living possible in an increasingly interdependent world. For better or for worse, the world has abjured the Hobbesian solution of throwing up hastily contrived institutional structures resting upon nothing more substantial than desperate fear of mutual destruction, adopting instead the Ciceronian ideal of establishing institutions of common life upon the limited but solid foundations of *consensus juris* and *utilitatis communione*. The builders of international organization have on occasion overestimated the extent of international agreement upon fundamental issues of right and justice and international preparedness to sustain joint approaches to mutual advantage, but they have not subordinated considerations of foundational adequacy to conceptions of architectural grandeur.

The proliferation of agencies in the United Nations system, the simultaneous exploration of approaches to peace ranging from preventive diplomacy to technical assistance and from regulation of civil aviation to dissemination of artistic masterpieces, is evidence not merely of a weakness for indiscriminate experimentation but also of a growing recognition of the multifaceted character of the problem of world order and of the essential interconnectedness of the parts of its solution. The world is truly beginning to see its problems "in the round";[3] international organization provides "a world's eye view" [4] of basic problems which can hardly fail to affect the perspectives of governments. Awareness of the scope and complex interrelatedness of the problems at hand is the necessary starting point for satisfactory solutions.

The world is not only developing a more sophisticated conception of its problems, but it is also beginning to recognize that global problems require global solutions. International organization is something more than a gathering of national governments; it is, in a very rudimentary sense, an expression of the concept that there is an international community which bears responsibility for dealing with matters which refuse to be confined within national boundaries. Statesmen assemble at the United Nations to promote the interests of their national constituencies, but they cannot altogether escape the tendency to feel that they compose a collective body whose constituency is mankind. The international community has become a little bit more than a dream of idealists. There is a limited sense in which it is meaningful to speak of a United Nations which imposes a principle of international accountability upon its member states, asserts its jurisdiction in areas previously encompassed by the functional boundaries of sovereignty, and assumes responsibility for doing as much of what must be done as can be done, on behalf of humanity.

The long-range effects of international organization upon the multistate system cannot be confidently predicted. It may be regarded as a

---

[3] Feller, *United Nations and World Community*, p. 119.

[4] Philip V. Cardon, "The Earth's Resources in the Service of Man," *United Nations Review*, July 1955, p. 20.

process of evolutionary unification; yet, it functions now to support the fragmentation of empires into groups of newly independent states. It may be regarded as a process of gradual replacement of national governments as the major agencies for the management of human affairs; yet, it operates now less to deprive governments of their domestic functions than to assist them in acquiring the competence to do their jobs more effectively. It may be regarded as a process leading to the eventual transcendence of the multistate system; yet, its immediate function is to reform and supplement the system, so as to make the maintenance of legal, political, and administrative pluralism compatible with the requirements of an interdependent world.

It is perhaps necessary to stress again the distinction between international *organizations* and international *organization*. Particular organizations may be nothing more than playthings of power politics and handmaidens of national ambitions. But international organization, considered as an historical process, represents a secular trend toward the systematic development of an enterprising quest for political means of making the world safe for human habitation. It may fail, and peter out ignominiously. But if it maintains the momentum which it has built up in the twentieth century, it may yet effect a transformation of human relationships on this planet which will at some indeterminate point justify the assertion that the world has come to be governed—that mankind has become a community capable of sustaining order, promoting justice, and establishing the conditions of that good life which Aristotle took to be the supreme aim of politics.

This is the conception of international organization that Arthur Sweetser had in mind when, on the occasion of his retirement after thirty-four years of active membership in the first generation of international civil servants, he addressed his colleagues of the United Nations staff:

> You were born out of the labor and travail of these older days [of the League]; you are the successors of those who tried to build before you, got swept temporarily away, but still left foundations to which you could anchor. You have built prodigiously upon them; I would not, in those first days of 1920, have dared dream you would get so far so fast. Don't underestimate this progress.
>
> The great lesson of all this effort and suffering, even frequent disappointment, is that you are right, eternally right, in the fight you are making. You have got hold of the big things of life; you are on the road to the future; you are working for all the ends that make life worth while on this planet—for peace, for the eradication of war, for human advancement, for human rights and decencies, for better living standards, better education, better health, better food, better homes, better labor conditions, better travel and communications—in short, for the world as it ought to be.
>
> This is the highest secular cause on earth. You deserve to be

> immensely proud of what you are doing, especially that you are privileged to be part of the permanent staff. During your low and grim moments, lift your eyes, I beg you, to these vaster horizons beyond; rise up out of the irritations and anxieties of the moment and realize that you have opportunities permitted to very few indeed.
>
> You cannot feel too strongly that the right is on your side and that your cause will win in the long run; it is your opponents who are wrong and on the losing side.[5]

Sweetser's words proved nothing. They were an expression of faith—that faith in the moral capacity and the rational capacity of man which provides the philosophical underpinning of international organization. That faith may be mistaken, but it is not wrong, or ignoble, or unworthy of any man. It represents modern man at something very near his best.

SUGGESTED READINGS

Carr, E. H., *Nationalism and After,* London: Macmillan, 1945.

Commission to Study the Organization of Peace (Arthur N. Holcombe, Chairman), *Strengthening the United Nations,* New York: Harper, 1957.

Feller, A. H., *United Nations and World Community,* Boston: Little, Brown, 1952.

Jessup, Philip C., *The International Problem of Governing Mankind,* Claremont, Calif.: Claremont College, 1947.

Niebuhr, Reinhold, *The Children of Light and the Children of Darkness,* New York: Scribner's, 1950.

[5] *United Nations Bulletin,* February 1, 1953, p. 123.

Appendixes

APPENDIX I

The Covenant of the League of Nations*

The High Contracting Parties

In order to promote international co-operation and to achieve international peace and security

by the acceptance of obligations not to resort to war,
by the prescription of open, just and honourable relations between nations,
by the firm establishment of the understandings of international law as the actual rule of conduct among Governments,
and by the maintenance of justice and a scrupulous respect for all treaty obligations in the dealings of organised peoples with one another,
Agree to this Covenant of the League of Nations.

Article 1

1. The original Members of the League of Nations shall be those of the Signatories which are named in the Annex to this Covenant and also such of those other States named in the Annex as shall accede without reservation to this Covenant. Such accession shall be effected by a Declaration deposited with the Secretariat within two months of the coming into force of the Covenant. Notice thereof shall be sent to all other Members of the League.

2. Any fully self-governing State, Dominion or Colony not named in the Annex may become a Member of the League if its admission is agreed to by two-thirds of the Assembly, provided that it shall give effective guarantees of its sincere

---

* The texts printed in italics indicate amendments adopted by the League.

intention to observe its international obligations, and shall accept such regulations as may be prescribed by the League in regard to its military, naval and air forces and armaments.

3. Any Member of the League may, after two years' notice of its intention so to do, withdraw from the League, provided that all its international obligations and all its obligations under this Covenant shall have been fulfilled at the time of its withdrawal.

Article 2

The action of the League under this Covenant shall be effected through the instrumentality of an Assembly and of a Council, with a permanent Secretariat.

Article 3

1. The Assembly shall consist of Representatives of the Members of the League.

2. The Assembly shall meet at stated intervals and from time to time as occasion may require at the Seat of the League or at such other place as may be decided upon.

3. The Assembly may deal at its meetings with any matter within the sphere of action of the League or affecting the peace of the world.

4. At meetings of the Assembly, each Member of the League shall have one vote, and may have not more than three Representatives.

Article 4

1. The Council shall consist of Representatives of the Principal Allied and Associated Powers, together with Representatives of four other Members of the League. These four Members of the League shall be selected by the Assembly from time to time in its discretion. Until the appointment of the Representatives of the four Members of the League first selected by the Assembly, Representatives of Belgium, Brazil, Spain and Greece shall be members of the Council.

2. With the approval of the majority of the Assembly, the Council may name additional Members of the League whose Representatives shall always be Members of the Council; the Council with like approval may increase the number of Members of the League to be selected by the Assembly for representation on the Council.

2. *bis. The Assembly shall fix by a two-thirds majority the rules dealing with the election of the non-permanent Members of the Council, and particularly such regulations as relate to their term of office and the conditions of re-eligibility.*

3. The Council shall meet from time to time as occasion may require, and at least once a year, at the Seat of the League, or at such other place as may be decided upon.

4. The Council may deal at its meetings with any matter within the sphere of action of the League or affecting the peace of the world.

5. Any Member of the League not represented on the Council shall be invited to send a Representative to sit as a member at any meeting of the Council during the consideration of matters specially affecting the interests of that Member of the League.

6. At meetings of the Council, each Member of the League represented on the Council shall have one vote, and may have not more than one Representative.

Article 5

1. Except where otherwise expressly provided in this Covenant or by the terms of the present Treaty, decisions at any meeting of the Assembly or of the Council shall require the agreement of all the Members of the League represented at the meeting.

2. All matters of procedure at meetings of the Assembly or of the Council,

including the appointment of Committees to investigate particular matters, shall be regulated by the Assembly or by the Council and may be decided by a majority of the Members of the League represented at the meeting.

3. The first meeting of the Assembly and the first meeting of the Council shall be summoned by the President of the United States of America.

Article 6

1. The permanent Secretariat shall be established at the Seat of the League. The Secretariat shall comprise a Secretary-General and such secretaries and staff as may be required.

2. The first Secretary-General shall be the person named in the Annex; thereafter the Secretary-General shall be appointed by the Council with the approval of the majority of the Assembly.

3. The secretaries and staff of the Secretariat shall be appointed by the Secretary-General with the approval of the Council.

4. The Secretary-General shall act in that capacity at all meetings of the Assembly and of the Council.

5. *The expenses of the League shall be borne by the Members of the League in the proportion decided by the Assembly.*

Article 7

1. The Seat of the League is established at Geneva.

2. The Council may at any time decide that the Seat of the League shall be established elsewhere.

3. All positions under or in connection with the League, including the Secretariat, shall be open equally to men and women.

4. Representatives of the Members of the League and officials of the League when engaged on the business of the League shall enjoy diplomatic privileges and immunities.

5. The buildings and other property occupied by the League or its officials or by Representatives attending its meetings shall be inviolable.

Article 8

1. The Members of the League recognise that the maintenance of peace requires the reduction of national armaments to the lowest point consistent with national safety and the enforcement by common action of international obligations.

2. The Council, taking account of the geographical situation and circumstances of each State, shall formulate plans for such reduction for the consideration and action of the several Governments.

3. Such plans shall be subject to reconsideration and revision at least every ten years.

4. After these plans have been adopted by the several Governments, the limits of armaments therein fixed shall not be exceeded without the concurrence of the Council.

5. The Members of the League agree that the manufacture by private enterprise of munitions and implements of war is open to grave objections. The Council shall advise how the evil effects attendant upon such manufacture can be prevented, due regard being had to the necessities of those Members of the League which are not able to manufacture the munitions and implements of war necessary for their safety.

6. The Members of the League undertake to interchange full and frank information as to the scale of their armaments, their military, naval and air programmes and the condition of such of their industries as are adaptable to warlike purposes.

Article 9

A permanent Commission shall be constituted to advise the Council on the execution of the provisions of Articles 1 and 8 and on military, naval and air questions generally.

Article 10

The Members of the League undertake to respect and preserve as against external aggression the territorial integrity and existing political independence of all Members of the League. In case of any such aggression or in case of any threat or danger of such aggression, the Council shall advise upon the means by which this obligation shall be fulfilled.

Article 11

1. Any war or threat of war, whether immediately affecting any of the Members of the League or not, is hereby declared a matter of concern to the whole League, and the League shall take any action that may be deemed wise and effectual to safeguard the peace of nations. In case any such emergency should arise, the Secretary-General shall, on the request of any Member of the League, forthwith summon a meeting of the Council.

2. It is also declared to be the friendly right of each Member of the League to bring to the attention of the Assembly or of the Council any circumstance whatever affecting international relations which threatens to disturb international peace or the good understanding between nations upon which peace depends.

Article 12

1. The Members of the League agree that if there should arise between them any dispute likely to lead to a rupture they will submit the matter either to arbitration *or judicial settlement* or to enquiry by the Council, and they agree in no case to resort to war until three months after the award by the arbitrators *or the judicial decision* or the report by the Council.

2. In any case under this article the award of the arbitrators *or the judicial decision* shall be made within a reasonable time, and the report of the Council shall be made within six months after the submission of the dispute.

Article 13

1. The Members of the League agree that whenever any dispute shall arise between them which they recognise to be suitable for submission to arbitration *or judicial settlement,* and which cannot be satisfactorily settled by diplomacy, they will submit the whole subject-matter to arbitration *or judicial settlement.*

2. Disputes as to the interpretation of a treaty, as to any question of international law, as to the existence of any fact which, if established, would constitute a breach of any international obligation, or as to the extent and nature of the reparation to be made for any such breach, are declared to be among those which are generally suitable for submission to arbitration *or judicial settlement.*

3. *For the consideration of any such dispute, the court to which the case is referred shall be the Permanent Court of International Justice, established in accordance with Article* 14, *or any tribunal agreed on by the parties to the dispute or stipulated in any Convention existing between them.*

4. The Members of the League agree that they will carry out in full good faith any award *or decision* that may be rendered, and that they will not resort to war against a Member of the League which complies therewith. In the event of any failure

to carry out such an award *or decision,* the Council shall propose what steps should be taken to give effect thereto.

Article 14

The Council shall formulate and submit to the Members of the League for adoption plans for the establishment of a Permanent Court of International Justice. The Court shall be competent to hear and determine any dispute of an international character which the parties thereto submit to it. The Court may also give an advisory opinion upon any dispute or question referred to it by the Council or by the Assembly.

Article 15

1. If there should arise between Members of the League any dispute likely to lead to a rupture, which is not submitted to arbitration *or judicial settlement* in accordance with Article 13, the Members of the League agree that they will submit the matter to the Council. Any party to the dispute may effect such submission by giving notice of the existence of the dispute to the Secretary-General, who will make all necessary arrangements for a full investigation and consideration thereof.

2. For this purpose, the parties to the dispute will communicate to the Secretary-General, as promptly as possible, statements of their case with all the relevant facts and papers, and the Council may forthwith direct the publication thereof.

3. The Council shall endeavour to effect a settlement of the dispute, and if such efforts are successful, a statement shall be made public giving such facts and explanations regarding the dispute and the terms of settlement thereof as the Council may deem appropriate.

4. If the dispute is not thus settled, the Council either unanimously or by a majority vote shall make and publish a report containing a statement of the facts of the dispute and the recommendations which are deemed just and proper in regard thereto.

5. Any Member of the League represented on the Council may make public a statement of the facts of the dispute and of its conclusions regarding the same.

6. If a report by the Council is unanimously agreed to by the members thereof other than the Representatives of one or more of the parties to the dispute, the Members of the League agree that they will not go to war with any party to the dispute which complies with the recommendations of the report.

7. If the Council fails to reach a report which is unanimously agreed to by the members thereof, other than the Representatives of one or more of the parties to the dispute, the Members of the League reserve to themselves the right to take such action as they shall consider necessary for the maintenance of right and justice.

8. If the dispute between the parties is claimed by one of them, and is found by the Council, to arise out of a matter which by international law is solely within the domestic jurisdiction of that party, the Council shall so report, and shall make no recommendation as to its settlement.

9. The Council may in any case under this article refer the dispute to the Assembly. The dispute shall be so referred at the request of either party to the dispute provided that such request be made within fourteen days after the submission of the dispute to the Council.

10. In any case referred to the Assembly, all the provisions of this article and of Article 12 relating to the action and powers of the Council shall apply to the action and powers of the Assembly, provided that a report made by the Assembly, if concurred in by the Representatives of those Members of the League represented on the Council and of a majority of the other Members of the League, exclusive in each

case of the Representatives of the parties to the dispute, shall have the same force as a report by the Council concurred in by all the members thereof other than the Representatives of one or more of the parties to the dispute.

Article 16

1. Should any Member of the League resort to war in disregard of its covenants under Articles 12, 13 or 15, it shall, *ipso facto,* be deemed to have committed an act of war against all other Members of the League, which hereby undertake immediately to subject it to the severance of all trade or financial relations, the prohibition of all intercourse between their nationals and the nationals of the Covenant-breaking State, and the prevention of all financial, commercial or personal intercourse between the nationals of the Covenant-breaking State and the nationals of any other State, whether a Member of the League or not.

2. It shall be the duty of the Council in such case to recommend to the several Governments concerned what effective military, naval or air force the Members of the League shall severally contribute to the armed forces to be used to protect the covenants of the League.

3. The Members of the League agree, further, that they will mutually support one another in the financial and economic measures which are taken under this article, in order to minimise the loss and inconvenience resulting from the above measures, and that they will mutually support one another in resisting any special measures aimed at one of their number by the Covenant-breaking State, and that they will take the necessary steps to afford passage through their territory to the forces of any of the Members of the League which are co-operating to protect the covenants of the League.

4. Any member of the League which has violated any covenant of the League may be declared to be no longer a Member of the League by a vote of the Council concurred in by the Representatives of all the other Members of the League represented thereon.

Article 17

1. In the event of a dispute between a Member of the League and a State which is not a member of the League or between States not members of the League, the State or States not members of the League shall be invited to accept the obligations of membership in the League for the purposes of such dispute, upon such conditions as the Council may deem just. If such invitation is accepted, the provisions of Articles 12 to 16 inclusive shall be applied with such modifications as may be deemed necessary by the Council.

2. Upon such invitation being given, the Council shall immediately institute an enquiry into the circumstances of the dispute and recommend such action as may seem best and most effectual in the circumstances.

3. If a State so invited shall refuse to accept the obligations of membership in the League for the purposes of such dispute, and shall resort to war against a Member of the League, the provisions of Article 16 shall be applicable as against the State taking such action.

4. If both parties to the dispute when so invited refuse to accept the obligations of membership in the League for the purposes of such dispute, the Council may take such measures and make such recommendations as will prevent hostilities and will result in the settlement of the dispute.

Article 18

Every treaty or international engagement entered into hereafter by any Member of the League shall be forthwith registered with the Secretariat and shall, as soon as possible, be published by it. No such treaty or international engagement shall be binding until so registered.

Article 19

The Assembly may from time to time advise the reconsideration by Members of the League of treaties which have become inapplicable and the consideration of international conditions whose continuance might endanger the peace of the world.

Article 20

1. The Members of the League severally agree that this Covenant is accepted as abrogating all obligations or understandings *inter se* which are inconsistent with the terms thereof, and solemnly undertake that they will not hereafter enter into any engagements inconsistent with the terms thereof.

2. In case any Member of the League shall, before becoming a Member of the League, have undertaken any obligations inconsistent with the terms of this Covenant, it shall be the duty of such Member to take immediate steps to procure its release from such obligations.

Article 21

Nothing in this Covenant shall be deemed to affect the validity of international engagements, such as treaties of arbitration or regional understandings like the Monroe doctrine, for securing the maintenance of peace.

Article 22

1. To those colonies and territories which as a consequence of the late war have ceased to be under the sovereignty of the States which formerly governed them and which are inhabited by peoples not yet able to stand by themselves under the strenuous conditions of the modern world, there should be applied the principle that the well-being and development of such peoples form a sacred trust of civilisation and that securities for the performance of this trust should be embodied in this Covenant.

2. The best method of giving practical effect to this principle is that the tutelage of such peoples should be entrusted to advanced nations who, by reason of their resources, their experience or their geographical position, can best undertake this responsibility, and who are willing to accept it, and that this tutelage should be exercised by them as Mandatories on behalf of the League.

3. The character of the mandate must differ according to the stage of the development of the people, the geographical situation of the territory, its economic conditions and other similar circumstances.

4. Certain communities formerly belonging to the Turkish Empire have reached a stage of development where their existence as independent nations can be provisionally recognised subject to the rendering of administrative advice and assistance by a Mandatory until such time as they are able to stand alone. The wishes of these communities must be a principal consideration in the selection of the Mandatory.

5. Other peoples, especially those of Central Africa, are at such a stage that the Mandatory must be responsible for the administration of the territory under conditions which will guarantee freedom of conscience and religion, subject only to the maintenance of public order and morals, the prohibition of abuses such as the slave trade, the arms traffic and the liquor traffic, and the prevention of the establishment of fortifications or military and naval bases and of military training of the natives for other than police purposes and the defence of territory, and will also secure equal opportunities for the trade and commerce of other Members of the League.

6. There are territories, such as South West Africa and certain of the South Pacific Islands, which, owing to the sparseness of their population, or their small size, or their remoteness from the centres of civilisation, or their geographical contiguity to the territory of the Mandatory, and other circumstances, can be best administered under the laws of the Mandatory as integral portions of its territory, subject to the safeguards above mentioned in the interests of the indigenous population.

7. In every case of mandate, the Mandatory shall render to the Council an annual report in reference to the territory committed to its charge.

8. The degree of authority, control or administration to be exercised by the Mandatory shall, if not previously agreed upon by the Members of the League, be explicitly defined in each case by the Council.

9. A permanent Commission shall be constituted to receive and examine the annual reports of the Mandatories and to advise the Council on all matters relating to the observance of the mandates.

Article 23

Subject to and in accordance with the provisions of international Conventions existing or hereafter to be agreed upon, the Members of the League:

(*a*) will endeavour to secure and maintain fair and humane conditions of labour for men, women and children, both in their own countries and in all countries to which their commercial and industrial relations extend, and for that purpose will establish and maintain the necessary international organisations;
(*b*) undertake to secure just treatment of the native inhabitants of territories under their control;
(*c*) will entrust the League with the general supervision over the execution of agreements with regard to the traffic in women and children, and the traffic in opium and other dangerous drugs;
(*d*) will entrust the League with the general supervision of the trade in arms and ammunition with the countries in which the control of this traffic is necessary in the common interest;
(*e*) will make provision to secure and maintain freedom of communications and of transit and equitable treatment for the commerce of all Members of the League. In this connection, the special necessities of the regions devastated during the war of 1914-1918 shall be borne in mind;
(*f*) will endeavour to take steps in matters of international concern for the prevention and control of disease.

Article 24

1. There shall be placed under the direction of the League all international bureaux already established by general treaties if the parties to such treaties consent. All such international bureaux and all commissions for the regulation of matters of international interest hereafter constituted shall be placed under the direction of the League.

2. In all matters of international interest which are regulated by general Conventions but which are not placed under the control of international bureaux or commissions, the Secretariat of the League shall, subject to the consent of the Council and if desired by the parties, collect and distribute all relevant information and shall render any other assistance which may be necessary or desirable.

3. The Council may include as part of the expenses of the Secretariat the expenses of any bureau or commission which is placed under the direction of the League.

Article 25

The Members of the League agree to encourage and promote the establishment and co-operation of duly authorised voluntary national Red Cross organisations having as purposes the improvement of health, the prevention of disease and the mitigation of suffering throughout the world.

Article 26

1. Amendments to this Covenant will take effect when ratified by the Members of the League whose Representatives compose the Council and by a majority of the Members of the League whose Representatives compose the Assembly.

2. No such amendments shall bind any Member of the League which signifies its dissent therefrom, but in that case it shall cease to be a Member of the League.

APPENDIX II

The Charter of the United Nations

We the peoples of the United Nations determined

to save succeeding generations from the scourge of war, which twice in our lifetime has brought untold sorrow to mankind, and

to reaffirm faith in fundamental human rights, in the dignity and worth of the human person, in the equal rights of men and women and of nations large and small, and

to establish conditions under which justice and respect for the obligations arising from treaties and other sources of international law can be maintained, and

to promote social progress and better standards of life in larger freedom,

and for these ends

to practice tolerance and live together in peace with one another as good neighbors, and

to unite our strength to maintain international peace and security, and

to ensure, by the acceptance of principles and the institution of methods, that armed force shall not be used, save in the common interest, and

to employ international machinery for the promotion of the economic and social advancement of all peoples,

have resolved to combine our efforts to accomplish these aims.

Accordingly, our respective Governments, through representatives assembled in the city of San Francisco, who have exhibited their full powers found to be in good and due form, have agreed to the present Charter of the United Nations and do hereby establish an international organization to be known as the United Nations.

CHAPTER I *Purposes and Principles*

Article 1

The Purposes of the United Nations are:

1. To maintain international peace and security, and to that end: to take effective collective measures for the prevention and removal of threats to the peace, and for the suppression of acts of aggression or other breaches of the peace, and to bring about by peaceful means, and in conformity with the principles of justice and international law, adjustment or settlement of international disputes or situations which might lead to a breach of the peace;

2. To develop friendly relations among nations based on respect for the principle of equal rights and self-determination of peoples, and to take other appropriate measures to strengthen universal peace;

3. To achieve international cooperation in solving international problems of an economic, social, cultural, or humanitarian character, and in promoting and encouraging respect for human rights and for fundamental freedoms for all without distinction as to race, sex, language, or religion; and

4. To be a center for harmonizing the actions of nations in the attainment of these common ends.

Article 2

The Organization and its Members, in pursuit of the Purposes stated in Article 1, shall act in accordance with the following Principles.

1. The Organization is based on the principle of the sovereign equality of all its Members.

2. All Members, in order to ensure to all of them the rights and benefits resulting from membership, shall fulfil in good faith the obligations assumed by them in accordance with the present Charter.

3. All Members shall settle their international disputes by peaceful means in such a manner that international peace and security, and justice, are not endangered.

4. All Members shall refrain in their international relations from the threat or use of force against the territorial integrity or political independence of any state, or in any other manner inconsistent with the Purposes of the United Nations.

5. All Members shall give the United Nations every assistance in any action it takes in accordance with the present Charter, and shall refrain from giving assistance to any state against which the United Nations is taking preventive or enforcement action.

6. The Organization shall ensure that states which are not Members of the United Nations act in accordance with these Principles so far as may be necessary for the maintenance of international peace and security.

7. Nothing contained in the present Charter shall authorize the United Nations to intervene in matters which are essentially within the domestic jurisdiction of any state or shall require the Members to submit such matters to settlement under the

present Charter; but this principle shall not prejudice the application of enforcement measures under Chapter VII.

CHAPTER II *Membership*

Article 3

The original Members of the United Nations shall be the states which, having participated in the United Nations Conference on International Organization at San Francisco, or having previously signed the Declaration by United Nations of January 1, 1942, sign the present Charter and ratify it in accordance with Article 110.

Article 4

1. Membership in the United Nations is open to all other peace-loving states which accept the obligations contained in the present Charter and, in the judgment of the Organization, are able and willing to carry out these obligations.

2. The admission of any such state to membership in the United Nations will be effected by a decision of the General Assembly upon the recommendation of the Security Council.

Article 5

A Member of the United Nations against which preventive or enforcement action has been taken by the Security Council may be suspended from the exercise of the rights and privileges of membership by the General Assembly upon the recommendation of the Security Council. The exercise of these rights and privileges may be restored by the Security Council.

Article 6

A Member of the United Nations which has persistently violated the Principles contained in the present Charter may be expelled from the Organization by the General Assembly upon the recommendation of the Security Council.

CHAPTER III *Organs*

Article 7

1. There are established as the principal organs of the United Nations: a General Assembly, a Security Council, an Economic and Social Council, a Trusteeship Council, an International Court of Justice, and a Secretariat.

2. Such subsidiary organs as may be found necessary may be established in accordance with the present Charter.

Article 8

The United Nations shall place no restrictions on the eligibility of men and women to participate in any capacity and under conditions of equality in its principal and subsidiary organs.

CHAPTER IV *The General Assembly*

COMPOSITION

Article 9

1. The General Assembly shall consist of all the Members of the United Nations.

2. Each Member shall have not more than five representatives in the General Assembly.

FUNCTIONS AND POWERS

Article 10

The General Assembly may discuss any questions or any matters within the scope of the present Charter or relating to the powers and functions of any organs provided for in the present Charter, and, except as provided in Article 12, may make recommendations to the Members of the United Nations or to the Security Council or to both on any such questions or matters.

Article 11

1. The General Assembly may consider the general principles of cooperation in the maintenance of international peace and security, including the principles governing disarmament and the regulation of armaments, and may make recommendations with regard to such principles to the Members or to the Security Council or to both.

2. The General Assembly may discuss any questions relating to the maintenance of international peace and security brought before it by any Member of the United Nations, or by the Security Council, or by a state which is not a Member of the United Nations in accordance with Article 35, paragraph 2, and, except as provided in Article 12, may make recommendations with regard to any such questions to the state or states concerned or to the Security Council or to both. Any such question on which action is necessary shall be referred to the Security Council by the General Assembly either before or after discussion.

3. The General Assembly may call the attention of the Security Council to situations which are likely to endanger international peace and security.

4. The powers of the General Assembly set forth in this Article shall not limit the general scope of Article 10.

Article 12

1. While the Security Council is exercising in respect of any dispute or situation the functions assigned to it in the present Charter, the General Assembly shall not make any recommendations with regard to that dispute or situation unless the Security Council so requests.

2. The Secretary-General, with the consent of the Security Council, shall notify the General Assembly at each session of any matters relative to the maintenance of international peace and security which are being dealt with by the Security Council and shall similarly notify the General Assembly, or the Members of the United

Nations if the General Assembly is not in session, immediately the Security Council ceases to deal with such matters.

Article 13

1. The General Assembly shall initiate studies and make recommendations for the purpose of:

a. promoting international cooperation in the political field and encouraging the progressive development of international law and its codification;

b. promoting international cooperation in the economic, social, cultural, educational, and health fields, and assisting in the realization of human rights and fundamental freedoms for all without distinction as to race, sex, language, or religion.

2. The further responsibilities, functions, and powers of the General Assembly with respect to matters mentioned in paragraph 1 (b) above are set forth in Chapters IX and X.

Article 14

Subject to the provisions of Article 12, the General Assembly may recommend measures for the peaceful adjustment of any situation, regardless of origin, which it deems likely to impair the general welfare or friendly relations among nations, including situations resulting from a violation of the provisions of the present Charter setting forth the Purposes and Principles of the United Nations.

Article 15

1. The General Assembly shall receive and consider annual and special reports from the Security Council; these reports shall include an account of the measures that the Security Council has decided upon or taken to maintain international peace and security.

2. The General Assembly shall receive and consider reports from the other organs of the United Nations.

Article 16

The General Assembly shall perform such functions with respect to the international trusteeship system as are assigned to it under Chapters XII and XIII, including the approval of the trusteeship agreements for areas not designated as strategic.

Article 17

1. The General Assembly shall consider and approve the budget of the Organization.

2. The expenses of the Organization shall be borne by the Members as apportioned by the General Assembly.

3. The General Assembly shall consider and approve any financial and budgetary arrangements with specialized agencies referred to in Article 57 and shall examine the administrative budgets of such specialized agencies with a view to making recommendations to the agencies concerned.

VOTING

Article 18

1. Each member of the General Assembly shall have one vote.

2. Decisions of the General Assembly on important questions shall be made by a two-thirds majority of the members present and voting. These questions shall include: recommendations with respect to the maintenance of international peace and security, the election of the non-permanent members of the Security Council, the election of the members of the Economic and Social Council, the election of members of the Trusteeship Council in accordance with paragraph 1 (c) of Article 86, the admission of new Members to the United Nations, the suspension of the rights and privileges of membership, the expulsion of Members, questions relating to the operation of the trusteeship system, and budgetary questions.

3. Decisions on other questions, including the determination of additional categories of questions to be decided by a two-thirds majority, shall be made by a majority of the members present and voting.

Article 19

A Member of the United Nations which is in arrears in the payment of its financial contributions to the Organization shall have no vote in the General Assembly if the amount of its arrears equals or exceeds the amount of the contributions due from it for the preceding two full years. The General Assembly may, nevertheless, permit such a Member to vote if it is satisfied that the failure to pay is due to conditions beyond the control of the Member.

PROCEDURE

Article 20

The General Assembly shall meet in regular annual sessions and in such special sessions as occasion may require. Special sessions shall be convoked by the Secretary-General at the request of the Security Council or of a majority of the Members of the United Nations.

Article 21

The General Assembly shall adopt its own rules of procedure. It shall elect its President for each session.

Article 22

The General Assembly may establish such subsidiary organs as it deems necessary for the performance of its functions.

CHAPTER V *The Security Council*

COMPOSITION

Article 23

1. The Security Council shall consist of eleven Members of the United Nations. The Republic of China, France, the Union of Soviet Socialist Republics, the United Kingdom of Great Britain and Northern Ireland, and the United States of America shall be permanent members of the Security Council. The General Assembly shall elect six other Members of the United Nations to be non-permanent members of the Security Council, due regard being specially paid, in the first instance to the contribution of Members of the United Nations to the maintenance of international peace and security and to the other purposes of the Organization, and also to equitable geographical distribution.

2. The non-permanent members of the Security Council shall be elected for a term of two years. In the first election of the non-permanent members, however, three shall be chosen for a term of one year. A retiring member shall not be eligible for immediate re-election.

3. Each member of the Security Council shall have one representative.

FUNCTIONS AND POWERS

Article 24

1. In order to ensure prompt and effective action by the United Nations, its Members confer on the Security Council primary responsibility for the maintenance of international peace and security, and agree that in carrying out its duties under this responsibility the Security Council acts on their behalf.

2. In discharging these duties the Security Council shall act in accordance with the Purposes and Principles of the United Nations. The specific powers granted to the Security Council for the discharge of these duties are laid down in Chapters VI, VII, VIII, and XII.

3. The Security Council shall submit annual and, when necessary, special reports to the General Assembly for its consideration.

Article 25

The Members of the United Nations agree to accept and carry out the decisions of the Security Council in accordance with the present Charter.

Article 26

In order to promote the establishment and maintenance of international peace and security with the least diversion for armaments of the world's human and economic resources, the Security Council shall be responsible for formulating, with the assistance of the Military Staff Committee referred to in Article 47, plans to be submitted to the Members of the United Nations for the establishment of a system for the regulation of armaments.

VOTING

Article 27

1. Each member of the Security Council shall have one vote.

2. Decisions of the Security Council on procedural matters shall be made by an affirmative vote of seven members.

3. Decisions of the Security Council on all other matters shall be made by an affirmative vote of seven members including the concurring votes of the permanent members; provided that, in decisions under Chapter VI, and under paragraph 3 of Article 52, a party to a dispute shall abstain from voting.

PROCEDURE

Article 28

1. The Security Council shall be so organized as to be able to function continuously. Each member of the Security Council shall for this purpose be represented at all times at the seat of the Organization.

2. The Security Council shall hold periodic meetings at which each of its members may, if it so desires, be represented by a member of the government or by some other specially designated representative.

3. The Security Council may hold meetings at such places other than the seat of the Organization as in its judgment will best facilitate its work.

Article 29

The Security Council may establish such subsidiary organs as it deems necessary for the performance of its functions.

Article 30

The Security Council shall adopt its own rules of procedure, including the method of selecting its President.

Article 31

Any Member of the United Nations which is not a member of the Security Council may participate, without vote, in the discussion of any question brought before the Security Council whenever the latter considers that the interests of that Member are specially affected.

Article 32

Any Member of the United Nations which is not a member of the Security Council or any state which is not a Member of the United Nations, if it is a party to a dispute under consideration by the Security Council, shall be invited to participate, without vote, in the discussion relating to the dispute. The Security Council shall lay down such conditions as it deems just for the participation of a state which is not a Member of the United Nations.

CHAPTER VI *Pacific Settlement of Disputes*

Article 33

1. The parties to any dispute, the continuance of which is likely to endanger the maintenance of international peace and security, shall, first of all, seek a solution by negotiation, enquiry, mediation, conciliation, arbitration, judicial settlement, resort to regional agencies or arrangements, or other peaceful means of their own choice.

2. The Security Council shall, when it deems necessary, call upon the parties to settle their dispute by such means.

Article 34

The Security Council may investigate any dispute, or any situation which might lead to international friction or give rise to a dispute, in order to determine whether the continuance of the dispute or situation is likely to endanger the maintenance of international peace and security.

Article 35

1. Any Member of the United Nations may bring any dispute, or any situation of the nature referred to in Article 34, to the attention of the Security Council or of the General Assembly.

2. A state which is not a Member of the United Nations may bring to the attention of the Security Council or of the General Assembly any dispute to which it is a party if it accepts in advance, for the purposes of the dispute, the obligations of pacific settlement provided in the present Charter.

3. The proceedings of the General Assembly in respect of matters brought to its attention under this Article will be subject to the provisions of Articles 11 and 12.

Article 36

1. The Security Council may, at any stage of a dispute of the nature referred to in Article 33 or of a situation of like nature, recommend appropriate procedures or methods of adjustment.

2. The Security Council should take into consideration any procedures for the settlement of the dispute which have already been adopted by the parties.

3. In making recommendations under this Article the Security Council should also take into consideration that legal disputes should as a general rule be referred by the parties to the International Court of Justice in accordance with the provisions of the Statute of the Court.

Article 37

1. Should the parties to a dispute of the nature referred to in Article 33 fail to settle it by the means indicated in that Article, they shall refer it to the Security Council.

2. If the Security Council deems that the continuance of the dispute is in fact likely to endanger the maintenance of international peace and security, it shall decide whether to take action under Article 36 or to recommend such terms of settlement as it may consider appropriate.

Article 38

Without prejudice to the provisions of Articles 33 to 37, the Security Council may, if all the parties to any dispute so request, make recommendations to the parties with a view to a pacific settlement of the dispute.

CHAPTER VII *Action with Respect to Threats to the Peace, Breaches of the Peace, and Acts of Aggression*

Article 39

The Security Council shall determine the existence of any threat to the peace, breach of the peace, or act of aggression and shall make recommendations, or decide what measures shall be taken in accordance with Articles 41 and 42, to maintain or restore international peace and security.

Article 40

In order to prevent an aggravation of the situation, the Security Council may, before making the recommendations or deciding upon the measures provided for in Article 39, call upon the parties concerned to comply with such provisional measures as it deems necessary or desirable. Such provisional measures shall be without prejudice to the rights, claims, or position of the parties concerned. The Security Council shall duly take account of failure to comply with such provisional measures.

Article 41

The Security Council may decide what measures not involving the use of armed force are to be employed to give effect to its decisions, and it may call upon the Members of the United Nations to apply such measures. These may include complete or partial interruption of economic relations and of rail, sea, air, postal, telegraphic, radio, and other means of communication, and the severance of diplomatic relations.

Article 42

Should the Security Council consider that measures provided for in Article 41 would be inadequate or have proved to be inadequate, it may take such action by air, sea, or land forces as may be necessary to maintain or restore international peace and security. Such action may include demonstrations, blockade, and other operations by air, sea, or land forces of Members of the United Nations.

Article 43

1. All Members of the United Nations, in order to contribute to the maintenance of international peace and security, undertake to make available to the Security Council, on its call and in accordance with a special agreement or agreements, armed forces, assistance, and facilities, including rights of passage, necessary for the purpose of maintaining international peace and security.
2. Such agreement or agreements shall govern the numbers and types of forces, their degree of readiness and general location, and the nature of the facilities and assistance to be provided.
3. The agreement or agreements shall be negotiated as soon as possible on the initiative of the Security Council. They shall be concluded between the Security Council and Members or between the Security Council and groups of Members and shall be subject to ratification by the signatory states in accordance with their respective constitutional processes.

Article 44

When the Security Council has decided to use force it shall, before calling upon a Member not represented on it to provide armed forces in fulfillment of the obligations assumed under Article 43, invite that Member, if the Member so desires, to participate in the decisions of the Security Council concerning the employment of contingents of that Member's armed forces.

Article 45

In order to enable the United Nations to take urgent military measures, Members shall hold immediately available national air-force contingents for combined international enforcement action. The strength and degree of readiness of these contingents and plans for their combined action shall be determined, within the limits laid down in the special agreement or agreements referred to in Article 43, by the Security Council with the assistance of the Military Staff Committee.

Article 46

Plans for the application of armed force shall be made by the Security Council with the assistance of the Military Staff Committee.

Article 47

1. There shall be established a Military Staff Committee to advise and assist the Security Council on all questions relating to the Security Council's military requirements for the maintenance of international peace and security, the employment and command of forces placed at its disposal, the regulation of armaments, and possible disarmament.

2. The Military Staff Committee shall consist of the Chiefs of Staff of the permanent members of the Security Council or their representatives. Any Member of the United Nations not permanently represented on the Committee shall be invited by the Committee to be associated with it when the efficient discharge of the Committee's responsibilities requires the participation of that Member in its work.

3. The Military Staff Committee shall be responsible under the Security Council for the strategic direction of any armed forces placed at the disposal of the Security Council. Questions relating to the command of such forces shall be worked out subsequently.

4. The Military Staff Committee, with the authorization of the Security Council and after consultation with appropriate regional agencies, may establish regional subcommittees.

Article 48

1. The action required to carry out the decisions of the Security Council for the maintenance of international peace and security shall be taken by all the Members of the United Nations or by some of them, as the Security Council may determine.

2. Such decisions shall be carried out by the Members of the United Nations directly and through their action in the appropriate international agencies of which they are members.

Article 49

The Members of the United Nations shall join in affording mutual assistance in carrying out the measures decided upon by the Security Council.

Article 50

If preventive or enforcement measures against any state are taken by the Security Council, any other state, whether a Member of the United Nations or not, which finds itself confronted with special economic problems arising from the carry-

ing out of those measures shall have the right to consult the Security Council with regard to a solution of those problems.

Article 51

Nothing in the present Charter shall impair the inherent right of individual or collective self-defense if an armed attack occurs against a Member of the United Nations, until the Security Council has taken the measures necessary to maintain international peace and security. Measures taken by Members in the exercise of this right of self-defense shall be immediately reported to the Security Council and shall not in any way affect the authority and responsibility of the Security Council under the present Charter to take at any time such action as it deems necessary in order to maintain or restore international peace and security.

CHAPTER VIII *Regional Arrangements*

Article 52

1. Nothing in the present Charter precludes the existence of regional arrangements or agencies for dealing with such matters relating to the maintenance of international peace and security as are appropriate for regional action, provided that such arrangements or agencies and their activities are consistent with the Purposes and Principles of the United Nations.

2. The Members of the United Nations entering into such arrangements or constituting such agencies shall make every effort to achieve pacific settlement of local disputes through such regional arrangements or by such regional agencies before referring them to the Security Council.

3. The Security Council shall encourage the development of pacific settlement of local disputes through such regional arrangements or by such regional agencies either on the initiative of the states concerned or by reference from the Security Council.

4. This Article in no way impairs the application of Articles 34 and 35.

Article 53

1. The Security Council shall, where appropriate, utilize such regional arrangements or agencies for enforcement action under its authority. But no enforcement action shall be taken under regional arrangements or by regional agencies without the authorization of the Security Council, with the exception of measures against any enemy state, as defined in paragraph 2 of this Article, provided for pursuant to Article 107 or in regional arrangements directed against renewal of aggressive policy on the part of any such state, until such time as the Organization may, on request of the Governments concerned, be charged with the responsibility for preventing further aggression by such a state.

2. The term enemy state as used in paragraph 1 of this Article applies to any state which during the Second World War has been an enemy of any signatory of the present Charter.

Article 54

The Security Council shall at all times be kept fully informed of activities undertaken or in contemplation under regional arrangements or by regional agencies for the maintenance of international peace and security.

CHAPTER IX *International Economic and Social Cooperation*

Article 55

With a view to the creation of conditions of stability and well-being which are necessary for peaceful and friendly relations among nations based on respect for the principle of equal rights and self-determination of peoples, the United Nations shall promote:

a. higher standards of living, full employment, and conditions of economic and social progress and development;

b. solutions of international economic, social, health, and related problems; and international cultural and educational cooperation; and

c. universal respect for, and observance of, human rights and fundamental freedoms for all without distinction as to race, sex, language, or religion.

Article 56

All Members pledge themselves to take joint and separate action in cooperation with the Organization for the achievement of the purposes set forth in Article 55.

Article 57

1. The various specialized agencies, established by intergovernmental agreement and having wide international responsibilities, as defined in their basic instruments, in economic, social, cultural, educational, health, and related fields, shall be brought into relationship with the United Nations in accordance with the provisions of Article 63.

2. Such agencies thus brought into relationship with the United Nations are hereinafter referred to as specialized agencies.

Article 58

The Organization shall make recommendations for the coordination of the policies and activities of the specialized agencies.

Article 59

The Organization shall, where appropriate, initiate negotiations among the states concerned for the creation of any new specialized agencies required for the accomplishment of the purposes set forth in Article 55.

Article 60

Responsibility for the discharge of the functions of the Organization set forth in this Chapter shall be vested in the General Assembly and, under the authority of the General Assembly, in the Economic and Social Council, which shall have for this purpose the powers set forth in Chapter X.

CHAPTER X *The Economic and Social Council*

COMPOSITION

Article 61

1. The Economic and Social Council shall consist of eighteen Members of the United Nations elected by the General Assembly.

2. Subject to the provisions of paragraph 3, six members of the Economic and Social Council shall be elected each year for a term of three years. A retiring member shall be eligible for immediate re-election.

3. At the first election, eighteen members of the Economic and Social Council shall be chosen. The term of office of six members so chosen shall expire at the end of one year, and of six other members at the end of two years, in accordance with arrangements made by the General Assembly.

4. Each member of the Economic and Social Council shall have one representative.

FUNCTIONS AND POWERS

Article 62

1. The Economic and Social Council may make or initiate studies and reports with respect to international economic, social, cultural, educational, health, and related matters and may make recommendations with respect to any such matters to the General Assembly, to the Members of the United Nations, and to the specialized agencies concerned.

2. It may make recommendations for the purpose of promoting respect for, and observance of, human rights and fundamental freedoms for all.

3. It may prepare draft conventions for submission to the General Assembly, with respect to matters falling within its competence.

4. It may call, in accordance with the rules prescribed by the United Nations, international conferences on matters falling within its competence.

Article 63

1. The Economic and Social Council may enter into agreements with any of the agencies referred to in Article 57, defining the terms on which the agency concerned shall be brought into relationship with the United Nations. Such agreements shall be subject to approval by the General Assembly.

2. It may coordinate the activities of the specialized agencies through consultation with and recommendations to such agencies and through recommendations to the General Assembly and to the Members of the United Nations.

Article 64

1. The Economic and Social Council may take appropriate steps to obtain regular reports from the specialized agencies. It may make arrangements with the Members of the United Nations and with the specialized agencies to obtain reports on the steps taken to give effect to its own recommendations and to recommendations on matters falling within its competence made by the General Assembly.

2. It may communicate its observations on these reports to the General Assembly.

Article 65

The Economic and Social Council may furnish information to the Security Council and shall assist the Security Council upon its request.

Article 66

1. The Economic and Social Council shall perform such functions as fall within its competence in connection with the carrying out of the recommendations of the General Assembly.

2. It may, with the approval of the General Assembly, perform services at the request of Members of the United Nations and at the request of specialized agencies.

3. It shall perform such other functions as are specified elsewhere in the present Charter or as may be assigned to it by the General Assembly.

VOTING

Article 67

1. Each member of the Economic and Social Council shall have one vote.

2. Decisions of the Economic and Social Council shall be made by a majority of the members present and voting.

PROCEDURE

Article 68

The Economic and Social Council shall set up commissions in economic and social fields and for the promotion of human rights, and such other commissions as may be required for the performance of its functions.

Article 69

The Economic and Social Council shall invite any Member of the United Nations to participate, without vote, in its deliberations on any matter of particular concern to that Member.

Article 70

The Economic and Social Council may make arrangements for representatives of the specialized agencies to participate, without vote, in its deliberations and in those of the commissions established by it, and for its representatives to participate in the deliberations of the specialized agencies.

Article 71

The Economic and Social Council may make suitable arrangements for consultation with non-governmental organizations which are concerned with matters within its competence. Such arrangements may be made with international organizations and, where appropriate, with national organizations after consultation with the Member of the United Nations concerned.

Article 72

1. The Economic and Social Council shall adopt its own rules of procedure, including the method of selecting its President.

2. The Economic and Social Council shall meet as required in accordance with its rules, which shall include provision for the convening of meetings on the request of a majority of its members.

CHAPTER XI *Declaration Regarding Non-Self-Governing Territories*

Article 73

Members of the United Nations which have or assume responsibilities for the administration of territories whose peoples have not yet attained a full measure of self-government recognize the principle that the interests of the inhabitants of these territories are paramount, and accept as a sacred trust the obligation to promote to the utmost, within the system of international peace and security established by the present Charter, the well-being of the inhabitants of these territories, and, to this end:

a. to ensure, with due respect for the culture of the peoples concerned, their political, economic, social, and educational advancement, their just treatment, and their protection against abuses;

b. to develop self-government, to take due account of the political aspirations of the peoples, and to assist them in the progressive development of their free political institutions, according to the particular circumstances of each territory and its peoples and their varying stages of advancement;

c. to further international peace and security;

d. to promote constructive measures of development, to encourage research, and to cooperate with one another, and, when and where appropriate, with specialized international bodies with a view to the practical achievement of the social, economic, and scientific purposes set forth in this Article; and

e. to transmit regularly to the Secretary-General for information purposes, subject to such limitation as security and constitutional considerations may require, statistical and other information of a technical nature relating to economic, social, and educational conditions in the territories for which they are respectively responsible other than those territories to which Chapters XII and XIII apply.

Article 74

Members of the United Nations also agree that their policy in respect of the territories to which this Chapter applies, no less than in respect of their metropolitan areas, must be based on the general principle of good-neighborliness, due account being taken of the interests and well-being of the rest of the world, in social, economic, and commercial matters.

CHAPTER XII *International Trusteeship System*

Article 75

The United Nations shall establish under its authority an international trusteeship system for the administration and supervision of such territories as may be placed thereunder by subsequent individual agreements. These territories are hereinafter referred to as trust territories.

Article 76

The basic objectives of the trusteeship system, in accordance with the Purposes of the United Nations laid down in Article 1 of the present Charter, shall be:

a. to further international peace and security;

b. to promote the political, economic, social, and educational advancement of the inhabitants of the trust territories, and their progressive development towards self-government or independence as may be appropriate to the particular circumstances of each territory and its peoples and the freely expressed wishes of the peoples concerned, and as may be provided by the terms of each trusteeship agreement;

c. to encourage respect for human rights and for fundamental freedoms for all without distinction as to race, sex, language, or religion, and to encourage recognition of the interdependence of the peoples of the world; and

d. to ensure equal treatment in social, economic, and commercial matters for all Members of the United Nations and their nationals, and also equal treatment for the latter in the administration of justice, without prejudice to the attainment of the foregoing objectives and subject to the provisions of Article 80.

Article 77

1. The trusteeship system shall apply to such territories in the following categories as may be placed thereunder by means of trusteeship agreements:

a. territories now held under mandate;

b. territories which may be detached from enemy states as a result of the Second World War; and

c. territories voluntarily placed under the system by states responsible for their administration.

2. It will be a matter for subsequent agreement as to which territories in the foregoing categories will be brought under the trusteeship system and upon what terms.

Article 78

The trusteeship system shall not apply to territories which have become Members of the United Nations, relationship among which shall be based on respect for the principle of sovereign equality.

Article 79

The terms of trusteeship for each territory to be placed under the trusteeship system, including any alteration or amendment, shall be agreed upon by the states directly concerned, including the mandatory power in the case of territories held under mandate by a Member of the United Nations, and shall be approved as provided for in Articles 83 and 85.

Article 80

1. Except as may be agreed upon in individual trusteeship agreements, made under Articles 77, 79, and 81, placing each territory under the trusteeship system, and until such agreements have been concluded, nothing in this Chapter shall be construed in or of itself to alter in any manner the rights whatsoever of any states or any peoples or the terms of existing international instruments to which Members of the United Nations may respectively be parties.

2. Paragraph 1 of this Article shall not be interpreted as giving grounds for delay or postponement of the negotiation and conclusion of agreements for placing mandated and other territories under the trusteeship system as provided for in Article 77.

Article 81

The trusteeship agreement shall in each case include the terms under which the trust territory will be administered and designate the authority which will exercise the administration of the trust territory. Such authority, hereinafter called the administering authority, may be one or more states or the Organization itself.

Article 82

There may be designated, in any trusteeship agreement, a strategic area or areas which may include part or all of the trust territory to which the agreement applies, without prejudice to any special agreement or agreements made under Article 43.

Article 83

1. All functions of the United Nations relating to strategic areas, including the approval of the terms of the trusteeship agreement and of their alteration or amendment, shall be exercised by the Security Council.

2. The basic objectives set forth in Article 76 shall be applicable to the people of each strategic area.

3. The Security Council shall, subject to the provisions of the trusteeship agreements and without prejudice to security considerations, avail itself of the assistance of the Trusteeship Council to perform those functions of the United Nations under the trusteeship system relating to political, economic, social, and educational matters in the strategic areas.

Article 84

It shall be the duty of the administering authority to ensure that the trust territory shall play its part in the maintenance of international peace and security. To this end the administering authority may make use of volunteer forces, facilities, and assistance from the trust territory in carrying out the obligations towards the Security Council undertaken in this regard by the administering authority, as well as for local defense and the maintenance of law and order within the trust territory.

Article 85

1. The functions of the United Nations with regard to trusteeship agreements for all areas not designated as strategic, including the approval of the terms of the trusteeship agreements and of their alteration or amendment, shall be exercised by the General Assembly.

2. The Trusteeship Council, operating under the authority of the General Assembly, shall assist the General Assembly in carrying out these functions.

CHAPTER XIII *The Trusteeship Council*

COMPOSITION

Article 86

1. The Trusteeship Council shall consist of the following Members of the United Nations:

a. those Members administering trust territories;

b. such of those Members mentioned by name in Article 23 as are not administering trust territories; and

c. as many other Members elected for three-year terms by the General Assembly as may be necessary to ensure that the total number of members of the Trusteeship Council is equally divided between those Members of the United Nations which administer trust territories and those which do not.

2. Each member of the Trusteeship Council shall designate one specially qualified person to represent it therein.

FUNCTIONS AND POWERS

Article 87

The General Assembly and, under its authority, the Trusteeship Council, in carrying out their functions, may:

a. consider reports submitted by the administering authority;

b. accept petitions and examine them in consultation with the administering authority;

c. provide for periodic visits to the respective trust territories at times agreed upon with the administering authority; and

d. take these and other actions in conformity with the terms of the trusteeship agreements.

Article 88

The Trusteeship Council shall formulate a questionnaire on the political, economic, social, and educational advancement of the inhabitants of each trust territory, and the administering authority for each trust territory within the competence of the General Assembly shall make an annual report to the General Assembly upon the basis of such questionnaire.

VOTING

Article 89

1. Each member of the Trusteeship Council shall have one vote.

2. Decisions of the Trusteeship Council shall be made by a majority of the members present and voting.

PROCEDURE

Article 90

1. The Trusteeship Council shall adopt its own rules of procedure, including the method of selecting its President.

2. The Trusteeship Council shall meet as required in accordance with its rules, which shall include provision for the convening of meetings on the request of a majority of its members.

Article 91

The Trusteeship Council shall, when appropriate, avail itself of the assistance of the Economic and Social Council and of the specialized agencies in regard to matters with which they are respectively concerned.

CHAPTER XIV *The International Court of Justice*

Article 92

The International Court of Justice shall be the principal judicial organ of the United Nations. It shall function in accordance with the annexed Statute, which is based upon the Statute of the Permanent Court of International Justice and forms an integral part of the present Charter.

Article 93

1. All Members of the United Nations are *ipso facto* parties to the Statute of the International Court of Justice.

2. A state which is not a Member of the United Nations may become a party to the Statute of the International Court of Justice on conditions to be determined in each case by the General Assembly upon the recommendation of the Security Council.

Article 94

1. Each Member of the United Nations undertakes to comply with the decision of the International Court of Justice in any case to which it is a party.

2. If any party to a case fails to perform the obligations incumbent upon it under a judgment rendered by the Court, the other party may have recourse to the Security Council, which may, if it deems necessary, make recommendations or decide upon measures to be taken to give effect to the judgment.

Article 95

Nothing in the present Charter shall prevent Members of the United Nations from entrusting the solution of their differences to other tribunals by virtue of agreements already in existence or which may be concluded in the future.

Article 96

1. The General Assembly or the Security Council may request the International Court of Justice to give an advisory opinion on any legal question.

2. Other organs of the United Nations and specialized agencies, which may at any time be so authorized by the General Assembly, may also request advisory opinions of the Court on legal questions arising within the scope of their activities.

CHAPTER XV *The Secretariat*

Article 97

The Secretariat shall comprise a Secretary-General and such staff as the Organization may require. The Secretary-General shall be appointed by the General Assembly upon the recommendation of the Security Council. He shall be the chief administrative officer of the Organization.

Article 98

The Secretary-General shall act in that capacity in all meetings of the General Assembly, of the Security Council, of the Economic and Social Council and of the Trusteeship Council, and shall perform such other functions as are entrusted to him by these organs. The Secretary-General shall make an annual report to the General Assembly on the work of the Organization.

Article 99

The Secretary General may bring to the attention of the Security Council any matter which in his opinion may threaten the maintenance of international peace and security.

Article 100

1. In the performance of their duties the Secretary-General and the staff shall not seek or receive instructions from any government or from any other authority external to the Organization. They shall refrain from any action which might reflect on their position as international officials responsible only to the Organization.

2. Each Member of the United Nations undertakes to respect the exclusively international character of the responsibilities of the Secretary-General and the staff and not to seek to influence them in the discharge of their responsibilities.

Article 101

1. The staff shall be appointed by the Secretary-General under regulations established by the General Assembly.

2. Appropriate staffs shall be permanently assigned to the Economic and Social Council, the Trusteeship Council, and, as required, to other organs of the United Nations. These staffs shall form a part of the Secretariat.

3. The paramount consideration in the employment of the staff and in the determination of the conditions of service shall be the necessity of securing the highest standards of efficiency, competence, and integrity. Due regard shall be paid to the importance of recruiting the staff on as wide a geographical basis as possible.

CHAPTER XVI *Miscellaneous Provisions*

Article 102

1. Every treaty and every international agreement entered into by any Member of the United Nations after the present Charter comes into force shall as soon as possible be registered with the Secretariat and published by it.

2. No party to any such treaty or international agreement which has not been registered in accordance with the provisions of paragraph 1 of this Article may invoke that treaty or agreement before any organ of the United Nations.

Article 103

In the event of a conflict between the obligations of the Members of the United Nations under the present Charter and their obligations under any other international agreement, their obligations under the present Charter shall prevail.

Article 104

The Organization shall enjoy in the territory of each of its Members such legal capacity as may be necessary for the exercise of its functions and the fulfillment of its purposes.

Article 105

1. The Organization shall enjoy in the territory of each of its Members such privileges and immunities as are necessary for the fulfillment of its purposes.

2. Representatives of the Members of the United Nations and officials of the Organization shall similarly enjoy such privileges and immunities as are necessary for the independent exercise of their functions in connection with the Organization.

3. The General Asembly may make recommendations with a view to determining the details of the application of paragraphs 1 and 2 of this Article or may propose conventions to the Members of the United Nations for this purpose.

CHAPTER XVII *Transitional Security Arrangements*

Article 106

Pending the coming into force of such special agreements referred to in Article 43 as in the opinion of the Security Council enable it to begin the exercise of its responsibilities under Article 42, the parties to the Four-Nation Declaration, signed at Moscow, October 30, 1943, and France, shall, in accordance with the provisions of paragraph 5 of that Declaration, consult with one another and as occasion requires with other Members of the United Nations with a view to such joint action on behalf of the Organization as may be necessary for the purpose of maintaining international peace and security.

Article 107

Nothing in the present Charter shall invalidate or preclude action, in relation to any state which during the Second World War has been an enemy of any signatory to the present Charter, taken or authorized as a result of that war by the Governments having responsibility for such action.

CHAPTER XVIII *Amendments*

Article 108

Amendments to the present Charter shall come into force for all Members of the United Nations when they have been adopted by a vote of two-thirds of the members of the General Assembly and ratified in accordance with their respective constitutional processes by two-thirds of the Members of the United Nations, including all the permanent members of the Security Council.

Article 109

1. A General Conference of the Members of the United Nations for the purpose of reviewing the present Charter may be held at a date and place to be fixed by a two-thirds vote of the members of the General Assembly and by a vote of any seven members of the Security Council. Each Member of the United Nations shall have one vote in the conference.

2. Any alteration of the present Charter recommended by a two-thirds vote of the conference shall take effect when ratified in accordance with their respective constitutional processes by two-thirds of the Members of the United Nations including all the permanent members of the Security Council.

3. If such a conference has not been held before the tenth annual session of the General Assembly following the coming into force of the present Charter, the proposal to call such a conference shall be placed on the agenda of that session of the General Assembly, and the conference shall be held if so decided by a majority vote of the members of the General Assembly and by a vote of any seven members of the Security Council.

CHAPTER XIX *Ratification and Signature*

Article 110

1. The present Charter shall be ratified by the signatory states in accordance with their respective constitutional processes.

2. The ratifications shall be deposited with the Government of the United States of America, which shall notify all the signatory states of each deposit as well as the Secretary-General of the Organization when he has been appointed.

3. The present Charter shall come into force upon the deposit of ratifications by the Republic of China, France, the Union of Soviet Socialist Republics, the United Kingdom of Great Britain and Northern Ireland, and the United States of America, and by a majority of the other signatory states. A protocol of the ratifications deposited shall thereupon be drawn up by the Government of the United States of America which shall communicate copies thereof to all the signatory states.

4. The states signatory to the present Charter which ratify it after it has come into force will become original Members of the United Nations on the date of the deposit of their respective ratifications.

Article 111

The present Charter, of which the Chinese, French, Russian, English, and Spanish texts are equally authentic, shall remain deposited in the archives of the Government of the United States of America. Duly certified copies thereof shall be transmitted by that Government to the Governments of the other signatory states.

IN FAITH WHEREOF the representatives of the Governments of the United Nations have signed the present Charter.

DONE at the city of San Francisco the twenty-sixth day of June, one thousand nine hundred and forty-five.

APPENDIX III

The North Atlantic Treaty

The Parties to this Treaty reaffirm their faith in the purposes and principles of the Charter of the United Nations and their desire to live in peace with all peoples and all governments.

They are determined to safeguard the freedom, common heritage and civilization of their peoples, founded on the principles of democracy, individual liberty and the rule of law.

They seek to promote stability and well-being in the North Atlantic area.

They are resolved to unite their efforts for collective defense and for the preservation of peace and security.

They therefore agree to this North Atlantic Treaty:

Article 1

The Parties undertake, as set forth in the Charter of the United Nations, to settle any international dispute in which they may be involved by peaceful means in such a manner that international peace and security, and justice, are not endangered, and to refrain in their international relations from the threat or use of force in any manner inconsistent with the purposes of the United Nations.

Article 2

The Parties will contribute toward the further development of peaceful and friendly international relations by strengthening their free institutions, by bringing about a better understanding of the principles upon which these institutions are founded, and by promoting conditions of stability and well-being. They will seek to eliminate conflict in their international economic policies and will encourage economic collaboration between any or all of them.

Article 3

In order more effectively to achieve the objectives of this Treaty, the Parties, separately and jointly, by means of continuous and effective self-help and mutual aid, will maintain and develop their individual and collective capacity to resist armed attack.

Article 4

The Parties will consult together whenever, in the opinion of any of them, the territorial integrity, political independence or security of any of the Parties is threatened.

Article 5

The Parties agree that an armed attack against one or more of them in Europe or North America shall be considered an attack against them all; and consequently they agree that, if such an armed attack occurs, each of them, in exercise of the right of individual or collective self-defense recognized by Article 51 of the Charter of the United Nations, will assist the Party or Parties so attacked by taking forthwith, individually and in concert with the other Parties, such action as it deems necessary, including the use of armed force, to restore and maintain the security of the North Atlantic area.

Any such armed attack and all measures taken as a result thereof shall immediately be reported to the Security Council. Such measures shall be terminated when the Security Council has taken the measures necessary to restore and maintain international peace and security.

Article 6

For the purpose of Article 5 an armed attack on one or more of the Parties is deemed to include an armed attack on the territory of any of the Parties in Europe or North America, on the Algerian departments of France, on the occupation forces of any Party in Europe, on the islands under the jurisdiction of any Party in the North Atlantic area north of the Tropic of Cancer or on the vessels or aircraft in this area of any of the Parties.

Article 7

This Treaty does not affect, and shall not be interpreted as affecting, in any way the rights and obligations under the Charter of the Parties which are members of the United Nations, or the primary responsibility of the Security Council for the maintenance of international peace and security.

Article 8

Each Party declares that none of the international engagements now in force between it and any other of the Parties or any third state is in conflict with the provisions of this Treaty, and undertakes not to enter into any international engagement in conflict with this Treaty.

Article 9

The Parties hereby establish a council, on which each of them shall be represented, to consider matters concerning the implementation of this Treaty. The council shall be so organized as to be able to meet promptly at any time. The council shall set up such subsidiary bodies as may be necessary; in particular it shall establish immediately a defense committee which shall recommend measures for the implementation of Articles 3 and 5.

Article 10

The Parties may, by unanimous agreement, invite any other European state in a position to further the principles of this Treaty and to contribute to the security of the North Atlantic area to accede to this Treaty. Any state so invited may become a party to the Treaty by depositing its instrument of accession with the Government of the United States of America. The Government of the United States of America will inform each of the Parties of the deposit of each such instrument of accession.

Article 11

This Treaty shall be ratified and its provisions carried out by the Parties in accordance with their respective constitutional processes. The instruments of ratification shall be deposited as soon as possible with the Government of the United States of America, which will notify all the other signatories of each deposit. The Treaty shall enter into force between the states which have ratified it as soon as the ratifications of the majority of the signatories, including the ratifications of Belgium, Canada, France, Luxembourg, the Netherlands, the United Kingdom and the United States, have been deposited and shall come into effect with respect to other states on the date of the deposit of their ratifications.

Article 12

After the Treaty has been in force for ten years, or at any time thereafter, the Parties shall, if any of them so requests, consult together for the purpose of reviewing the Treaty, having regard for the factors then affecting peace and security in the North Atlantic area, including the development of universal as well as regional arrangements under the Charter of the United Nations for the maintenance of international peace and security.

Article 13

After the Treaty has been in force for twenty years, any Party may cease to be a Party one year after its notice of denunciation has been given to the Government of the United States of America, which will inform the Governments of the other Parties of the deposit of each notice of denunciation.

Article 14

This Treaty, of which the English and French texts are equally authentic, shall be deposited in the archives of the Government of the United States of America. Duly certified copies thereof will be transmitted by that Government to the Governments of the other signatories.

April 4, 1949.

Appendix IV

Poster 22

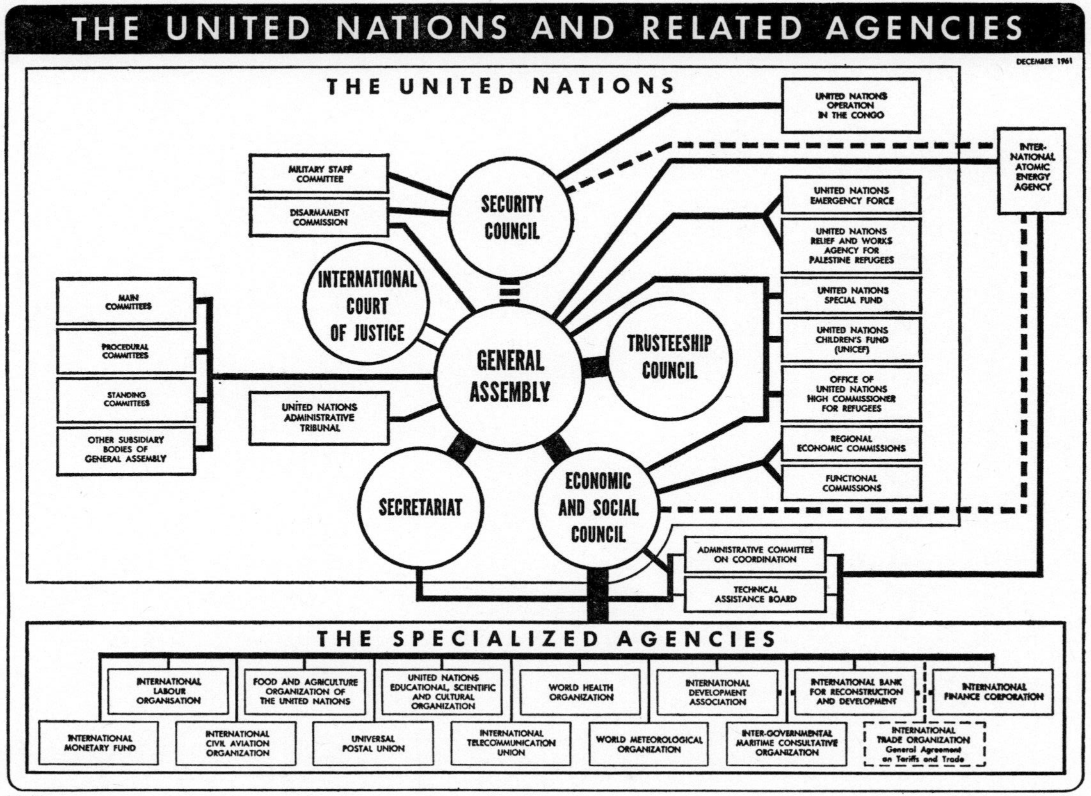

Litho in U.N.
11446—May 1963—5M

APPENDIX

IV

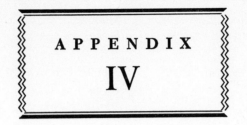

Membership in the United Nations

(As of January 1964)

Original Members

Argentina
Australia
Belgium
Bolivia
Brazil
Byelorussian Soviet Socialist Republic
Canada
Chile
China
Colombia
Costa Rica
Cuba
Czechoslovakia
Denmark
Dominican Republic
Ecuador
Egypt (United Arab Republic)
El Salvador
Ethiopia
France
Greece
Guatemala
Haiti
Honduras
India
Iran
Iraq
Lebanon
Liberia
Luxembourg
Mexico
Netherlands
New Zealand
Nicaragua
Norway
Panama
Paraguay
Peru
Philippines
Poland
Saudi Arabia
Syria
Turkey
Ukrainian Soviet Socialist Republic

Union of South Africa
Union of Soviet Socialist Republics
United Kingdom of Great Britain and Northern Ireland
United States of America
Uruguay
Venezuela
Yugoslavia

Admitted in 1946

Afghanistan
Iceland
Sweden
Thailand

Admitted in 1947

Pakistan
Yemen

Admitted in 1948

Burma

Admitted in 1949

Israel

Admitted in 1950

Indonesia

Admitted in 1955

Albania
Austria
Bulgaria
Cambodia
Ceylon
Finland
Hungary
Ireland
Italy
Jordan
Laos
Libya
Nepal
Portugal
Romania
Spain

Admitted in 1956

Japan
Morocco
Sudan
Tunisia

Admitted in 1957

Ghana
Malaya (Malaysia)

Admitted in 1958

Guinea

Admitted in 1960

Cameroun
Central African Republic
Chad
Congo (Brazzaville)
Congo (Leopoldville)
Cyprus
Dahomey
Gabon
Ivory Coast
Madagascar
Mali
Niger
Nigeria
Senegal
Somalia
Togo
Upper Volta

Admitted in 1961

Mauritania
Mongolia
Sierra Leone
Tanganyika

Admitted in 1962

Algeria
Burundi
Jamaica
Rwanda
Trinidad and Tobago
Uganda

Admitted in 1963

Kenya
Kuwait
Zanzibar

APPENDIX V

Costs of the United Nations System

United Nations, specialized agencies and special programs total expenditures, calendar years 1946-61

[In thousands]

	1946	1947	1948	1949	1950	1951	1952	1953	1954	1955	1956	1957	1958	1959	1960	1961	Total
A. United Nations and specialized agencies:																	
United Nations	$19,330	$27,290	$38,388	$42,575	$43,746	$48,628	$50,270	$49,292	$48,510	$50,090	$50,508	$53,173	$62,506	$61,946	$65,264	$72,696	$784,212
Food and Agriculture Organization	377	5,173	4,174	4,655	4,505	4,582	4,830	5,064	5,500	5,974	6,397	7,006	9,147	10,530	10,665	10,872	99,451
Intergovernmental Maritime Consultative Organization	......	......	......	......	......	......	......	......	......	......	......	......	......	164	256	233	653
International Civil Aviation Organization	719	1,690	2,285	2,345	2,946	3,021	3,192	3,150	3,087	3,255	3,349	3,900	3,999	4,497	4,666	4,880	50,981
International Labor Organization	2,711	3,721	4,148	5,034	5,267	5,835	6,390	6,510	6,575	7,041	7,291	7,706	8,521	9,096	9,617	10,414	105,877
International Telecommunication Union	......	......	897	2,994	1,639	1,382	1,592	1,456	1,327	1,291	1,685	1,471	1,890	2,696	2,414	2,920	25,654
United Nations Educational, Scientific and Cultural Organization	1,053	6,213	6,697	7,780	7,163	7,989	8,726	7,973	9,019	9,151	11,437	10,613	12,316	12,591	13,779	15,095	147,595
Universal Postal Union	132	168	866	297	302	354	417	435	433	429	441	523	452	619	635	798	7,301
World Health Organization	116	1,719	4,443	4,777	6,108	6,259	7,939	8,113	8,135	9,275	9,983	12,091	13,961	15,379	16,919	18,975	144,192
World Meteorological Organization	......	......	......	......	......	186	179	272	327	395	371	418	441	502	655	671	4,417
Subtotal	24,438	45,974	61,898	70,457	71,676	78,236	83,535	82,265	82,913	86,901	91,462	96,901	113,233	118,020	124,870	137,554	1,370,333
B. United Nations Emergency Force	......	......	......	......	......	......	......	......	......	......	......	29,909	23,914	18,949	19,096	19,000	110,868
C. United Nations operations in the Congo:																	
Military	......	......	......	......	......	......	......	......	......	......	......	......	......	......	60,000	100,000	160,000
Economic	......	......	......	......	......	......	......	......	......	......	......	......	......	......	1,902	35,000	36,902
Subtotal	......	......	......	......	......	......	......	......	......	......	......	......	......	......	61,902	135,000	196,902
D. International Refugee Organization	......	75,676	132,167	119,402	85,447	......	......	......	......	......	......	......	......	......	......	......	412,692
E. Special programs financed by voluntary contributions:																	
International Civil Aviation Organization joint support program	......	......	......	2,018	906	1,376	1,515	1,604	1,595	1,606	1,789	2,089	2,253	1,899	1,858	1,984	22,492
United Nations Childrens' Fund	......	815	31,454	46,665	35,933	22,571	13,526	12,506	14,474	14,161	18,005	21,349	22,436	23,784	23,006	27,000	327,685

SOURCE: *Information on the Operations and Financing of the United Nations,* Joint Committee Print of the Committee on Foreign Relations, U. S. Senate, and the Committee on Foreign Affairs, U. S. House of Representatives, 87th Congress, 2d Session (Washington: Government Printing Office, 1962), pp. 69-70.

	1946	1947	1948	1949	1950	1951	1952	1953	1954	1955	1956	1957	1958	1959	1960	1961	Total
E. Special programs financed by voluntary contributions—Continued																	
United Nations Educational, Scientific, and Cultural Organization—Aid to Africa	......	......	......	......	......	......	......	......	......	......	......	......	......	......	......	$1,504	$1,504
United Nations expanded technical assistance program	......	......	......	......	......	$6,642	$22,306	$22,662	$19,465	$25,405	$30,483	$31,574	$33,825	$32,829	$34,413	43,737	303,341
United Nations High Commissioner for Refugees [1]	......	......	......	......	......	......	......	848	400	1,129	1,241	3,460	5,480	4,614	4,981	6,000	28,153
United Nations Korean Reconstruction Agency [2]	......	......	......	......	......	497	4,133	58,219	46,654	31,515	3,574	2,596	1,156	345	211	......	148,900
United Nations Relief for Hungarian Refugees	......	......	......	......	......	......	......	......	......	......	739	6,967	2,217	1,067	664	253	11,907
United Nations Relief and Works Agency for Palestine Refugees in the Near East [3]	......	......	......	$39,116	$19,220	42,131	26,779	29,192	29,223	32,280	32,199	52,046	31,776	34,138	34,701	39,334	442,135
United Nations Special Fund	......	......	......	......	......	......	......	......	......	......	......	......	......	694	2,771	31,531	34,996
World Health Organization, community water development program	......	......	......	......	......	......	......	......	......	......	......	......	......	......	55	300	355
World Health Organization, malaria eradictation program	......	......	......	......	......	......	......	......	......	......	......	28	3,027	3,749	3,895	5,769	16,468
World Health Organization, medical research program	......	......	......	......	......	......	......	......	......	......	......	......	55	245	341	1,620	2,261
Subtotal	......	815	31,454	87,799	56,059	73,217	68,259	125,031	111,811	106,096	88,030	120,109	102,225	103,364	106,896	159,032	1,340,197
Total	24,438	122,465	225,519	277,658	213,182	151,453	151,794	207,296	194,724	192,997	179,492	246,919	239,372	240,333	312,764	450,586	3,430,992

[1] The figure shown for the United Nations High Commissioner for Refugees includes expenditures of the 4-year U.N. refugee fund (1955-58) and funds received in connection with the world refugee year program (1959-60).

[2] The fiscal year for UNKRA is July 1-June 30. In each case, the fiscal year is shown under the calendar year in which it ends. Figures represent obligations incurred for annual programs.

[3] Prior to 1957, the fiscal year for UNRWA was July 1-June 30. From 1949 through 1956, the fiscal year is shown under the calendar year in which it ends. The 1957 figure covers the 18-month period from July 1 to December 31, 1957.

Index

About the Author

INIS L. CLAUDE, JR., a native of Arkansas, graduated from Hendrix College and received his master's and doctor's degrees from Harvard, where he taught from 1949 to 1956. He also taught at the University of Delaware before going to the University of Michigan, where he became Professor of Political Science in 1960. Professor Claude has served as a consultant to the Department of State, and is presently Chairman of the Committee on International Organization of the Social Science Research Council. He is a member of the Board of Editors of *International Organization* and of the *Journal of Conflict Resolution.* He is also the author of *National Minorities: An International Problem* and of *Power and International Relations,* for which he received the Woodrow Wilson Foundation Award of the American Political Science Association in 1962.

A Note on the Type

The text of this book was set on the Linotype in a face called TIMES ROMAN, designed by Stanley Morison for *The Times* (London), and first introduced by that newspaper in 1932.

Among typographers and designers of the twentieth century, Stanley Morison has been a strong forming influence, as typographical advisor to the English Monotype Corporation, as a director of two distinguished English publishing houses, and as a writer of sensibility, erudition, and keen practical sense.